The Abraham Accords

The Gulf States in International Affairs

Series Editor

Robert Mason, Arab Gulf States Institute in Washington and the Gulf Research Center in Jeddah

This series focuses on the contemporary Gulf region with special reference to its politics, economics and international relations, as well as its projection of influence and engagement with influences from around the world. Books in this series might include research on topics such as, but not limited to: foreign policy analysis; ethno-religious conflict; economic and military interventionism; energy politics; alliance patterns and the regional balance of power; nationalism, regionalism and the Gulf milieu; rentier, late-rentier and post-rentier models; trade and investment relations (including engagement with China's Belt and Road Initiative); political transition and consolidation; arms control and non-proliferation.

The scope of the series encompasses members of the Gulf Cooperation Council (GCC): Saudi Arabia, UAE, Bahrain, Kuwait, Oman and Qatar, as well as Iraq, Iran and Yemen. Volumes which refer substantially to the Gulf region, states or related foreign actors (which might typically involve the US, European powers, Russia and East Asian partners) will also be considered from across the social sciences and the humanities. The series welcomes volumes which shed new light on areas of theoretical, conceptual and empirical inquiry to advance our understanding of the region during a period of rapid change. All books will undergo double-blind peer review and adhere to high quality and rigorous standards.

Titles in the series

The Abraham Accords: National Security, Regional Order, and Popular Representation
By Robert Mason, Guy Burton, and Banafsheh Keynoush

The Abraham Accords

National Security, Regional Order, and Popular Representation

Robert Mason, Guy Burton, and
Banafsheh Keynoush

LEXINGTON BOOKS
Lanham • Boulder • New York • London

Published by Lexington Books
An imprint of The Rowman & Littlefield Publishing Group, Inc.
4501 Forbes Boulevard, Suite 200, Lanham, Maryland 20706
www.rowman.com

86-90 Paul Street, London EC2A 4NE

British Library Cataloguing in Publication Information Available

Library of Congress Cataloging-in-Publication Data Available

ISBN 978-1-66690-325-6 (cloth : alk. paper)
ISBN 978-1-66690-326-3 (ebook)

♾™ The paper used in this publication meets the minimum requirements of American
National Standard for Information Sciences—Permanence of Paper for Printed Library
Materials, ANSI/NISO Z39.48-1992.

Contents

Introduction

Robert Mason

The Abraham Accords Declaration between the United Arab Emirates (UAE), and Bahrain and Israel, signed on August 13, 2020, set a precedent for the normalization of relations between Israel and the Arab Gulf States and made explicit the interests of some of those states in pursuing new forms of cooperation with Israel. These accords followed decades of the Arab-Israeli/Israel-Palestine conflict and almost two decades since Saudi Arabia tabled the Arab Peace Initiative (API), endorsed by the Arab League at the Beirut Summit in 2002 (and re-endorsed at the 2007 and 2017 Arab League Summits). The API publicly stated for the first time Arab recognition of Israel in return for full withdrawal by Israel from the occupied territories (i.e., pre-1967 borders), a "just settlement" of the Palestinian refugee problem based on UN Resolution 194 and the establishment of a Palestinian state with East Jerusalem as its capital.

Despite the API, normalization between Gulf Cooperation Council (GCC) states and Israel has taken a contrary route. The Abraham Accords mark a moment where GCC states have adopted a diverse set of responses toward Israel as well as other challenges in their region, including the United States and some GCC state perception of Iran as a threat due to its ballistic and nuclear programs, as well as regional behavior. In December 2022, the most far-right Israeli government in the history of the country came to power raising questions about the durability of the Abraham Accords. By November 2023, Hamas had killed or captured hundreds of Israelis. Israel had in turn invaded northern Gaza, killed more than 11,000 people, and internally displaced more than one million.[1] With the United States seemingly preoccupied with the war in Ukraine and the rise of China, the Biden administration appeared unwilling to assume the mantle of honest peace broker that marked out the Carter administration, even when the threat of regional escalation was possible. The lack of progress in the peace process has underscored US Mideast policy as being what Steven Simon, former US National Security Council member, describes as "delusional" and the "superimposition of grand ideas" on the region.[2] The fallout from this conflict comes in rapid succession to US and NATO military withdrawal from Afghanistan, where Qatar also played an important mediation and facilitation role.

This book is one of the first to attempt to pull the experience of GCC normalization with Israel together and explain what it also means to the Jewish state, Iran and Palestine. It aims to fully contextualize the drivers, issues, and challenges in the boycott, resistance or normalization of relations between Israel and the GCC states (including Saudi Arabia, the UAE, Qatar, Kuwait, Bahrain, and Oman), and the relevance to Iran and Palestine. Although many forms of regional cooperation with Israel are covert and remain secret, this book utilizes a broad range of sources to chart how, over time, GCC state positions remain intact, have evolved, or encountered potential or real obstacles. Against this backdrop, the book dwells in separate chapters on Israel and Palestine, the Iranian-Israeli connection, and individual GCC state's relations with Israel and the Palestinians.

The book is guided by two primary research questions: What are the leading drivers of normalization or anti-normalization with Israel in the context of the Abraham Accords? For those participating in the accords, are the accords sustainable, and more so after the outbreak of war between Hamas and Israel in October 2023? Since the advancement of the accords remains a priority for recent and current administrations in the United States and for participating states, the accords' impact are bound to evolve. Each chapter in the present book hence provides a comprehensive "snapshot" of dynamics involved in states and actors reaching decisions regarding relations or disassociation with Israel. Chapters examine relevant history, threat perception, leadership, socioeconomic interaction, security relations, and other specific factors in each case. Different conceptual and theoretical frameworks are explored for this study in the individual chapters. Realism and its focus on power politics through balancing, bandwagoning, and hedging and the influences that affect them guide the authors, as do security theories. These influences may also include factors such as leadership, threat perception, and security trends, as well as societal conceptions about peace in the Middle East.

ARAB GULF RESPONSE TO PALESTINIAN-ISRAELI CONFLICT

The roots of cooperation, or lack thereof, between Israel and its Arab neighbors stem from the 1917 Balfour Declaration which announced support for the establishment of a "national home for the Jewish people" in Palestine. The false assumption by David Lloyd George, then British prime minister, that a Zionist "national home" under British protection could attract support for the Allied cause from Jews in Europe and neutral countries during the First World War, and act as a land bridge between India and Egypt to sustain British imperialism, was ill-founded. London's perfidy during this period, including the secret 1916 Sykes-Picot Agreement which established British and French spheres of influence and areas of control after the dissolution of the Ottoman Empire by 1922, drew Arab and Jewish attention to overriding imperial interests at the time rather than a considered foreign policy toward the Middle East.

What may have been the first major direct political link in the twentieth century between the Arab Gulf States and Palestinians occurred a few weeks after an Arab general strike began in Palestine in April 1936. The strike degenerated into violence and the 1936–1939 Arab revolt in Palestine. At this time a letter sent from possibly the Palestinians or the Arab Higher Committee, a central political organ of the Palestinians in the League of Nations termed Mandatory Palestine (1920–1948), to the ruler of Kuwait Sheikh Sir Ahmad bin Jaber Al-Sabah asked for a financial contribution to support the strike in Palestine.[3] Kuwait's ruler forbade public contributions, but money was collected and sent via Al Nas newspaper in Basra to Palestine.[4] The British Agent in Kuwait, Captain G. S. de Gaury noted a discrepancy between the Arab Bedouin who had little information on Palestine and the more informed Kuwaiti townspeople who felt an affinity toward the Palestinians.[5] Subsequently, a committee of leading Kuwaiti merchants and notables was established to help Palestinians, whose fundraising efforts were curtailed once the strike ended.

Bahrain's ruler Sheikh Hamad bin Isa Al-Khalifah also received a letter asking for help from the Palestinians. The letter was shown to British Political Agent Tom Hickinbotham who responded that "the [the Sheikh] would be ill advised to associate himself with [it] in any way." The advice was heeded,[6] perhaps more so because anti-British sentiment was spreading from Palestine into the Gulf, and compromising British protection and influence governed by treaties such as the Exclusive Agreement between Britain and Bahrain (1892), the Trucial States (1892), and Qatar (1916). This forbade Arab Gulf States from entering into any agreement or correspondence with powers other than with Britain. Kuwait could correspond directly with the Palestinians, but not receive representation from any other country other than from Britain, and was therefore the only Gulf entity able to lobby the British government and the League of Nations on partition plans for Palestine. Despite Oman's commercial agreements with the United States (1833) and France (1844), the sheikhdom was a British protectorate.[7]

President Woodrow Wilson's Fourteen Points of principles for peace to end the First World War (1914–1918), including freedom of the seas and self-determination, continued to erode British authority in the Gulf. Equally concerning was emerging news which undermined British prestige. An Iraqi newspaper reported about anti-British uprisings by tribes in the North-West frontier of India in sympathy with Palestinians that left more than 1,000 people dead.[8] The wider impact of the relatively open Iraqi media, the higher education of the Kuwaiti merchant class in Iraq, and a wave of Arab nationalism that spread through Iraq ultimately impacted Gulf response to Palestine. Kuwaiti opposition groups were linked to Palestine, which was instrumental in the creation of the Kuwaiti legislative council in 1938, similar to a body created earlier by the Kuwaiti leader's grandfather Mubarak Al-Sabah (Mubarak "the Great"). Council membership and voting, however, was restricted to 150 leading families of Kuwait whose competing economic and political interests ultimately led to its collapse.

Meanwhile, a paper written by a Shia alim (Islamic scholar) in the Iraqi city of Najaf, by the name of Shaykh Muhammad Husayn Al-Kashif al Ghata, appealed to the Muslim world to save Palestine and circulated to Bahrain via Dubai.[9] In 1937, a man from Sharjah, Mubarak bin Sayf, delivered a speech in a Dubai mosque and in Sharjah about Palestine, appealing for help for the Palestinians.[10] The content of the speech was communicable by radio and newspapers. The more pragmatic ruler of Oman, Said bin Taymur, viewed the 1937 British-devised Peel Commission Report investigating the causes of unrest in Mandatory Palestine as a workable solution because it maintained that it was not possible to expel either the Arabs or the Jews from Palestine.

After the Arab press blamed the Sunnis and Shias of Bahrain for taking only limited interest in Palestinian affairs, a brother to Bahrain's ruler Sheikh Abdullah bin Isa chaired a fundraising event for Palestine. Saudi interest in Palestine would form a substantial part of discussions between King Abd al-Aziz Al Saud and President Franklin D. Roosevelt in 1945 on board the USS Quincy in the Suez Canal. President Roosevelt argued for a Jewish state, while Abd al-Aziz thought the Jews could benefit by building themselves a new state in Bavaria, Germany.[11]

On November 29, 1947, the United Nations General Assembly (UNGA) passed Resolution 181 which suggested the creation of two states, one Jewish and one Arab. The United Nations (UN) Partition Plan for Palestine envisioned a Jewish state on an area representing roughly 56.47 percent of the total land, inhabited by 300,000 Jews and 400,000 Arab-Palestinians, and an Arab state covering 42.88 percent of the total land with 10,000 Jews and 800,000 Arab-Palestinians.[12] Jerusalem was to be subject to a Special International Regime under UN control.[13] The resolution was controversial when it passed due to a range of territorial, demographic, and existential claims over the land in question, and a rise in the immigrant Jewish population and decline in the Arab-Palestinian population resulting from their immigration to South America.[14]

The May 1948 Arab-Israeli War that broke out when the British mandate in Palestine expired, involved Egypt, Lebanon, Syria, Jordan, and Iraq against the newly formed Israeli state. The newly founded Israeli Defense Forces repelled the Arab troops. In the Gulf, states' attitudes reflected growing dissatisfaction with the British among the merchant class in places such as Kuwait and Bahrain. For example, after partition resulting from Israel's proclamation of independent statehood in May 1948, Bahrain declared a Palestine Day, closed shops and fundraised to help Palestinians retain lands rather than sell them to Jewish immigrants. Cultural hubs and societies served as centers of political ideas and dissemination, inclusive of businessmen, students, and employees from major enterprises such as the Bahrain Petroleum Company.[15]

For the most part, however, the small Jewish community in Bahrain expressed willingness to go along with decisions taken by Sheikh Abdullah bin Isa Al Khalifa, in the Committee for the Liberation of Palestine.[16] The Bahraini leader was a politician, cabinet minister, and from 1938, chief judge of the Court of Cassation (the final court of appeal for all civil, commercial, and criminal matters). Sheikh Salman bin Hamad Al Khalifa, then ruler of Bahrain, received Palestinian delegates. But he did not see them off at the airport or pay return visits, thereby showing sympathy for the Palestinian cause but not enough to warrant further action.

ARAB-ISRAELI RELATIONS AFTER THE SECOND WORLD WAR

What the Palestinians call the Nakba ("disaster," "catastrophe") took place between 1947 and 1949. It involved the permanent displacement of the majority of Palestinian Arabs, estimated at around 700,000, who fled or were expelled.[17] Palestinian refugees were received in tents and camps throughout the Arab world, changing their identity and helping to crystalize political opposition to Israel in Kuwait and Bahrain. The status of Jewish citizens in Arab states consequently worsened. Most Jews migrated or were expelled in acts of Arab solidarity with the Palestinians from 1948 to the early 1970s, starting in Iraq, Yemen, and Libya. Many Jews would later leave Iran after its Islamic Revolution of 1979. From a peak of 100,000 to 150,000 before the revolution, by 2018 that number had dwindled to around 12,000 and continues to fall amid unresolved geopolitical tensions.[18]

By the end of the First Arab-Israeli War in 1949, a number of armistice lines were established, creating the Gaza Strip which was occupied by Egypt,

East Jerusalem, and the West Bank occupied by Jordan. Since none of Israel's neighbors recognized Israel at the time, the borders remained unset. Egypt closed the narrow passage between the Sinai and Arabian Peninsula known as the Straits of Tiran when the State of Israel was created in 1948, up to the Suez Crisis in 1956. At that time, Israel deemed the closure casus belli for joint action with Britain and France, which led to the Suez Crisis. Following the Sinai War (or the Second Arab-Israeli War) in late 1956, the UNGA set up a peacekeeping UN Emergency Force (UNEF) on the border between Egypt and Israel. Tensions remained, including over control of the headwaters of the Jordan River and the issue of increased terrorism activity against Israel from bases in Syria and Jordan. Subsequently, Egyptian President Gamal Abdel Nasser ordered UNEF to leave Egypt.[19]

Israel carried out a preemptive attack against Egypt (and Syria) between June 5 and 10, 1967. Following the attack, it took the Gaza Strip, a slice of territory on the Mediterranean coast formerly administered by Egypt. Due to the rapid territorial acquisition, Israel became complacent to the idea of accommodation and territorial compromise with its Arab neighbors.[20] The Six-Day War, also known as the Third Arab-Israeli War, enabled Israel to control the Straits of Tiran, drawing in Jordan, Syria, and Egypt into the conflict. A small contingent of troops from Saudi Arabia assisted the Jordanian military, but arrived too late to fight.[21] Israel captured the Sinai Peninsula, Gaza Strip, West Bank, East Jerusalem including the Old City, and the Golan Heights. An unwavering Israeli occupation created a deadlock to diplomatic solutions. Israeli leverage over Syria and Egypt immediately subordinated Arab interests regarding Palestinians to more immediate national interests of territorial recovery.

Saudi Arabia supported an Iraqi proposal to cut oil production, a precursor to the more effective use of the oil embargo in the 1973 Yom Kippur/Ramadan War (or the Fourth Arab-Israeli War) when the United States and Europe were more dependent on the Gulf region for energy supplies. The legacy of the war was the fundamental reorientation of Saudi foreign policy toward the Arab world. Although Saudi Arabia played no significant role in the June War, Saudi thinking shifted in favor of working with President Nasser to help recover Arab control of East Jerusalem which had been lost by Jordan.[22]

The Kingdom of Saudi Arabia proceeded to back Yasser Arafat, the Palestinian political leader and chairman of the Palestinian Liberation Organization (PLO) from 1969 to 2004. The PLO is a nationalist coalition that is recognized as the official representative of the Palestinian people, before the PLO and State of Israel agreed that Palestinian National Authority (PNA) which was envisaged as an interim body, established in 1994, to help deliver a two-state solution. Arafat was president of the PNA from 1994 to 2004. Saudi Arabia supported Palestinian statehood and sought to create pan-Islamic movements. Riyadh also backed an Islamic summit in Morocco after an arson attack on the Al-Aqsa Mosque, a move that led to the founding of the Organisation of the Islamic Conference in 1969, later renamed the Organisation of Islamic Cooperation (OIC).

The 1973 war fought by Egypt and Syria against Israel aimed at recovering the Sinai Peninsula and the Golan Heights. Egypt would eventually reclaim the Sinai through the Camp David Accords in 1979, by making peace with Israel at the cost of abandoning the cause of Palestinian self-determination. Syria refused to build peace with Israel unless it regained possession of the Golan Heights. In the Gulf, the Organization of Arab Petroleum Exporting Countries (OAPEC) implemented an oil embargo against Israel and its allies who provided military aid to the Jewish state, including the United States, Netherlands, Portugal, and South Africa. The embargo was undertaken in an attempt to persuade the United States to bring about peace between Israel and its Arab neighbors. It ended in 1974, when Egyptian president Anwar Sadat reported to the Saudi leader, King Faisal bin Abd al-Aziz Al Saud, that the United States was being more even-handed over the Arab-Israel conflict. The US secretary of state Henry Kissinger proceeded to agree to sell Saudi Arabia weapons previously blocked by the US Congress over fears they might be used against Israel, once Riyadh and Cairo worked together to promote peace through the Camp David Accords.

Following the 1967 war, once Israel took control of the West Bank and Gaza, Israeli settlement activity expanded into Hebron, the old city of Jerusalem, and in the southern part of the Golan Heights.[23] Settlements increased when the Israeli right-wing Likud party came to power in 1977.[24] Partly in response to such developments, Palestinian frustration grew, resulting in the first Intifada in the form of a sustained series of protests and violent riots, beginning in December 1987. Over the following years, PLO leaders met secretly with Israeli officials, culminating in the announcement of the Oslo I Accord or the Declaration of Principles (DoP) on Interim Self-Government Arrangements in September 1993. The DoP was an attempt to set up a framework that would lead to the resolution of the Israel-Palestine conflict and was the first face-to-face agreement between the PLO and the State of Israel, supported by then President Bill Clinton.

Earlier in 1989, the administration of US president George H. W. Bush proposed a measured policy toward Israel aimed at halting Israeli settlement activity. This was a departure from conventional US foreign policy wisdom in providing Israel with unconditional diplomatic and military support. The US secretary of state, James Baker III, stated that Israel should abandon its expansionist policies in the West Bank and reach out to Arabs.[25]

The lead up to the Gulf War (1990-91), resulted in a US-led and Arab-funded international military coalition to repel the advancement of the Iraqi forces, and put pressure on Israel and the PLO to commit to a peace conference.[26] Russia and the US co-sponsored the Madrid Conference in October 1991, in which Israel, Jordanian-Palestinian delegates, Egypt, the European Community, the GCC, and the UN took part. Lebanon and Syria did not participate although they were invited.[27]

The desired outcome of the conference—bilateral talks between Israeli, Syrian, Jordanian, and Palestinian representatives—became deadlocked. But secret Israeli-Palestinian and Israeli-Jordanian talks picked up, leading to the Oslo I Accord. Major issues such as the status of Jerusalem, the right of return for Palestinian refugees, Israeli settlements, security, and borders would fall under permanent status negotiations. The settlement of the Palestinian refugee crisis, a major theme since the Nakba, remained unclear, but refugees had grown in the millions living in camps in Jordan, Lebanon, Syria, the Gaza Strip, and the West Bank.[28] Many other Palestinians left their homes to travel abroad and settled in the GCC states in search of work. On November 4, 1995, after attending an anti-violence rally in support of the Oslo peace process, Yitzhak Rabin, then prime minister of Israel, was assassinated by a far-right law student. The Oslo Accords represented a gradualist approach and an effort at building trust, and even if Rabin had survived, there is evidence to suggest that concluding final status issues depended on compromises that both leaders may not have been ready to make within the five-year timeframe.[29]

By the end of President Bill Clinton's second term in office (1996–2000), Washington embarked on inviting PLO Chairman Yasser Arafat and Israeli prime minister Ehud Barak to Camp David in an effort to reach a conflict-ending accord. Differences between the three sides pushed them apart, including Clinton's and Arafat's individual concerns about their legacies, and Barak's prioritization of peace with Syria over the Palestinians. Furthermore, Arafat needed the support of the Arab states including mainly Saudi Arabia and Egypt whose officials were not in attendance.[30] The failure of the negotiations, including Israeli prime minister Ehud Barak's lack of concessions (including on withdrawal of settlers, Palestinian sovereignty over mosques in the Old City, and allowing a Palestinian capital in East Jerusalem[31]), Yasser Arafat's tolerance for Palestinian militant groups, and wider Palestinian discontent with Oslo I, were additional challenges at Camp David. The failure of the negotiations was uniquely leveled at Arafat.

As intolerance in Israel over the prospects of peace with the Arabs grew, conditions on the ground worsened. Likud leader Aerial Sharon's provocative walk in Al-Aqsa on September 28, 2000, triggered the second Palestinian Intifada that lasted through February 8, 2005. In this new securitized environment, Sharon became the prime minister in March 2001. Tensions only subsided in 2005 when the PNA presidential elections were held in the

West Bank and Gaza, soon after Arafat died on November 11, 2004. By April 2006, Sharon was himself incapacitated by a massive stroke. Meanwhile, Hamas, the violent Islamist movement with regional links, especially support from Iran, sustained its resistance against Israel from its popular base in Gaza.[32] The group went on to achieve electoral victory in the 2006 Palestinian legislative election, securing seventy-four seats against forty-three seats for Fatah.[33] A unity government was formed in Gaza in 2007, but Hamas broke the deal and took control of the Gaza Strip, creating a Palestinian political and territorial cleavage that endures.

FROM ARAB PEACE INITIATIVE TO ABRAHAM ACCORDS

The Saudi-led API adopted by the Arab League in 2002 stated an intent to recognize Israel in exchange for its withdrawal from occupied Arab territories in the West Bank, Gaza, and the Golan Heights. Seeking a "just settlement" of the Palestinian refugee problem based on 1948 UN Resolution 194, and the establishment of a sovereign and economically viable Palestinian state with East Jerusalem as its capital, the initiative was ignored by Israel and in Washington. Since the majority of the 9/11 terror suspects were Saudi citizens, the timing of the API initiative matched a hawkish neoconservative and particularly pro-Israeli agenda in Washington in the lead up to the 2003 Iraq War, and was tabled during the Second Intifada. It was not the paradigm shifting moment that it should have been.

The Palestinian issue was also marginal at the time because the GCC states began paying more attention to their own internal security and enhanced political and security ties with the US and other Western powers post-9/11. In particular, the G. W. Bush administration promoted a Greater Middle East Initiative (GMEI) in April 2004 via the G-8 industrialized states and aimed at advancing democracy in the region but it was largely undermined by the US-led intervention in Iraq. By 2011, when dissident internal fractions generated by the Arab Spring emerged across the GCC as Iran's influence in Iraq grew, the Arab Gulf States understood that preserving their internal security was paramount. President Barack Obama's policies during the Arab Spring, including indirectly supporting the ouster of a long-time GCC ally, Egyptian president Hosni Mubarak, increased GCC threat perceptions. The announcement of a US "pivot" to Asia in 2010 and, from 2013, the lead-up to the 2015 Joint Comprehensive Plan of Action (JCPOA) nuclear deal with Iran set the tone for the GCC to refocus on preserving regional security, as Saudi leader King Abdullah bin Abd Al-Aziz Al Saud urged the United States to halt the advancement of Iran's nuclear program.[34]

When Abdullah's successors King Salman bin Abd al-Aziz Al Saud and Crown Prince Mohammed bin Salman bin Abd al-Aziz Al Saud assumed power in 2015 and 2017 respectively, they stressed the need to contain Iranian nuclear ambitions and regional influence.

Israeli prime minister Netanyahu, who rose to power on the back of opposing peace talks which he saw as risking Israeli security, challenged the Obama administration for its pursuit of a nuclear agreement with Iran and its tough stance on Israeli settlement activity, which—along with relegating the Palestinian statehood issue—were prerequisites to the prime minister's ability to retain a right-wing majority in the Knesset. Having "waited out" President Obama over his policies with Iran and on the issue of the Arab Spring,[35] Saudi Arabia and the UAE also proceeded to publicly turn against President Obama's policies, by showing support for President Donald J. Trump's unilateral decision to withdraw the United States from the JCPOA in May 2018. However, Saudi Arabia called for caution on the issue and the need to maintain a nuclear deal with Iran. Israel criticized the deal for falling short of preventing Iran from developing a nuclear weapon. The GCC states, led by Saudi Arabia, reluctantly backed the JCPOA in a possible quid pro quo involving the United States backing for the war on the Houthis in Yemen from March 2015.

Saudi, Emirati, and Israeli opinions in fact converged on two points of containing Iran and maintaining the regional status quo in the GCC states post-Arab Spring. President Trump's carte blanche and transactional approach enabled Saudi and UAE influence on regional issues to expand, especially viz-à-viz the isolation of Qatar and the GCC Crisis 2017–2021. Meanwhile, the Saudi-led military coalition war in Yemen against the Iranian-backed Houthis escalated, and the Trump administration's "maximum pressure" policy against Iran further incentivized Tehran to steadfastly increase its outreach to its network, including Hamas and the Palestinian Islamic Jihad.

In 2018, the Trump administration declared that it would move the US embassy to Jerusalem and withdrew US funding from the United Nations Relief and Works Agency (UNRWA), the primary UN agency tasked with assisting Palestinian refugees. A much-touted US "economy first" peace plan for Arab-Israeli normalization was launched in Bahrain in June 2019. Although many of the GCC states paid lip service in support of it, pressure from the Palestinian leadership ensured a more nuanced approach. For example, Saudi Arabia and PNA agreed to form a joint economic committee in November 2019 to develop concrete collaborative projects.[36] Qatar is a staunch supporter of Hamas, and the UAE has found a greater impact on Palestinian politics through supporting Mohammed Dahlan, a former Palestinian official. While ostensibly serving Palestine, the variety of these inputs reflects the intra-GCC competition taking place. President Trump's follow-up "Peace to Prosperity" plan, launched in January 2020 to improve the lives of the Palestinian and Israeli people now with both a political and an economic framework, was criticized for being vague and not providing a clear linkage between stopping Israeli annexation and proceeding with negotiations.[37]

The Trump administration thus enabled the Israeli 2020 annexation plan in parts of the West Bank to go ahead unimpeded. The Abraham Accords was another missed opportunity to constrain Israeli settlement activity and provide a solid basis for dialogue and actions that support a two-state solution. The accords are supposed to promote interfaith and intercultural dialogue, support tolerance and respect, boost cooperation, and end radicalization and conflict.[38] While its first signatories, Bahrain and the UAE, were in support of measures to sustain a possible two-state solution, the accords have not addressed the underlying conflict. Escalation in places such as Sheikh Jarrah, a neighborhood in East Jerusalem, where Israeli settlers had moved in, has become a regular occurrence.

Furthermore, amid a deteriorating regional security environment following Iran-sponsored attacks on Saudi oil installations at Abqaiq and Khurais in 2019, ongoing Houthi and Iranian attacks on Gulf shipping, and the Iranian-sponsored attack on US troops at al-Asad base in Iraq in response to the assassination of General Soleimani in 2021, US credibility in the region has been deteriorating. This has caused Saudi Arabia to shift policy to prize regionalism and pursue "strategic autonomy" in a number of ways: ending the GCC Crisis with Qatar in January 2021; opening a dialogue with Iran in Baghdad, engaging with Turkey, and bringing Assad's Syria back into the Arab fold.

President Joseph R. Biden Jr. continued to work on expanding the accords through meetings and military exercises to counter the Iranian missile and drone threat, policies which the Trump administration had earlier encouraged. Military drills included top-level personnel from Israel, the UAE, Saudi Arabia, Bahrain, Egypt, and Jordan.[39] But the more contained Iran felt in the region, the less likely it appeared that either the Iran nuclear crisis or the Palestinian issue could be resolved peacefully.

On October 7, 2023, Hamas carried out an attack against Israel, killing and wounding hundreds, engaging in sexual violence, and then abducting 253 Israeli citizens.[40] Iran congratulated the Palestinian group for its ability to penetrate Israel's tightly secure borders. By then, the general view in the Middle East was that the Abraham Accords were temporarily derailed and that the ensuing Israel-Hamas war discouraged Saudi Arabia from joining the accords. Bahrain, meanwhile, distanced itself from the accords as the death toll of Palestinians in Gaza mounted, and cut off its economic ties with Israel.

APPLICATION OF THEORY TO CASE STUDIES

A single theory fails to sufficiently explain the complexity of Israel's ties with the GCC states, and its policies toward the Palestinians and Iran. The present book introduces theory in separate chapters. Israeli and Palestinian policies are discussed in two separate chapters, followed by case studies on Israel's connections with Iran and the individual GCC states.

A long-standing debate affecting this book's theoretical perspectives involves the issue of whether or not Israel's ties with the Gulf region could precede Israel-Palestine peace or not. There is no straightforward answer to this question, mindful of the intractable Palestinian conflict and yet a desire by the GCC states to retain strong ties with the United States and possibly by extension with Israel down the road in order to keep Iranian power and influence contained. Much is set to depend on the reach for strategic autonomy that many of the GCC states are now engaged in and the extent to which external actors, such as China, will continue to engage in the region. So far, China's impact has been limited to Saudi-Iranian normalization and remains dependent on the US-led hard power architecture established over decades.

The chapters set out in this book reveal the complexities of forming ties with Israel without peace in Palestine in place, and in the absence of an honest broker to build and maintain the peace. Variables including the impact of pan-Arab public opinion on the Abraham Accords, geostrategic considerations and US policy preferences, and Iranian behavior are examined to show their significant constraint or impact on the direction, persistence, and expansion of the Abraham Accords.

Shifts in the Middle East order since 9/11, coupled with generational and leadership challenges after the Arab Spring are critical to the better understanding of Israel's position specifically in the Gulf region. Earlier, when Washington entered its "unipolar moment" in 1991 immediately after the collapse of the former Soviet Union, and "Gulf moment" at around the same time to forge stronger partnerships with the GCC, it was briefly successful in forging a more balanced Middle East policy between the Arabs and Israel. But Washington no longer operates in a unipolar world. More importantly, the breadth and depth of negotiations that take place now to resolve the Arab-Israeli conflict involve a range of stakeholders and an asymmetry in power relations encouraged upheld by Iran and its allies, which thwart peace with Israel.

In 2017, Arab public opposition to diplomatic recognition of Israel was found to range from 65 percent in Saudi Arabia and 74 percent in Egypt, up to 99 percent in Algeria.[41] Some 45.3 percent of those polled cited reasons related to the occupation of Palestinian lands by Israel and the repression of Palestinian rights.[42] The swearing-in of Israel's most far-right government in history at the end of 2022 was set to create further ruptures across the Gulf region and in Palestine on the issue of normalization and peace, as settlement expansion became almost a norm.

Beyond the broader historical, regional, and political contexts in which Israel-Palestinian-GCC relations have developed and operated, and tensions between Israel and Iran persisted, this book assumes a broadly defined realist foreign policy behavior by different actors. However, its realist as well as structural realist underpinnings, in which power and state security matter the most, are challenged by a thorough analysis of domestic forces and relevant theories that shape Israel's relations with the GCC and Iran.[43] Israel's relations with Iraq, another major Gulf state, are left out simply because of the absence of formal ties between the two, and Iraq's complex relations with its Gulf neighbors to ensure internal Iraqi security first before it is able to become a major regional player next. But Iraq and Syria are discussed if and when they relate to events covered in the chapter discussions.

Barry Buzan's regional security complex theory (RSCT) attests that a regional perspective is needed to account for the constraints and opportunities therein.[44] In the context of the Gulf region, since the Arab Spring, the next big issue complicating a regional perspective on the topic of ties with Israel is Iran's nuclear program and relationship with non-state actors such as the Lebanese Hezbollah and Hamas. These complexities are explored in terms of their influence on the security choices that the GCC states, the Palestinians, and Israel make, and the Iranian stance in relation to these choices. Furthermore, core-periphery ties between the Arab core and the non-Arab so-called periphery states of the Middle East region—mainly Israel and Iran—and the shift in these ties due to the Arab Spring and the Abraham Accords are explored in several chapters.

Motivated by a desire for survival and security, states operating according to a realist perspective are said to develop military capabilities and hard power (military power) to constrain the most powerful state that represents a potential threat. Small states like Bahrain, Qatar, and the UAE which may lack such capacities can adopt a range of different behaviors to ensure security as well. They may bandwagon, whereby they accept the power of another party like the United States and join with it. Or they may choose to reject that party's power and seek to counter its influence by joining with others to contain regional conflicts. Meanwhile, they may advance balancing strategies to ensure that they can retain ties with different regional stakeholders while building up hard power. While balancing may be largely motivated by external or international factors, omni-balancing can enable states to pursue relative autonomy by identifying the connections between addressing threats at the domestic, regional, and international levels.[45] Some states, like Qatar and the UAE, have been found to follow this pattern.[46]

Alternatively, a number of Gulf States may opt to hedge, a midpoint tactic between bandwagon and balancing, in which they adopt a number of different and apparently contradictory forms of behavior that include cooperating with stronger actors while also avoiding confrontation with them or other strong but rival actors, to reduce the cost of conflict. In sum, hedging may be seen as a way of maintaining ambiguity and freedom of maneuver in such conflictual circumstances.[47]

In a period when US conditionality was expected from the Biden administration in contrast to the more transactional approach of the Trump administration toward the issue of Arab-Israeli peace, the Saudi and UAE balancing has gone into overdrive by building security-related ties in parallel. While many of the security opportunities in the international environment also besetting the Gulf region represent familiar patterns of balancing, the timing and number of switches to alternative sources of arms, joint ventures, or security agreements for example (including with regional states such as Iran) point to a significant element of hedging (since their outcome or effect is unknown). In a period of more intense international competition in the Middle East, there is also a degree of signaling to the United States for concessions toward Palestine and the recognition that GCC state ambitions as autonomous actors cannot be contained.

Political consolidation in the Gulf region domestically has potentially reduced external and domestic threats and increased the degree of autonomy of younger leaders including Crown Prince Mohammed bin Salman Al Saud and the UAE leader Mohammed bin Zayed Al Nahyan. Saudi Arabia and the UAE, ahead in their economic diversification compared to many other states in the GCC, have used their respective development visions and plans to capture economic and security opportunities relevant to their long-term autonomy, such as the creation and expansion of military-industrial complexes. More broadly in the GCC, member states have coalesced primary around common security goals.[48]

This selective bandwagon tactic by the GCC states has run concurrently with more ingrained and widespread practices of balancing with the United States as the primary security guarantor for the Gulf region and balancing with European states such as the United Kingdom and France as secondary security providers, against perceived or actual threats from Iran. Rents and rentierism, however, historically central concepts in understanding the dependent nature of Gulf governments and societies on protection guarantees, remain insufficiently developed to address state power and societal ties in recent years.[49] Rapid GCC state diversification and the necessity to engage in the global economy more broadly (e.g., by attracting trade and investment, tourism, and expat labor) are now also segments to the better understanding of the GCC normalization drive with Israel.

Since the Arab Spring, the number and intensity of perceived ontological threats—such as those based on identities similar to the Shia-state of Iran and the Sunni branches of the Muslim Brotherhood[50]—influence Gulf-Israeli relations. Iran and countries that it backs such as Syria, as well as the Brotherhood stand accused of creating instability across the Middle East and Gulf region.[51] Presumably, hence, the Abraham Accords are rooted in realist assumptions about the need to contain Iran and the Brotherhood. The fact that Saudi Arabia and the UAE welcomed Syrian president Bashar al-Assad back to the Arab fold and entertained it rejoining the Arab League, after nearly a decade-long bloody Syrian civil war since 2011, spoke toward renewed leadership by the GCC to address any challenges from within the region that might trigger future conflicts. The GCC also contained the Egyptian Muslim Brotherhood's brief rise to power after the Arab Spring and signaled to Iran that its foreign policy behavior had to accommodate the interests of the Arab Gulf States.[52]

Tacit Security Regimes (TSRs) reflect economic and military power which are not entirely about the "security dilemma" faced by the GCC, but about converging interests to contain threats.[53] TSRs are described as "interest-based, limited, and informal mechanisms of cooperation between states for the purpose of deconflicting their respective interests" over specific security issues.[54] The exploration of Israel's relations with the GCC states in the present book sheds further light on the function of TSRs or its failure to function in the face of other intervening factors involving Gulf-Israeli ties.

STRUCTURE OF THE VOLUME

In chapter 1, Banafsheh Keynoush explains the strategic relevance of the Abraham Accords through shifting periphery-core constructs, designed to show how Iran and Israel were different from other countries in the Middle East that had a shared core pan-Arab identity. Rationalizing periphery-core relations through improved ties between Israel and the core Arab Gulf States, as her chapter shows, could take place only by considering the larger framework of world systems theory and its examination of the Gulf region's asymmetrical economic dependency and sociopolitical inequality patterns within the context of the Arab Spring, the Abraham Accords, and the challenge to the Gulf region from Iran. The chapter therefore discusses a host of relevant security, leadership, and social factors impacting the Iranian-Israeli connection.

In chapter 2, Guy Burton provides an overview of Israel-GCC state relations, locating the Abraham Accords as an extension of Israel's "periphery doctrine" from the 1950s designed to reach out to non-hostile regional states in the Middle East, normalization with formerly hostile states in the Arab world that began in 1979, and more recent clandestine relationships in the Arab Gulf with an emphasis on national security. He asserts that regional instability from the Arab Spring that enhanced Iranian influence coincided with perceived uncertainties about US influence in the wider region and that both are key in contextualizing the Abraham Accords, along with its bridging role through Israel's special relationship with the United States.

In chapter 3, Guy Burton explores the divided Palestinian polity and the opportunities that such divisions have created for the GCC states to engage with Fatah and/or Hamas. These are found to have developed over time from more passive aid transfers to more prominent roles played by Saudi Arabia, Qatar, and the UAE. The chapter notes the de-prioritization of the Palestine cause vis-à-vis Arab identity and major national interests of the GCC states, a feature that is pertinent to the signing of the Abraham Accords in the cases of Bahrain and the UAE.

Chapter 4 explores UAE-Israeli relations. Robert Mason determines that UAE foreign policy orientation has undergone a radical shift in recent years reflecting its changes in leadership, visceral responses to Islamist groups in the region, and a sustained threat perception vis-à-vis Iran. The UAE is relatively unusual among GCC states in that it has gained significant hard and soft power status in recent years. However, growing military assertiveness has come at a cost, particularly with regard to its vulnerability from Houthi attacks from Yemen and from escalations in the Gulf. The UAE government has used economic statecraft to contribute to its alliance formations and consolidation of relations with the United States, Israel, and others. Israel also fills an important security gap in terms of surveillance technology and in missile defense. The ongoing question for signatories to the Abraham Accords such as the UAE is to what extent elite politics can manage the normalization process in the context of Israel's far-right governments and policies that continue to expand settlements in pursuit of a one-state hegemonic "solution."

Chapter 5 by Banafsheh Keynoush reviews the reasons why Bahrain embraced normalization with Israel, and its consequences for Bahraini-Israeli security, economic, leadership, social, and cultural ties. The author looks at the ties not only through the "economy first" model designed to promote the Abraham Accords but also through defense-layered security partnerships between Bahrain and Israel. In addition, she reviews the impact of the relations in view of Bahrain's complex social and cultural fabric, and Bahraini vulnerabilities as a small Gulf state.

Chapter 6 by Guy Burton draws attention to the long-standing and pragmatic relations between Qatar and Israel even if these states are yet to normalize their relations. Qatar has led on transfers of aid to Hamas-controlled Gaza, and as a small state with significant soft power capabilities, it is able to hedge and advance a series of policy positions simultaneously. A key mediator but one with a divergent position from other actors such as Saudi Arabia and the UAE, especially its hospitality to the Muslim Brotherhood, Qatar has remained an outlier in accepted norms of GCC state relations within the region. Doha's close relations with the United States and an ongoing rapprochement within the GCC hold out possibilities for more aligned policies into the future, conditioned by Qatar's policy of adhering to the two-state solution competition with Egypt/UAE for influence over Hamas/Gaza, and therefore the future of the Palestinian polity.

In chapter 7, Banafsheh Keynoush reviews the connection between Saudi Arabia and Israel in the context of the Abraham Accords through realist calculations including the need to contain Iran and end the conflict in Palestine. She examines a host of complex security, political, economic, leadership, social, and cultural factors to unravel the details of the Saudi-Israeli connection, and she introduces military and non-military aspects of problem-solving to better understand this connection in the fluid security spheres in which the two countries operate.

In chapter 8, Robert Mason delves into the historic connections between Oman and Israel. Still short of recognition, relations are shown to be rooted in the Dhofar Rebellion, Oman's balanced foreign policy (including consistent contact with PLO, Israeli and Iranian officials) and contact with Israeli officialdom through regional forums such as the Middle East Desalination Research Center based in Muscat. Oman continues to play the role of valued interlocutor in regional affairs, but must carefully balance that role with premature recognition. Lessons may be learned by Oman and others in the GCC as to the sequencing of moves to recognize and normalize relations, as in the case of Syria being welcomed back into the Arab League.

Robert Mason explores Kuwait and Israel in chapter 9, from PLO Chairman Arafat's alignment with Saddam Hussein during the Gulf War to Kuwait's adherence to the API and the role of Palestinians in the Kuwaiti economy. He also looks to the relatively unique role played by the Kuwaiti National Assembly, the continuity of the Kuwaiti leadership on the Palestinian cause, and how Arab solidarity informs policy despite some evidence of dissenting views in Kuwaiti media outlets. The chapter also draws attention to the potential role played by GCC states at different stages of economic diversification and their absorptive capacity of new sources of FDI.

The conclusion to the book returns to several of the points set out in the introduction as well as in the individual chapters themselves to offer a conceptually rich interpretation of the Abraham Accords relevant to the GCC states and possibly other Arab states that have embarked on the recognition and normalization process. It answers the research question as to what the leading drivers of the accords are and on which points they are most or least sustainable. It also takes into consideration the extent to which GCC states and Israel are occupied in efforts at bandwagoning, (omni)balancing, and hedging when it comes to the question of normalization. In sum, the book looks beyond the current empirical tapestry to lay out a framework which supports our understanding of the myriad of domestic, regional, and international political, social, security, and economic issues that play into elite decision-making and could yet form pressures for recalculation and recalibration.

NOTES

1. United Nations, "Gaza: 'Thousands of Children Killed' Within a Few Weeks, Says UN's Guterres," November 20, 2023, https://news.un.org/en/story/2023/11/1143772#:~:text=According%20to%20the%20UN%20agency%2C%20more%20than%20880%2C000,11%2C000%20people%20in%20Gaza%20according%20to%20health%20authorities.
2. Lisa Anderson, "The Forty-Year War," *Foreign Affairs,* May/June 2023, https://www.foreignaffairs.com/reviews/middle-east-forty-year-war-china.
3. Rosemarie Said Zahlan, "The Gulf States and the Palestine Problem, 1936–48," *Arab Studies Quarterly,* 3(1) (Winter 1981): 1.
4. Ibid, 1–2.
5. Ibid, 3.
6. Ibid, 2.
7. Ibid, 3.
8. Ibid, 4.
9. Ibid, 5.
10. Ibid, 6.
11. Bruce Riedel, "75 Years after a Historic Meeting on the USS Quincy, US-Saudi Relations are in Need of a True Rethink," *Brookings,* February 10, 2020, https://www.brookings.edu/blog/order-from-chaos/2020/02/10/75-years-after-a-historic-meeting-on-the-uss-quincy-us-saudi-relations-are-in-need-of-a-true-re-think/.
12. Lorenzo Kamel, "Framing the Partition Plan for Palestine," *The Cairo Review of Global* Affairs, Winter 2022, https://www.thecairoreview.com/essays/framing-the-partition-plan-for-palestine/.
13. Ibid.
14. Ibid.
15. Zahlan, "The Gulf States and the Palestine Problem, 1936-48," 16.
16. Ibid.
17. Rashid Khalidi, "Contrasting Narratives of Palestinian Identity," in *Palestinian Identity: The Construction of Modern National Consciousness* (New York: Columbia University Press, 2009), 21.
18. Kim Hjelmgaard, "Iran's Jewish Community is the Largest in the Mideast Outside Israel – and Feels Safe and Respected," *USA Today,* August 2, 2018, https://www.usatoday.com/in-depth/news/world/inside-iran/2018/08/29/iran-jewish-population-islamic-state/886790002/.

19. Government of Canada, "United Nations Emergency Force 1 (UNEF 1)," https://www.canada.ca/en/department-national-defence/services/military-history/history-heritage/past-operations/middle-east/united-nations-emergency-force-i.html.

20. Martin Bunton, "Occupation 1967-87," in *The Palestinian-Israeli Conflict: A Very Short Introduction* (Oxford: Oxford University Press, 2013), 70–86.

21. Bruce Riedel, "How the 1967 War Dramatically Re-orientated Saudi Arabia's Foreign Policy," *Brookings*, May 30, 2017, https://www.brookings.edu/blog/markaz/2017/05/30/how-the-1967-war-dramatically-re-oriented-saudi-arabias-foreign-policy/.

22. Ibid.

23. United Nations, "Israeli Settlements in Gaza and the West Bank," https://www.un.org/unispal/document/auto-insert-205221/.

24. Ibid.

25. Thomas L. Friedman, "Baker, in a Middle East Blueprint, Asks Israel to Reach Out to Arabs," *The New York Times,* May 23, 1989, https://www.nytimes.com/1989/05/23/world/baker-in-a-middle-east-blueprint-asks-israel-to-reach-out-to-arabs.html.

26. Ibid.

27. United Nations, "Invitation to Madrid Middle East Conference ('Madrid Principles') – US, USSR Letter (Non-UN Document)," https://www.un.org/unispal/document/auto-insert-208112/.

28. United Nations Relief and Works Agency for Palestinian Refugees in the Near East, "Palestinian Refugees," https://www.unrwa.org/palestine-refugees.

29. "The Life and Legacy of Yitzhak Rabin: 25 Years Later," *Council on Foreign Relations*, October 29, 2020, https://www.cfr.org/event/life-and-legacy-yitzhak-rabin-25-years-later.

30. Aaron David Miller, "Lost in the Woods: A Camp David Retrospective," *Carnegie Endowment for International Peace*, July 13, 2020, https://carnegieendowment.org/2020/07/13/lost-in-woods-camp-david-retrospective-pub-82287.

31. Jerome Slater, "Camp David, Taba, and the Clinton Parameters, 2000-2001," in *Mythologies Without End: The US, Israel, and the Arab-Israeli Conflict, 1917–2020* (Oxford: Oxford University Press, 2020), 241–273.

32. Beverley Milton-Edwards and Stephen Farrell, *Hamas: The Islamic Resistance Movement* (Cambridge: Polity, 2013).

33. Fred Kaplan, "How George W. Bush Helped Hamas Come to Power," *Slate,* October 24, 2023, https://slate.com/news-and-politics/2023/10/was-hamas-elected-to-govern-gaza-george-w-bush-2006-palestinian-election.html.

34. Ian Black and Simon Tisdall, "Saudi Arabia Urges US Attack on Iran to Stop Nuclear Programme," *The Guardian,* November 28, 2010, https://www.theguardian.com/world/2010/nov/28/us-embassy-cables-saudis-iran.

35. Ben Rhodes, "A Fatal Abandonment of American Leadership," *The Atlantic,* October 12, 2018, https://www.theatlantic.com/ideas/archive/2018/10/jamal-khashoggi-and-us-saudi-relationship/572905/.

36. Moran Zaga, "The Intra-GCC Competition Over the Palestinian Heart," *Middle East Institute*, December 18, 2019, https://www.mei.edu/publications/intra-gcc-competition-over-palestinian-heart

37. Salam Fayyad, "Trump's Middle East Peace Plan: What's There to be Upset About?," *Brookings*, February 21, 2020, https://www.brookings.edu/blog/order-from-chaos/2020/02/21/trumps-middle-east-peace-plan-whats-there-to-be-upset-about/#cancel.

38. US Department of State, "The Abraham Accords," https://www.state.gov/the-abraham-accords/.

39. Michael R. Gordon and David S. Cloud, "US Held Secret Meeting with Israel, Arab Military Chiefs to Counter Iran Air Threat," *The Wall Street Journal,* June 26, 2022, https://www.wsj.com/articles/u-s-held-secret-meeting-with-israeli-arab-military-chiefs-to-counter-iran-air-threat-11656235802.

40. "Hamas Hostages: Stories of the People Taken from Israel," *BBC News*, April 6, 2024, https://www.bbc.com/news/world-middle-east-67053011.

41. Arab Center DC, "The 2019–2020 Arab Opinion Index: Main Results in Brief," Figure 35. https://arabcenterdc.org/resource/the-2019-2020-arab-opinion-index-main-results-in-brief/.

42. Ibid, Figure 36.

43. For a broad range of discussions on Israel and US foreign policy choices and on realism and neo-realism, see John Mearsheimer, *The Great Delusion: Liberal Dreams and International Realities* (New Haven, CT: Yale University Press, 2019); John Mearsheimer and Stephen Walt, *The Israeli Lobby and US Foreign Policy.* (New York: Farrar, Straus and Giroux, 2008).

44. Barry Buzan and Ole Waever, *Regions and Powers: The Structure of International Security* (Cambridge: Cambridge University Press, 2004).

45. Gerd Nonneman, "Determinants and Patterns of Saudi Foreign Policy: 'Omni-balancing' and 'Relative Autonomy' in Multiple Environments," in *Saudi Arabia in the Balance: Political Economy, Society, Foreign Affairs,* Paul Aarts and Gerd Nonneman, eds. (New York: New York University Press, 2005), 315–351.

46. Jessica Watkins, "Identity Politics, Elites and Omni-balancing: Reassessing Arab Gulf State Interventions in the Uprisings from the Inside Out," *Conflict, Security and Development*, 20(5) (2020): 653–675.

47. Cheng-Chwee Kuik and Gilbert Rozman, "Light or Heavy Hedging: Positioning between China and the US," in *Joint US-Korea Academic Studies 2015,* Gilbert Rozman, ed. (Washington DC: Korea Economic Institute of America, 2015), 1–9, http://www.keia.org/sites/default/files/publications/introduction_-_light_or_heavy_hedging.pdf; Gustaaf Geeraets and Mohammed Salman, "Measuring Strategic Hedging Capability by Second-Tier States Under Unipolarity," *Chinese Political Science Review*, 1(1) (2016): 60–80; Kei Koga, "The Concept of 'Hedging' Revisited: the Case of Japan's Foreign Policy Strategy in East Asia's power Shift," *International Studies Review,* 20(4) (2018): 633–660.

48. Steven Wright, "Foreign Policy in the GCC," in *International Politics of the Persian Gulf*, Mehran Kamrava, ed. (Syracuse, NY: Syracuse University Press, 2011), 74.

49. Matthew Gray, "A Theory of "Late Rentierism" in the Arab States of the Gulf," Center for International and Regional Studies, Georgetown University, Occasional Paper 7, 36–37, https://repository.library.georgetown.edu/bitstream/handle/10822/558291/CIRSOccasionalPaper7MatthewGray2011.pdf.

50. May Darwich, "The Ontological (In) Security of Similarity: Wahhabism Versus Islamism in Saudi Foreign Policy," *Foreign Policy Analysis,* 12(3) (July 2016): 469–488.

51. Kenneth M. Pollack and Bilal Y. Saab, "US Strategy Options for Iran's Regional Challenge," Atlantic Council (2017), 9, https://www.atlanticcouncil.org/in-depth-research-reports/report/us-strategy-options-for-iran-s-regional-challenge/.

52. Christopher M. Davidson, *From Sheikhs to Sultanism: Statecraft and Authority in Saudi Arabia and the United Arab Emirates* (London: Hurst, 2021); Robert Mason, *Saudi Arabia and the United Arab Emirates: Foreign Policy and Strategic Alliances in an Uncertain World* (Manchester: Manchester University Press, 2023).

53. Clive Jones and Yoel Guzansky, *Fraternal Enemies: Israel and the Gulf States* (London: Hurst, 2019).

54. Asaf Siniver and Scott Lucas, "Understanding Tacit Security Regimes," *Journal of Global Security Studies,* 4(4) (October 2019): 510–525.

REFERENCES

Anderson, Lisa, "The Forty-Year War," *Foreign Affairs,* May/June 2023, https://www.foreignaffairs.com/reviews/middle-east-forty-year-war-china.

Arab Center DC, "The 2019-2020 Arab Opinion Index: Main Results in Brief," Figure 35. https://arabcenterdc.org/resource/the-2019-2020-arab-opinion-index-main-results-in-brief/.

BBC News, "Hamas Hostages: Stories of the People Taken from Israel," April 6, 2024, https://www.bbc.com/news/world-middle-east-67053011

Black, Ian, and Simon Tisdall, "Saudi Arabia Urges US Attack on Iran to Stop Nuclear Programme," *The Guardian,* November 28, 2010, https://www.theguardian.com/world/2010/nov/28/us-embassy-cables-saudis-iran.

Bunton, Martin, *The Palestinian-Israeli Conflict: A Very Short Introduction* (Oxford: Oxford University Press, 2013).

Buzan, Barry, and Ole Waever, *Regions and Powers: The Structure of International Security* (Cambridge: Cambridge University Press, 2004).

Council on Foreign Relations, "The Life and Legacy of Yitzhak Rabin: 25 Years Later," October 29, 2020, https://www.cfr.org/event/life-and-legacy-yitzhak-rabin-25-years-later.

Darwich, May, "The Ontological (In) Security of Similarity: Wahhabism Versus Islamism in Saudi Foreign Policy," *Foreign Policy Analysis,* 12(3) (July 2016): 469–488.

Davidson, Christopher M., *From Sheikhs to Sultanism: Statecraft and Authority in Saudi Arabia and the United Arab Emirates* (London: Hurst, 2021).

Fayyad, Salam, "Trump's Middle East Peace Plan: What's There to be Upset About?," *Brookings,* February 21, 2020, https://www.brookings.edu/blog/order-from-chaos/2020/02/21/trumps-middle-east-peace-plan-whats-there-to-be-upset-about/#cancel.

Friedman, Thomas L., "Baker, in a Middle East Blueprint, Asks Israel to Reach Out to Arabs," *The New York Times,* May 23, 1989, https://www.nytimes.com/1989/05/23/world/baker-in-a-middle-east-blueprint-asks-israel-to-reach-out-to-arabs.html.

Geeraets, Gustaaf, and Mohammed Salman, "Measuring Strategic Hedging Capability by Second-Tier States Under Unipolarity," *Chinese Political Science Review,* 1(1) (2016): 60–80.

Gordon, Michael R., and David S. Cloud, "US Held Secret Meeting with Israel, Arab Military Chiefs to Counter Iran Air Threat," *The Wall Street Journal,* June 26, 2022, https://www.wsj.com/articles/u-s-held-secret-meeting-with-israeli-arab-military-chiefs-to-counter-iran-air-threat-11656235802.

Government of Canada, "United Nations Emergency Force 1 (UNEF 1)," https://www.canada.ca/en/department-national-defence/services/military-history/history-heritage/past-operations/middle-east/united-nations-emergency-force-i.html.

Gray, Matthew, "A Theory of "Late Rentierism" in the Arab States of the Gulf," Center for International and Regional Studies, Georgetown University, Occasional Paper 7, 36–37, https://repository.library.georgetown.edu/bitstream/handle/10822/558291/CIRSOccasionalPaper7MatthewGray2011.pdf.

Hjelmgaard, Kim, "Iran's Jewish Community is the Largest in the Mideast Outside Israel—and Feels Safe and Respected," *USA Today,* August 2, 2018, https://www.usatoday.com/in-depth/news/world/inside-iran/2018/08/29/iran-jewish-population-islamic-state/886790002/.

Jones, Clive, and Yoel Guzansky, *Fraternal Enemies: Israel and the Gulf States* (London: Hurst, 2019).

Kamel, Lorenzo, "Framing the Partition Plan for Palestine," *The Cairo Review of Global Affairs,* Winter 2022, https://www.thecairoreview.com/essays/framing-the-partition-plan-for-palestine/.

Kaplan, Fred. "How George W. Bush Helped Hamas Come to Power," *Slate,* October 24, 2023, https://slate.com/news-and-politics/2023/10/was-hamas-elected-to-govern-gaza-george-w-bush-2006-palestinian-election.html.

Khalidi, Rashid, "Contrasting Narratives of Palestinian Identity," in *Palestinian Identity: The* Construction of Modern National Consciousness (New York: Columbia University Press, 2009): 9–34.

Koga, Kei, "The Concept of 'Hedging' Revisited: The Case of Japan's Foreign Policy Strategy in East Asia's power Shift," *International Studies Review,* 20(4) (2018): 633–660.

Kuik, Cheng-Chwee, and Gilbert Rozman, "Light or Heavy Hedging: Positioning between China and the US," in *Joint-Korea Academic Studies 2015,* Gilbert Rozman, ed. (Washington, DC: Korea Economic Institute of America, 2015), 1–9, http://www.keia.org/sites/default/files/publications/introduction_-_light_or_heavy_hedging.pdf.

Mason, Robert, *Saudi Arabia and the United Arab Emirates: Foreign Policy and Strategic Alliances in an Uncertain World* (Manchester: Manchester University Press, 2023).

Mearsheimer, John, *The Great Delusion: Liberal Dreams and International Realities* (New Haven, CT: Yale University Press, 2019).

Mearsheimer, John, and Stephen Walt, *The Israeli Lobby and US Foreign Policy* (New York: Farrar, Straus and Girouz, 2008).

Miller, Aaron David, "Lost in the Woods: A Camp David Retrospective," *Carnegie Endowment for International Peace*, July 13, 2020, https://carnegieendowment.org /2020/07/13/lost-in-woods-camp-david-retrospective-pub-82287.

Milton-Edwards, Beverley, and Stephen Farrell, *Hamas: The Islamic Resistance Movement.* (Cambridge: Polity, 2013).

Nonneman, Gerd, "Determinants and Patterns of Saudi Foreign Policy: "Omni-balancing" and "Relative Autonomy" in Multiple Environments," in *Saudi Arabia in the Balance: Political Economy, Society, Foreign Affairs,* Paul Aarts and Gerd Nonneman, eds. (New York: New York University Press, 2005), 315–351.

Pollack, Kenneth M., and Bilal Y. Saab, "US Strategy Options for Iran's Regional Challenge," Atlantic Council, 2017, https://www.atlanticcouncil.org/in-depth -research-reports/report/us-strategy-options-for-iran-s-regional-challenge/.

Rhodes, Ben, "A Fatal Abandonment of American Leadership," *The Atlantic,* October 12, 2018, https://www.theatlantic.com/ideas/archive/2018/10/jamal-khashoggi -and-us-saudi-relationship/572905/.

Riedel, Bruce, "75 Years after a Historic Meeting on the USS Quincy, US-Saudi Relations are in Need of a True Rethink," *Brookings*, February 10, 2020, https:// www.brookings.edu/blog/order-from-chaos/2020/02/10/75-years-after-a-historic -meeting-on-the-uss-quincy-us-saudi-relations-are-in-need-of-a-true-re-think/.

Riedel, Bruce, "How the 1967 War Dramatically Re-orientated Saudi Arabia's Foreign Policy," *Brookings*, May 30, 2017, https://www.brookings.edu/blog/markaz /2017/05/30/how-the-1967-war-dramatically-re-oriented-saudi-arabias-foreign -policy/.

Siniver, Asaf, and Scott Lucas, "Understanding Tacit Security Regimes," *Journal of Global Security Studies,* 4(4) (October 2019): 510–525.

Slater, Jerome, "Camp David, Taba, and the Clinton Parameters, 2000-2001," in *Mythologies Without End: The US, Israel, and the Arab-Israeli Conflict, 1917– 2020* (Oxford: Oxford University Press, 2020), 241–273.

The Trump White House Archive, "Peace to Prosperity: A Vision to Improve the Lives of the Palestinian and Israeli People," January 2020, https://trumpwhitehouse .archives.gov/wp-content/uploads/2020/01/Peace-to-Prosperity-0120.pdf.

United Nations, "Gaza: 'Thousands of Children Killed' Within a Few Weeks, Says UN's Guterres," November 20, 2023, https://news.un.org/en/story/2023 /11/1143772#:~:text=According%20to%20the%20UN%20agency%2C%20more %20than%20880%2C000,11%2C000%20people%20in%20Gaza%20according %20to%20health%20authorities.

United Nations, "Israeli Settlements in Gaza and the West Bank," https://www.un.org /unispal/document/auto-insert-205221/.

United Nations, "Invitation to Madrid Middle East Conference ("Madrid Principles")—US, USSR Letter (Non-UN Document)," https://www.un.org/unispal/ document/auto-insert-208112/.

United Nations Relief and Works Agency for Palestinian Refugees in the Near East, "Palestinian Refugees," https://www.unrwa.org/palestine-refugees.

US Department of State, "The Abraham Accords," https://www.state.gov/the-abra-ham-accords/.

Watkins, Jessica, "Identity Politics, Elites and Omni-balancing: Reassessing Arab Gulf State Interventions in the Uprisings from the Inside Out," *Conflict, Security and Development*, 20(5) (2020): 653–675.

Wright, Steven, "Foreign Policy in the GCC," in *International Politics of the Persian Gulf*, Mehran Kamrava, ed. (Syracuse, NY: Syracuse University Press, 2011), 72–93.

Zaga, Moran. "The Intra-GCC Competition Over the Palestinian Heart," *Middle East Institute*, December 18, 2019, https://www.mei.edu/publications/intra-gcc-compe-tition-over-palestinian-heart.

Zahlan, Rosemarie Said, "The Gulf States and the Palestine Problem, 1936–48," *Arab Studies Quarterly,* 3(1) (Winter 1981): 1–21.

Chapter 1

Iran and Israel

A Distorted Connection

Banafsheh Keynoush

Decades of traumatic shocks from four major wars between the Arab states of the Middle East and Israel (i.e., the 1948 War, 1956 Suez War, 1967 Six-Day War, and 1973 Yom Kippur War) drew the latter closer to Iran before the Iranian Islamic revolution of 1979. The region's periphery-core construct, a rationally based analytical template that divided it between its non-Arab and Arab states, encouraged the Iranian-Israeli connection as two non-Arab countries in the Middle East.[1]

The Iranian parliament had granted recognition to Israel in March 1950, on grounds that Tehran aimed through this recognition to protect the interests of Iranian nationals residing in Palestine, where an estimated 20,000 to 100,000 Iranian Jews lived, many of whom had settled in kibbutzim in Gaza prior to Israel's recognition by Iran. In July 1951, Iran's clerical establishment pressured then Prime Minister Mohammad Mossadegh to withhold the recognition, which led to the closure of Iran's consulate in Jerusalem, citing financial constraints. Iran's de facto recognition of Israel remained unscathed.[2]

The Arab world challenged Iran over its close ties with Israel, despite Iranian refusal to grant de jure recognition to the State of Israel. When Tehran proceeded to sell oil to Israel following the outbreak of the 1956 Suez crisis, Egypt broke its ties off with Iran and called on the Arab League to take similar action. Tehran refused to condemn Britain, France, and Israel for invading Egypt in October, although it offered to mediate the conflict. In April 1960, Tehran contemplated sending an ambassador to Israel, which caused fears in the Arab world of Israel's de jure recognition by Iran. When Egypt and Syria launched a war to reclaim the Sinai and the Golan Heights from Israel in October 1973, Iran allowed a limited number of Soviet planes to cross its airspace to aid Egypt. But Tehran also sent oil to Israel.

Iran and Israel maintained their strategic partnership until the Iranian revolution which overthrew a monarchy under the Pahlavi dynasty. Israel cautiously avoided fully abandoning the Iranian-Israeli periphery connection after the revolution. Demolishing revolutionary Iran's regional ambitions, as desirable as it was for Israel, underserved the key task to prevent potential threats from the Arab core. Consequently, the State of Israel failed to quickly come to terms with the sudden rupture of its security ties with Iran or recognize the scale of an emerging Iranian threat when Tehran built military strongholds in Lebanon and aided militant Palestinian groups. Reeling from the revolution, Israel observed the magnitude of Iran's revisionist agenda for the Middle East but opted to contain Iraq under Saddam Hussein, through a lobbying campaign to encourage the United States to briefly supply arms to Iran in the course of the Iran-Iraq War (1980–1988).

ISRAEL'S RESPONSE TO REVOLUTIONARY IRAN'S INFLUENCE IN MIDDLE EAST

After the Iran-Iraq War, the Iranian-Israeli connection was rife with strategic ambiguities over a clandestine Iranian nuclear program and Israel's alleged possession of a nuclear arsenal. Meanwhile, Iran's ideational power designed to export its revolution called for a form of utopian global justice that required it to take revisionist action, by disrupting the regional status quo in the Middle East. According to the revolutionaries, this served to expedite the return of justice to earth through the return to Jerusalem (which Tehran referred to as Al-Quds) of Jesus Christ or the messiah (whom the revolutionaries believed was never crucified but ascended to Heaven to return to earth in an unknown time in the future) and his companion, that is, the last Shia saint-like figure, Imam Mahdi (believed to be in a state of spiritual occultation since 941 CE). This belief system encouraged actions to contain Iran by Israel and the Gulf Cooperation Council (GCC) states of Saudi Arabia, Kuwait, Bahrain, Oman, Qatar, and the United Arab Emirates (UAE).

Concerned in part by Tehran's calls to dismantle the GCC monarchies (which backed Iraq in the war) and interference in the Levant and Palestinian affairs, the GCC tried to end the Israeli-Palestinian conflict as quickly as possible. Two Saudi-led policy initiatives, that is, the 1981 Fahd Peace Plan and the 2002 Abdullah Peace Plan (also known as the Arab Peace Initiative) helped partially converge Israeli-GCC positions. Combined, the two initiatives would ultimately endorse an independent Palestinian state and Arab recognition of Israel in return for its withdrawal from territories occupied during the 1967 Arab-Israeli Six-Day War, including East Jerusalem. But Israel disregarded the proposals and decided that its security was best served by attacking Palestinian Liberation Organization (PLO) strongholds in southern Lebanon, expanding Israeli settlements in occupied lands, and later by rejecting Palestinian statehood.

Iran's regional influence increased the longer it took to resolve the Palestinian crisis, and after the United States invaded Iraq in 2003 and the Arab Spring in 2011. Iran's backing for the Iraqi Shias post-invasion, the Houthis in Yemen, and the Syrian government during the Arab Spring reinforced in the GCC a sense of strategic isolation especially when Hamas and the Iranian-backed militant group, the Palestinian Islamic Jihad (a branch of the Egyptian Muslim Brotherhood that emerged after the Iranian revolution in 1979), fired missiles from Gaza at Israel. The US military support for its GCC allies as well as Israel's ability to intercept most missiles, however, forced Tehran to recognize that its actions to export its revolutionary ideology by force did not match its limited material capabilities.[3]

With the golden age of the Arab Spring quickly in decline by 2014, Iran's influence over Palestinian groups declined. Hamas's backing for anti-Syrian government forces during the Syrian Arab Spring had cut back Tehran's financial support for the group. In July 2014, Iran's lukewarm ties with the Palestinian National Authority (PA or PNA, set up under the terms of the Oslo Accords to administer the West Bank and the Gaza Strip) deteriorated when President Mahmoud Abbas took part at a peace conference in Tel Aviv.

Hamas leaders were invited back to Tehran to repair ties. By December 2014, the Hamas military branch Izz al-Din al-Qassam Brigades vowed to target Tel Aviv, Haifa, and Jerusalem with rockets, pushing Egypt into a race to de-escalate tensions through a short ceasefire. Hamas praised Iran for supplying weapons and money.[4] In March 2015, Iran's parliament speaker Ali Larijani met with Hamas leader Khaled Mashal in Qatar to work out differences over Hamas and Qatari support for the Syrian Muslim Brotherhood that opposed the Iranian-backed Syrian president Bashar al-Assad, shortly before the seizure of the Yarmouk Palestinian refugee camp in the vicinity of Damascus a month later by the Islamic State in Syria and Iraq (ISIS), which Tehran blamed on the anti-Assad forces and their foreign patrons.[5]

Iran reached out to Hamas again in 2016, when the group itself increasingly grew larger and more complex to operate. Reports pointed out that Iran sent millions of dollars into Gaza.[6] Iran, meanwhile, expanded its security cooperation with Syria as well, calculating that Israel would not eliminate Assad for fear it could cause a succession problem in Damascus that ISIS could take advantage of.[7] Tehran proceeded to mobilize proponents of extreme ideologies in the ranks of the Lebanese Hezbollah (established by Iran in 1981–1982), the Afghan Fatemiyoun, and Pakistani Zainabiyoun brigades it had created near Syria's borders to monitor Israeli actions in the Golan Heights. By 2017, Hamas and Tehran renewed contacts again, and within a year the group declared that their relations were closer than in any period since the start of the Syrian civil war. In 2018 Russia stepped in to encourage Iran to pull back its forces along Syria's borders with Israel, after Iran's Islamic Revolutionary Guards Corps (IRGC) Quds Force reportedly helped launch thirty-two rockets at Israel's defensive line on the Golan Heights border.[8]

Along Iran's borders, Israel reportedly trained armed Iranian Kurdish opposition groups, a well-known secret that was observed by both Turkish journalists who spoke to this author and by the Iranians.[9] Tel Aviv built ties with the Iraqi Kurdistan Democratic Party and backed its 2017 bid for a referendum of independence for the Kurdistan Region of Iraq.[10] Iran discouraged the referendum on grounds that it disregarded the Iraqi constitution and territorial integrity.

In September, the United States set up an air defense base in the Negev desert in Israel. In May 2018, the Trump administration withdrew the United States as a party to the 2015 Iran nuclear deal called the Joint Comprehensive Plan of Action (JCPOA). Meanwhile, to undermine the JCPOA, Israel revealed details of how Mossad smuggled 110,000 documents from Iran proving its nuclear proliferation program. In April 2019, Israel identified 350 fake Iranian Twitter accounts aiming to influence the outcome of the Israeli general elections in retaliation for Israel's sabotage attacks on Iranian nuclear facilities.[11] That same year, the US-Israel Security Assistance Authorization Act increased the pressure on Iran, as did the Caesar Syria Civilian Protection Act targeting foreign persons aiding Damascus. Hezbollah vowed not to let the Syrian government suffer as a result of the Caesar Act, which combined with Iranian defiance over its nuclear program, increased tensions with Israel.[12] Hamas visits to Iran picked up, with reports emerging that Iran offered monthly payments to the group in exchange for information on the location of Israeli weapons and missiles stockpiles.[13]

FRAMING IRANIAN-ISRAELI SECURITY FILES THROUGH LENS OF IR THEORY

Following the Iranian revolution, Israel contended with building new periphery-core relationships with the GCC states. Israel's choice could be explained by world-systems theory which frames, for example, the Middle East region's asymmetrical economic dependency and sociopolitical inequality patterns due to conflicts, the Arab Spring, and rifts between Tehran and Tel Aviv, as sufficient reasons to rationally draw the Jewish state closer to GCC markets and political systems. Constructivist factors shaped the new periphery-core contacts between Israel and the GCC states, where a younger generation of leaders was emerging.[14] Consequently, shifts in economic dependency patterns between Israel and the Arab core after the September 2020 Abraham Accords, political inequality between Israel and Iran, and emerging Gulf leaders weakened the historic Iranian-Israeli bonds.

Iran tried to correct trends that tipped an emerging regional imbalance of power against it. Due to the disruption in its periphery-periphery ties with Israel, from a neorealist or structural realist theoretical point of view, the two countries would seek predominant power to contain threats from each other. To realize this goal, Iran funded and armed substate and non-state actors, including Palestinian factions and Hezbollah (established in Lebanon in 1981–1982). Iran's actions encouraged the gradual formation of an Israeli-GCC partnership. Three factors contributed to Israel's decision to embrace the new ties with the GCC. First, Israel had to support the Gulf region's social and political changes and economic dependency patterns in response to rising Iranian power after it concluded a nuclear deal with the world powers in 2015. Second, the periphery-core template was not impenetrable, and Washington influenced it by backing the GCC against Iran, even after the JCPOA, thereby encouraging Israel to reassess its ties with the bloc, in the process of which Tel Aviv openly shaped a new semi-periphery identity to converge some of its interests with the Arab core.[15] Third, hardliners unwilling to recognize Israel radicalized the Iranian political landscape which led to uncompromising views about the Jewish state. Tehran's ideational power which verged on apocalyptic views made its potential access to sophisticated nuclear weapons especially dangerous when these hardliners argued that *zohur*, or the return of the Mahdi, was not too far away. According to the cleric Alireza Panahian who led a think tank initiative under the *beyt-e rahbari* run by the hardline Iranian supreme leader Ayatollah Ali Khamenei, Iran would destroy Israel before the *zohur*.[16]

This radical view enabled Iranian allies such as Hamas to negotiate from a position of power, despite being a paradiplomatic non-state actor, when dealing with the GCC countries to discourage Arab-Israeli normalization.[17] Iran, in fact, supported a wide network of para-diplomatic non-state and substate actors with the capability to negotiate with state actors in the region. In 1985, for example, when Israel withdrew its forces from Lebanon, having first sent an army to southern Lebanon in 1982, Hezbollah took credit for this withdrawal under the terms of a nonbelligerence agreement that enabled Israel control over a twelve-mile stretch of land. In 1988, Israel expelled Palestinians linked with the Islamic Jihad. The group relocated to Lebanon where it built contacts with Iran, and its members played a role in the first Palestinian uprising or Intifada (1987–1993) before a truce could be had through regional talks to appease the riots.[18] Meanwhile, although Hamas would reluctantly constitute the core of the Iranian-backed Axis of Resistance along with Hezbollah, and the two groups remained ideologically distant, the PLO-linked Fatah as well as Hamas both led parallel diplomatic representations in Tehran.[19]

Despite these Iranian efforts to be seen by the international community as a key party to the Arab-Israeli conflict, in the 1990s, international negotiations to end Arab-Israeli tensions ignored Iran. Tehran was a bystander during the October 1991 Madrid Conference which granted Israel peace in return for a commitment to resolve tensions with Arab countries. By then, Iran had lost some of its influence over the PLO, and it often ignored its representatives in Tehran, after a fall out with its leader Yasser Arafat over his links to Saddam Hussein during the Iran-Iraq War and the Gulf War (1990–1991). Shia Iran's ties to the Sunni Muslim Brotherhood that shaped the core of Hamas was less defined in this period, and the group diplomatically worked with Egypt when Washington enforced a dual containment policy in 1993–1994 to exclude Iran and Iraq from regional arrangements that led to the Oslo Accords in September 1993.[20]

Tehran continued its backing for Hezbollah and Palestinian factions. It played a key role in enabling Hezbollah's battlefront victories during the 2006 Lebanon War with Israel and supplied Hamas with money, rockets, and arms. This support came when Hamas won a legislative election in 2006, but an international peace quartet led by the United States, Russia, the United Nations, and the European Union conditioned financial aid to a new Hamas-led government on its ending of violence and possible recognition of Israel. Failing to gain sufficient international recognition for its electoral victory, Hamas parted ways with the defeated Fatah party which administered the PA that controlled the West Bank and the Gaza Strip. Hamas took over the administration of Gaza, and Iranian backing enabled it to fight Israel after it imposed a blockade to trigger a collapse of Gaza's economy, in the three-week 2008–2009 Gaza War that ended with a temporary ceasefire.[21]

In 2010, a Stuxnet cyberattack on Iran's nuclear enrichment facilities that was reportedly carried out jointly by American and Israeli intelligence services set back the Iranian nuclear program. Tensions between Iran and Israel briefly subsided when Tehran negotiated the 2015 nuclear deal with the world powers during the Obama administration. But Prime Minister Benjamin Netanyahu's rejection of the JCPOA, for failing to offer sufficient security guarantees, influenced the Trump administration's decision to withdraw the United States from the Iran nuclear deal. Israel proceeded to promote the Abraham Accords by signing new security partnerships with the Kingdom of Bahrain and the UAE. However, the hesitation by other GCC states to join the accords increased Israel's security problems because of a prevailing sense of strategic ambiguity across the region toward Tehran. The collective bargaining between Israel and the GCC to manage the Iranian nuclear threat post-JCPOA in fact failed to translate into collective security, despite Israel's frequent derailing of Iran's nuclear activities through cyber and other sabotage attacks. This forced Israel and the GCC to tolerate Iran's peaceful nuclear ambitions, which seemed to border on acquiring know-how to produce a nuclear bomb, until Washington could work out how to prevent Iran's potential nuclear weaponization program.[22]

In the absence of a strong balance of nuclear deterrence regime between Iran and Israel, and mindful of Iran's stated ability to produce a nuclear bomb in late 2023, peace eluded the Gulf region.[23] As much as Iran's hostile assertions or Israel's bellicose reactions may have been mere posturing to discourage a more serious regional conflagration, their opposing views undermined a deterrent balance of military power between the two states. Preventing conflict between the two proved challenging due to Israeli attacks on Iranian nuclear facilities and the Iranian drive to safeguard the know-how to produce nuclear weapons.[24]

Furthermore, an unresolved Palestinian conflict with Israel and the nuclearization drive of Saudi Arabia complicated the deterrent value of an emerging nuclear regime between Iran and Israel. As a result, the region faced an emerging anarchical nonpolar based nuclear regime. Proclamations by Iran's supreme leader that the regional balance of power was tilting in favor of Iran's Axis of Resistance and against regimes close to the United States and Israel (in reference to GCC countries) was one of many heralding a hazardous regional future.[25]

Iran and its allies, however, possessed limited military capabilities to rise as dominant regional powers as offensive realism would prescribe. Iran's middle power status was backed by financial resources to build asymmetrical capabilities through proxy operations. This meant that offensive realism's focus on conflict and rivalry, along with Tehran's antagonism in response to sustained US and Israeli hostility, undermined the prospects of Iran rising as a peaceful nation. This in turn promised to lead to regional chaos if Iran attempted to advance hegemonic goals in order to thwart the prospect of regime change that Israel and the United States advocated.[26] Although Iran and Israel tried to contain immediate threats as defensive realism would prescribe, the GCC, being wary of incurring the cost of challenging Iran, was expected to buck pass and let Israel balance the Iranian threat so as not to gravely endanger Gulf security, thereby promoting defensive realist strategies across the Arab Gulf region.[27]

Since Iran and Israel were experiencing the disintegration of their shared transnational identity bond as periphery states in the Middle East, this meant that patterns of conflict formation between them would constantly be shaped by a fear of war and the expectation of the use of violence.[28] In response, the Biden administration hastily encouraged normalization between Israel and Saudi Arabia in September 2021 and after. Seizing the momentum, Israel took the step to announce that it would rally Iran's Arab neighbors to prepare for a more "violent" Middle East.[29] On October 7, 2023, a key member of Iran's Axis of Resistance, Hamas, took the first step to prepare the region for a more violent future, when it crossed into Israel and killed and took hostage Israeli citizens. The October war demonstrated that a security architecture in the region excluding Iranian allies could fail. For the GCC, this meant that it could not sufficiently rely on either Israel or Iran to guarantee the regional security if the two battled directly or through proxy wars. Even the Chinese-brokered deal leading to the resumption of diplomatic relations between Iran and Saudi Arabia in March 2023 could not be expected to ensure peace when regional wars broke out, despite Saudi assertions of maintaining strategic autonomy to build the ties with both Tehran and Israel.

The emergent trial and error of security regimes in the Gulf region, especially after the outbreak of the October war, was not desirable for any regional actor. The notion of balance of security forwarded by Iran to encourage Israel and the Arab core to accept the inevitability of Iranian power in region-wide strategic paradigms fell short of building Iranian coalitions with US regional allies, as hard as Tehran tried to insert itself in peace negotiations over Gaza. Furthermore, Iran's nuclear posturing undermined the future of the Gulf region's security. Another unaddressed issue between Iran and Israel was the balance of nuclear deterrence between them. The possibility of Iran possessing nuclear breakout capacity called for building deterrent threshold capability for emerging nuclear regimes in the Middle East. As of the time of this writing, however, tensions in the Iranian and Israeli connection were not conducive to ensuring a basic balance of nuclear deterrence among the regional states. Therefore, the threat of an emerging anarchical nonpolar nuclear regime in the Middle East seemed real. Consequently, this pitted the Iranian and Israeli regimes against each other.

IRAN AND ISRAEL AFTER THE ABRAHAM ACCORDS

The Trump administration concluded the Abraham Accords nine months after US forces killed Iran's Quds Force commander Qasim Soleimani in the vicinity of Baghdad's airport on January 3, 2020. Israel's former military intelligence chief, Major General Tamir Heyman, confirmed Iranian suspicions that his country was involved in the assassination.[30] Iran expressed concern about the potential for conflict breaking out after the accords, and it called on the UAE to reduce contacts with Israel. The call came after an Iranian vessel accident in the Red Sea and Iranian strikes on Israeli vessels.[31]

Hamas, which exchanged fire with Israel in the West Bank after the accords, joined voices with Iran to isolate Israel despite the PA calling for negotiations with the Jewish state.[32] The May 2021 Sief al-Quds (Sword of Jerusalem) operation that lasted for 11 days involved the use of 4,000 missiles shot by Iranian-backed Palestinian factions at Israel. The Izz al-Din al-Qassam Brigades showcased some of the missiles on street parades while the Iranian-backed Rezvan Brigade carried out military operations in southern Lebanon.[33] In March 2022, the Jenin resistance faction, formed in the Jenin Camp in the northern sector of the West Bank, vowed to increase attacks on Israel.[34] That same month, when the IRGC launched ballistic missiles at opposition Kurdish strongholds in Erbil in Iraq, Iran said it had targeted Israeli and Mossad operations.[35]

A regional summit meeting in late March held in Israel, and in which Arab countries and the United States took part, brought to light the scope of the Iranian operational capacity after Tehran claimed it had foiled an Israeli attack on its Fordow nuclear facility mid-month. The meeting overlapped with the twentieth anniversary of the Beirut Declaration, an Arab League initiative approved by the Palestinians to normalize Israeli-Arab ties but conditioned on a two-state solution and the return of Palestinian refugees. But with peace prospects faltering in the Middle East, in September, Israel's defense minister Benny Gantz disclosed that Iran was using Syria as a weapons production facility.[36] Iran's counternarrative focused on condemning the US decision to connect Israel to CENTCOM (the US Central Command which brought Israel under its sphere of responsibility for the Middle East in 2021 and assumed responsibility for the small number of US forces in Israel). Iran subsequently offered warnings in writing to regional countries hosting US military forces. The warnings discouraged forming military alliances with Israel under the CENTCOM umbrella, which according to Tehran, could lead the United States to provide spycraft, intelligence, and operational capacities to its partners.[37] Earlier on June 14, Israel had called for the formation of a US-led Middle East military coalition against Iran.[38]

In response, on June 14, Israel called for the formation of a US-led Middle East military coalition against Iran including a regional air defense plan.[39] Iran continued to issue warnings after Israeli jets escorted two US B-52 bombers en route to the Persian Gulf in September. A year prior, the B-52 bomber had joined escort aircraft of Israel, Qatar, and Saudi Arabia over the waterway, which alarmed Tehran and led to its calls for a new region-wide security system with Iran instead. In October, Hamas resumed ties with Syria after leaving the country in 2012 to relocate its office to Qatar following the Syrian Arab Spring, while Iran enhanced its aerial, naval, and intelligence operations, conducted military exercises, and attacked vessels or tankers linked with Israeli businesses. In North Africa, Iran used Hamas contacts to expand ties with local governments opposed to Israel which held joint naval drills in the Red Sea with the United States and its Arab allies.[40]

In January 2023, Iran's foreign minister Hussein Amirabdollahian traveled to Lebanon to meet with Hezbollah leader Hassan Nasrullah and Ziyad Al-Nakhalah.[41] The visit came as Israel's outgoing army chief Aviv Kochavi unveiled three operational plans to neutralize the Iranian nuclear program, extending from a retaliatory strike unrelated to the nuclear issue to taking out nuclear installations and auxiliary sites.[42] Late that month, an Iranian Defense Ministry ammunition site exploded, and in retaliation, Iran struck an Israeli-linked tanker in February. This was followed by Israel attacking targets near Damascus where Iranian and Hezbollah fighters operated.[43]

Meanwhile, an Israeli disinformation watchdog found a network of eighty fake Twitter accounts linked to illegal acts affecting the country's judicial reform protests. Iran had also reportedly infiltrated the anti-Netanyahu Black Flags movement, disbanded in 2021, before the Israeli November 2022 elections.[44] In addition, Tehran succeeded in recruiting Israelis for espionage purposes, including a former minister of energy Gonen Segev, and it identified dozens of Israeli spy networks inside Iran, some of which it blamed for the killing of Iranian nuclear scientists.

With diminished prospects for a nuclear deal with Iran, and an uncertain Iranian commitment to a deal that would halt the advancement of its nuclear program, the Iranian problem for Israel mounted. On the occasion of an approaching Palestine Land Day on March 30, 2023, secretary general of the Palestinian Islamic Jihad Ziad Al-Nakhalah condemned the Abraham Accords and reaffirmed that Iran supported the Palestinian cause, stressing that it was the only country that was willing to pay a price for the people of Palestine. Al-Nakhalah's concerns about the Abraham Accords were doubled by the fact that the Palestinian resistance was generally divided internally, which made building peace with Israel harder for any Arab country.[45]

Meanwhile, the issue of physical regional security in the context of nuclear weaponization remained by and large an unaddressed topic in the Iranian-Israeli connection. Tamir Heyman as well as many other former Israeli officials argued strongly that a nuclear deal between Iran and the world powers could delay the building of an Iranian nuclear time bomb despite flaws and buy time for other countries to develop technology to conduct precision attacks on Iranian nuclear facilities. Most of these voices stood openly opposed to policies pursued by Benjamin Netanyahu to undermine a nuclear deal and build a coalition to get rid of the Iranian threat as soon as possible. In March 2023, Netanyahu said that a statement by the head of the International Atomic Energy Agency (IAEA), Rafael Grossi, outlawing possible Israeli strikes on Iranian nuclear facilities was an "unworthy" remark made by a worthy person, as Tehran vowed to grant the IAEA additional oversight and monitoring of its nuclear activities and stay committed to the Nuclear Non-Proliferation Treaty and the Safeguards Agreement. Tehran would later withdraw a level of access to the IAEA.[46] The IRGC meanwhile promised that by the following year on the International Quds Day of 2024, an annual pro-Palestinian event that Iran holds on the last Friday of the month of Ramadan, the Abraham Accords would fall to pieces.[47]

LEADERSHIP AND SOCIOECONOMIC ASPECTS OF IRANIAN-ISRAELI RELATIONS

The end-of-time theory that Iran subscribed to, which is essentially an apocalyptic worldview, would mean drawing Israel into a quagmire on its borders in order to expedite the return of a messiah or Mahdi. This Mahdi, who is expected to return with Christ, will fight evil and manage to restore justice and a brief period of peace on earth prior to the end of the world and the resurrection of the dead for the final Day of Judgment. In a distorted way, this theory is embedded in Evangelical ideas of restoring Israel's borders for the return of Christ as the messiah. That the coming of a messiah, possibly descending from King David, would lead to the rebuilding of Jerusalem for all believers was a part of the Jewish belief system as well.[48] But as far as Tehran was concerned, the coming of the messiah would mean increased evangelically driven and Jewish-led support for Israel, morally, financially, and militarily, so much so that untying US and Israeli security interests would eventually become impossible, thereby weakening the United States and placing its forces within closer range in the Middle East for Axis of Resistance forces to attack and defeat. This mother of all battles would expedite the return of the Mahdi, but at a lower cost for Iran than if it were to engage in any form of direct military confrontation with Israel, the United States, and its GCC allies.

Iran's revolutionary leaders had long hoped and planned to lead the Muslim march onto Israel, by first forcing the United States to step into Israel to defend the land when it witnesses the final face-off with Muslims that Iran recruits as members of its Axis of Resistance. In the meantime, Tehran believed that signs of the coming of the messiah emerged in Israel's growing weakness at home due to its own discriminatory practices against Arab citizens as well as the Palestinians, the rise of right-wing politics in Israel, and the Israeli state's undemocratic measures to alter the structure of the Israeli judiciary in order to expand the powers of Prime Minister Netanyahu and his right-wing military and defense appointees in 2023.

The Israeli state's near obsession with Iran, in the meantime, probably meant that while some strategic concerns about Iran were legitimate, others of them derived from Israel's domestic crises.[49] The Iranian Jews in Israel, roughly around 250,000 people and many who migrated to avoid repression in Iran, specifically feared that Israel might turn into another poor example of democracy and descend into irreparable chaos which could then make it easier for Tehran to develop its end of time strategy to weaken the Israeli state. Not surprisingly, many of these Jews were uplifted by the prospects for regime change that the 2022–2023 nationwide anti-government protests in Iran offered, and its potential to facilitate normal exchanges with Israel after the IRI collapsed. The speed by which Iranian opposition groups outside Iran mobilized in this period, and the secrecy of some of their activities, suggested that a larger project was in the making to expedite regime change in Iran, with Israel in the know. The Iranian Jews of Israel, however, also stood opposed for the most part to any military confrontation between Israel and Iran. Sociologically identified as Mizrahim (or Oriental Jews), and despite many supporting Israeli right-leaning parties and having little sympathy for the Palestinian cause, they also rejected Prime Minister Netanyahu's policies toward Tehran.[50]

The average Iranian's lesser sympathy for the Palestinian cause compared to those by Arabs was a pervasive sentiment inside Iran, a country which knew more about Israel than Palestine before the revolution, and saw Tehran's advocacy on behalf of radical Palestinian groups post-revolution as a policy that compromised Iranians' welfare and security. In Iran, many, in fact, missed the good ties the country once had with Israel prior to the revolution, as well as the close bonds between the Iranian Jewish community and the Iranian Jews residing in Israel and the West.

Attracted to Israel's frontier settlements and newly developed towns where pockets of poverty emerged, the Iranian Jews in Israel were, however, ways apart from the wealthier Iranian Jews who moved to the West. Both groups were keen on preserving their Persian heritage, and for many, intermarriages outside the Persian Jewish community were forbidden in order to preserve this Persian legacy. Moreover, deep bonds that had previously led to blossoming trade and business contacts between Iran and Israel were being missed by these communities. Iran once exported oil and received Israeli technology to develop its infrastructures and agricultural and health sectors (the money owed to Iran in the tune of nearly US$1 billion by Israel for some of these projects was never returned after the revolution).[51]

Unsurprisingly, the Iranians and Israelis never ceased to connect after the revolution. Israel broadcasts a radio program in Iran, often containing misinformation or propaganda material to undermine the Iranian revolution, while entertaining its Iranian audience with news, music, and cultural programs. Iran continued to offer representation in parliament to one member of the local Jewish community. Judaism officially remained recognized under Iranian law as a divine monotheistic religion, and the local Jewish community of once nearly 100,000 people and now roughly 25,000, some of whom converted to Islam or turned into staunch revolutionaries or served in the Iran-Iraq War, continually runs its own synagogues and civic and educational programs. In Israel, the local community of Iranian descent runs Persian restaurants and food stores, holds art and media programs and community activities, and has even designated a site to serve as an imaginary embassy of Iran in the country, hoping the measure would encourage Israelis not to view Iranians as an enemy at all times.[52]

Rediscovering more similarities between Iranians and Israelis is blocked due to political tensions and intelligence concerns that hinder people-to-people contacts. For a brief period, Iranians and the Israeli-Iranians hoped that tensions between the two countries might someday subside, especially during the presidency of the reformist Mohammad Khatami which partly overlapped with the presidency of the Iranian-born Israeli Likud Party leader Moshe Katsav. In an interview in 2022, Katsav said he still believed a day would come when relations between Israel and Iran would be friendly. He confirmed that he shook hands with Khatami in a meeting and discussed his hometown in Yazd. Khatami too was born near Yazd.[53]

Years earlier, Iran and Israel held deep intellectual bonds. The Jewish communists of Iran, for example, were prominent activists in left-leaning circles inside Iran in the 1950s. A number of Iranian intellectuals viewed the Jewish kibbutz life as a socialist trend that Iran could also replicate in an effort to rid the country of its poverty and a Western-oriented capitalist agenda, and revolutionary Jews took part in the 1979 Iranian Islamic revolution to overthrow the Pahlavi monarchy.[54] In more recent years, a number of Iranian journalists, activists, and athletes tried to reach out to Israelis, despite Iranian laws criminalizing all contacts with people and entities from Israel.[55] In the meantime, persistent condemnation of Israel by Iranian presidents, leaders, and the IRGC, Iran's rejection of Zionism, especially in its political form, and official Israeli hostility toward Tehran left little to explore by way of easing tensions.

Leadership factors in Iran and Israel were as important a driver as security factors affecting the two countries, as both countries were forced to adapt to the Middle East region's transitory events after the Arab Spring as well as the US decision to withdraw from engaging in large military expeditions in the region. The Abraham Accords, however, altered periphery-core relations, by boosting the socioeconomic and leadership aspects of the connections between Israel and its Gulf Arab neighbors. This challenged world-systems theory to the extent that its focus on political inequalities and wealth distribution now shifted toward strengthening periphery-core partnerships, excluding Iran. As a state increasingly suffering from political inequality at home and economic disadvantages, Iran and its revolutionary leaders thus failed to fully prevent emerging patterns of periphery ties between Israel and the Arab world.

CONCLUSION

The Middle East region's tensions due to costly military ventures and arms proliferation threatened to change the regional and global order, and bring anarchy to the regional subsystem of the Persian Gulf, especially if the Abraham Accords isolated Iran and led to a military confrontation with the IRI. Before then, the emerging chaos in the Iranian-Israeli connection that is outlined in this chapter was addressed through deterrence and preemption capabilities by the two sides in the security sphere. Yet, even these steps failed to explain simple questions such as why Iran's nuclear deal impasse had not led to a complete breakdown of the region's current security architecture through escalating clashes between Iran and Israel. As this chapter shows, the United States continued to play a pivotal role in upholding this regional security architecture to protect the interests of its allies, which meant that without Washington on board, Israel would find it extremely difficult to build a coalition to confront Iran militarily.

The emerging Hobbesian space in the region in which Israel and Iran operated meant that the former attempted to unite the GCC through the Abraham Accords and the latter used its Axis of Resistance to contain Israel, under the shadow of the Iranian nuclear program. Iran's military balance of power calculations meshed with its ideational and material power to control Israeli hostility. But it served only to delay the problem of a potential breakdown of regional security structures that had to date prevented a new war, and regime change in Tehran.

NOTES

1. For core-periphery constructs, see Arlene B. Tickner, "Core, Periphery and (Neo)imperialist International Relations," *European Journal of International Relations,* 19(3) (September 2013): 627–646, https://journals.sagepub.com/toc/ejta/19/3.

2. Banafsheh Keynoush, *Saudi Arabia and Iran: Friends or Foes?* (New York: Palgrave Macmillan, 2016), 64-65; Masoud Koohestani Nejad, "ravabet iran va Israel dar doreh dr. Mossadegh" ["Relations between Iran and Israel under Dr. Mossadegh]," *faslnameh tarikh ravabet khareji [Quarterly on History of Foreign Relations],* 15 (tabestan 1382/Summer 2003): 107, 110–111, 145–148, cited from Documents of the Foreign Ministry File no. 1332-9-78 and "rouznameh rasmi keshvar shahanshai iran [Official Newspaper of the Kingdom of Iran]," s. 1828, Khordad 8, 1330/May 30, 1951, p. 3; Morteza Ghanoun, diplomacy penhan: jastari dar ravabet

iran va israel dar asr pahlavi [*Secret Diplomacy: Preview of Relations between Iran and Israel in the Pahlavi Era*] (Tehran: tabarestan 1381/1991–1992), 182.

3. For the alignment of ideational power and limited material capabilities see John Lewis Gaddis, *Grand Strategy* (New York: Penguin Press, 2018).

4. Nidal al-Mughrabi, "Hamas Holds Gaza Military Parade, Vows Israel's Destruction," *Reuters*, December 14, 2014, https://www.reuters.com/article/us-mideast-hamas-israel/hamas-holds-gaza-military-parade-vows-israels-destruction-idU SKBN0JS0LO20141215.

5. Hassan Hashemian, "Ups and Downs of Hamas Ties with Islamic Republic," *Radio Farda*, Mordad 12, 1394, https://www.radiofarda.com/a/f35_iran_hamas /27166377.html.

6. "Tehran Encourages Palestinian National Reconciliation," *IRDiplomacy*, Aban 6, 1396, http://www.irdiplomacy.ir/fa/news/1972748/%D8%AA%D9%87%D8%B1 %D8%A7%D9%86-%D8%AA%D8%B1%D8%BA%DB%8C%D8%A8-%DA%A9 %D9%86%D9%86%D8%AF%D9%87-%D8%A2%D8%B4%D8%AA%DB%8C- %D9%85%D9%84%DB%8C-%D9%81%D9%84%D8%B3%D8%B7%DB%8C%D9 %86%DB%8C%D8%A7%D9%86; "Iran, Hamas & Palestinian Islamic Jihad", Wilson Center, October 11, 2023, https://www.wilsoncenter.org/article/iran-hamas-and-palestinian-islamic-jihad

7. "Behind the Scenes of Israel's Attacks on Syria," *Fararu*, Shahrivar 16, 1401, https://fararu.com/fa/news/573364/%D9%BE%D8%B4%D8%AA-%D9%BE%D8 %B1%D8%AF%D9%87-%D8%AD%D9%85%D9%84%D8%A7%D8%AA-%D8 %A7%D8%B3%D8%B1%D8%A7%D8%A6%DB%8C%D9%84-%D8%A8%D9 %87-%D8%B3%D9%88%D8%B1%DB%8C%D9%87.

8. "Russia Tells Iran to Immediately Remove Militias from Syrian-Israel Border," *The Times of Israel*, May 30, 2018, https://www.timesofisrael.com/russia-tells -iran-to-immediately-remove-militias-from-syrian-israel-border/; "Russia: Iranian Troops in Syria to be Kept 85 Kilometers from Israel Border," *The Times of Israel*, August 1, 2018, https://www.timesofisrael.com/russia-iranian-troops-in-syria-to-be -kept-85-kilometers-from-israel-border/; Daniel Levin, "Iran, Hamas & Palestinian Islamic Jihad," *Wilson Center*, May 21, 2021, https://gbv.wilsoncenter.org/article/ iran-hamas-and-palestinian-islamic-jihad.

9. See also Zachary Keyser, "Fars News: Kurdish Forces Are Being Sent to Israel to Train with Mossad," *The Jerusalem Post*, June 16, 2019, https://www.jpost.com/middle -east/fars-news-kurdish-forces-are-being-sent-to-israel-to-train-with-mossad-592667.

10. Hogr Tarkhani, "Strengthening Relations Between Israel and Iraqi Kurdistan," *The Jerusalem Post*, June 12, 2021, https://www.jpost.com/opinion/strengthening -relations-between-israel-and-iraqi-kurdistan-670829.

11. Ofir Barel, "Is Iran Encouraging Illegal Acts in Israel over Judicial Reform?," *The Jerusalem Post*, January 31, 2023, https://www.jpost.com/opinion/article-730207.

12. Yaniv Kubovich, "Israel Attacked 1,000 Iranian and Hezbollah Targets in Syria since 2017," *Haaretz*, August 13, 2020, https://www.haaretz.com/israel-news /2020-08-13/ty-article/.premium/israel-attacked-1-000-iranian-and-hezbollah-targets -in-syria-since-2017/0000017f-f0ca-df98-a5ff-f3ef434c0000.

13. Levin, "Iran, Hamas & Palestinian Islamic Jihad."

14. For world-system theory, see Frank F. Klink, "Rationalizing Core-Periphery Relations: The Analytical Foundations of Structural Inequality in World Politics," *International Studies Quarterly,* 34(2) (June 1990): 183–209, https://doi.org/10.2307/2600708.

15. For semi-periphery theory, see "Glossary of World Systems Theory" dividing economic nations into the core, the semi-periphery, and the periphery, in Immanuel Wallerstein, *World-Systems Analysis: An Introduction* (Durham, NC: Duke University Press, 2004); Klink, "Rationalizing Core-Periphery Relations: The Analytical Foundations of Structural Inequality in World Politics."

16. "Panahian: Based on Narratives, Iranians Will Destroy Israel Prior to Zohur," *Hamshahri Online*, October 14, 1401, https://www.hamshahrionline.ir/news/710417/
%D8%A8%D8%A8%DB%8C%D9%86%DB%8C%D8%AF-%D9%BE%D9%86
%D8%A7%D9%87%DB%8C%D8%A7%D9%86-%D8%A8%D8%B1%D8%A7
%D8%B3%D8%A7%D8%B3-%D8%B1%D9%88%D8%A7%DB%8C%D8%A7
%D8%AA-%D8%A7%DB%8C%D8%B1%D8%A7%D9%86%DB%8C-%D9%87
%D8%A7-%D8%A7%D8%B3%D8%B1%D8%A7%D8%A6%DB%8C%D9%84-
%D8%B1%D8%A7-%D9%82%D8%A8%D9%84-%D8%A7%D8%B2.

17. For details on the evolution of the concept of para-diplomacy see Iñaki Aguirre, "Making Sense of Para-Diplomacy? An Intertextual Enquiry About a Concept in Search of a Definition," *Regional and Federal Studies,* 9(1) (December 1999): 185–209; for details on how para-diplomacy affects international security see Noé Cornago, "Diplomacy and Para-Diplomacy in the Redefinition of International Security: Dimensions of Conflict and Cooperation," *Regional and Federal Studies,* 9(1) (December 2009): 40–57.

18. Rachel Brandenberg, "Iran Primer: Iran and the Palestinians," *PBS Frontline*, October 28, 2010, https://www.pbs.org/wgbh/pages/frontline/tehranbureau/2010/10/iran-primer-iran-and-the-palestinians.html.

19. Hashemian, "Ups and Downs of Hamas Ties with Islamic Republic."

20. Ezatollah Ezati, *tahlili bar geopolitic iran va Iraq* [An Analysis of Iran-Iraq Geopolitics] (Tehran: daft motaleat siyasi va beinolmellalo 1384/2005), 218–220.

21. Ariel Farrar Wellman, "Iran Hamas Relationship in 2008," Critical Threats, https://www.criticalthreats.org/analysis/iran-hamas-relationship-in-2008.

22. For Iranian views on what a regional balance of interest could look like, see Kayhan Barzegar, "The Balance of Power in the Persian Gulf: An Iranian View," Belfer Center, Fall 2010, https://www.belfercenter.org/publication/balance-power-persian-gulf-iranian-view.

23. For nuclear deterrence regimes, see Yair Evron, "An Israeli-Iran Balance of Nuclear Deterrence: Seeds of Instability," Institute for National Security Studies, 2008, https://www.jstor.org/stable/pdf/resrep08946.6.pdf.

24. Alexandre Debs and Nuno P. Monteiro, "Nuclear Politics: The Strategic Logic of Nuclear Proliferation," *International Security*, 39(2) (October 2014): 7–51, https://direct.mit.edu/isec/article/39/2/7/12309/The-Strategic-Logic-of-Nuclear-Proliferation.

25. Michael Segall, "Iran's Supreme Leader: The Global Balance of Power is Tilting Toward 'Palestine' and Muslims," *Jerusalem Center for Public Affairs*, May

19, 2021, https://jcpa.org/irans-supreme-leader-the-global-balance-of-power-is-tilting-toward-palestine-and-muslims/.

26. John J. Mearsheimer, *The Tragedy of Great Power Politics* (New York: W. W. Norton & Company, 2001).

27. For defensive realism see Stephen M. Walt, "The Enduring Relevance of the Realist Tradition," in *Political Science: The State of the Discipline III*, eds. Ira Katznelson and Helen V. Milner (New York: W. W. Norton & Company, 2002).

28. Emmanuel Adler and Michael Barnett, "Taking Identity and Our Critics Seriously," *Cooperation and Conflict*, 35(3) (September 2000): 321–329, https://www.jstor.org/stable/45083947; Barry Buzan and Ole Waever, *Regions and Powers: The Structure of International Security* (Cambridge: Cambridge University Press, 2004); Hakan Edstrom and Jacob Westberg, "The Defense Strategies of Middle Powers: Competing for Security Influence and Status in an Era of Unipolar Demise," *Comparative Strategy*, 39(2) (2020): 171–190, https://www.tandfonline.com/doi/full/10.1080/01495933.2020.1718992.

29. "Egypt, UAE, Israeli Leaders Meet for First Ever Three-Way Summit," *AlJazeera*, March 22, 2022, https://www.aljazeera.com/news/2022/3/22/egypt-uae-israel-address-energy-and-food-stability-at-summit.

30. "Ex-Intel Chief Confirms Israel's Role in Soleimani Killing," *AP News*, December 21, 2021, https://apnews.com/article/middle-east-iran-jerusalem-israel-military-intelligence-cfba78c69ae656697684ab92c4cac5b9; Maziar Motamedi, "Iran Implicates UK Firm, US Base in Germany in Soleimani Killing," *AlJazeera*, December 31, 2020, https://www.aljazeera.com/news/2020/12/31/iran-implicates-uk-firm-us-base-in-germany-in-soleimanis-murder.

31. "Israeli Forces Carried Out Strike on Iran Spy Ship in Red Sea, NY Times Reports," *The Times of Israel*, April 7, 2021, https://www.timesofisrael.com/israeli-forces-carried-out-strike-on-iranian-ship-in-red-sea-new-york-times/.

32. "Hamas Has Unified and Stable Ties with Iran," *Mehr News Agency*, December 7, 1400, https://www.mehrnews.com/news/5385787/%D8%B1%D8%A7%D8%A8%D8%B7%D9%87-%D8%AD%D9%85%D8%A7%D8%B3-%D8%A8%D8%A7-%D8%A7%DB%8C%D8%B1%D8%A7%D9%86-%D8%A7%D8%B2-%D8%AA%D8%B5%D9%85%DB%8C%D9%85-%D8%B1%D8%A7%D9%87%D8%A8%D8%B1%D8%AF%DB%8C-%DB%8C%DA%A9%D9%BE%D8%A7%D8%B1%DA%86%D9%87-%D9%88-%D8%AB%D8%A7%D8%A8%D8%AA-%D8%A8%D8%B1%D8%AE%D9%88%D8%B1%D8%AF%D8%A7%D8%B1.

33. "One-year Victory of Resistance Axis; From "Seif" Quds to "Hesan" Hezbollah," *Fars News Agency*, December 15, 1400, https://www.farsnews.ir/news/14001205000182/%D9%BE%DB%8C%D8%B1%D9%88%D8%B2%DB%8C%E2%80%8C%D9%87%D8%A7%DB%8C-%DB%8C%DA%A9%D8%B3%D8%A7%D9%84%D9%87%E2%80%8C%DB%8C-%D9%85%D8%AD%D9%88%D8%B1-%D9%85%D9%82%D8%A7%D9%88%D9%85%D8%AA-%D8%A7%D8%B2-%D8%B3%DB%8C%D9%81-%D9%90-%D9%82%D8%AF%D8%B3-%D8%AA%D8%A7-%D8%AD%D8%B3%D8%A7%D9%86%D9%90-%D8%AD%D8%B2%D8%A8%E2%80%8C%D8%A7%D9%84%D9%84%D9%87.

34. "Announcing Preparedness by Janin Brigade Against Zionist Regime," *Fars News Agency*, December 13, 1400, https://www.farsnews.ir/news/14001213000587/%D8%A7%D8%B9%D9%84%D8%A7%D9%85-%D8%A2%D9%85%D8%A7%D8%AF%D9%87E2%80%8C%D8%A8%D8%A7%D8%B4-%DA%AF%D8%B1%D8%AF%D8%A7%D9%86-%D8%AC%D9%86%DB%8C%D9%86-%D8%B9%D9%84%DB%8C%D9%87-%D8%B1%DA%98%DB%8C%D9%85-%D8%B5%D9%87%DB%8C%D9%88%D9%86%DB%8C%D8%B3%D8%AA%DB%8C.

35. "Mossad in Iraqi Kurdistan; From Secret Ties in Framework of Trade to Hosting Iranian Opposition," *Fars News Agency*, March 4, 1401, https://www.farsnews.ir/news/14010104000289/%D9%85%D9%88%D8%B3%D8%A7%D8%AF-%D8%AF%D8%B1-%DA%A9%D8%B1%D8%AF%D8%B3%D8%AA%D8%A7%D9%86-%D8%B9%D8%B1%D8%A7%D9%82-%D8%A7%D8%B2-%D8%B1%D9%88%D8%A7%D8%A8%D8%B7-%D9%BE%D9%86%D9%87%D8%A7%D9%86%DB%8C-%D8%AF%D8%B1-%D9%82%D8%A7%D9%84%D8%A8-%D8%AA%D8%AC%D8%A7%D8%B1%D8%AA-%D8%AA%D8%A7-%D9%85%DB%8C%D8%B2%D8%A8%D8%A7%D9%86%DB%8C-%D8%A7%D8%B2.

36. "Israeli Minister Says Iran Using Syria Facilities for Weapons Production," *Reuters*, September 12, 2022, https://www.reuters.com/world/middle-east/israeli-minister-says-iran-using-syria-facilities-weapons-production-2022-09-12/.

37. "Chief of Armed Forces of Iran: We Have Given Written Warning to Countries Hosting US Army," *BBC Farsi*, September 7, 2022, https://www.bbc.com/persian/articles/c9rk416v661o.

38. Dan Williams and Aziz El Yaakoubi, "Israel Says It's Building Regional Air Defense Alliance Under US," *Reuters*, June 20, 2022, https://www.reuters.com/world/middle-east/israel-says-building-regional-air-defence-alliance-under-us-2022-06-20/.

39. Ibid.

40. "Iran Accuses Israel of Fomenting Unrest as Regime Struggles to Contain Protestors," *Israel Hayom*, November 19, 2022, https://www.israelhayom.com/2022/11/19/iran-accuses-israel-of-fomenting-unrest-as-regime-struggles-to-contain-protesters/.

41. "Amir Abdollahian Meets Senior Syrian Officials," *Tehran Times*, January 14, 2023, https://www.tehrantimes.com/news/480836/Amir-Abdollahian-meets-senior-Syrian-officials.

42. "Israel Has 3 Plans to 'Neutralize' Iran's Nuclear Program," *i24*, January 13, 2023, https://www.i24news.tv/en/news/israel/defense/1673599013-israel-has-3-plans-to-neutralize-iran-s-nuclear-program-army-chief.

43. "More than a Dozen Killed in Israel's 'Deadliest Attack' on Syrian Capital Damascus," *France24*, February 19, 2023, https://www.france24.com/en/middle-east/20230219-more-than-a-dozen-people-killed-in-israel-s-deadliest-attack-on-syrian-capital-of-damascus.

44. Ofir Barel, "Is Iran Encouraging Illegal Acts in Israel over Judicial Reform?" *The Jerusalem Post*, January 31, 2023, https://www.jpost.com/opinion/article-730207.

45. "Islamic Jihad: Iran is the Only Real Supporter of Palestinian Resistance," *Fars News Agency*, Farvardeen 6, 1401, https://www.farsnews.ir/news/14010106000400/%D8%AC%D9%87%D8%A7%D8%AF-%D8%A7%D8%B3%D9%84%D8%A7%D9%85%DB%8C-%D8%A7%DB%8C%D8%B1%D8%A7%D9%86-%D8%AA%D9%86%D9%87%D8%A7-%D8%AD%D8%A7%D9%85%DB%8C-%D9%88%D8%A7%D9%82%D8%B9%DB%8C-%D9%85%D9%82%D8%A7%D9%88%D9%85%D8%AA-%D9%81%D9%84%D8%B3%D8%B7%DB%8C%D9%86-%D8%A7%D8%B3%D8%AA.

46. "Israeli Minister sees Possible Attack on Iran 'in Two or Three Years,'" *Reuters*, December 28, 2022, https://www.reuters.com/world/middle-east/israeli-minister-sees-possible-attack-iran-two-or-three-years-2022-12-28/; "Ex-IDF Intel Chief Backs Nuke Deal as Vital to Delay Iranian Program, Prepare Strike," *The Times of Israel*, August 19, 2022, https://www.timesofisrael.com/ex-idf-intel-chief-backs-nuke-deal-as-vital-to-delay-iranian-program-prepare-strike/; "Netanyahu Slams IAEA Chief for Saying Attacks on Nuclear Facilities 'Outlawed'," *The Times of Israel*, March 5, 2023, https://www.timesofisrael.com/netanyahu-slams-iaea-chief-for-saying-attacks-on-nuclear-facilities-outlawed/.

47. "IRGC Spokesperson Appoints 'Day'/Announces Timing of 'End of Shameful Abraham Accords,'" *Khabar Online*, March 13, 2023, https://www.khabaronline.ir/news/1742629/%D8%B3%D8%AE%D9%86%DA%AF%D9%88%DB%8C-%D8%B3%D9%BE%D8%A7%D9%87-%D8%B1%D9%88%D8%B2-%D8%AA%D8%B9%DB%8C%DB%8C%D9%86-%DA%A9%D8%B1%D8%AF-%D8%A7%D8%B9%D9%84%D8%A7%D9%85-%D8%B2%D9%85%D8%A7%D9%86-%D9%BE%D8%A7%DB%8C%D8%A7%D9%86-%D9%BE%DB%8C%D9%85%D8%A7%D9%86-%D9%86%D9%86%DA%AF%DB%8C%D9%86.

48. For similar views see "Mahdisim, the Jews, and the Iranians," Al Islam, https://www.al-islam.org/al-imam-al-mahdi-just-leader-humanity-ibrahim-amini/chapter-3-mahdiism-jews-and-iranians, or Robert Leonhard, "Visions of Apocalypse: What Jews, Christians, and Muslims Believe About the End Times, and How Those Beliefs Affect Our World," The John Hopkins University, May 2010, https://www.jhuapl.edu/Content/documents/ApocalypseVision.pdf.

49. See Haggai Ram, *Iranophobia: The Logic of an Israeli Obsession* (Stanford, CA: Stanford University Press, 2009).

50. See also Lior Sternfeld, "Iranian Jews in Israel, Protests, and the Palestinians," Foreign Policy Research Institute, December 6, 2022, https://www.fpri.org/article/2022/12/iranian-jews-in-israel-protests-and-the-palestinians/.

51. "Economic and Commercial Relations Between Iran and Israel Before the Islamic Republic," *Voice of America*, May 7, 1397, https://ir.voanews.com/a/4367674.html.

52. Daniel Estrin, "Torn Between Native and Adoptive Lands, Israel's Iranian Jews Hope for Peace," *NPR*, July 26, 2015, https://www.npr.org/sections/parallels/2015/07/26/425968487/torn-between-native-and-adoptive-lands-israels-iranian-jews-hope-for-peace.

53. Tobias Siegal, "Ex-President Katsav Gives His First Interview Since Jail – to Iranian Opposition TV," *The Times of Israel*, February 3, 2022, https://www.timesofisrael.com/ex-president-katsav-gives-his-first-interview-since-jail-to-iranian-opposition-tv/.

54. "Pahlavi Iran and Zionism: An Intellectual Elite's Short-Lived Love Affair with the State of Israel," *Ajam Media Collective*, March 7, 2013, https://ajammc.com /2013/03/07/pahlavi-iran-and-zionism-an-intellectual-elites-short-lived-love-affair -with-israel/.

55. "Kanaani: US Has No Merit to Directly Negotiate," *Shargh Daily*, March 6, 1401, https://www.sharghdaily.com/%D8%A8%D8%AE%D8%B4-%D8%B3%DB %8C%D8%A7%D8%B3%D8%AA-6/871529-%DA%A9%D9%86%D8%B9%D8 %A7%D9%86%DB%8C-%D8%A2%D9%85%D8%B1%DB%8C%DA%A9%D8 %A7-%D8%B4%D8%A7%DB%8C%D8%B3%D8%AA%DA%AF%DB%8C- %D9%84%D8%A7%D8%B2%D9%85-%D8%A8%D8%B1%D8%A7%DB%8C- %D9%85%D8%B0%D8%A7%DA%A9%D8%B1%D9%87-%D9%85%D8%B3 %D8%AA%D9%82%DB%8C%D9%85-%D8%B1%D8%A7-%D9%86%D8%AF %D8%A7%D8%B1%D8%AF.

REFERENCES

Adler, Emmanuel and Michael Barnett, "Taking Identity and Our Critics Seriously," *Cooperation and Conflict*, 35(3) (September 2000): 321–329, https://www.jstor .org/stable/45083947.

Aguirre, Iñaki, "Making Sense of Para-diplomacy? An Intertextual Enquiry About a Concept in Search of a Definition," *Regional and Federal Studies*, 9(1) (December 1999): 185–209.

Alikhani, Alinaqi, *yad dasht ha-yi asadollah alam, jeld seh, 1352* [The Diaries of Alam], vol. 3, *1972-1973* (Tehran: entesharat maziar va moin, 1377), 190–205.

Buzan, Barry and Ole Waever, *Regions and Powers: The Structure of International Security* (Cambridge: Cambridge University Press, 2004).

Cornago, Noé, "Diplomacy and Paradiplomacy in the Redefinition of International Security: Dimensions of Conflict and Cooperation," *Regional and Federal Studies*, 9(1) (December 2009): 40–57.

Edstrom, Hakan and Jacob Westberg, "The Defense Strategies of Middle Powers: Competing for Security Influence and Status in an Era of Unipolar Demise," *Comparative Strategy*, 39(2) (2020): 171–190, https://www.tandfonline.com/doi/full/10 .1080/01495933.2020.1718992.

Ezati, Ezatollah, *tahlili bar geopolitic iran va Iraq* [An Analysis of Iran-Iraq Geopolitics] (Tehran: daft motaleat siyasi va beinolmellalo 1384/2005), 218–220.

Gaddis, John Lewis, *Grand Strategy* (New York: Penguin Press, 2018).

Ghanoun, Morteza, *diplomacy penhan: jastari dar ravabet iran va israel dar asr pahlavi* [Secret Diplomacy: Preview of Relations between Iran and Israel in the Pahlavi Era] (Tehran: tabarestan, 1381/1991–1992), 182.

Katznelson, Ira and Helen V. Milner, *Political Science: The State of the Discipline* (New York: W. W. Norton & Company, 2002).

Keynoush, Banafsheh, "Revolutionary Iran's Africa Policy," *King Faisal Center for Research and Islamic Studies*, June 2021, https://kfcris.com/pdf/dd448fcd67b35ab 48903bd18c6fcffd160d99d2290923.pdf.

Keynoush, Banafsheh, *Saudi Arabia and Iran: Friends or Foes?* (New York: Palgrave Macmillan, 2016).

Keynoush, Banafsheh and Hamad AlBloshi, "Iran's Axis of Influence in Levant and Iraq," in *Iran's Interregional Dynamics in the Near East*, ed. Banafsheh Keynoush (New York: Peter Lang, 2021), 47.

Klink, Frank F., "Rationalizing Core-Periphery Relations: The Analytical Foundations of Structural Inequality in World Politics," *International Studies Quarterly*, 34(2) (June 1990): 183–209, https://doi.org/10.2307/2600708.

Koohestani Nejad, Masoud, "ravabet iran va Israel dar doreh dr. Mossadegh" ["Relations between Iran and Israel under Dr. Mossadegh]," *faslnameh tarikh ravabet khareji [Quarterly on History of Foreign Relations]* 15 (tabestan 1382/ Summer 2003): 107, 110–111, 145–148, cited from Documents of the Foreign Ministry File no. 1332-9-78 and "rouznameh rasmi keshvar shahanshai iran [Official Newspaper of the Kingdom of Iran]," s. 1828, Khordad 8, 1330/May 30, 1951.

Leonhard, Robert, "Visions of Apocalypse: What Jews, Christians, and Muslims Believe About the End Times, and How Those Beliefs Affect Our World," The John Hopkins University, May 2010, https://www.jhuapl.edu/Content/documents /ApocalypseVision.pdf.

Levin, Daniel, "Iran, Hamas & Palestinian Islamic Jihad," *Wilson Center*, May 21, 2021, https://gbv.wilsoncenter.org/article/iran-hamas-and-palestinian-islamic -jihad.

Mearsheimer, John J., *The Tragedy of Great Power Politics* (New York: W. W. Norton & Company, 2001).

Ram, Haggai, *Iranophobia: The Logic of an Israeli Obsession* (Stanford, CA: Stanford University Press, 2009).

Segall, Michael, "Iran's Supreme Leader: The Global Balance of Power is Tilting Toward 'Palestine' and Muslims," *Jerusalem Center for Public Affairs*, May 19, 2021, https://jcpa.org/irans-supreme-leader-the-global-balance-of-power-is-tilting -toward-palestine-and-muslims/.

Sternfeld, Leon, "Iranian Jews in Israel, Protests, and the Palestinians," *Foreign Policy Research Institute*, December 6, 2022, https://www.fpri.org/article/2022/12 /iranian-jews-in-israel-protests-and-the-palestinians/.

Terrill, W. Andrew. "Iran's Strategy for Saving Assad," *The Middle East Journal,* 69(2) (Spring 2015): 222–236.

Tickner, Arlene B. "Core, Periphery and (Neo)imperialist International Relations," *European Journal of International Relations*, 19(3) (September 2013): 627–646, https://journals.sagepub.com/toc/ejta/19/3.

Wallerstein, Immanuel, *World-Systems Analysis: An Introduction* (Durham, NC: Duke University Press, 2004).

Walt, Stephen M. "The Enduring Relevance of the Realist Tradition," in *Political Science: The State of the Discipline III*, ed. Ira Katznelson and Helen V. Milner (New York: W. W. Norton & Company, 2002).

Chapter 2

Israel-Arab Normalization Drive

Guy Burton

Israel's normalization with the Arab world is not a new phenomenon. Although the Abraham Accords constitute the most recent and visible manifestation, Israeli normalization as a process has a long history. Indeed, it echoes part of Israel's wider "periphery doctrine" by its leaders, who starting in the 1950s, began looking for sought partnerships and allies by states and minorities in the region and beyond its immediate and hostile Arab neighbors.[1] That objective has remained, even as Israel eventually managed to make peace with several of those core Arab states, beginning with Egypt in 1979.

The 1979 peace agreement between Israel and Egypt constituted the first case of normalization with a previously hostile Arab state. It became the model for subsequent searches at normalization, in particular, between Israel and the Palestinians via the Oslo Accords, which were signed in 1993. The Oslo Accords were significant because they marked the beginning of direct talks between Israel and the Palestinians in which the two sides recognized the existence of the other and in the eyes of its signatories, appeared willing to work toward the establishment of a Palestinian state alongside Israel and existing in peace with each other.

The Oslo Accords provided space for other states in the region to rethink their position toward Israel, including in the Gulf. If it was possible for the Palestinians, who were most directly affected by Israeli actions to work with Israel, then surely it was possible for other Arabs to similarly do so? As a result, normalization began to gather pace between Israel and several Arab Gulf states during the 1990s. That process continued, even as the Oslo Accords appeared to come to a juddering halt following a collapse in trust between Israel and the Palestinians and the outbreak of violence in the form of the Second Intifada between 2000 and 2005.

However, despite the violence, the door between Israel and the Gulf Cooperation Council (GCC) states never completely closed. Normalization remained on the cards after 2005 and gathered pace after 2011, albeit tacitly and due largely to their common fears and suspicions surrounding Iran and its nuclear program.[2] Indeed, what helped normalization remain a viable prospect between Israel and some of the GCC states was the changing nature of the regional environment, especially following the instability generated by the uprisings in the Arab world after 2011 and the role of different actors, both supposed partners like the United States, and rivals like Iran. As a result—and as this chapter demonstrates—the overall structure of the region and its politics, along with shared perceptions of security threats by Israel and several GCC states have prompted the current push toward normalization.

Since 2011 Iran has increased its regional influence and embraced various proxy states and groups while the perception of American regional hegemony is perceived to have declined. That is due in large part to US failure to impose itself in Iraq and Afghanistan while also looking further afield, to redirect resources and focus toward the Indo-Pacific. As a result, the United States is judged as being a less reliable and committed partner and guarantor of regional security.

What makes these challenges so significant is that they were not unique to either Israel or GCC states such as the UAE, Saudi Arabia, or Bahrain. Rather, they were shared, which made the two sides recognize the importance of each other as a potential security partner. Both sides saw the other as a useful way of countering Iranian influence and making up for the apparent shortfall of American interest. For Israel, normalized relations with GCC states could mean greater cooperation to derail Iranian actions and proxies, for example, through their own influence with actors in Gaza, Lebanon, and Syria. Israel offers GCC access both to advanced technology in the field of surveillance and to political cachet or benefits with the United States, via their special relationship. Indeed, among such calculations is that normalization might enable GCC states to acquire certain weapons and weapons systems, as well as bringing them together with Israel and the United States in a more explicitly constructed joint regional security architecture.[3]

The convergence of interests between Israel and several GCC states meant that clandestine relationships have grown between them during the past decade—although one which was trumpeted more by Israel and treated with greater reticence by the Arabs in the Gulf.[4] Those interactions eventually culminated in a joint statement between Israel and the UAE to normalize relations in August 2020 (which was signed into effect a month later), followed by similar normalization agreements between Israel and Bahrain (which was also signed in September 2020) and with Sudan (October 2020) and Morocco (December 2020). Until now, the UAE and Bahrain remain the only two

GCC states to have fully recognized Israel. Although Israel also wishes to sign an accord with Saudi Arabia, that has not happened so far.[5] Indeed, even if the expectation is that it will eventually happen, the prospects for it doing so seem later than planned following the outbreak of war between Israel and Hamas in October 2023.

The trend toward normalization between Israel and several of the GCC states is one that has generated strong support in Israel. Soon after the announcement of the Abraham Accords, large majorities of Israeli society believed that normalization would generate benefits for the country.[6] Moreover, that support transcended the political divide, with both leftists and rightists approving of the move. In short, support for normalization in Israel transcends individual political leaders and parties in Israel, which meant that that momentum between Israel and its new partners (especially the UAE) was sustained despite the change of political parties in power in Israel during these years. Against that, however, is the variable character of normalization: While it has been especially vibrant in relation to Israel and the UAE, it has been slower to expand and consolidate in relation to other Arab signatories, including Bahrain, Morocco, and Sudan. Among the reasons why this may be so is the difference in priorities and scope between the UAE and others; for instance, the wider range of potential interaction between Israel and the UAE (including mutual economic interest as well as countering Iran) and Bahrain's more limited focus on countering Iran.[7] Finally, the outbreak of the Hamas-Israel war of October 2023 explains why normalization is not an easy path, even as GCC states like Saudi Arabia and the UAE—who have little sympathy for Hamas—have felt a need to put some distance between themselves and Israel following its military campaign in Gaza.

US ROLE AND ISRAEL-GCC STATE TIES

Israel's leaders have long focused on ensuring national security to the extent that it has been described as "primarily a security state . . . to provide security for the Jewish population."[8] A major part of that equation has been the United States, which has been a strong and close supporter of Israel since 1948, although it was only in the years leading up to the 1967 Arab-Israeli War that Washington began to acquire the strategic depth that it holds today in Israel. Until that point, Israel's primary foreign partner had been France. But with Washington replacing Paris, the United States quickly contributed to the establishment of Israel as a regional power.[9]

Over the decades, Israel has become the largest recipient of American aid, and the bulk of it has been military. Between 1948 and 2019, American aid to Israel totaled more than $150 billion, of which $108 billion was military and

$34 billion economic assistance, the latter of which was contributed between 1971 and 2007.[10] According to the Stockholm International Peace Research Institute, American equipment made up over 80 percent of Israeli arms purchases between 1950 and 2020.[11]

The relationship has not been one way, however. The two have collaborated on mutually beneficial projects, even as they have found difficulties in fully integrating their equipment. A notable recent example is Israel's air-defense Iron Dome System. Following pressure from American politicians, the US Army tested the system but rejected it. As well as not being able to intercept cruise missiles, it is so far difficult to integrate it alongside current American radar and control systems.[12]

Notwithstanding these challenges at home, there remains a strong American determination to ensure that Israel retains a "qualitative edge" over other militaries in the Middle East region. In addition, the US-Israeli relationship is a unique one, involving close personal ties and interests which transcend the main political parties on both sides.

While close and deep, there remains no scholarly consensus regarding the nature of the US-Israel relationship. Some observers suggest that American policy has sometimes been conditional, with the United States at times attempting to restrain Israel from behaving in a bellicose manner and at other times pushing reluctant Israeli leaders toward peace talks.[13] On the other hand, American policy has sometimes seemed to be unconditional, to the point of appearing detrimental to wider American strategic and moral concerns. Much of the reason for this is due to the strong influence of the Israel lobby in Washington, which seeks to advance Israeli interests within the executive and legislature.[14]

Both Israel and the United States generally share a concern about regional threats, in particular Iran. This issue is also a major concern that some of the GCC states similarly have, creating a convergence in threat perception between all three. Like Israel, the GCC states have historically looked toward Washington for protection—a priority that placed normalization with Israel a largely secondary concern until Iran's regional threat increased.[15]

However, those calculations have changed as both Israel and the Arab Gulf states judged successive American administrations as a less reliable security partner. Indeed, it may well be that normalization with Israel was one way of building stronger security ties with a regional power that was less dependent on the whims and vicissitudes of individual American presidents. The election of President Barack Obama in 2009 seemed to indicate the United States would be a global hegemon less concerned with maintaining its regional footprint in the Middle East and keen to retreat the United States from regional conflicts in Iraq and Afghanistan after invading the two countries respectively in 2003 and 2001. Then, following the Arab Spring of 2011, the Americans were unwilling to step in to shape their course in theatres deemed vital to the national interests of some of the GCC states in particular, such as Syria.

Israel, Saudi Arabia, and the UAE therefore found it difficult to work with President Obama. Consequently, when he was succeeded by President Donald J. Trump in 2017, Israeli, Saudi, and Emirati policymakers were more positive about the new president, believing that he was more sympathetic to their interests—or could at least be swayed through lobbying and transactional measures to adopt a similar viewpoint. Those hopes seemed confirmed when Trump visited Saudi Arabia in his first overseas visit as president in May 2017. He was persuaded to support Saudi Arabia and the UAE in their opposition toward Qatar, which enabled them to put in motion a diplomatic and economic boycott against Doha in part for its desire to accommodate Iran in the region.

For Israel, Trump offered a more sympathetic ear and voice on the peace process, even though he had campaigned for a more isolationist foreign policy. Trump arguably suffered from a lack of interest in foreign policy making. That disinterest left space for officials around him to become more proactive in policymaking and supportive of Israel and its objectives. They included Jason Greenblatt (Trump's special envoy to the Middle East), David Friedman (Trump's ambassador to Israel), Vice President Mike Pence, and Secretary of State Mike Pompeo.[16]

In December 2017, the president announced that the US embassy would move from Tel Aviv to Jerusalem, undoing the international consensus that no change be made until a final peace agreement be reached with the Palestinians. Trump said that American assistance to the Palestinians would be cut, in order to press them to talk to Israel. He also proposed a "deal of the century" to cut through the lack of negotiations, the bulk of which, when they were published in early 2020, reflected Israeli preferences.

On Iran, Israeli, Saudi, and Emirati policymakers all welcomed Trump's shared dissatisfaction with the nuclear deal, the details of which had been agreed upon by Obama between 2013 and 2015. While all agreed that Iran should not be able to advance its nuclear program, the narrow nature of the nuclear deal with the country did little to counter Iran's wider regional ambitions. Indeed, the removal of sanctions on Iran per the deal in exchange for freezing parts of its nuclear program could only serve to boost its economy and generate greater revenues for the government to carry out what Israelis, Saudis, and Emiratis saw as disruptive regional behavior designed to advance the Iranian influence.[17]

In October 2017, the Trump administration demanded changes to the nuclear deal with Iran. Without those changes, the United States threatened to withdraw from the deal and subsequently did so on May 8, 2018, reimposing earlier sanctions and imposing new ones amounting to a "maximum pressure" campaign against Iran.[18] But while the US president was arguably a high point when it came to handling Iran for the Israelis, Saudis, and Emiratis and leveraging their interests in American foreign policy, he did not constitute an unequivocal transformation in US behavior toward the Middle East region and a consistent guarantee of security—thereby making clearer to Jerusalem, Abu Dhabi, and Riyadh that they would need to look elsewhere to maximize their protection.

The Saudis and Emiratis soon learned of Trump's unreliability. Not long after accepting their reasons for boycotting and blockading Qatar in 2017, he soon changed tack and spent the rest of his presidency persuading them to resolve their differences.[19] Later, despite drone attacks against Saudi oil installations at Abqaiq and Khurais in September 2019, which Iran was believed to have helped carry out, his initial response was a defensive one; he did little to boost Saudi defense other than sending several hundred troops to the region.[20] That reticence was also echoed in the limitations of the American withdrawal from the Iran nuclear deal: although the new policy of "maximum pressure" prevented Iranian oil sales and much-needed revenue, it did little to stop Tehran's production and stockpiling of nuclear material, which exceeded agreed-upon levels in 2019.[21]

Notwithstanding Trump's capriciousness, he was initially viewed by America's Middle East allies in a more favorable light than his successor, President Joseph Biden. For one, despite Biden's commitment to Arab-Israeli normalization, he did not see it as a substitute for a final Palestinian-Israeli peace settlement. During his campaign to be the president, he was extremely critical of the Saudis, and of Crown Prince Mohammed bin Salman bin Abd al Aziz Al Saud in particular, for his suspected part in the murder of the dissident Saudi journalist, Jamal Khashoggi, in 2018. In Israel, support for Trump was higher than it has been for Biden, even as the latter was perceived to be less "dangerous."[22] Biden arguably compounded that sentiment upon taking office, when he declared his intention to return to the Iran nuclear deal. Although the process proved protracted and at the time of writing incomplete, American willingness to talk fueled Israeli and Saudi unease.[23] By the midpoint of his presidency, it was debatable if Biden had achieved much in relation to Iran. He had also begun to row back with the Saudis. In July 2022, President Biden visited Riyadh, reaffirming the alliance even if he would not give the Saudis (or indeed, other American partners) the depth of commitment that they sought.[24] The visit was considered unsuccessful at the time, although months later his government would seek to secure legal immunity for Muhammed bin Salman in relation to the Khashoggi killing while also stressing areas of mutual American-Saudi interest, including regional security and counter-terrorism. Increasingly, he began to see Saudi-Israel normalization as a means toward this end and encouraged Riyadh's entry into the Abraham Accords.[25]

President Biden's limits were also evident in the difficulties he faced in persuading his Israeli and GCC partners to align with the West in opposition to Russia and its invasion of Ukraine. Since the start of the war in February 2022, Israel and the GCC states have broadly sought nonalignment, so as to provide them with room for maneuver. For Israel, former prime minister Naftali Bennett attempted to mediate between Russia and Ukraine while current prime minister Netanyahu maintained the line he adopted in 2015, whereby he sought to keep Israel's rivalry with Iran separate from other great power competitions. Meanwhile, the GCC states broadly saw the conflict as a European one and which had little direct impact on their own security. Moreover, given their perception of diminishing American regional influence or commitment, they saw a need to maintain good relations with Russia, given its status as an important external actor in the Middle East.[26]

FROM BOYCOTT TO PARTIAL NORMALIZATION

Even before the Abraham Accords, Israel did have economic ties with the GCC states. That it did so reflects an earlier period of normalization in the wake of the signing of the Oslo Accords and several countries' preparedness to boost trade, beginning in the 1990s. Moreover, that opening continued, even as relations deteriorated between Israel and the Palestinians during the Second Intifada.

For the Arab Gulf states, part of the motivation to trade with Israel could be attributed toward their regimes' economic diversification efforts to offset their reliance on hydrocarbon production and the growing global consensus to move away from such forms of energy. In order to do so, they needed to invest in new industries and sectors that could generate similarly high amounts of revenues to support their substantial cradle-to-grave welfare states for their citizens. Israel's successful start-up culture and technology were widely admired across the Gulf region for achieving similar results.[27]

That several GCC states had been willing to enter into an economic exchange with Israel since the 1990s was in marked contrast to previous decades, when a boycott was in place—although one which had been only partial in its implementation and effectiveness against Israel. Besides the anti-Israel boycott was also another one that took shape in the late 1960s and 1970s which was targeted against other mostly Western states which backed Israel—and which had the effect of bringing Arab Gulf state concerns into their chancelleries.

Although boycotts were used against the Jewish community in historic Palestine prior to 1948, they took on an added impetus after the creation of Israel that year. The Arab League agreed in a collective decision to impose a boycott on the new state with the aim of undermining it and contributing to its collapse.[28] In 1951, a Central Boycott Office was established in Damascus. It investigated potential transgressions of the boycott and made recommendations to member states, but it had little power of enforcement.[29]

Regional boycotts against Israel have consisted of three types over the years. The first form of boycott banned citizens of an Arab country from entering into direct contact with Israel, via a contract with an Israeli state or non-state entity. A second level of the boycott was more indirect, extending the first boycott worldwide, to any company that did business in Israel. The third level prevented citizens from an Arab country from doing business with a company which was blacklisted for doing business in Israel.[30]

Even during the heyday of the Arab boycott against Israel, the secondary and tertiary components of the boycott were the least used. Meanwhile, from the 1970s, cracks began to appear within the primary boycott through exemptions and conditions. This was due in part to both an increase in trade between Western countries (and particularly the United States) and Arab countries from the mid-1960s and the efforts of individual businesses, especially in response to the inconsistent application and administration of the boycott at the mid- and lower levels.[31]

Undoubtedly, an important reason for the failure of the Arab boycotts was the presence of clandestine economic relations with Israel. Certainly, at the official level there was virtually no trade between Israel and the Gulf. In practice, however, there was some slippage, especially in the more indirect forms of boycott and the absence of enforcement and because its implementation fell to individual states. While some states, such as Kuwait and Bahrain, were more active in their support of the boycott, other GCC states like Oman were less restrained and did not impose the boycott as rigorously as might have been expected prior to Oslo.[32] In this period before the Oslo Accords then, some forms of informal and indirect trade did take place between Israel and the Gulf. During this time, "straw companies, offshore addresses and other legal mechanisms" were set up and used to enable economic exchange, including a mostly one-way form of trade from Israel to the UAE, specifically in high-end technology and diamonds.[33]

Beyond the direct boycott against Israel, others emerged in the late 1960s and early 1970s which more directly targeted Israel's international supporters. In 1967, the Arabs imposed an oil boycott on those countries which had supported Israel in the course of the war. Along with Saudi Arabia and Kuwait, the leaders of Bahrain, Qatar, and Abu Dhabi also expressed their support. However, a range of factors ensured that it did not have much impact, including insufficient Arab unity, coordination, and implementation; the Arabs in the Gulf in particular were hesitant at extending the boycott beyond a limited period of time. Notwithstanding their hesitancy, the experience was psychologically important and laid the groundwork for another attempt after the 1973 war.[34]

Despite the failure of the 1967 boycott, the decision was made to cut oil production after the 1973 war again. This time Arab oil producers committed to cutting production month by month in order which had the consequence of reducing supply and driving up prices while also imposing an embargo on sales to the United States. The Arabs' purpose was primarily political, by sending a message to the international community about the Palestinian question.[35]

Although the embargo came to an end almost half a year later, in March 1974, the impact was felt in both higher energy prices and longer queues at the petrol pump. The boycott had the added effect of making American policymakers more sensitive to Arab demands, owing in large part to greater level of trade and contact between the two sides since the mid-1960s. Increasingly, the political message associated with the embargo and boycott cut through in Washington; it was realized that oil could be a weapon on behalf of the Palestinians, which prompted the United States to factor in Saudi concerns on the Palestinian and Israeli file.[36]

Yet still there were limits to the Arab boycott and the oil embargo. The Arabs themselves were also sensitive to the impact of using oil and trade as a weapon. They began to appreciate American sensitivity toward their actions, especially given through their increasing interconnectedness. At the same time, there may have been an understanding that the primary objectives of these measures had not been achieved: not only had successive boycotts and the oil embargo failed to undermine Zionist ambitions, but they had also failed to dislodge Israel.[37]

The signing of the Oslo Accords marked a change in Israel's position in the Middle East region. The PLO's recognition of Israel, along with the establishment of the Palestinian Authority and Jordan's signing of a peace agreement with Israel in 1994, meant that both, along with Egypt which had signed an earlier treaty with Israel in 1979, were open to economic exchanges with the Jewish state. But while the boycott with Israel ended for these entities, the prospect of economic normalization in the Gulf was more halting. Although the indirect boycotts effectively ended, the direct one remained in place, awaiting a final peace settlement with the Palestinians.[38]

Yet even with these limited changes, there was a palpable shift between Israel and the GCC states. Oman and Qatar led the way in opening up with Israel. Their willingness to engage Israel stood out from other Arab Gulf states like Saudi Arabia and the UAE, who were more reticent and less involved.[39]

Israeli officials made visits to both countries and trade offices were opened. Bahrain was also visited by Israeli officials, and Kuwait indicated its willingness to allow a trade office. Meanwhile, Israeli firms indicated their interest in exploring potential commercial opportunities across the region.[40]

Notwithstanding the lack of uniformity in Israel's economic ties with the Arab world and the Gulf States, overall economic contact grew. In 1990, for instance, Israeli trade with the Middle East and Central Asia stood at $11.3 million. In 1993, it leaped to $68.8 million and rose to $228.9 million by 2000 (figure 2.1).[41] However, these figures were not definitive and could well have overlooked the full range of products, especially those which may have used third-party intermediaries. Consequently, an early estimate of Israeli-Arab Gulf economic exchange could have been anywhere between $60 million to $4.8 billion a year during the first few years of Oslo.[42]

Despite the outbreak of the Second Intifada in 2000, economic normalization with Israel continued. By 2014, it peaked at $1.2 billion but then declined, settling at just over $800 million by 2020.[43] At the same time, it is important to set Israel's trade relationship with the region in context. Overall, the Middle East and Central Asia accounted for a small proportion of Israel's overall global trade, worth 0.2 percent in 1993 and peaking at just under 1.2 percent by 2009 after which it dropped off, to around 0.7 percent by 2020.[44]

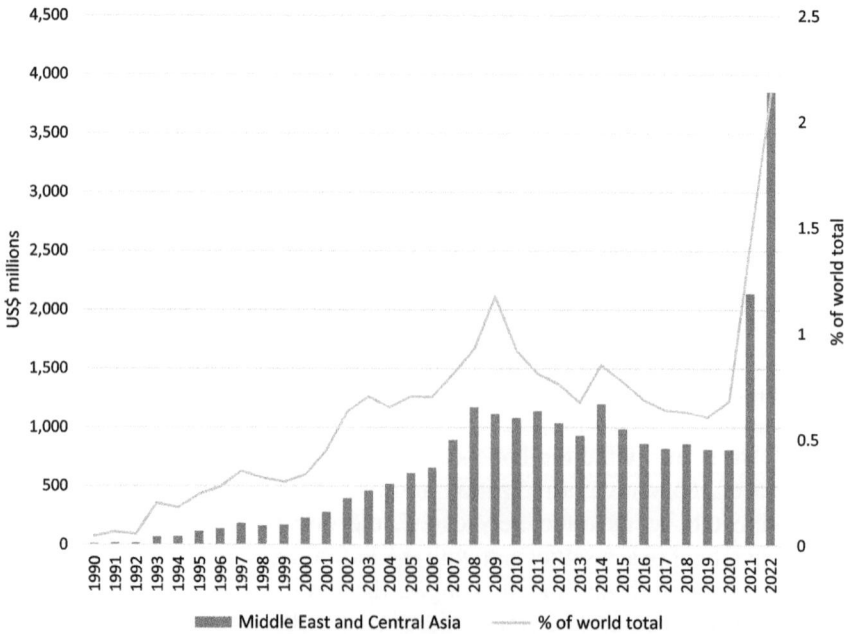

Figure 2.1   Israel's Trade with the Middle East and Central Asia, 1990–2022. *Source:* IMF Statistics.

Within this regional trade, GCC states made up Israel's third-largest market in the Middle East after Turkey and the Palestinian Authority. Added to that, virtually none of that trade was direct and was instead done through third-party intermediaries. The amount was uncertain but was estimated at anywhere between $500 million and $1 billion a year.[45] However, since then trade with the region has exploded, more than doubling in the year after the Abraham Accords, to $2.1 billion in 2021 and $3.85 billion in 2022. The bulk of that increase, which led to the Middle East and Central Asia constituting 2.1 percent of Israel's trade with the world, was with the UAE, amounting to over $1 billion in 2021 and $2.6 billion in 2022[46] (figure 2.1).

MUTUAL SECURITY CONCERNS BETWEEN ISRAEL AND ARAB GULF STATES

Both Israel and the Arab Gulf states like Saudi Arabia and the UAE have historically looked toward the United States for regional protection. However, American commitment to them is perceived to be lacking. Meanwhile, Iran has been a common security threat for both Israel and its GCC partners. Israel's perception of Iran has shifted substantially: Whereas Tehran was an important pillar of Israel's periphery diplomacy after independence, that changed after the 1979 Islamic revolution when it became a radical ideological threat. Iran's threat was judged to be growing: By 1999, Iran had developed missiles capable of reaching Israel and in 2002 Iran's nuclear program was exposed. Israel and the GCC states now had a mutual interest in containing Iran's nuclearization, which was subsequently revealed in cables between 2005 and 2009 which were published by Wikileaks.[47]

Beyond the nuclear threat, Tehran constituted a regional one, which Arab Gulf states—Saudi Arabia in particular—portrayed in sectarian terms, between a Shia Iran and its proxies and the wider Sunni and Arab world.[48] To compound the point further, other Arab leaders, including King Abdullah of Jordan, made similar observations, including his 2004 presentation of an Iran-promoted Shia crescent stretching across the Middle East, including Iraq and Syria.[49]

For many, the Arab Spring in 2011 only served to enhance Iranian influence. It expanded support from long-standing proxy groups like Hezbollah in Lebanon to include Hamas in Gaza and the Houthis in Yemen.[50] These actors threatened Israel and the Arab Gulf states including the UAE and Saudi Arabia. Their clandestine cooperation may have encouraged the Abraham Accords.[51] Among the GCC states, however, such concerns may have varied in their order of priority, with such region-wide developments being given greater consideration by Emirati leaders compared to Bahrain's, where engagement with and pressure from the US may have been more significant. In the latter instance, this included Bahrain's shuttering of an anti-normalization office alongside acting as host for the Trump administration's Prosperity for Peace conference in 2019.[52]

While Iran's support for insurgent groups posed an indirect threat to some GCC states and Israel (at least until October 2023), Tehran's missile and nuclear programs were a more direct one. Consequently, neither Israel, the Saudis nor the UAE welcomed President Obama's attempt to freeze Iran's nuclear program through the nuclear deal fashioned between them, Russia, China, and the Europeans in 2015.[53] They feared that not only would it not stop Iran from acquiring the knowledge to build a nuclear bomb, but it also showed a disjuncture between American objectives and those of its regional allies and partners in terms of their security threat perceptions. While building an agreement with Iran, the United States also showed unwillingness to contain the Iran-backed Bashar al-Assad regime in Syria, even after it crossed America's red lines by using chemical weapons against his people in 2013.

Beyond Iran, both Israel and the Arab Gulf states have had to deal with an increasingly unstable regional environment since the Arab Spring of 2011. Across the Middle East, several states and societies have broken down, leading to conflicts that have spilled across borders and sucked in regional powers like Iran, the Saudis, Emiratis, and Qataris, from Libya to Syria and Yemen, in an attempt to support parties that can advance the regional states' interests.

Looking to extend their footprint in the region, the Arab countries have sought to simultaneously ensure their security at home. Among the ways they have sought to build security is through the use of surveillance technology to monitor populations. Especially important in this process are Israeli firms and their development of such technology, which has the added appeal of having relatively few end-use restrictions that other Western technologies often face.[54] Meanwhile, for Israeli policymakers, Arab Gulf interest in such technology was seen as a potential route to develop contact and connections within the wider Arab world.[55]

Finally, one hope among Arab leaders who have normalized is the possibility that Israel might play in securing and sustaining American commitment in the region in the form of financial and military assistance. They look at what happened to Egypt after its decision to exit the Soviet orbit and embrace the Western camp following the Camp David peace process that led to peace with Israel in the 1970s, and also to substantial increases in US aid to enable Cairo to influence Middle East regional events and address the challenge from Iran.[56]

Despite American wishes to see closer interactions between Israel and the GCC states, a key challenge in this process is that there is no overall consensus regarding the principal threats facing the Middle East or action to be taken. This is compounded further by other factors including the break out of the Hamas-Israel war in late 2023, which makes building peace in that part of the region with Israel harder. Meanwhile, the GCC states' tendency to purchase military equipment and weapons systems from a variety of suppliers undermines interoperability, as well as wariness at sharing information and working together. Indeed, this latter point is particularly significant, since many Arab governments discourage the disparate parts of their national security services from coordinating with each other, in an effort to prevent potential coups.[57]

LEADERSHIP CHANGES IN ISRAEL AND IMPACT ON NORMALIZATION

Israel's outreach and normalization with the Arab Gulf have taken place regardless of the political complexion of the government and the intensification of conflict with the Palestinians, primarily Hamas in Gaza. Indeed, so strong has been the consensus on normalization that the issue of diplomatic outreach to Arab states like the UAE and Bahrain has generated very little electoral or political advantage either for Benjamin Netanyahu, who signed on to the Abraham Accords, or for his political rivals. That this has been the case may arguably point to the consolidation and institutionalization of those normalized ties from the Israeli perspective, since it would appear that normalization is a subject that transcends parties and individual leaders across the political spectrum.

The strong consensus over normalization with the Arab world is in marked contrast to Israel's approach to the Palestinians. There, changes in Israeli governments have shifted since the Oslo Accords were first signed. Generally, Labor-led governments have been more inclined toward talks and reaching an agreement with the Palestinians, while right-wing governments led by Netanyahu, Ariel Sharon, and Likud have been less engaged and more unilateral in their actions. Yet even those differences over tactics and behavior toward the Palestinians mask a broader similarity across the Israeli political spectrum, between both the political parties and the wider public. In short, the majority has been more in favor of maintaining the status quo in which Israel is dominant; any separate Palestinian state that emerges would be subordinate, including having limited autonomy and demilitarized.[58] The origins of Israel's wider normalization with the Arab world began with the 1991 Madrid conference (and as opposed to the bilateral peace agreement achieved with Egypt in 1979). The event marked the moment when Israeli representatives were brought into direct and public contact with their Arab counterparts for the first time and at a time when the First Intifada (1987–1993) was starting to wind down. The Israeli government was led by Likud, following the end of a national unity government with Labor in 1990. On the Arab side, front-line Arab states like Egypt, Jordan, Lebanon, and Syria were present, along-side other Arab countries, including the GCC as an observer and Tunisia, Morocco, and Mauritania from the Maghreb and North Africa, to help with normalization. While the conference and subsequent bilateral and multilateral talks hosted in Washington and Moscow the following year did little to close the distance between Israel and its Arab rivals, it was an important symbolic moment and a further opportunity for GCC states to be present, via the GCC's observer status.[59]

Taking place clandestinely and in parallel, the talks which eventually resulted in the Oslo Accords were overseen by Prime Minister Yitzhak Rabin and the Labor Party. But just as his Palestinian interlocutors had their own veto player in the form of Hamas, Rabin also faced opposition toward Oslo, from the right-wing Likud Party and the settler movement which backed it.

In November 1995, Rabin was assassinated by an Israeli ultranationalist. Soon after, Likud won the 1996 elections. The new prime minister, Benjamin Netanyahu, aimed to maintain the diplomatic and commercial opportuni-ties offered by Oslo, but without making concessions to the Palestinians.[60] Negotiations between the two began to slow down, and by early 1997, the door between Israel and the Gulf states looked to be closing. There was a brief respite in 1999–2000 when Ehud Barak and the Labor Party returned to power. However, Barak's efforts to sign a comprehensive peace agreement at Camp David in July 2000 proved illusionary. The breakdown of trust was exacerbated by the violence that erupted in September 2000, which marked the start of the Second Intifada and an end to direct talks.[61]

For much of the Second Intifada, Israel's government was led by Likud's Ariel Sharon. He became prime minister in February 2001, following his special election victory over Labor's Ehud Barak and subsequently reinforced by parliamentary elections a month later. A hawk, as defense minister he had instigated Israel's invasion of Lebanon in 1982. As the Second Intifada increased in intensity, he rejected Palestinian claims of identity or demands. He gave no quarter, being accused of "politicide" in his determination to eliminate what he saw as the Palestinian threat.[62]

It was during this period that Saudi Arabia put forward the Arab Peace Initiative in 2002. In several respects it looked similar to the Saudis' own Fahd Plan from twenty years previously. It included reference to UN General Assembly Resolution 194 as a starting point for resolving the refugee issue, Israeli withdrawal from southern Lebanon and the establishment of "normal relations" rather than "normalization."[63] Although Sharon did not reject the plan out of hand, his government showed little willingness to publicly endorse it. Much of the reason for this was the intransigence of both Sharon's government and unenthusiastic public opinion at the time, given the violence of the Second Intifada.[64]

Even when Israel offered no official response to the Arab Peace Initiative, it was undertaking unilateral action against the Palestinians and seemingly also to appease them. In 2003, the Sharon government proposed to dismantle Israeli settlements and withdraw from Gaza. But the move sought to establish a clear separation between Israelis and Palestinians and avert a perceived demographic threat in the form of a future Palestinian majority. The plan generated considerable ruction within the government, leading to several parties removing their support. In response, Sharon established Kadima, a new centrist party in 2005 which brought together his base from Likud and moderates from other parties. That same year the pull-out from Gaza began.

In January 2006, Sharon collapsed and became permanently incapacitated. He was replaced by Ehud Olmert, whose premiership saw an attempt to reach a settlement with the Palestinians. His efforts were partly thwarted by the intra-Palestinian conflict that resulted in Hamas becoming the principal Palestinian party in Gaza, following its defeat of Fatah in late 2006.

The split of the Palestinian territory meant that West Bank–controlled Fatah remained within the Oslo peace process and committed to talking with Israel while Hamas stood outside it. Over the next decade, the focus of Israeli military operations became dominated by Gaza, as it responded disproportionately to missile attacks from Hamas (and later other militants) inside the territory. In one of his last acts as prime minister, Olmert launched Operation Cast Lead in December 2008–January 2009, after which Prime Minister Netanyahu's Likud governments oversaw Operation Pillar of Defense in November 2012, Operation Protective Edge in August 2014, Operation Wall Guardian in May 2021, and Operation Swords of Iron in October 2023.[65]

In the wake of the 2012 confrontation, Qatar offered to provide aid to the Gaza territory to help reconstruction efforts, which began sometime after that year. Initially, Israeli leaders disliked the proposal, especially if it propped Hamas up. Over time, however, Israeli leaders came around to Qatari involvement in Gaza since it provided the population with income and thereby limited prospects for an internal collapse[66]—a position that it looked to have abandoned in the wake of the surprise Hamas attack on October 2023. Qatari involvement may also have appeared to offset potential Iranian outreach toward Hamas.[67]

By the start of the Arab Spring, Israel looked to be in a relatively solid position. It had weathered the collapse of Oslo, the violence of the Second Intifada, and a possible agreement with the Palestinians. Under Netanyahu, Sharon, and then under Netanyahu again after 2009, it had foresworn dialogue for unilateralism toward the Palestinians. In so doing, Netanyahu captured wider Israeli public opinion, which was itself divided over what alternative course to take toward the Palestinians other than that Israel should maintain its dominant position.[68] This has remained the case among the Israeli public since the outbreak of the Israel-Hamas war in October 2023; following US president Biden's attempt to link continued American aid to progress on a two-state solution, a majority (52 percent) of Jewish Israelis rejected the demand.[69] Such opinion has been the prevailing one even as Israel remained largely apart from the wider ructions engulfing the Arab world and later the domestic political tensions that resulted in five elections between 2019 and 2022.

Israel's electoral turmoil had little to do with Israel's Palestinian, regional or wider foreign policy and everything to do with domestic actors positioning themselves in relation to Netanyahu. Trump's proposed "deal of the century" to end the Israeli-Palestinian conflict made little impression on the Israeli political scene for instance; indeed, it was barely raised in the 2020 election campaign.

The Abraham Accords were signed several months later and received cross-party support in Israel. Despite this, there were questions from both the left and the right. The left questioned the timing of the agreements and whether they were designed to compensate for Netanyahu's poor handling of the coronavirus pandemic and to boost President Trump's electoral prospects in the forthcoming presidential election in the United States. On the right, meanwhile, settler leaders were angry that the agreement with the UAE coincided with the government stepping back from its earlier promise to annex the West Bank.[70]

Both sets of criticisms had an impact on Netanyahu's political prospects at the March 2021 elections. His broken promise on annexation may have undermined his standing on the right, which, along with the broad antipathy toward him across the political spectrum, contributed to a multiparty coalition that combined to keep him from retaining power. His failure to form a new government led to one led by his former chief of staff and a former settler leader, Naftali Bennett.

Both Bennett and his principal coalition partner, Foreign Minister Yair Lapid of the centrist Yesh Atid party, remained committed to the normalization process. That commitment not only demonstrated the extent to which normalization transcended the political spectrum, but it was also not reliant on any individual personalities. This was reinforced by a series of visits and meetings between Bennett and Lapid and key figures in the UAE and Bahrain in the year before the Bennett-Lapid government fell in June 2022. Months later, Netanyahu and his partners won the November election, following which he received calls from the UAE president and Bahrain that included further development of relations between their countries.[71]

ISRAEL-GCC STATE RELATIONS SINCE THE ABRAHAM ACCORDS

The signing of the Abraham Accords in August 2020 was a surprise to many. They generated both celebration among the participants and their backers and dismay by its opponents, including the Palestinians. For Israel, it constituted a variation on the long-standing policy of periphery diplomacy, in which its leaders pursued ties with potential partners to counter states hostile to it. Whereas previously that entailed Arab neighbors like Egypt, Jordan, and Syria, today that involves Iran and the pursuit of like-minded Arab partners to counter it from the Gulf.

To date, the bulk of the exchanges that have taken place have been dominated largely by Israel and the UAE, with the other signatories—Bahrain, Morocco, and Sudan—following further behind. That this is so perhaps reflects the greater degree of prior interaction between the two, including a clandestine dialogue that existed before 2020 and echoed shared interests and concerns.

The Israeli-UAE agreement which led the way stated that they would recognize each other and establish cooperation across a range of sectors, including tourism, education, healthcare, trade, and security. On the political question of the Palestinians, the Emiratis claimed that the agreement did not eliminate the "viability" of a two-state solution and that it had halted previously announced Israeli plans to annex the West Bank. For Israel's part, Netanyahu claimed that the agreement did no such thing, suggesting that the decision not to annex was only temporary. Meanwhile, Trump played up the agreement by calling it a "peace agreement" despite the absence of any hostilities between the two countries.[72]

In December 2021, slightly more than a year after the Abraham Accords were signed, the new Israeli prime minister, Naftali Bennett, traveled to Abu Dhabi. The enthusiasm generated by his visit and meetings with UAE leaders distinguished Israel's normalization with the UAE from other, earlier efforts, most notably Egypt, Jordan, and the PLO.

Although the treaties signed between Israel and Egypt and Jordan respectively established peace between them, they were forms of "cold" or "negative" peace in that while they halted the threat of physical violence, they did little to build a more constructive set of relations between the two sides that extended beyond the elite level (i.e., a "positive" peace). In short, the peace that took shape was "frozen," with little noticeable change in the dynamics between and within the countries themselves.

Despite the absence of any substantial thaw at the societal level, the elites pressed ahead. In March 2022, the foreign ministers of Israel, Egypt, Bahrain, Morocco, and the UAE all met in the Negev, along with the US secretary of state, Antony Blinken. For Israel and Arab states, the main concern was the Iran threat and how to counter it. Both sides saw each other as potential partners, especially in a context of perceived American decline and commitment in the region.[73] Toward that end, the participants said the summit "would become a permanent, rotating forum."[74]

Beyond these broad, common positions, Israel's engagement with the Abraham Accords signatories in the Gulf has been varied. Between the UAE and Bahrain, the level of interaction has been more substantial in relation to the latter. Indeed, it has included forms of contact that have gone beyond the official, governmental level to include the pursuit of commercial opportunities and some people-to-people contacts.[75]

Viewed more broadly, some observers suggested that the Abraham Accords might encourage greater integration in a region that has seen relatively little of it. Around 13 percent of trade happens between countries in the Middle East, compared to 66 percent in Europe. RAND Corporation suggests that were the four Arab normalization countries—the UAE, Sudan, Morocco, and Bahrain—to sign a plurilateral free trade agreement among themselves, their individual economies would grow by 2–3 percent and stimulate employment while adding another 2.3 percent to Israel's economy over ten years.[76] In addition to this regional boost, the accords could also stimulate interest from other Muslim-majority countries outside the Middle East to operate with Israel.[77] So promising was the prospect of greater economic exchange with Israel based on the pace at which Israel-UAE trade was growing, that other Abraham Accord signatories have begun to take a more active interest. Ahead of a meeting between the foreign ministers of the five countries in March 2022, Moroccan business and trade associations sent delegations to Israel to explore ways of increasing economic opportunities.[78]

Despite the mutual interest and exchange between Israel and its Arab partners, the Palestinian issue remains a sticking point. While Israeli leaders can scarcely contemplate the notion of full Palestinian autonomy and sovereignty, that is a position strongly held by many Arab publics, including in the Gulf. That point of contention was exacerbated by ongoing violence between Israel and Palestinians in 2021 and 2022. A first test took place in April and May 2021 when an upsurge of communal violence took place between Arabs and Jews in "mixed" cities across Israel, between Israeli security forces and Palestinian protestors in east Jerusalem and between Israel and Hamas around Gaza.

All the normalizing states criticized Israel and its treatment of the Palestinians in Jerusalem following the protests at Al-Aqsa. By contrast, the reactions toward the fighting between Israel and Palestinian groups like Hamas and Islamic Jihad were more muted. For example, during the fighting between Israel and Hamas in 2021, the *Al-Ittihad* newspaper in the UAE was less explicit in its condemnation or support for the Palestinians. Part of the reason for this may be due to Emirati aversion both toward Hamas and its Qatari backers.[79] Later, in 2022, following months of tensions, mobilizing among Palestinian groups and attacks against Israelis in the West Bank, Israel retaliated against Islamic Jihad in Gaza. For several days in early August, it bombed the territory, killing nearly fifty Palestinians, including seventeen children. While Qatar denounced the attacks and identified Israel's involvement, the Arab Abraham Accord signatories were more reticent;[80] the UAE's foreign ministry, for instance, appealed for "calm" and to "reduce escalation" and made no direct reference to either Israel or the Palestinians.[81]

Following the fighting in 2021, the GCC states have kept the Palestinian issue on the agenda with their new Israeli partner. While Israeli attention was focused on Iran at the March 2022 Negev summit of foreign ministers, the Arab representatives refused to discount the Palestinians and stressed the need for Israel to resolve the conflict with them: a statement that the American secretary of state reiterated when summarizing the details of the talks to press.[82]

Following the summit, the United States, Israel, Egypt, Bahrain, Morocco, and the UAE established the Negev Forum to support multilateral projects between the parties. Jordan chose not to join so long as the Palestinians refused to participate. Following a meeting in Bahrain in June 2022 and a virtual one in October, the signatories met in Abu Dhabi in January 2023 to plan for the next summit, scheduled for Dakhla in Morocco-controlled Western Sahara in March. The Arabs were keen to keep the Palestinian issue on the agenda, but the summit was subsequently postponed following Israeli attacks against Palestinians and the decision to expand settlements in the West Bank, with no date set for it to happen.[83]

CONCLUSION

The Abraham Accords constitute only the latest form of Israeli normalization and periphery diplomacy. The prospect and application of Israeli-Arab normalization have happened before, most especially during the Oslo period. What makes the Abraham Accords notable is that they differ from this earlier period in several ways. Although the regional international system is currently in a state of flux, it differs from the immediate post-Cold War period. Then, the Middle East was experiencing change, but one in which the United States was the dominant and hegemonic power. By contrast, in today's Middle East, the uncertainty generated by the Arab Spring has also combined with increasingly autonomous regional state actors and a perceived decline in American power and commitment to the region.

That suspicion and fear of the American retreat along with Iran's growing regional influence is one that is shared by Israel and several Arab Gulf states. This remains an ongoing concern, along with what effect the Accords might have on the security architecture of the Gulf. Indeed, notwithstanding Saudi Arabia and Iran's own normalization agreement in early 2023, the reasons for it and events do not suggest a complete thawing of relations.[84] Not only will the two continue to be suspicious of each other, but Iran has given tacit backing to groups opposed to Saudi Arabia, Israel, and others like the UAE, such as Hamas Gaza and the Houthis in Yemen. Perhaps because of this, neither Israel nor the other Accord signatories have made much headway to date in coordinating their position in relation to conflicts across the region, with relations between Israel and each of the other states being largely ad hoc and an absence of any institutionalized mechanism which could respond to regional crises.

The ad hoc and bilateral nature of Israeli-Arab normalization is also reflected in the variable nature of the relationships. So far, they are most extensive and deepest with the UAE: both moved quickly to explore opportunities that overlapped with and moved beyond the security sector, including cyber surveillance and other high-value technological and economic exchange. By contrast, those with other signatories, like Sudan, appear similar to Israel's previous agreements with Egypt, Jordan, and the PLO, where the agreements achieved a cold or "negative" peace. At the same time, the range of these relations does not have much to say with regard to Iran and its regional role; despite the common Israeli and Emirati distrust of Tehran, the depth of their growing relationship has offered little to curb or contain Iranian ambitions.[85]

Beyond the limitations of the Abraham Accords themselves is the wider regional uncertainty generated by the fighting between Israel and Hamas in Gaza since October 2023. While the outbreak of war disrupted the growing closeness of Saudi-Israeli normalization, it has arguably not dented its trajectory. At the same time, the fighting has shown both those who have normalized relations with Israel (the UAE and Bahrain) and those who have not (Saudi Arabia) that such a development cannot take place without acknowledgment of the Palestinians and their plight and a change in their situation.[86] While it cannot be said at the time of writing what the outcome of the Israel-Hamas conflict will be and whether the majority of the Israeli public and its political leadership could or will move on from their commitment to Israeli domination over the Palestinians, it is unlikely that this pre-bellum arrangement will remain untested, along with Israel's previous siege of a Hamas-controlled Gaza. At the time of writing, there is considerable speculation as to whether the political and legal limbo that the Palestinians in the occupied territories have experienced will remain or place or change, the consequences of which will have wider effects at the regional and international levels, including in the Gulf and for the Abraham Accords themselves.

While that remains in the future, the principal message of the chapter has been to illustrate the extent to which Israeli normalization has taken place thus far and the hurdles it will face if it is to venture further. While the Abraham Accords constitute a substantial change in Israel's relations with the Arab world, they are by no means comprehensive and there are still a number of important parties and issues that will need to be addressed if Israel is ever to become accepted as a full state member of the Middle East with strong ties to other regional states.

NOTES

1. Yossi Alpher, *Periphery: Israel's Search for Middle East Allies* (Lanham, MD: Rowman & Littlefield, 2015).

2. Yoel Guzansky, "Israel and the Arab Gulf States: from tacit cooperation to reconciliation?," *Israel Affairs,* 21(1) (2015): 131–147; Ian Black, "Just Below the Surface: Israel, the Arab Gulf states and the Limits of Cooperation," LSE Middle East Centre Report (March 2019), https://eprints.lse.ac.uk/100313/; Masami Nishino, "Progress in the Normalization of Relations between the Arab Countries and Israel," in *East Asian Strategic Review*, ed. National Institute for Defense Studies (Tokyo: National Institute for Defense Studies, 2022), 44–67.

3. Creede Newton, "Israel Ties That Bind: What is the US Giving Gulf Arab States?," *Al Jazeera*, September 14, 2020, https://www.aljazeera.com/news/2020 /9/14/israel-ties-that-bind-what-is-the-us-giving-gulf-arab-states; Bradley Bowman and Ryan Brobst, "How Arming Saudi Arabia Helped Israel and the United States," *Defense News*, November 2, 2023, https://www.defensenews.com/opinion/2023/11 /02/how-arming-saudi-arabia-helped-israel-and-the-united-states/.

4. Omar Rahman, "What's Behind the Relationship Between Israel and the Arab Gulf States?," *Brookings*, January 28, 2019, https://www.brookings.edu/blog/order -from-chaos/2019/01/28/whats-behind-the-relationship-between-israel-and-arab-gulf -states/.

5. Bruce Riedel, "How to Understand Israel and Saudi Arabia's Secretive Relationship," *Brookings*, July 11, 2022, https://www.brookings.edu/blog/order-from-chaos /2022/07/11/how-to-understand-israel-and-saudi-arabias-secretive-relationship/.

6. Jewish Federations of North America, "Israeli Reactions to the Abraham Peace Accords with the UAE and Bahrain," October 6, 2020, https://cdn.fedweb.org/fed-42 /2212/Abraham%2520Accords_Israeli%2520Reactions_Sep30.pdf.

7. Hussein Ibish, "Why Bahrain is Embracing Normalization with Israel," Arab Gulf States Institute in Washington, September 14, 2020, https://agsiw.org/why-bahrain-is-embracing-normalization-with-israel/.

8. David Sorenson, *An Introduction to the Modern Middle East*, 2nd ed. (Boulder, CO: Westview, 2014), 395.

9. Joel Peters, "Israel in the World: The quest for legitimacy," in *Understanding Israel: Political, Societal and Security Challenges*, eds. Joel Peters and Rob Geist Pinfold (Abingdon: Routledge, 2019), 247, 260.

10. Jeremy Sharp, *US Foreign Aid to Israel* (Washington DC: Congressional Research Service, 2022).

11. Stockholm International Peace Research Institute [SIPRI], "Importer/Exporter TIV Tables," https://armstrade.sipri.org/armstrade/page/values.php.

12. Oded Yaron and Ben Samuels, "US Marines Tested Israel's Iron Dome. Here's What They Really Proved," *Haaretz*, 31 July 2022, https://www.haaretz.com/israel -news/security-aviation/2022-07-31/ty-article/u-s-marines-tested-israels-iron-dome -heres-what-they-really-proved/00000182-3f89-dbf9-a7f3-bfd9c8d20001.

13. Sorenson, *An Introduction to the Middle East*, 336.

14. John Mearsheimer and Stephen Walt, *The Israel Lobby and US Foreign Policy* (New York: Farrar, Straus and Giroux, 2007): 17-8.

15. Elisheva Rosman-Stollman, "Balancing Acts: The Gulf States and Israel," *Middle Eastern Studies,* 40(4) (2004): 185–208.

16. Oliver Holmes, "Will Trump's Major Foreign Policy Legacy be Israel and Palestine?," *Guardian*, November 19, 2020, https://www.theguardian.com/us-news /2020/nov/19/will-trumps-major-foreign-policy-legacy-be-israel-and-palestine.

17. "Why Saudi Arabia and Israel Oppose Iran Nuclear Deal," *Al Jazeera*, April 14, 2015, https://www.aljazeera.com/news/2015/4/14/why-saudi-arabia-and-israel -oppose-iran-nuclear-deal.

18. Julian Borger, Saeed Kamali Dehghan, and Peter Beaumont, "Trump Threat-ens to Rip Up Iran Nuclear Deal Unless US and Allies 'Fix Serious Flaws,'" *Guard-ian*, October 13, 2017, https://www.theguardian.com/us-news/2017/oct/13/trump -iran-nuclear-deal-congress.

19. Nawaf Obaid, "Trump Will Regret Changing His Mind About Qatar," *Foreign Policy*, August 15, 2018, https://foreignpolicy.com/2018/08/15/trump-will-regret -changing-his-mind-about-qatar/.

20. Phil Stewart and Idrees Ali, "United States Sending Troops to Bolster Saudi Defenses after Attack," *Reuters*, September 21, 2019, https://www.reuters.com/article /us-saudi-aramco-usa-pentagon-idUSKBN1W52K3.

21. Kali Robinson, "What Is the Iran Nuclear Deal?," *Council on Foreign Rela-tions*, July 20, 2020, https://www.cfr.org/backgrounder/what-iran-nuclear-deal.

22. Jacob Magid, "Biden Less Popular Among Israelis than Trump, But Seen as Less Dangerous," *The Times of Israel*, July 11, 2022, https://www.timesofisrael.com /biden-less-popular-among-israelis-than-trump-but-seen-as-less-dangerous/.

23. Josh Boak, Josef Federman, and Aamer Madhani, "Biden Arrives in Mideast Jittery About Iran Nuclear Program," *Time*, July 13, 2022, https://time.com/6196604/ biden-trip-mideast-iran-nuclear-program/; Ali Harb, "Israel-Palestine US Policy: What Changed under Biden, What Didn't," *Al Jazeera*, July 12, 2022, https://www.aljazeera .com/news/2022/7/12/israel-palestine-us-policy-what-changed-under-biden-what-didnt.

24. Kirsten Fontenrose, "Why Biden's Mideast Trip Was Much Ado About Very Little," *Atlantic Council*, July 19, 2022, https://www.atlanticcouncil.org/blogs/new -atlanticist/why-bidens-mideast-trip-was-much-ado-about-very-little/.

25. Dan Whitcomb and Steve Holland, "Biden Administration Says Saudi Prince Has Immunity in Khashoggi Killing Lawsuit," *Reuters*, November 18, 2022, https://www.reuters.com/legal/biden-admin-says-saudi-prince-has-immunity-khashoggi-killing-lawsuit-court-2022-11-18/; Jon Alterman, "Biden's Efforts to Bring Saudi Arabia into the Abraham Accords," *CSIS*, September 21, 2023, https://www.csis.org/analysis/bidens-efforts-bring-saudi-arabia-abraham-accords.

26. George Cafiero, "Where has the Ukraine Conflict Left Gulf States?" Italian Institute for International Political Studies, February 22, 2023, https://www.ispionline.it/en/publication/where-has-the-ukraine-conflict-left-gulf-states-116712; Samuel Ramani, "One Year on: The GCC's Balancing Act in the Ukraine War," *The New Arab*, March 2, 2023, https://www.newarab.com/analysis/one-year-gccs-balancing-act-ukraine-war; Daniel Rakov, "The Netanyahu Government's Approach to Russia and the Ukraine," *Fikra Forum*, February 28, 2023, https://www.washingtoninstitute.org/policy-analysis/netanyahu-governments-approach-russia-and-ukraine.

27. Kristian Coates Ulrichsen, *Israel and the Arab Gulf States: Drivers and Directions of Change* (Houston, TX: Baker Institute for Public Policy, Rice University, 2016), 11.

28. Gil Feiler, *From Boycott to Economic Cooperation: The Political Economy of the Arab Boycott of Israel* (Abingdon: Routledge, 1999).

29. Nancy Turck, "The Arab Boycott of Israel," *Foreign Affairs,* 55(3) (1977): 472–493.

30. Martin Weiss, *Arab League Boycott of Israel* (Washington, DC: Congressional Research Service, 2017), 2.

31. Turck, "The Arab Boycott of Israel"; Feiler, *From Boycott to Economic Cooperation.*

32. Rosman-Stollman, "Balancing Act"; Ibrahim Abed and Peter Hellyer, *United Arab Emirates: A New Perspective* (London: Trident Press, 2001), 173.

33. Jonathan Fulton and Roie Yellinek, "UAE-Israel Diplomatic Normalization: A Response to a Turbulent Middle East Region," *Comparative Strategy,* 40(5) (2021): 499–515; Niels de Hoog, "Israel-UAE Trade Normalisation," *Atradius*, April 1, 2021, https://group.atradius.com/publications/economic-research/israel-uae-trade-relations.html.

34. M. S. Daoudi and M. S. Dajani, "The 1967 Oil Embargo Revisited," *Journal of Palestine Studies,* 13(2) (1984): 65–90.

35. Timothy Mitchell, "The Resources of Economics: The Making of the 1973 Oil Crisis," *Journal of Cultural Economy,* 3(2) (2010): 189–204; Giuliano Garavini, "Completing Decolonization: The 1973 'Oil Shock' and the Struggle for Economic Rights," *International History Review,* 33(3) (2011): 473–487.

36. Uzi Rabi and Chelsi Mueller, "The Gulf Arab States and Israel since 1967: From 'No Recognition' to Tacit Cooperation," *British Journal of Middle Eastern Studies,* 44(4) (2017): 576–592.

37. Feiler, *From Boycott to Economic Cooperation.*

38. Yoel Guzansky, "Israel and the Arab Gulf States: From Tacit Cooperation to Reconciliation?," *Israel Affairs,* 21(1) (2015): 131–147; Weiss, *Arab League Boycott of Israel*, 2.

39. Rabi and Mueller, "The Gulf Arab States and Israel since 1967."

40. Rosman-Stollman, "Balancing Acts."

41. Data extracted and calculated by the author, from IMF, Direction of Trade Statistics (DOTS), https://data.imf.org/?sk=9d6028d4-f14a-464c-a2f2 -59b2cd424b85.

42. Colin MacKinnon, "The Party's Over for Israeli Economic Integration Into the Middle East," Washington Report On Middle East Affairs, January/February 1998, https://www.wrmea.org/1998-january-february/the-mena-summit-conference -in-doha-two-views.html.

43. Data extracted and calculated by the author from IMF, Direction of Trade Statistics.

44. Ibid.

45. Guzansky, "Israel and the Arab Gulf States"; Elie Podeh, "Saudi Arabia and Israel: From Secret to Public Engagement, 1948-2018," *Middle East Journal,* 72(4) (2018): 563–586.

46. Data extracted and calculated by the author from IMF, Direction of Trade Statistics.

47. Guzansky, "Israel and the Arab Gulf States"; Efraim Inbar, *Israel's National Security: Issues and challenges since the Yom Kippur War* (Abingdon: Routledge, 2008), 109.

48. Joseph Massad, "How the Iran 'Threat' Led to Arab-Israeli Alliance," *Middle East Eye*, January 28, 2022, https://www.middleasteye.net/opinion/iran-theat-arab -israel-alliance-led-how.

49. Kahyan Barzegar, "Iran and the Shiite Crescent: Myths and Realities," Brown Journal of World Affairs Fall/Winter, 2008, https://www.belfercenter.org/publication /iran-and-shiite-crescent-myths-and-realities.

50. In the case of the Houthis, their contact with Iran predates the uprisings but remained slight, both following the outbreak of fighting between them and the former Saleh regime in 2004 and then again, in relation to the post-Saleh regime in 2014. See Thomas Juneau, "Iran's Policy Toward the Houthis in Yemen: A Limited Return on a Modest Investment," *International Affairs,* 92(3) (2016): 647–663.

51. Fatiha Dazi-Héni, "The Gulf States and Israel after the Abraham Accords," *Arab Reform Initiative*, November 6, 2020, https://www.arab-reform.net/publica- tion/the-gulf-states-and-israel-after-the-abraham-accords/; Kenneth Katzman, *The United Arab Emirates (UAE): Issues for US Policy* (Washington, DC: Congressional Research Service, 2021).

52. Dana El Kurd, "The Paradox of Peace: The Impact of Normalization with Israel on the Arab World," *Global Studies Quarterly*, 3(3) (2023): 1–11.

53. Ibid.

54. Omar Rahman, "The Emergence of GCC-Israel Relations in a Changing Middle East," *Brookings*, July 28, 2021, https://www.brookings.edu/research/the -emergence-of-gcc-israel-relations-in-a-changing-middle-east/.

55. Fulton and Yellinek, "UAE-Israel Diplomatic Normalization."

56. Rahman, "The Emergence of GCC-Israel Relations in a Changing Middle East."

57. Yasmine Farouk, "The Middle East Strategic Alliance Has a Long Way to Go," Carnegie Endowment for International Peace, February 8, 2019, https://carn-egieendowment.org/2019/02/08/middle-east-strategic-alliance-has-long-way-to-go-pub-78317; Chyrine Mezher, "'Mission Impossible?' Interoperability Across Arab States," *Breaking Defense*, November 5, 2020, https://breakingdefense.com/2020/11/mission-impossible-interoperability-across-arab-states/.

58. See, for instance, Ilan Pappe, "A Palestinian State in Zionist and Israeli Thought," *Palestine-Israel Journal,* 6(2) (1999), https://www.pij.org/articles/924/a-palestinian-state-in-zionist-and-israeli-thought; Toby Greene, "Israel's Two State Debate," International Affairs 91(5) (2015): 1009-1026.

59. Ahmed Nasser Al-Thani, "The Gulf Cooperation Council's Foreign Policy toward the Middle East Peace Process (1991-2005) with Special Reference to Qatar's Foreign Policy," PhD Dissertation (Cheltenham: University of Gloucestershire, 2017), 126–127.

60. Rabi and Mueller, "The Gulf Arab States and Israel since 1967"; Rosman-Stollman, "Balancing Acts."

61. Guzansky, "Israel and the Arab Gulf States."

62. Baruch Kimmerling, *Politicide: Ariel Sharon's War Against the Palestinians* (London: Verso Books, 2006).

63. Guzansky, "Israel and the Arab Gulf States."

64. Ibid.

65. In terms of casualties, the number killed on the Israeli/civilian side were 13, 2, 73, 14, and 1 in the 2008–2009, 2012, 2014, 2021, and May 2023 confrontations while the estimates of the dead in Gaza were 1,100–1,400, 150–200, 2,200, 256, and 33, respectively. At the time of writing in mid-November 2023, the fighting that began on October 7, 2023, had resulted in the deaths of over 1,300 Israelis and 14,000 Palestinians in Gaza.

66. Yoel Guzansky and Yohanan Tzoreff, "Gaza, Qatar, and the UAE: The Abraham Accords After Operation Guardian of the Walls," Washington Institute, June 16, 2021, https://www.washingtoninstitute.org/policy-analysis/gaza-qatar-and-uae-abraham-accords-after-operation-guardian-walls.

67. Elia Zureik, "Qatar's Humanitarian Aid to Palestine," *Third World Quarterly,* 39(4) (2017): 786–798.

68. Greene, "Israel's Two State Debate."

69. Tamar Hermann and Or Anabi, "Israelis Sharply Divided on the Question of a Two-State Solution in Return for US Assistance," Israel Democracy Institute, War in Gaza Survey 6, December 5, 2023, https://en.idi.org.il/articles/51746.

70. Jewish Federations of North America, "Israeli Reactions to the Abraham Peace Accords with the UAE and Bahrain."

71. "Israel's Netanyahu Says UAE President Invited Him to Visit," *Reuters*, November 10, 2022, https://www.reuters.com/world/middle-east/israels-netanyahu-says-uae-president-invited-him-visit-2022-11-10/; "Netanyahu Speaks to Bahrain Crown Prince of 'Great Opportunities' for Cooperation," *The Times of Israel*, November 13, 2022, https://www.timesofisrael.com/netanyahu-speaks-to-bahrain-crown-prince-of-great-opportunities-for-cooperation/.

72. Oliver Holmes and Julian Borger, "Israel Signs Hhistoric Deal with UAE that Will 'Suspend' West Bank Annexation," *Guardian*, August 13, 2020, https://www.theguardian.com/world/2020/aug/13/israel-and-uae-to-form-diplomatic-ties-says-donald-trump.

73. Amr Hamzawy, "The Negev Summit's Participants Had Wildly Different Goals," *Atlantic Council*, April 6, 2022, https://carnegieendowment.org/2022/04/06/negev-summit-s-participants-had-wildly-different-goals-pub-86826.

74. Lucy Kurtzer-Ellenborgen and Hesham Youssef, "The Negev Summit Furthers Arab-Israeli Normalization," United States Institute for Peace, March 31, 2022, https://www.usip.org/publications/2022/03/negev-summit-furthers-arab-israeli-normalization.

75. Aaron David Miller, "Three Takeaways From the Israeli Prime Minister's UAE Trip," *Carnegie Endowment for International Peace*, December 14, 2021, https://carnegieendowment.org/2021/12/14/three-takeaways-from-israeli-prime-minister-s-uae-trip-pub-85990.

76. Michael Singh, "Axis of Abraham: Arab-Israeli Normalization Could Remake the Middle East," *Foreign Affairs*, March/April, 2022, https://www.foreignaffairs.com/articles/middle-east/2022-02-22/axis-abraham?utm_medium=newsletters&utm_source=twofa&utm_campaign=Invasions%20Are%20Not%20Contagious&utm_content=20220304&utm_term=FA%20This%20Week%20-%20112017.

77. Singh, "Axis of Abraham"; Daniel Egel, Shira Efron, and Linda Robinson, *Peace Dividend: Widening the Economic Growth and Development Benefits of the Abraham Accords* (Santa Monica, CA: RAND, 2021), https://www.rand.org/pubs/perspectives/PEA1149-1.html.

78. Danny Zaken, "Israeli Business Leaders Expect Surge in Trade with Morocco," *Al-Monitor*, March 31, 2022, https://www.al-monitor.com/originals/2022/03/israeli-business-leaders-expect-surge-trade-morocco.

79. Guzansky and Tzoreff, "Gaza, Qatar, and the UAE."

80. David Weinberg, "Abraham Accords: Israel is a Role Model for Arab Countries – Opinion," *Jerusalem Post*, September 16, 2022, https://www.jpost.com/opinion/article-717280.

81. "'Restraint and Common Sense': Reaction to Israel's Gaza Attack," *Al Jazeera*, August 5, 2022, https://www.aljazeera.com/news/2022/8/5/restraint-and-common-sense-reaction-to-israels-gaza-attack; UAE Ministry of Foreign Affairs and International Cooperation, "UAE Calls for De-escalation in Gaza," August 7, 2022, https://www.mofaic.gov.ae/en/mediahub/news/2022/8/7/07-08-2022-uae.

82. Rina Bassist and Jared Szuba, "Israeli, Arab Summit Seeks 'New Regional Architecture' against Iran," *Al-Monitor*, March 28, 2022, https://www.al-monitor.com/originals/2022/03/israeli-arab-summit-seeks-new-regional-architecture-against-iran; Kurtzer-Ellenborgen and Youssef, "The Negev Summit Furthers Arab-Israeli Normalization."

83. Rina Bassist, "Negev Forum Convenes in UAE with Jordan Absent from Arab-Israeli Meeting," *Al-Monitor*, January 9, 2023, https://www.al-monitor.com/originals/2023/01/negev-forum-convenes-uae-jordan-absent-arab-israeli-meeting; Mohamed Chtatou, "Morocco, Israel, and the Future of the Negev Forum," *Fikra*

Forum, February 16, 2023, https://www.washingtoninstitute.org/policy-analysis /morocco-israel-and-future-negev-forum; Middle East Monitor, "Negev Forum Meeting Delayed Due to Israeli Escalation against Palestinians," February 20, 2023, https://www.middleeastmonitor.com/20230220-negev-forum-meeting-delayed-due -to-israeli-escalation-against-palestinians/; Rina Bassist, "Morocco cancels Negev summit with Israel over settlement expansion," Al-Monitor, June 21, 2023, https:// www.al-monitor.com/originals/2023/06/morocco-cancels-negev-summit-israel-over -settlement-expansion.

84. George Cafiero, "Iranian-Saudi Deal: They Didn't Do It for Llove," Responsible Statecraft, September 8, 2023, https://responsiblestatecraft.org/china-iran-saudi-arabia/.

85. See, for instance, Omar Rahman, "Five Reasons Why the Abraham Accords Are Ceding Ground to Arab-Iranian De-escalation," Baker Institute for Public Policy, July 11, 2023, https://www.bakerinstitute.org/research/five-reasons-why-abraham -accords-are-ceding-ground-arab-iranian-de-escalation.

86. Abdullah Alrebh, "Is Saudi-Israeli Normalization Still on the Table?," Middle East Institute, December 22, 2023, https://www.mei.edu/publications/saudi-israel -normalization-still-table.

REFERENCES

Abed, Ibrahim, and Peter Hellyer, *United Arab Emirates: A New Perspective* (London: Trident Press, 2001).

Al Jazeera, "'Restraint and Common Sense': Reaction to Israel's Gaza Attack," August 5, 2022, https://www.aljazeera.com/news/2022/8/5/restraint-and-common -sense-reaction-to-israels-gaza-attack.

Al Jazeera, "Why Saudi Arabia and Israel Oppose Iran Nuclear Deal," April 14, 2015, https://www.aljazeera.com/news/2015/4/14/why-saudi-arabia-and-israel-oppose -iran-nuclear-deal.

Alpher, Yossi Alpher, *Periphery: Israel's Search for Middle East Allies* (Lanham, MD: Rowman & Littlefield, 2015).

Alterman, Jon, "Biden's Efforts to Bring Saudi Arabia into the Abraham Accords," *CSIS*, September 21, 2023, https://www.csis.org/analysis/bidens-efforts-bring -saudi-arabia-abraham-accords.

Al-Thani, Ahmed Nasser, "The Gulf Cooperation Council's Foreign Policy toward the Middle East Peace Process (1991-2005) with Special Reference to Qatar's Foreign Policy," PhD Dissertation (Cheltenham: University of Gloucestershire, 2017), 126–127.

Barzegar, Kahyan, "Iran and the Shiite Crescent: Myths and Realities," *Brown Journal of World Affairs*, Fall/Winter, 2008, https://www.belfercenter.org/publication/ iran-and-shiite-crescent-myths-and-realities.

Bassist, Rina, "Morocco Cancels Negev Summit with Israel Over Settlement Expansion," *Al-Monitor*, June 21, 2023, https://www.al-monitor.com/originals/2023/06/ morocco-cancels-negev-summit-israel-over-settlement-expansion.

Bassist, Rina, "Negev Forum Convenes in UAE with Jordan Absent from Arab-Israeli Meeting," *Al-Monitor*, January 9, 2023, https://www.al-monitor.com/originals/2023/01/negev-forum-convenes-uae-jordan-absent-arab-israeli-meeting.

Bassist, Rina, and Jared Szuba, "Israeli, Arab Summit Seeks 'New Regional Architecture' against Iran," *Al-Monitor*, March 28, 2022, https://www.al-monitor.com/originals/2022/03/israeli-arab-summit-seeks-new-regional-architecture-against-iran.

Boak, Josh, Josef Federman, and Aamer Madhani, "Biden Arrives in Mideast Jittery About Iran Nuclear Program," *Time*, July 13, 2022, https://time.com/6196604/biden-trip-mideast-iran-nuclear-program/.

Borger, Julian, Saeed Kamali Dehghan, and Peter Beaumont, "Trump Threatens to Rip up Iran Nuclear Deal Unless US and Allies 'Fix Serious Flaws'," *Guardian*, October 13, 2017, https://www.theguardian.com/us-news/2017/oct/13/trump-iran-nuclear-deal-congress.

Cafiero, George, "Where has the Ukraine Conflict Left Gulf States?" Italian Institute for International Political Studies, February 22, 2023, https://www.ispionline.it/en/publication/where-has-the-ukraine-conflict-left-gulf-states-116712.

Chtatou, Mohamed, "Morocco, Israel, and the Future of the Negev Forum," Fikra Forum, February 16, 2023, https://www.washingtoninstitute.org/policy-analysis/morocco-israel-and-future-negev-forum.

Daniel, Shira Efron, and Linda Robinson, *Peace Dividend: Widening the Economic Growth and Development Benefits of the Abraham Accords* (Santa Monica, CA: RAND, 2021), https://www.rand.org/pubs/perspectives/PEA1149-1.html.

Daoudi, M. S., and M. S. Dajani, "The 1967 Oil Embargo Revisited," *Journal of Palestine Studies,* 13(2) (1984): 65–90.

Dazi-Héni, Fatiha, "The Gulf States and Israel after the Abraham Accords," *Arab Reform Initiative*, November 6, 2020, https://www.arab-reform.net/publication/the-gulf-states-and-israel-after-the-abraham-accords/.

De Hoog, Niels, "Israel-UAE trade normalisation," *Atradius*, April 1, 2021, https://group.atradius.com/publications/economic-research/israel-uae-trade-relations.html.Egel.

Farouk, Yasmine, "The Middle East Strategic Alliance Has a Long Way to Go," *Carnegie Endowment for International Peace*, February 8, 2019, https://carnegieendowment.org/2019/02/08/middle-east-strategic-alliance-has-long-way-to-go-pub-78317.

Feiler, Gil, *From Boycott to Economic Cooperation: The Political Economy of the Arab Boycott of Israel* (Abingdon: Routledge, 1999).

Fontenrose, Kirsten, "Why Biden's Mideast Trip was Much Ado About Very Little," *Atlantic Council*, July 19, 2022, https://www.atlanticcouncil.org/blogs/new-atlanticist/why-bidens-mideast-trip-was-much-ado-about-very-little/.

Fulton, Jonathan, and Roie Yellinek, "UAE-Israel Diplomatic Normalization: A Response to a Turbulent Middle East Region," *Comparative Strategy*, 40(5) (2021): 499–515.

Garavini, Giuliano, "Completing Decolonization: The 1973 'Oil Shock' and the Struggle for Economic Rights," *International History Review,* 33(3) (2011): 473–487.

Guzansky, Yoel, and Yohanan Tzoreff, "Gaza, Qatar, and the UAE: The Abraham Accords After Operation Guardian of the Walls," Washington Institute, June

16, 2021, https://www.washingtoninstitute.org/policy-analysis/gaza-qatar-and-uae
-abraham-accords-after-operation-guardian-walls.

Guzansky, Yoel, "Israel and the Arab Gulf States: From Tacit Cooperation to Reconciliation?," *Israel Affairs,* 21(1) (2015): 131–147.

Hamzawy, Amr, "The Negev Summit's Participants Had Wildly Different Goals,"
Atlantic Council, April 6, 2022, https://carnegieendowment.org/2022/04/06/negev
-summit-s- participants-had-wildly-different-goals-pub-86826.

Harb, Ali, "Israel-Palestine US Policy: What Changed under Biden, What Didn't," *Al
Jazeera*, 12 July 2022, https://www.aljazeera.com/news/2022/7/12/israel-palestine
-us-policy-what-changed-under-biden-what-didnt.

Holmes, Oliver, "Will Trump's Major Foreign Policy Legacy be Israel and
Palestine?," *Guardian*, November 19, 2020, https://www.theguardian.com
/us-news/2020/nov/19/will-trumps-major-foreign-policy-legacy-be-israel-and
-palestine.

Holmes, Oliver, and Julian Borger, "Israel Signs Historic Deal with UAE That Will
'Suspend' West Bank Annexation," *Guardian*, August 13, 2020, https://www
.theguardian.com/world/2020/aug/13/israel-and-uae-to-form-diplomatic-ties-says
-donald-trump.

Ibish, Hussein, "Why Bahrain is Embracing Normalization with Israel," Arab Gulf
States Institute in Washington, September 14, 2020, https://agsiw.org/why-bahrain
-is-embracing-normalization-with-israel/.

IMF, "Direction of Trade Statistics (DOTS)," https://data.imf.org/?sk=9d6028d4
-f14a-464c-a2f2-59b2cd424b85.

Inbar, Efraim, *Israel's National Security: Issues and Challenges since the Yom Kippur War* (Abingdon: Routledge, 2008).

Jewish Federations of North America, "Israeli Reactions to the Abraham Peace
Accords with the UAE and Bahrain," October 6, 2020, https://cdn.fedweb.org/fed
-42/2212/Abraham%2520Accords_Israeli%2520Reactions_Sep30.pdf.

Juneau, Thomas, "Iran's Policy toward the Houthis in Yemen: A Limited Return on a
Modest Investment," *International Affairs,* 92(3) (2016): 647–663.

Katzman, Kenneth, *The United Arab Emirates (UAE): Issues for US Policy* (Washington DC: Congressional Research Service, 2021).

Kimmerling, Baruch, *Politicide: Ariel Sharon's War Against the Palestinians* (London: Verso Books, 2006).

Kurtzer-Ellenborgen, Lucy, and Hesham Youssef, "The Negev Summit Furthers
Arab-Israeli Normalization," *United States Institute for Peace*, March 31, 2022,
https://www.usip.org/publications/2022/03/negev-summit-furthers-arab-israeli
-normalization.

MacKinnon, Colin, "The Party's Over for Israeli Economic Integration Into the
Middle East," Washington Report On Middle East Affairs, January/February 1998,
https://www.wrmea.org/1998-january-february/the-mena-summit-conference-in
-doha-two-views.html.

Magid, Jacob, "Biden Less Popular Among Israelis than Trump, but Seen as Less
Dangerous," *The Times of Israel*, July 11, 2022, https://www.timesofisrael.com/
biden-less-popular-among-israelis-than-trump-but-seen-as-less-dangerous/.

Massad, Joseph, "How the Iran 'Threat' Led to Arab-Israeli Alliance," *Middle East Eye*, January 28, 2022, https://www.middleeasteye.net/opinion/iran-theat-arab -israel-alliance-led-how.

Mearsheimer, John, and Stephen Walt, *The Israel Lobby and US Foreign Policy* (New York: Farrar, Straus and Giroux, 2007), 17–18.

Mezher, Chyrine, "'Mission Impossible?' Interoperability Across Arab States," *Breaking Defense*, November 5, 2020, https://breakingdefense.com/2020/11/mis sion-impossible-interoperability-across-arab-states/.

Middle East Monitor, "Negev Forum Meeting Delayed Due to Israeli Escala- tion against Palestinians," February 20, 2023, https://www.middleeastmonitor .com/20230220-negev-forum-meeting-delayed-due-to-israeli-escalation-against -palestinians/.

Miller, Aaron David, "Three Takeaways From the Israeli Prime Minister's UAE Trip," *Carnegie Endowment for International Peace*, December 14, 2021, https:// carnegieendowment.org/2021/12/14/three-takeaways-from-israeli-prime-minister -s-uae-trip-pub-85990.

Mitchell, Timothy, "The Resources of Economics: The Making of the 1973 Oil Cri- sis," *Journal of Cultural Economy,* 3(2) (2010): 189–204.

Obaid, Nawaf, "Trump Will Regret Changing His Mind About Qatar," *Foreign Policy*, August 15, 2018, https://foreignpolicy.com/2018/08/15/trump-will-regret -changing-his-mind-about-qatar/.

Peters, Joel, "Israel in the World: The Quest for Legitimacy," in *Understanding Israel: Political, Societal and Security Challenges*, eds. Joel Peters and Rob Geist Pinfold (Abingdon: Routledge, 2019), 247, 260.

Podeh, Elie, "Saudi Arabia and Israel: From Secret to Public Engagement, 1948- 2018," *Middle East Journal,* 72(4) (2018): 563–586.

Rabi, Uzi, and Chelsi Mueller, "The Gulf Arab States and Israel since 1967: From 'No Recognition' to Tacit Cooperation," *British Journal of Middle Eastern Studies,* 44(4) (2017): 576–592.

Rahman, Omar, "The Emergence of GCC-Israel Relations in a Changing Middle East," *Brookings*, July 28, 2021, https://www.brookings.edu/research/the-emer gence-of-gcc-israel-relations-in-a-changing-middle-east/.

Rahman, Omar, "What's Behind the Relationship between Israel and the Arab Gulf States?," *Brookings*, January 28, 2019, https://www.brookings.edu/blog/order -from-chaos/2019/01/28/whats-behind-the-relationship-between-israel-and-arab -gulf-states/.

Rakov, Daniel, "The Netanyahu Government's Approach to Russia and the Ukraine," *Fikra Forum*, February 28, 2023, https://www.washingtoninstitute.org/policy -analysis/netanyahu-governments-approach-russia-and-ukraine.

Ramani, Samuel, "One Year on: The GCC's Balancing Act in the Ukraine War," *The New Arab*, March 2, 2023, https://www.newarab.com/analysis/one-year-gccs -balancing-act-ukraine-war.

Reuters, "Israel's Netanyahu Says UAE President Invited Him to Visit," *Reuters,* November 10, 2022, https://www.reuters.com/world/middle-east/israels-netanyahu -says-uae-president-invited-him-visit-2022-11-10/.

Riedel, Bruce, "How to Understand Israel and Saudi Arabia's Secretive Relationship," *Brookings*, July 11, 2022, https://www.brookings.edu/blog/order-from-chaos/2022/07/11/how-to-understand-israel-and-saudi-arabias-secretive-relationship/.

Robinson, Kali, "What Is the Iran Nuclear Deal?," *Council on Foreign Relations*, July 20, 2020, https://www.cfr.org/backgrounder/what-iran-nuclear-deal.

Rosman-Stollman, Elisheva, "Balancing Acts: The Gulf States and Israel," *Middle Eastern Studies,* 40(4) (2004): 185–208.

Sharp, Jeremy, *US Foreign Aid to Israel* (Washington, DC: Congressional Research Service, 2022).

Singh, Michael, "Axis of Abraham: Arab-Israeli Normalization Could Remake the Middle East," *Foreign Affairs*, March/April, 2022, https://www.foreignaffairs.com/articles/middle-east/2022-02-22/axis-abraham?utm_medium=newsletters&utm_source=twofa&utm_campaign=Invasions%20Are%20Not%20Contagious&utm_content=20220304&utm_term=FA%20This%20Week%20-%20112017.

Sorenson, David, *An Introduction to the Modern Middle East*, 2nd ed. (Boulder, CO: Westview Press, 2014).

Stewart, Phil, and Idrees Ali, "United States Sending Troops to Bolster Saudi Defenses after Attack," *Reuters*, September 21, 2019, https://www.reuters.com/article/us-saudi-aramco-usa-pentagon-idUSKBN1W52K3.

Stockholm International Peace Research Institute [SIPRI], "Importer/Exporter TIV Tables," https://armstrade.sipri.org/armstrade/page/values.php.

The Times of Israel, "Netanyahu Speaks to Bahrain Crown Prince of 'Great Opportunities' for Cooperation," *The Times of Israel*, November 13, 2022, https://www.timesofisrael.com/netanyahu-speaks-to-bahrain-crown-prince-of-great-opportunities-for-cooperation/.

Turck, Nancy, "The Arab Boycott of Israel," *Foreign Affairs,* 55(3) (1977): 472–493.

UAE Ministry of Foreign Affairs and International Cooperation, "UAE Calls for De-escalation in Gaza," August 7, 2022, https://www.mofaic.gov.ae/en/mediahub/news/2022/8/7/07-08-2022-uae.

Ulrichsen, Kristian Coates, *Israel and the Arab Gulf States: Drivers and Directions of Change* (Houston, TX: Baker Institute for Public Policy, Rice University, 2016).

Weinberg, David, "Abraham Accords: Israel is a role model for Arab Countries – Opinion," *Jerusalem Post*, September 16, 2022, https://www.jpost.com/opinion/article-717280.

Weiss, Martin, *Arab League Boycott of Israel* (Washington, DC: Congressional Research Service, 2017).

Whitcomb, Dan, and Steve Holland, "Biden Administration says Saudi Prince has Immunity in Khashoggi Killing Lawsuit," *Reuters*, November 18, 2022, https://www.reuters.com/legal/biden-admin-says-saudi-prince-has-immunity-khashoggi-killing-lawsuit-court-2022-11-18/.

Yaron, Oded, and Ben Samuels, "US Marines Tested Israel's Iron Dome. Here's What They Really Proved," *Haaretz*, July 31, 2022, https://www.haaretz.com/israel-news/security-aviation/2022-07-31/ty-article/u-s-marines-tested-israels-iron-dome-heres-what-they-really-proved/00000182-3f89-dbf9-a7f3-bfd9c8d20001.

Zaken, Danny, "Israeli Business Leaders Expect Surge in Trade with Morocco," *Al-Monitor*, March 31, 2022, https://www.al-monitor.com/originals/2022/03/israeli-business-leaders-expect-surge-trade-morocco.

Zureik, Elia, "Qatar's Humanitarian aid to Palestine," *Third World Quarterly,* 39(4) (2017): 786–798.

Chapter 3

Internal Fragmentation and External Penetration in Palestine

Guy Burton

Since 1948, Palestine has been a divided polity, first territorially, then politically. A significant reason for that is due to the Palestinian-Istraeli conflict, whereby Israel's political leadership and a majority of society favor Israeli dominance, with limited Palestinian autonomy at most. This has been a consistent position over the decades, even as Israeli leaders have indicated different means and models by which this may be achieved. Even at the outset of the Oslo period after 1993, Israeli leading politicians shared a common position that transcended party lines, that even if a Palestinian state were to be formed it should be so "only in name, not in substance."[1]

Israel's pursuit of dominance and control over the territory of Palestine and Palestinians has put pressure on Palestinian society and its policy, splintering Palestinians and their responses. In recent decades the splits that have become a prominent feature of the Palestinian experience have been further exposed to the actions of state and non-state actors in the Gulf. These have ranged from diplomacy, mediation, and financial assistance by governments to organization and agitation by groups supportive of the Boycott, Divestment, and Sanctions (BDS) movement. In general, these developments have had only limited benefit for Palestinians and do not indicate an overarching and consistent strategy for resolving the Israel-Palestine conflict. Indeed, they have done little to transform the prevailing structure of the Palestinians' conflict with Israel, which is overwhelmingly weighted toward the latter.

Another notable feature of Palestinian–Gulf Cooperation Council (GCC) state relations is the way that they have developed over time. Perhaps, the most significant aspect of this is the change in both the importance of the Israel-Palestine conflict and its impact on Palestine versus the GCC states, if not their societies. Whereas the Palestinian issue constituted the primary conflict in the Middle East in the decades after 1948 and provided a principal element of Arab identity, since the 1990s, both aspects have become less salient for GCC rulers. Whereas most Arab governments saw the Palestinian issue as a primarily military one in the first decades, after 1967, it became a more political one. This arguably paved the way to normalization with Israel, beginning with Egypt in 1979 and Jordan in 1994, followed by the GCC states of the United Arab Emirates (UAE) and Bahrain in 2020. At the same time, while Arab leaders have taken this view, this remains in contrast to their societies; Egyptian and Jordanian societies have remained cool toward Israel, while in the Gulf GCC citizens have not been enthusiastic supporters of the Abraham Accords Expression of public distaste has been limited, however, owing to the autocratic and repressive nature of GCC states, including campaigns against critics of the Abraham Accords in the UAE and Bahrain.[2]

To make sense of the relationship between the Palestinians and the GCC states, the chapter charts the Palestinians' relations with the Arab Gulf before and since the Abraham Accords. Early on, the Palestinian issue was an important political concern for Arab leaders and populations, the most tangible feature of Gulf-Palestinian engagement and exchange was societal in the form of the Palestinian diaspora in those countries. Among those who settled in the Gulf included the current Palestinian president, Mahmoud Abbas. Others were born there, like Jordan's queen Rania and Omar Barghouti, the co-founder of the BDS movement. Even former Israeli Knesset member Azmi Bishara and Hamas leader Ahmed Meshal have both lived in Qatar.

In the 1980s and then during the Oslo period in the 1990s, the GCC states contributed to Palestinian development and state-building through aid programs. Despite this, Gulf-Palestinian interaction remained politically distant. That began to change following the end of the Oslo era and the onset of the Second Intifada when GCC states began to play a more prominent and direct role in Palestinian politics. In particular, Saudi Arabia, Qatar, and later the United Arab Emirates (UAE) became more visible both as backers of rival Palestinian parties like Fatah and Hamas and as important potential and actual mediators and financiers.

While the Arab Gulf presence in Palestine has been steadily growing, the signing of the Abraham Accords heralded a new stage, not only in the Palestinians' conflict with Israel but also in the relationship between Palestinians and GCC states. Moreover, the Palestinian struggle is one that can go in a number of different directions, from the pursuit of a Palestinian state to the upholding and implementation of equal human rights for Palestinians. Important factors in this process are the role of the Palestinian political parties, especially Fatah and Hamas, as well as social movements such as the BDS campaign, and civil society more generally. The interplay between these forces, actors, and GCC states and societies may contribute significantly to the advancement or retreat of Palestinian ambitions and their results in the coming years.

US ROLE IN PALESTINIAN-GCC STATE RELATIONS

GCC state involvement was largely focused on the Arab boycott of Israel and providing financial assistance to Palestinian groups involved in the struggle against Israel or involved in supporting Palestinians living under occupation.[3] In 1981, the Saudis put forward the Fahd Plan. On the surface, it was no different from the land-for-peace principle that was enshrined in the international consensus of UN Security Council Resolution 242 (1967). What made it stand out was that it came from an Arab state. Before that point, the United States had largely ignored Arab Gulf considerations. The initiative did not advance, however, in part because of Israel's invasion and subsequent occupation of southern Lebanon in 1982 which overshadowed the Arab olive branch, and in part because the Americans were pursuing their own (largely unsuccessful) diplomatic efforts.[4]

The United States would return to the peace process in the wake of the Second Gulf War (1990–1991) and only do so reluctantly. Despite the convulsions surrounding the end of the Cold War, then president George H. W. Bush was a somewhat conservative figure; while he welcomed the prospect of an expansion of American values and leadership, he was wary of generating instability. Indeed, despite putting together and leading an international coalition against Iraq following its invasion of Kuwait, he refused to extend the fight into the country and remove Saddam Hussein from power.[5]

Even if the American administration saw limits to its involvement in the Middle East, regionally the crisis generated by Iraq's invasion of Kuwait exposed the vulnerability faced by some oil producers to regional security threats. More optimistically, however, the prospect of a peace settlement that would address one of the Middle East's pressing issues—namely the Arab-Israeli conflict—was highly appealing and offered the chance for a regional reset.[6] At the same time, the Gulf states saw the opportunity to cultivate ties with the United States—and through it, outreach with Israel—as a means to counter the threats they faced in the region, especially Iraq and Iran.[7]

The prospect of containing Iraq and Iran also influenced a Gulf presence as observers in the subsequent Madrid Conference. Later, the Oslo Accords provided space for the GCC states to engage with both Israel and the Palestinians—especially since the Palestinian representative entity, the Palestinian Liberation Organization (PLO), had effectively formalized recognition of Israel. In particular, it led to financial assistance from the GCC states toward the institutions set up during the Oslo process, especially the Palestinian

Authority. Overall though, Gulf involvement was largely secondary. There are several reasons for this. One was the absence of any formal recognition between GCC states and Israel, which limited the scope of exchange. Another was American dominance of the peace process as the primary mediator, with the Europeans taking up a secondary and supplementary status as a provider of economic aid.[8]

The limited scope for the GCC states was exacerbated by the collapse of Oslo process and the violence of the Second Intifada (2000–2005). In 2002, the Saudis proposed an Arab Peace Initiative, which was an upgrade of the Fahd Plan from twenty years earlier. Like its predecessor, it offered to normalize relations with Israel in exchange for a peace settlement and a Palestinian state along the 1967 borders.

Throughout this period, the United States remained the principal global and regional power. However, in the two decades since 2000, American power is generally perceived by its allies, partners, and rivals in the Middle East, to have declined. Several developments account for this, including the inability of US and allied forces to establish a stable and orderly political environment following the invasions of Afghanistan and Iraq; the emergence and increasingly assertive powers like Russia and China on both the global stage and in the Middle East; the fracture of states and fragmentation of societies across the Arab world after the Arab Spring from 2011; increasing autonomy of regional powers like Turkey, Iran, and Saudi Arabia, as well as several of the smaller Arab Gulf states such as Qatar and the UAE; and isolationist tendencies and transactional policies of the Trump administration.

Yet even though US power has, at times, felt to be relatively diminished, it has still dominated external engagement in the Israel-Palestine conflict, largely for domestic political reasons and the strength of the Israeli lobby in the United States and for the special relationship with Israel. After years in which there had been no movement on the Palestinian question, the Trump administration indicated that it would unilaterally move beyond the Oslo paradigm. This reflected its wider position that it neither saw the Israel-Palestine conflict as the main one in the Middle East nor that the United States needed to pay lip service to a two-state solution or take a balanced view as an honest broker if Arab normalization with Israel was to be achieved. Indeed, the administration saw Israel as a major democratic ally and largely blamed the Palestinians for not being willing to make peace.[9]

The first signs of the shift in American thinking took place in December 2017. The United States broke with the international consensus and announced it would move its embassy to Jerusalem. Then in early 2018, Trump announced US aid to the Palestinians would be cut in order to pressure them to negotiate with Israel.[10] Later, in June 2019 and January 2020, the Trump administration put forward its proposals for an alternative peace process.

The plan had been developed by Trump's adviser and son-in-law, Jared Kushner, who sought to work independently from the conflict parties.[11] However, its content echoed many Israeli preferences, including a highly circumscribed and demilitarized Palestinian state that would be subject to Israeli security interests, including Israel's control of the Jordan Valley and of land, sea, and air. In addition, Israeli settlements in the West Bank were to be linked to and absorbed into Israel proper.[12]

The plan received short shrift from the Palestinians, who immediately discounted it. Across the Arab world, however, the response was more mixed, with Egypt, Saudi Arabia, the UAE, Bahrain, Oman, Qatar, and Morocco offering qualified support to the Palestinians.[13] Yet some months earlier, the prospects had arguably been more promising. Saudi Arabia's king Salman and his son, Crown Prince Mohammad bin Salman, for instance, had hosted Palestinian president Abbas in February 2019, where they both declared their support for an independent Palestinian state with east Jerusalem as its capital and the Saudi foreign minister reiterated his country's commitment to its Arab Peace Initiative.[14].

Arguably, the more receptive stance by Arab states toward the downgrade of Palestinian autonomy in Trump's proposal may have been due to the state of regional politics. Indeed, differences between the Arab states could be distinguished between the GCC states which opposed Iran (and who wanted American protection) which were more willing to lend their support, and Syria, part of the so-called "resistance axis" with Iran, which opposed the plan.[15]

Despite questions about US power, American policy has remained important, confirmed by the reaction to Abbas's counterproposal: that the peace process be restarted through a supposedly more impartial and diplomatically balanced forum like an international conference involving the Quartet (made up of the United States, European Union, Russia, and the UN), thereby diminishing the US role. However, like his other earlier calls for an international conference, Abbas's words fell on deaf ears.[16] Months later, it would be upended with the announcement of the Abraham Accords.

Following President Trump's departure from office, his successor, President Joe Biden, did not lead any substantial change in US policy toward the Palestinians. Although he had previously expressed commitment to a two-state solution, he has so far done little to advance that goal. Moreover, even as he restored some of the American aid which had been cut by Trump and communicated with the Palestinian president Mahmoud Abbas, he did not reverse the US embassy move to Jerusalem. However, in May 2021, US secretary of state Anthony Blinken did announce that he would reestablish a consulate in East Jerusalem to handle direct contact with the Palestinian National Authority (PNA) in the West Bank. Still, President Biden's stance has been disappointing to date for the Palestinians, reflecting a realpolitik that the Israeli government is not interested in negotiations and that Washington is unwilling to use its political capital to achieve movement toward peace. This stance did not shift after the outbreak of the Israel-Hamas war in October 2023. Indeed, Israel's regional integration, an important Israeli regional policy, is being achieved via the Abraham Accords rather than through peace with the Palestinians.[17]

AID AND TRADE BETWEEN PALESTINE AND THE GCC STATES

Economic exchange between the Gulf and Palestine has been a combination of both aid and trade. Of the two, aid has long been the most prominent and significant component, both before, during, and after the Oslo period (1993–2000). At the same time, Palestinian trade with the Gulf has grown, especially since the end of the Second Intifada (2000–2005), from $15 million in 2008 to $46 million in 2009 and to nearly $200 million by 2019.[18] Saudi Arabia and the UAE have been especially important partners in this respect, followed some distance behind by Qatar.

Much of the early Gulf aid to the Palestinians was the result of growing oil rents, which was helped in part by the oil producers' embargo in the wake of the 1973 war. At a regional level, the Arab League coordinated aid to the "frontline" countries involved in the struggle against Israel, including Egypt, Jordan, Syria, and the PLO. Alongside this, regional multilateral organizations like the Arab Fund, Islamic Development Bank, and the Arab Gulf Fund for United Nations Development Organizations all received funding from Arab Gulf states like Saudi Arabia, Kuwait, and the UAE which made important contributions toward the Palestinians. The Arab League provided a monthly stipend of $43 million during the First Intifada to help Palestinians with their living costs.[19]

The signing of the Oslo Accords gave further impetus for foreign aid from the Gulf. Between 1994 and 2010, Saudi Arabia disbursed around $1 billion in grants toward the Palestinian Authority, far above the nearly $300 million allocated by the UAE and $200 million by Kuwait (Algeria was the only other Arab country to make a significant contribution, around $500 million). During the same period, Qatar also began to make an important contribution as well, although its total was slightly more modest than the other three Gulf states, slightly below $200 million—yet even this contribution was greater than most other Arab states, including those from outside the Gulf.[20]

Although important, Arab aid to the Palestinians constituted a smaller share than that of other donors, however. While the total amount from Gulf states ($2.2 billion) was greater than from North American sources ($1.5 billion), it was far less than from Europe ($6.6 billion).[21] In addition, whereas much of European and American money was directed toward development, the bulk of Arab assistance during the Oslo years was spent on general budget support for the Palestinian Authority.[22]

Beyond the Palestinian Authority, financial assistance from the Gulf was more modest. Palestinian civil society organizations, for instance, were not prominent beneficiaries of such aid. Instead, political parties received growing levels of direct support. In the case of Hamas, for instance, Gulf money was extremely important. While the figures remain incomplete and uncertain, it was believed to have received several tens of millions of dollars during the Oslo period and after. Of that, around $12 million was believed to originate from the Gulf, and especially sympathizers in Saudi Arabia.[23] Later, after the Second Intifada and Hamas's takeover of Gaza, Gulf support toward Hamas changed. Beginning in 2012, Qatar offered $400 million to rebuild roads and housing in Gaza. Both Israel and Egypt were opposed to the proposal, seeing the step as one that could only be beneficial for Hamas.[24]

Over time Israel changed its judgment of Qatari aid. Increasingly, Israeli officials came to see the funds as a source of stability for and in the territory.[25] At the same time, however, Israel was keen to tighten up the process, especially following the fighting in May–June 2021. Over several months they negotiated with Qatar and the UN to establish a mechanism whereby Qatari funds would be paid by the UN into beneficiaries' bank accounts directly, so as to prevent any of the money from reaching Hamas.[26]

Beyond aid, trade has also been an important driver of Gulf influence in Palestine. Between 2005 and 2019, Palestine's total trade more than doubled, from $3 billion to $7.7 billion. A significant proportion of that trade was with the Middle East and Central Asia, which nearly tripled in 2008–2022, from 3.1 percent to 8.5 percent (figure 3.1).[27] Within the Middle East, the Gulf became an increasingly important market to Palestinian importers and exporters. Between 2008 and 2009 trade jumped from $14.8 million to $46.2 million and then more than quadrupled by 2019, to $199 million.[28] Notwithstanding the slowdown in trade during the COVID pandemic in 2020, trade has continued to grow, reaching $345 million in 2022. Among the most important markets were the main financial backers of the Palestinian Authority and parties, including Saudi Arabia and the UAE, which were worth $213 million and $77.7 million respectively and followed some way behind by Qatar and Kuwait, with $13 million each in trade receipts respectively (figure 3.2).[29]

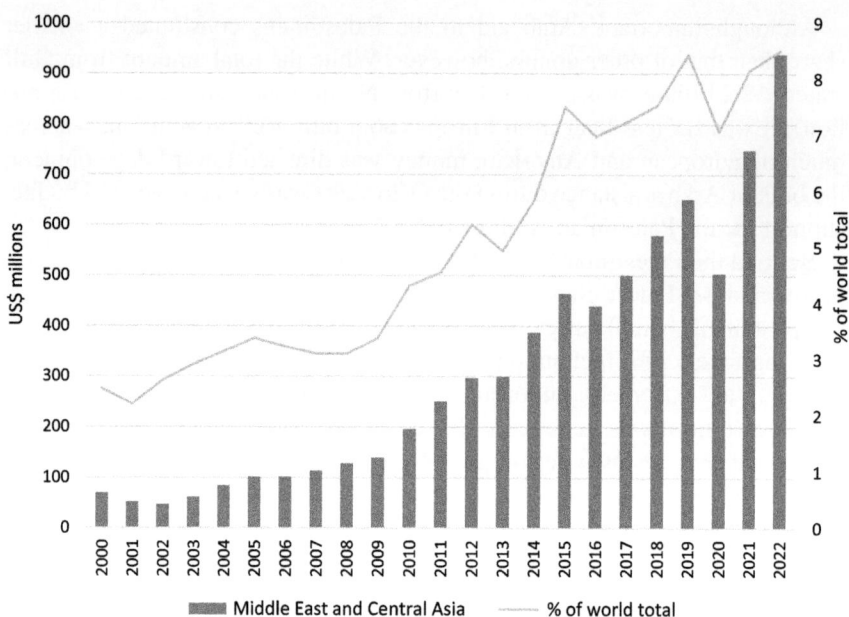

Figure 3.1   West Bank and Gaza Trade with the Middle East and Central Asia, 2000–2022. *Source*: IMF Statistics.

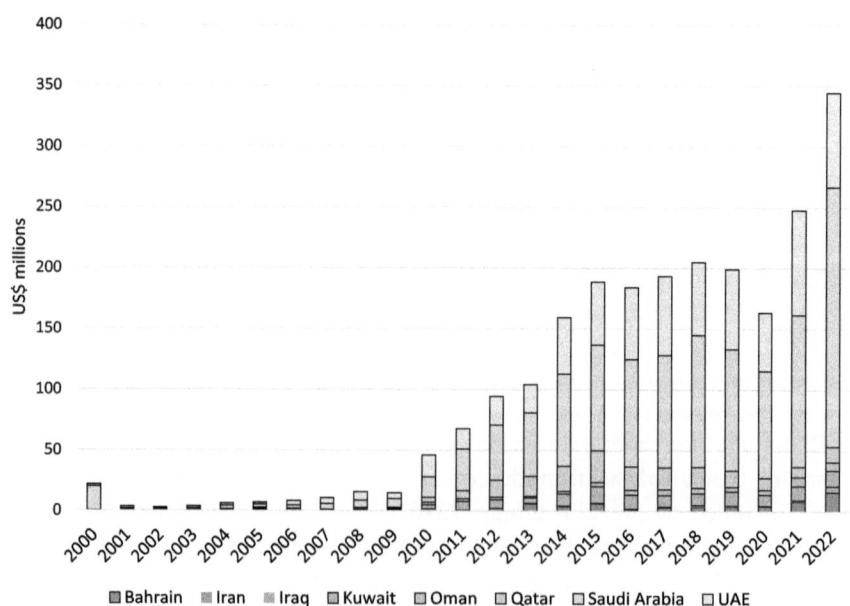

Figure 3.2   West Bank and Gaza Trade with Gulf Countries, 2000–2022. *Source:* IMF Statistics.

SECURITY CONCERNS OVER
PALESTINIAN DIASPORA

Despite a shared Arab identity and commitment to a Palestinian state, there has been underlying wariness between Palestinians and GCC state leadership. Those reservations go back decades and include GCC state unease about the nature and potential behavior of Palestinian populations within their respective countries before 1990; apparent Palestinian support for Iraq's invasion of Kuwait in 1990; and, splits within the Palestinian polity and between the GCC states themselves.

Ties between the Gulf regimes and the Palestinians deteriorated sharply in the wake of Iraq's invasion of Kuwait in August 1990. Iraq's actions under President Saddam Hussein were met with widespread opprobrium. In an effort to regain some credibility, he portrayed himself as an Arab nationalist and a defender of the Palestinian cause. Arafat's decision to accept Saddam's support put him at odds with the regimes in the Gulf, who feared Iraqi expansion and also weakened their support for the Palestinian cause.[30] Several Gulf states limited entrance visas and work permits for Palestinians. Thousands were forced to leave Iraq, Bahrain, and the UAE. Between August and September 1990, the General Federation of Palestinian Trade Unions reported that more than 56,000 Palestinians left the Gulf and between 20,000 and 30,000 returned to the West Bank or Gaza.[31] The exodus contributed to a fall in remittances back to the occupied territories, increasing the levels of hardship in the society, which were compounded by the boycott against Israel during the First Intifada. In addition, Arab aid, including assistance from Gulf states, fell.[32]

Although Arafat has received considerable censure, it has been suggested that procedural factors and an ambivalence may account for his position.[33] In this telling, the PLO's position was not intentional but was instead a consequence of Egyptian president Hosni Mubarak's decision to only count the votes of those who supported the Arab League motion which condemned the invasion and supported the deployment of American troops to the region in August 1990. Amendments, votes against, and abstentions were not allowed during the debate, which meant that the PLO's non-vote was taken to mean that it supported Iraq. Instead, PLO officials claimed that they would have abstained were it possible. They also stated their reasons for doing so: while they opposed Iraq's invasion, they also rejected any American military presence in the region.

If the 1990–1991 Gulf crisis and war constituted a low point for Palestinian-Gulf relations, Oslo offered a chance of rapprochement, including increased aid. But after Oslo's collapse and the split in the Palestinian polity, followed later by intra-Gulf rivalry, the result was a scenario in which Palestinian and

Arab Gulf actors used each other to overcome their own immediate rivals. In the Gulf, those differences were evident in the growing differences between Saudi Arabia and Qatar following the end of the Second Intifada, which began to be played out in Palestine. The political strife and conflict between Fatah and Hamas, which split the Palestinian territory in 2007 also became a means through which those tensions were channeled.

Once the Second Intifada ended, the outbreak of the Second Lebanese War in 2006 prompted the Saudis to apparently provide private support for Israel against Hezbollah.[34] Hezbollah's ability to resist Israel's attacks boosted both its stature and that of its backer, Iran, which was reported to have provided around $100 million a year in military assistance at the time, including 11,500 missiles and projectiles.[35] Iran's reflected stature arguably undermined its Saudi rival, which, concerned by this turn of events, may have led the Saudi leadership to become more active on the Palestinian file.[36] During this period, the Palestinian political scene also deteriorated. Hamas's election victory in March 2006 was not welcomed by many of the Palestinian Authority's western backers. There were several attempts at externally mediated reconciliation and the formation of a national unity government. But these efforts failed.

The split between the Palestinian factions began to align with the contrary positions being drawn in the Gulf. The Saudis, along with Egypt and the West, backed Fatah in their rivalry with Hamas. Hamas, meanwhile, looked toward other potential partners in the Gulf, including Qatar, for support. It helped that just as the Saudis began to focus more on domestic Palestinian politics, Qatar was also doing the same. Although prior relations with the Palestinian Authority had been relatively distant, Qatar's involvement in the Palestinian file had risen, especially through its hosting of the Al Jazeera news network which covered the Second Intifada extensively for Arab audiences. The coverage generated greater public awareness, irritated Israel, and boosted Qatar's international profile.[37]

Qatar's leadership took advantage of its rising soft power status in several ways. One was for Qatari foreign minister Sheikh Hamad bin Jassim Al-Thani to try and resolve the siege of Arafat's headquarters in Ramallah in 2002.[38] Another was that Qatar became more robust in its criticisms of "disproportionate" Israeli force in Lebanon in 2006.[39] Given their own rivalry at the time, both the Saudis and Qataris sought to project their influence by influencing Palestinian politics. After Doha attempted to mediate between Fatah and Hamas in late 2006, Riyadh did the same in February 2007, resulting in the similarly short-lived Mecca Agreement.[40]

Soon after, fighting broke out which was severe enough to result in Palestine's political split, leaving Fatah in control of the West Bank and Gaza in the hands of Hamas. Since then, Saudi backing for Fatah and Qatar for Hamas has been consolidated, the latter most notably through Qatari aid to Gaza after 2012—a position that Israel's Prime Minister Netanyahu backed as a way of keeping Hamas contained[41] while ensuring that the Palestinian polity remained split. At the same time, the Palestinian parties themselves have looked to cultivate their ties with Arab Gulf states, while also seeking ideological, diplomatic, and financial assistance as a means to counter the other. This was particularly apparent during the intra-Gulf crisis in 2017 when the Saudis and UAE imposed a blockade of Qatar.[42]

For the Fatah-led Palestinian Authority in the West Bank, there was private satisfaction regarding the 2017 GCC crisis and the impact it might have on both Hamas and Qatar. Fatah hoped that the blockade would force Doha to undertake a retrenchment of its foreign policy and curb its aid to Gaza. Relations between the two parties had deteriorated since 2011, partly owing to Al Jazeera's decision to publish the Palestine Papers, which exposed details of Palestinian and Israeli exchanges and dialogue between 1999 and 2010. Two stories in particular were embarrassing for the Fatah leadership: one in which Abbas was reported to have been informed in advance of Israel's plan to attack Gaza in 2008; the other, that the Palestinian Authority had tried to postpone the vote on the UN's fact-finding Goldstone Report following the end of the Gaza conflict.[43]

Qatar's ties to Hamas generated concerns beyond the Palestine Papers and the Gulf crisis and blockade, however. Especially worrying for Fatah (and Israeli) leaders was what less Qatari aid for Gaza might mean for Hamas. Would it lead to greater instability and a loss of control? If so, who might benefit? Fatah was by no means the sole option, with other, potentially more violent jihadi groups also staking a claim. Against that, though, was another scenario: if both Hamas and Qatar were defeated, it would signal a victory for Israel, the UAE, and the Saudis.[44]

THE GCC STATES, PALESTINIAN LEADERSHIP, AND BDS CAMPAIGN

The Saudi association with Fatah and opposition toward Qatar should have—on the face of it—neatly enjoined the UAE. Like them, the UAE has an antipathy toward the Muslim Brotherhood and therefore Hamas. However, that shared sentiment has not led to an easy correspondence between the two since the UAE hosts Mohammed Dahlan, a Fatah dissident and rival of President Mahmoud Abbas.[45] Dahlan has become a close associate of the UAE president, Muhammed bin Zayed Al Nahyan, whom he advises on Palestinian affairs. Dahlan shares the president's opposition toward political Islamists and especially Hamas, owing to his confrontation with the group in 2007. That year Dahlan and his partners in Fatah lost Gaza. Despite

Fatah's defeat, Dahlan retained strong popular support which made him a threat to Abbas, who he accused of corruption. Abbas had Dahlan arrested but before his court case began, he fled to the UAE where he was offered sanctuary.[46]

Just as the UAE's relationship with Fatah is complicated, so too is Qatar's with Hamas. Contrary to the assumption that its aid to Gaza marks it out as pro-Hamas, its concern has less to do with underlying sympathy for the party and its ideology and more with pragmatic concerns. In particular, it seeks access so as to be present at any dialogue or mediation. While that would be in line with wider Qatari policy, it may be lost in a zero-sum context where Fatah leaders see any support for their rival as a form of external legitimation and undermining their view of themselves as the primary Palestinian political actor.[47] Qatar has since come under pressure for its outreach toward Hamas following the latter's surprise attack against Israel in October 2023: its prime minister said that there could be "no more business as usual" with Hamas, even as its contacts with the group meant it was the main sole GCC country able to and actively mediating the possible return of some of the Israeli hostages taken into Gaza.[48]

The hostility that exists between Fatah and Hamas (and through them, the Saudis and UAE on one side and Qatar on the other) is somewhat ironic, since both broadly share similar objectives: in particular, the pursuit of a two-state outcome in the form of a Palestinian state. But whereas Fatah has sought to do this through Oslo—largely through negotiations and when those have failed, by appealing to the international community by seeking membership of international organizations for a Palestinian state—Hamas has adopted a more directly confrontational approach: although it could not hope to defeat Israel militarily through conflict in 2008–2009, 2012, 2014, 2021, and 2023, it has sought to sap Israeli resources and morale. Even when it has endorsed alternate, nonviolent efforts, such as the initially independently organized March to the Border protests which took place on most Fridays in 2018 and 2019, the consequences and impact were adverse, with over 200 Gazans killed and nearly 10,000 injured.

For both Fatah and Hamas, their approach may be termed as "stay the course!"[49] Against that is another strategy that emerged in the post-Second Intifada period, which recommends that Oslo be declared a failure and the PNA disbanded, in order to force Israel to take on its responsibilities as an occupying power.[50] It is based on the Palestinian intellectual and former Palestinian Authority representative in Jerusalem Sari Nusseibeh's earlier suggestion during the 1980s, that the Palestinians abandon the nationalist struggle in favor of one that pursues citizenship and equal rights inside Israel. To date, no Palestinian political party has adopted this strategy wholesale; instead, it has fallen to civil society and the BDS movement to articulate it.[51]

The BDS was founded in 2005 when over 170 Palestinian social movements, organizations, professional associations, and groups came together. Its emergence was ironically helped in part by the Oslo process, during which international attention and financial aid helped establish a flourishing civil society relative to that of the wider Middle East, where such space was largely constrained.[52] The BDS campaign is also evident in the GCC states, where the BDS Gulf group has gained support from individuals and groups in these countries; but so far, no official support from the regimes.

Part of the reason that regime backing has not been forthcoming for the BDS is due to its opposition toward Israel and its confrontational style. In July 2016, the BDS Gulf group went as far as to criticize a meeting between a Saudi delegation, headed by a former general, Anwar Eshki, to Israel. Eshki was accused of denying the visit had taken place, claiming that he had gone at the invitation of the Palestinians. In January the following year, pictures appeared of Israel's former foreign minister Tzipi Livni at Davos with the high-ranking Saudi prince Turki al-Faisal, a former Saudi ambassador to Washington and the long-standing head of Saudi intelligence.

The BDS Gulf group noted the repeated nature of these events and that it regretted "flirtations between the [Saudi] prince and Zionist officials." It noted the Saudi prince had met with senior Israelis in the previous year, alongside a high-level Saudi visit to Israel. The group also condemned secret arms sales between Israel and the UAE and stated that "We affirm . . . our firm and categorical rejection of any official or quasi-official effort to normalize relations with [Israel]."[53]

In November 2017, BDS Gulf held its first regional conference in Kuwait City to map out its strategy, campaigns, and actions for the years ahead. The conference was attended by the speaker of the Kuwait parliament and included a number of politicians from across the Gulf States. An important decision was to campaign against the private security company, G4S for providing Israeli-backed security equipment and training in the Gulf. The campaign also sought to encourage more ethical investments and divestment of Gulf sovereign wealth funds from companies involved in Israel's occupation.[54]

PALESTINIAN-GCC STATE RELATIONS AFTER THE ABRAHAM ACCORDS

Other tensions have constituted a challenge to Fatah and Hamas authority in the occupied territory since 2020, which led to Israeli aerial attacks in Gaza in August 2022 and May 2023. Israeli raids earlier in 2022 led to falling public support and the rise of armed groups that challenged the Fatah leadership in the West Bank and exposed its failure to confront Israel.[55] Among Israel's targets included leaders of Palestinian Islamic Jihad (PIJ), which retaliated with rocket attacks from their stronghold in Gaza in 2022. In May 2023 they launched further rockets following the death of their spokesperson, Khader Adnan, after a hunger strike in an Israeli prison.[56] Such attacks arguably undermined Hamas's authority in the strip.[57]

Over eighty Palestinians were killed during these attacks, including more than thirty children. Although Israel was condemned in the GCC states, some of it was relatively mild, most especially from the UAE and Saudi Arabia, where some media commentators accused PIJ of doing Iran's bidding. Instead, some of the strongest criticism came from Bahrain and—potentially worryingly for the UAE—from royalty, in the form of Sharjah's Princess Hend bint Faisal Al-Qasimi.[58] Qatar was the most vociferous in its denunciation of Israel. Representatives soon pledged humanitarian aid and assistance to rebuild destroyed and damaged homes.[59] However, that the confrontation had been engineered by PIJ rather than Hamas suggested that the latter's control over Gaza was not complete;[60] this could potentially bode problems for Qatar's relations in the strip, especially if Hamas's influence is eliminated, as appeared to become the Israeli objective following the surprise attack by the group in southern Israel on October 7, 2023.

Should this happen, however, it seems unlikely that the UAE would be a chief beneficiary. Following the 2021 fighting, Abu Dhabi offered itself as a potential patron in Gaza, in the form of reconstruction funds. However, that offer was undermined by several factors, including Qatar's current prominence as a donor in Gaza, the UAE's threat to withhold funds to Hamas if it did not curb the fighting and the UAE's long-held aversion toward Hamas's Islamist ideology, which in the wake of the 2022 and 2023 fighting, may also be extended to PIJ.[61]

At the same time, the UAE also faced difficulties, not only with Hamas's rival, Fatah, but also with Palestinian public opinion. The presence of Abbas's rival, Mohammed Dahlan, in Abu Dhabi has already been noted.[62] In addition, the UAE has failed to build bridges with the Fatah leadership or win over the public after the Abraham Accords. It has acted belligerently toward Fatah and its criticisms, by threatening to cut its contributions to the United Nations Relief and Works Agency from around $50 million in 2018 and 2019 to $1 million in 2020. Meanwhile, its financial assistance has had mixed reviews among the public: although nearly two-thirds of those surveyed welcomed Emirati aid to al Makasid Hospital in East Jerusalem, two-thirds also said that they did not welcome support for Palestinians by the countries that had normalized relations with Israel.[63]

Finally, the developments that have taken place within the Palestinian polity have prompted the two main parties to explore alternative options, including outreach toward the Gulf. In early 2022, the Algerian ambassador in Qatar invited the Hamas leader, Ismail Haniyeh, to Algiers for unity talks. Then in July, for the first time in six years, Haniyeh and the Palestinian Authority (PA) and Fatah president Mahmoud Abbas met each other for talks in the Algerian capital. The Algerians then hosted both Fatah and Hamas along with other Palestinian factions to sign a reconciliation agreement, which included holding presidential and parliamentary elections within a year.[64]

At home, the agreement was received skeptically by both analysts and the public.[65] Not only did they assume that the two main parties of Hamas and Fatah were too invested in the status quo to accept a change in their circumstances, it arguably echoed the growing disconnect that has developed between them and society in recent decades.

Meanwhile, Hamas has been looking to expand its international relations. Despite its differences with GCC states like the UAE, it has made overtures toward the Saudis. Toward that end, Haniyeh stressed his party's equidistance between Arab countries and refusal to interfere in their internal affairs.[66] The move seemed to pay off, at least symbolically. Following Hamas's signing of the reconciliation deal with Fatah, the Saudis released Mohammad al-Khudary, a Hamas official who had been detained in the kingdom for three years.[67]

At the same time, Hamas's surprise attack on Israel in October 2023 had the effect of freezing talk about the prospect of normalization between Israel and Saudi Arabia. It also reminded Arab leaderships that peace with Israel could not be achieved without resolving the Palestinian question. Indeed, Israel's subsequent military campaign in Gaza helped crystalize that point, as it obliged Arab leaderships to criticize it, including those countries who had already recognized it, like the UAE—even if they privately hoped that Israel's actions would ultimately eliminate Hamas.[68]

CONCLUSION

This chapter studied Palestinian ties to Israel and the Gulf, in the decades before, during, and after the Oslo Accords, as well as around and since the Abraham Accords were signed. From what was a relatively distant relationship, the ties have become much closer over the past two decades, helped in part by greater Gulf interaction with the principal Palestinian parties, their increased autonomy in the international sphere, and the political split that has emerged in the Palestinian polity since 2007.

However, the dynamics of that growing closeness do not appear to be subject to an overarching strategy, either by the Palestinians or by the Gulf states themselves. Rather, relations between the different actors look more improvised than preemptively thought out. At the same time though, the impact of these developments has not been felt equally. They have been more direct and adverse for the Palestinians than for those in the Gulf.

That the results have been detrimental for the Palestinians owes much to the internal political split between Fatah and Hamas, from which many of the other challenges have manifested. Their rivalry and struggle mean that there is no national unity or ability to form a consensus about how best to overcome the Palestinians' plight. In addition, the split has been supported—arguably even exacerbated—by the presence of external actors including from the Gulf who have backed one side or the other.

Both the Fatah-Hamas split and the Abraham Accords have given a boost to civil society activism in the form of the BDS movement. While the BDS's emergence predates the Abraham Accords, the movement's campaigns and statements prior to 2020 had an element of shadowboxing about them, owing to a general cloak of deniability afforded the clandestine nature of Israeli-Gulf ties. By contrast, the signing of the accords has made those ties more visible and campaigning more focused. That said, it is uncertain whether this change will have consequences for the wider Palestinian struggle. The fact is that the Palestinian political scene is becoming an increasingly complex one. Although it is dominated by the Fatah and Hamas parties, there are signs that they do not command sufficient levels of public support. Alongside grow-ing public disillusion and disaffection with their rule, there is also the recent emergence of more autonomous armed groups, which, over time, could potentially destabilize the two parties and their rule.

NOTES

1. Ilan Pappe, "A Palestinian State in Zionist and Israeli Thought," *Palestine-Israel Journal,* 6(2) (1999), https://www.pij.org/articles/924/a-palestinian-state-in -zionist-and-israeli-thought.

2. Hamas al-Shamsi, "How the UAE is Suppressing Criticism of Its Normaliza-tion with Israel," *Democracy for the Arab World Now*, June 2, 2021, https://dawn-mena.org/how-the-uae-is-suppressing-criticism-of-its-normalization-with-israel/; Aya Batrawy, "No Longer Silent, Gulf Arab Citizens Express Anger at Israel," *Asso-ciated Press*, May 19, 2021, https://apnews.com/article/africa-israel-middle-east-866 2c35ae1fac682b47cb08b3cbea2ea; Americans for Democracy and Human Rights in Bahrain, "Bahrain Suppresses Demonstrations Supporting Palestinians and Denounc-ing the Attack on Gaza," *IFEX*, November 14, 2023, https://ifex.org/bahrain-sup-presses-demonstrations-supporting-palestinians-and-denouncing-the-attack-on-gaza/; Yahya Alhadid, "What Was Really Behind Bahrain's Normalization with Israel?," *Democracy for the Arab World Now*, January 25, 2022, https://dawnmena.org/what -was-really-behind-bahrains-normalization-with-israel/.

3. See, for instance, Rex Brynen, *A Very Political Economy: Peacebuilding and Foreign Aid in the West Bank* (Washington, DC: United States Institute of Peace, 2000): 44-45.

4. Richard Herrman, "The Middle East and the New World Order: Rethinking US Political Strategy after the Gulf War," *International Security*, 16(2) (1991): 54.

5. Jeffrey Engel, "A Better World… but Don't Get Carried Away: The Foreign Policy of George H. W. Bush Twenty Years On," *Diplomatic History*, 34(1) (2010): 25–46.

6. Jerome Segal, "The Gulf War and the Israeli-Palestinian Conflict," *World Policy Journal*, 8(2) (1991): 351–362.

7. Elisheva Rosman-Stollman, "Balancing Acts: The Gulf States and Israel," *Middle Eastern Studies*, 40(4) (2004): 185–208.

8. Taylan Özgür Kaya, "The USA and EU as a Third Party in Middle East Peacemaking: An Asymmetric Division of Labour," *Journal of Transatlantic Studies*, 15 (2017): 143–160.

9. Douglas Feith and Lewis Libby, "How the Trump Plan Makes Peace Possible," *Middle East Quarterly*, 27(4) (2020): 1–15.

10. Jim Zanotti, *US Foreign Aid to the Palestinians* (Washington, DC: Congressional Research Service Report, 2018).

11. Jacob Magid, "In New Book, Trump's Israel Envoy Hammers 4 Rocky Years Into a Smooth Path to Peace," *The Times of Israel*, February 10, 2022, https://www.timesofisrael.com/in-new-book-trumps-israel-envoy-hammers-four-rocky-years-into-smooth-path-to-peace/; Chris McGreal, "'Don't Talk About History': How Jared Kushner Drafted his Middle East 'Peace' Plan," *Guardian*, January 28, 2020, https://www.theguardian.com/us-news/2020/jan/27/jared-kushner-israel-palestine-peace-plan.

12. Guy Burton, "Palestine Needs to Move Beyond Condemnation," *CGTN*, January 30, 2020, https://news.cgtn.com/news/2020-01-30/Palestine-needs-to-move-beyond-condemnation--NFzNNEpnHy/index.html.

13. Mohamed Abdelaziz, "Arab Reactions to Trump's Peace Plan: An Analysis and Recommendation," *Washington Institute*, January 31, 2020, https://www.washingtoninstitute.org/policy-analysis/arab-reactions-trumps-peace-plan-analysis-and-recommendation.

14. Adam Rasgon, "Saudi Ministers Says All at Warsaw Mideast Confab Agreed Iran the Major Problem," *Times of Israel*, February 18, 2019, https://www.timesofisrael.com/saudi-minister-says-all-at-warsaw-mideast-confab-agreed-iran-the-major-problem/; "Meeting Abbas, MBS Backs Palestinian State with East Jerusalem as its Capital," *Time of Israel*, February 13, 2019, https://www.timesofisrael.com/meeting-abbas-mbs-backs-palestinian-state-with-east-jerusalem-as-its-capital/;

15. Ibid.

16. Ahmad Melhem, "Low Chances of Success for Abbas' Alternative to US Peace Plan," *Al-Monitor*, February 13, 2020, https://www.al-monitor.com/originals/2020/02/palestinian-abbas-conference-peace-process-israel.html.

17. Ali Harb, "Israel-Palestine US Policy: What Changed Under Biden, What Didn't," *Al Jazeera*, July 12, 2022, https://www.aljazeera.com/news/2022/7/12/israel

-palestine-us-policy-what-changed-under-biden-what-didnt; Marwan Muasher, "The Two-State Lie," Carnegie Middle East Center, July 22, 2022, https://carnegie-mec.org/diwan/87558.

18. Data extracted and calculated by the author from IMF, Direction of Trade Statistics (DOTS), https://data.imf.org/?sk=9d6028d4-f14a-464c-a2f2-59b2cd424b85.

19. Guy Burton, "Revenue Without a Cause: Arab Financial Assistance in Palestine," Paper presented at Geographies of Aid Intervention Conference, Birzeit University, Birzeit, September 2010.

20. Ibid.

21. Ibid.

22. Ibid.

23. Matthew Levitt, *Hamas: Politics, Charity and Terrorism in the Service of Jihad* (Washington, DC: Washington Institute for Near East Policy, 2006).

24. Yoel Guzansky, "Israel and the Arab Gulf States: From Tacit Cooperation to Reconciliation?," *Israel Affairs,* 21(1) (2015): 131–147. It is notable that Israel and Egypt opposed Hamas since both have previously had reason to work with or at least tolerate it. For Israel, Hamas was initially seen as a "lesser evil" in its early years after it was formed in 1987, owing to its opposition toward the PLO, then seen as the principal Palestinian threat to Israel. For Egypt, pragmatism has been a central tenet of its relationship with Hamas. On the one hand, it opposes Hamas due to its similarity and historical links with the Muslim Brotherhood, the largest opposition force in the country. On the other hand, Hamas has been an important partner in containing the threat of Islamic State in the Sinai Peninsula. See Moonis Ahmar, "How and Why Israel Helped Create Hamas?," *Express Tribune*, May 30, 2021, https://tribune.com.pk/story/2302309/how-and-why-israel-helped-create-hamas; Maged Mandour, "Egypt's Shifting Hamas Policies," Carnegie Endowment for International Peace, July 26, 2021, https://carnegieendowment.org/sada/85037.

25. Al Jazeera, "Israel Approves Resumption of Qatar Aid to Gaza," August 19, 2021, https://www.aljazeera.com/news/2021/8/19/israel-approves-resumption-of-qatar-aid-to-gaza; Kobi Michael and Yoel Guzansky. "Might Qatar Join the Abraham Accords?," Institute for National Security Studies, Insight No. 1391, October 12, 2020, https://www.inss.org.il/publication/the-abraham-accords-and-qatar/.

26. Al Jazeera, "Israel Approves Resumption of Qatar Aid to Gaza."

27. Data extracted and calculated by the author from IMF, Direction of Trade Statistics (DOTS).

28. Ibid.

29. Ibid.

30. Uzi Rabi, "Qatar's Relations with Israel: Challenging Arab and Gulf Norms," *Middle East Journal,* 63(3) (2009): 443–459; Rosman-Stollman, "Balancing Acts."

31. Rashid Khalidi, "The Palestinians and the Gulf Crisis," *Current History,* 90(552) (1991): 18–20, 37.

32. Burton, "Revenue without a Cause."

33. Khalidi, "The Palestinians and the Gulf Crisis."

34. Middle East Monitor, "Saudi Supported Israel Against Hezbollah During 2006 War," February 16, 2019, https://www.middleeastmonitor.com/20190216-saudi-supported-israel-against-hezbollah-during-2006-war/.

35. Human Rights Watch, "Civilians Under Assault: Hezbollah's Rocket Attacks on Israel in the 2006 War," August 28, 2007, https://www.hrw.org/report/2007/08/28/civilians-under-assault/hezbollahs-rocket-attacks-israel-2006-war.

36. Ibid.

37. Mouin Rabbani, "Qatar and the Palestinians," *Perspectives: Political Analysis and Commentary from the Middle East & North Africa,* 4 (2012): 42–45.

38. Ibid.

39. Kristian Coates Ulrichsen, *Qatar and the Arab Spring* (Oxford: Oxford University Press, 2014), 74.

40. Federica D'Acunto, "The Brand of Peace: The Relations Between Qatar, Palestine and Israel," MSc Dissertation (Venice: Univeristà Ca'Foscari Venezia, 2016), 19.

41. Mark Mazzetti and Ronan Bergman, "'Buying Quiet': Inside the Israeli Plan That Propped Up Hamas," *New York Times*, December 10, 2023, https://www.nytimes.com/2023/12/10/world/middleeast/israel-qatar-money-prop-up-hamas.html.

42. David Hearst, "Why Hamas Was Not on the Saudi List of Demands for Qatar," *Middle East Eye*, June 28, 2017, https://www.middleeasteye.net/opinion/why-hamas-was-not-saudi-list-demands-qatar; Hussein Ibish, "Regional Winners and Losers in the Hamas-Fatah Deal," *Arab Gulf States Institute in Washington,* October 13, 2017, https://agsiw.org/regional-winners-losers-hamas-fatah-deal/.

43. D'Acunto, *"The Brand of Peace: The Relations Between Qatar, Palestine and Israel,"* 70.

44. Daoud Kuttab, "Hamas Could Lose Qatar's Support Amid GCC Strife," *Al-Monitor*, June 9, 2017, https://www.al-monitor.com/originals/2017/06/qatar-gulf-crisis-affect-hamas-palestine-gaza.html; Al Jazeera, "Will the GCC Crisis Undermine the Palestinian Cause?," June 11, 2017, https://www.aljazeera.com/features/2017/6/11/will-the-gcc-crisis-undermine-the-palestinian-cause.

45. Michael and Guzansky, "Might Qatar Join the Abraham Accords?"

46. George Cafiero, "Why the UAE Supports Mohammed Dahlan," *TRT World*, October 27, 2020, https://www.trtworld.com/opinion/why-the-uae-supports-mohammed-dahlan-40944; Jonathan Ferziger, "The UAE's Invisible Palestinian Hand," *Foreign Policy*, October 30, 2020, https://foreignpolicy.com/2020/10/30/mohammed-dahlan-uae-palestinians-israel/

47. Rabbani, "Qatar and the Palestinians."

48. Humeyra Pamuk, "Qatar Open to Reconsidering Hamas Presence in Qatar, US Official Says," *Reuters*, October 27, 2023, https://www.reuters.com/world/middle-east/qatar-told-us-it-is-open-reconsidering-hamas-presence-us-official-says-2023-10-27/; Andrew Mills and Ahmed Mohamed Hassan, "Exclusive: Qatar Seeking Israel-Hamas Deal to Free 50 Hostages and 3-Day-Truce," *Reuters*, November 15, 2023, https://www.reuters.com/world/middle-east/qatar-seeking-israel-hamas-deal-release-50-hostages-3-day-truce-sources-say-2023-11-15/.

49. Glenn Robinson, "The Death of the Two-State Solution: Israel, the Palestinians, and the Arab world in the Age of Netanyahu," in *Israel Under Netanyahu: Domestic Politics and Foreign Policy*, ed. Robert Freedoman (Abingdon: Routledge, 2020), 176–196.

50. Ibid.

51. Ibid, 184–186.

52. Eberhard Kienle, "Civil Society in the Middle East," in *The Oxford Handbook of Civil Society*, ed. Michael Edwards (Oxford: Oxford University Press, 2011), 146–158; Anne Le More, *International Assistance to the Palestinians after Oslo: Political Guilt, Wasted Money* (Abingdon: Routledge, 2008); Benoit Challand, *Palestinian Civil Society: Foreign Donors and the Power to Promote and Exclude* (London: Routledge 2009); Nithya Nagarajan, "Development Under Colonialism?," in editorial board of the Center for Development Studies (eds.) *Critical Readings of Development under Colonialism: Toward a Political Economy for Liberation in the Occupied Palestinian Territories* (Ramallah and Birzeit: Rosa Luxemburg Stiftung and Center for Development Studies, Birzeit University, 2015), 67–87.

53. Ali Abunimah, "Saudi-Israeli Courtship Heats Up with General's Visit," *Electronic Intifada*, July 27, 2016, https://electronicintifada.net/blogs/ali-abunimah/saudi-israeli-courtship-heats-generals-visit; Ali Abunimah, "Gulf Activists Reject Saudi-Israel "Flirtation" at Davos," *Electronic Intifada*, January 23, 2017, https://electronicintifada.net/blogs/ali-abunimah/gulf-activists-reject-saudi-israeli-flirtation-davos.

54. Abunimah, "Gulf Activists Reject Saudi-Israeli 'Flirtation' at Davos."

55. Mohammed Najib, "Poll Shows Decline in Popularity of Fatah Movement," *Arab News*, June 29, 2022, https://www.arabnews.com/node/2113551/middle-east; Ahmad Melhem, "Palestinians Alarmed by Lawlessness in West Bank," *Al-Monitor*, August 3, 2022, https://www.al-monitor.com/originals/2022/08/palestinians-alarmed-lawlessness-west-bank; Hani al-Masri, "The Jenin Brigades and the Lions' Den: Palestine's New Resistance," *Middle East Eye*, October 21, 2022, https://www.middleeasteye.net/opinion/phenomenon-jenin-brigades-and-lions-den; Sam Kiley, "West Bank Militants Threaten Israel, Urge Palestinian Leaders to Join Resistance as Tensions Rise," *CNN*, October 30, 2022, https://edition.cnn.com/2022/10/28/middleeast/palestinian-militants-jenin-west-bank-intl-cmd/index.html.

56. David Gritten, "Khader Adnan: Israel-Gaza Violence Flares after Palestinian Hunger Striker Dies," *BBC*, May 3, 2023, https://www.bbc.com/news/world-middle-east-65452946.

57. Monir Ghaedi, "What is the Palestinian Islamic Jihad?," *DW*, September 8, 2022, https://www.dw.com/en/what-is-the-palestinian-islamic-jihad/a-62746894.

58. Tobias Siegel, "Comparing Muslim Deaths to Holocaust, UAE Royal Suggests Jews are Hung Up on Shoah," *The Times of Israel*, August 7, 2022, https://www.timesofisrael.com/comparing-muslim-deaths-to-holocaust-uae-royal-suggests-jews-are-hung-up-on-shoah/; Haaretz, "UAE Urges 'Calm' in Gaza as Bahrain Condemns Israeli Strikes," August 7, 2022, https://www.haaretz.com/israel-news/2022-08-07/ty-article/uae-urges-calm-in-gaza-as-bahrain-condemns-israeli-strikes/00000182-78eb-d080-a9d7-7dfb17950000; Mosaic, "The Arab Press Blames Iran Rather Than Israel

for Gaza's Woes," August 10, 2022, https://mosaicmagazine.com/picks/israel-zion-ism/2022/08/the-arab-press-blames-iran-rather-than-israel-for-gazas-woes/.

59. "'Reaction and Common Sense': Reaction to Israel's Gaza Attack," *Al Jazeera*, August 5, 2022, https://www.aljazeera.com/news/2022/8/5/restraint-and -common-sense-reaction-to-israels-gaza-attack; Jack Khoury, "Qatar Agrees to Reconstruct Gaza Homes Destroyed by Israeli Operation," *Haaretz*, August 12, 2022, https://www.haaretz.com/middle-east-news/palestinians/2022-08-12/ty-article/ .premium/qatar-agrees-to-reconstruct-gaza-homes-destroyed-by-israeli-operation /00000182-9200-d9bc-affb-f39ea1960000.

60. "Tempers Flare Between Hamas, Islamic Jihad," *Al-Monitor*, September 4, 2022, https://www.al-monitor.com/originals/2022/09/tempers-flare-between-hamas -islamic-jihad.

61. Michael and Guzansky, "Might Qatar Join the Abraham Accords?"; The Times of Israel, "UAE Said to Warn Hamas Planned Gaza Infrastructure Projects Are in Danger," May 15, 2021, https://www.timesofisrael.com/uae-said-to-warn-hamas -planned-gaza-infrastructure-projects-are-in-danger/.

62. Guzansky and Tzoreff, "Gaza, Qatar and the UAE."

63. Palestinian Center for Survey and Policy Research, "Public Opinion Poll No (85)," September 13–17, 2022, https://pcpsr.org/en/node/920.

64. Hamas, "Hamas Delegation to Head to Algeria for Palestinian Unity Talks," January 15, 2022, https://hamas.ps/en/post/3870/Hamas-delegation-to-head-to-Alge-ria-for-Palestinian-unity-talks; Ahmad Abu Amer, "Palestinian Rivals Abbas, Hani-yeh Shake Hands in Algiers," *Al-Monitor*, July 8, 2022, https://www.al-monitor.com/ originals/2022/07/palestinian-rivals-abbas-haniyeh-shake-hands-algeria; Al-Monitor, "Palestinian Factions Sign Reconciliation Deal in Algiers," October 13, 2022, https:// www.al-monitor.com/originals/2022/10/palestinian-factions-sign-reconciliation-deal -algiers.

65. Hazem Balousha, "Little Success Seen in Algeria Dialogue for Palestinian Reconciliation," *Arab News*, October 4, 2022, https://www.arabnews.com/node /2175036/middle-east; Al Jazeera English, "Hamas & Fatah in Algeria for Reconcili-ation Talks," October 11, 2022, https://www.youtube.com/watch?v=XMAqp8kJbjM.

66. "Hamas Aims to Restore Saudi Arabia Relations," *Middle East Monitor*, September 17, 2022, https://www.middleeastmonitor.com/20220917-hamas-aims-to -restore-saudi-arabia-ties/.

67. "Senior Hamas Official Released From Saudi Arabia, Heads to Jordan," *Al Jazeera*, October 19, 2022, https://www.aljazeera.com/news/2022/10/19/saudi-arabia -frees-senior-hamas-official.

68. Alexander Cornwell, "Exclusive: UAE Plans to Maintain Ties with Israel Despite Gaza Outcry, Sources Say," *Reuters*, November 11, 2023, https://www .reuters.com/world/middle-east/uae-plans-maintain-ties-with-israel-despite-gaza-out-cry-sources-say-2023-11-11/; William Wechsler, "Dispatch from Abu Dhabi: Do the Israelis Know About the Basus War?," *Atlantic Council,* October 18, 2023, https:// www.atlanticcouncil.org/blogs/new-atlanticist/dispatch-from-abu-dhabi-do-the-israe-lis-know-about-the-basus-war/; Trinidad Deiros Bronte, "Israel-Hamas War Forces Saudi Arabia's Hand Over the Palestinian Cause," *El País*, November 3, 2023, https://

english.elpais.com/international/2023-11-03/israel-hamas-war-forces-saudi-arabias
-hand-over-the-palestinian-cause.html; Steven Cook, "Saudi Arabia is Mysteriously
Absent in the Israel-Hamas War," *Foreign Policy*, October 26, 2023, https://foreignpol-
icy.com/2023/10/26/saudi-arabia-mbs-israel-hamas-war-strategy-policy-diplomacy/.

REFERENCES

Abdelaziz, Mohamed, "Arab Reactions to Trump's Peace Plan: An Analysis and
  Recommendation," *Washington Institute*, January 31, 2020, https://www.wash-
  ingtoninstitute.org/policy-analysis/arab-reactions-trumps-peace-plan-analysis-and
  -recommendation.
Abu Amer, Ahmad, "Palestinian Rivals Abbas, Haniyeh Shake Hands in Algiers," *Al-
  Monitor*, July 8, 2022, https://www.al-monitor.com/originals/2022/07/palestinian
  -rivals-abbas-haniyeh-shake-hands-algeria.
Abunimah, Ali, "Gulf Activists Reject Saudi-Israel "Flirtation" at Davos," *Electronic
  Intifada*, January 23, 2017, https://electronicintifada.net/blogs/ali-abunimah/gulf
  -activists-reject-saudi-israeli-flirtation-davos.
Abunimah, Ali, "Israel-Palestine US Policy: What changed Under Biden, What
  Didn't," *Al Jazeera*, July 12, 2022, https://www.aljazeera.com/news/2022/7/12/
  israel-palestine-us-policy-what-changed-under-biden-what-didnt.
Ahmar, Moonis, "How and Why Israel Helped Create Hamas?" *Express Tribune*,
  May 30, 2021, https://tribune.com.pk/story/2302309/how-and-why-israel-helped
  -create-hamas.
Al Jazeera, "Hamas & Fatah in Algeria for Reconciliation Talks," *Al Jazeera English,*
  October 11, 2022, https://www.youtube.com/watch?v=XMAqp8kJbjM.
Al Jazeera, "Israel Approves Resumption of Qatar Aid to Gaza," *Al Jazeera*, August
  19, 2021, https://www.aljazeera.com/news/2021/8/19/israel-approves-resumption
  -of-qatar-aid-to-gaza.
Al Jazeera, "'Reaction and Common Sense': Reaction to Israel's Gaza Attack," *Al
  Jazeera*, August 5, 2022, https://www.aljazeera.com/news/2022/8/5/restraint-and
  -common-sense-reaction-to-israels-gaza-attack
Al Jazeera, "Senior Hamas Official Released From Saudi Arabia, Heads to Jordan,"
  Al Jazeera, October 19, 2022, https://www.aljazeera.com/news/2022/10/19/saudi
  -arabia-frees-senior-hamas-official.
Al Jazeera, "Will the GCC Crisis Undermine the Palestinian Cause?," *Al Jazeera*,
  June 11, 2017, https://www.aljazeera.com/features/2017/6/11/will-the-gcc-crisis
  -undermine-the-palestinian-cause.
Al-Masri, Hani, "The Jenin Brigades and the Lions' Den: Palestine's New Resis-
  tance," *Middle East Eye*, October 21, 2022, https://www.middleeasteye.net/opinion
  /phenomenon-jenin-brigades-and-lions-den.
Al-Monitor, "Palestinian Factions Sign Reconciliation Deal in Algiers," *Al-Monitor,*
  October 13, 2022, https://www.al-monitor.com/originals/2022/10/palestinian-fac-
  tions-sign-reconciliation-deal-algiers.

Al-Monitor, "Tempers Flare Between Hamas, Islamic Jihad," *Al-Monitor,* September 4, 2022, https://www.al-monitor.com/originals/2022/09/tempers-flare-between -hamas-islamic-jihad.

Balousha, Hazem, "Little Success Seen in Algeria Dialogue for Palestinian Reconciliation," *Arab News*, October 4, 2022, https://www.arabnews.com/node/2175036 /middle-east.

Bronte, Trinidad Deiros, "Israel-Hamas War Forces Saudi Arabia's Hand Over the Palestinian Cause," *El País*, November 3, 2023, https://english.elpais.com/international/2023-11-03/israel-hamas-war-forces-saudi-arabias-hand-over-the-palestinian-cause.html.

Brynen, Rex, *A Very Political Economy: Peacebuilding and Foreign Aid in the West Bank* (Washington, DC: United States Institute of Peace, 2000).

Burton, Guy, "Revenue Without a Cause: Arab Financial Assistance in Palestine," Paper presented at Geographies of Aid Intervention Conference, Birzeit University, Birzeit, September 2010.

Burton, Guy, "Palestine Needs to Move Beyond Condemnation," *CGTN*, January 30, 2020, https://news.cgtn.com/news/2020-01-30/Palestine-needs-to-move-beyond -condemnation--NFzNNEpnHy/index.html.

Cafiero, George, "Why the UAE Supports Mohammed Dahlan," *TRT World*, October 27, 2020, https://www.trtworld.com/opinion/why-the-uae-supports-mohammed -dahlan-40944.

Challand, Benoit, *Palestinian Civil Society: Foreign Donors and the Power to Promote and Exclude* (London: Routledge, 2009).

Cook, Steven, "Saudi Arabia is Mysteriously Absent in the Israel-Hamas War," *Foreign Policy*, October 26, 2023, https://foreignpolicy.com/2023/10/26/saudi-arabia -mbs-israel-hamas-war-strategy-policy-diplomacy/.

Cornwell, Alexander, "Exclusive: UAE Plans to Maintain Ties with Israel Despite Gaza Outcry, Sources Say," *Reuters*, November 11, 2023, https://www.reuters .com/world/middle-east/uae-plans-maintain-ties-with-israel-despite-gaza-outcry -sources-say-2023-11-11/.

D'Acunto, Federica, "The Brand of Peace: The Relations Between Qatar, Palestine and Israel," MSc Dissertation (Venice: Univerità Ca'Foscari Venezia, 2016).

David. "Khader Adnan: Israel-Gaza Violence Flares after Palestinian Hunger Striker Dies," *BBC*, May 3, 2023, https://www.bbc.com/news/world-middle-east -65452946.

Engel, Jeffrey, "A Better World... but Don't Get Carried Away: The Foreign Policy of George H. W. Bush Twenty Years On," *Diplomatic History*, 34(1) (2010): 25–46.

Feith, Douglas, and Lewis Libby, "How the Trump Plan Makes Peace Possible," *Middle East Quarterly,* 27(4) (2020): 1–15.

Ferziger, Jonathan, "The UAE's Invisible Palestinian Hand," *Foreign Policy,* October 30, 2020, https://foreignpolicy.com/2020/10/30/mohammed-dahlan-uae-palestinians-israel/

Ghaedi, Monir, "What is the Palestinian Islamic Jihad?," *DW*, September 8, 2022, https://www.dw.com/en/what-is-the-palestinian-islamic-jihad/a-62746894.Gritten.

Guzansky, Yoel, "Israel and the Arab Gulf States: From Tacit Cooperation to Reconciliation?," *Israel Affairs,* 21(1) (2015): 131–147.

Haaretz, "UAE Urges 'Calm' in Gaza as Bahrain Condemns Israeli Strikes," August 7, 2022, https://www.haaretz.com/israel-news/2022-08-07/ty-article/uae-urges-calm-in-gaza-as-bahrain-condemns-israeli-strikes/00000182-78eb-d080-a9d7-7dfb17950000.

Hamas, "Hamas Delegation to Head to Algeria for Palestinian Unity Talks," January 15, 2022, https://hamas.ps/en/post/3870/Hamas-delegation-to-head-to-Algeria-for-Palestinian-unity-talks.Harb.

Hearst, David, "Why Hamas Was Not on the Saudi List of demands for Qatar," *Middle East Eye*, June 28, 2017, https://www.middleeasteye.net/opinion/why-hamas-was-not-saudi-list-demands-qatar.

Herrman, Richard, "The Middle East and the New World Order: Rethinking US Political Strategy after the Gulf War," *International Security,* 16(2) (1991): 42–75.

Human Rights Watch, "Civilians Under Assault: Hezbollah's Rocket Attacks on Israel in the 2006 War," August 28, 2007, https://www.hrw.org/report/2007/08/28/civilians-under-assault/hezbollahs-rocket-attacks-israel-2006-war.

Ibish, Hussein, "Regional Winners and Losers in the Hamas-Fatah Deal," Arab Gulf States Institute in Washington, October 13, 2017, https://agsiw.org/regional-winners-losers-hamas-fatah-deal/.

IMF, Direction of Trade Statistics (DOTS), https://data.imf.org/?sk=9d6028d4-f14a-464c-a2f2-59b2cd424b85.

Kaya, Taylan Özgür, "The USA and EU as a Third Party in Middle East Peacemaking: An Asymmetric Division of Labour," *Journal of Transatlantic Studies,* 15 (2017): 143–160.

Khalidi, Rashid, "The Palestinians and the Gulf Crisis," *Current History,* 90(552) (1991): 18–20, 37.

Khoury, Jack, "Qatar Agrees to Reconstruct Gaza Homes Destroyed by Israeli Operation," *Haaretz*, August 12, 2022, https://www.haaretz.com/middle-east-news/palestinians/2022-08-12/ty-article/.premium/qatar-agrees-to-reconstruct-gaza-homes-destroyed-by-israeli-operation/00000182-9200-d9bc-affb-f39ea1960000.

Kienle, Eberhard, "Civil Society in the Middle East," in *The Oxford Handbook of Civil Society*, ed. Michael Edwards (Oxford: Oxford University Press 2011), 146–158.

Kiley, Sam, "West Bank Militants Threaten Israel, Urge Palestinian Leaders to Join Resistance as Tensions Rise," *CNN*, October 30, 2022, https://edition.cnn.com/2022/10/28/middleeast/palestinian-militants-jenin-west-bank-intl-cmd/index.html.

Kuttab, Daoud, "Hamas Could Lose Qatar's Support Amid GCC Strife," *Al-Monitor*, June 9, 2017, https://www.al-monitor.com/originals/2017/06/qatar-gulf-crisis-affect-hamas-palestine-gaza.html.

Le More, Anne, *International Assistance to the Palestinians after Oslo: Political Guilt, Wasted Money* (Abingdon: Routledge, 2008).

Levitt, Matthew, *Hamas: Politics, Charity and Terrorism in the Service of Jihad* (Washington, DC: Washington Institute for Near East Policy, 2006).

Magid, Jacob, "In New Book, Trump's Israel Envoy Hammers 4 Rocky Years Into a Smooth Path to Peace," *Times of Israel*, February 10, 2022, https://www.timesofisrael.com/in-new-book-trumps-israel-envoy-hammers-four-rocky-years-into-smooth-path-to-peace/.

Mandour, Maged, "Egypt's Shifting Hamas Policies," *Carnegie Endowment for International Peace*, July 26, 2021, https://carnegieendowment.org/sada/85037.

McGreal, Chris, "'Don't Talk About History': How Jared Kushner Drafted his Middle East 'Peace' plan," *Guardian*, January 28, 2020, https://www.theguardian.com/us-news/2020/jan/27/jared-kushner-israel-palestine-peace-plan.

Melhem, Ahmad, "Low Chances of Success for Abbas' Alternative to US Peace Plan," *Al-Monitor*, February 13, 2020, https://www.al-monitor.com/originals/2020/02/palestinian-abbas-conference-peace-process-israel.html.

Melhem, Ahmad, "Palestinians Alarmed by Lawlessness in West Bank," *Al-Monitor*, August 3, 2022, https://www.al-monitor.com/originals/2022/08/palestinians-alarmed-lawlessness-west-bank.

Michael, Kobi, and Yoel Guzansky, "Might Qatar Join the Abraham Accords?," Institute for National Security Studies, Insight No. 1391, October 12, 2020, https://www.inss.org.il/publication/the-abraham-accords-and-qatar/.

Middle East Monitor, "Hamas aims to Restore Saudi Arabia Relations," *Middle East Monitor*, September 17, 2022, https://www.middleeastmonitor.com/20220917-hamas-aims-to-restore-saudi-arabia-ties/.

Mills, Andrew, and Ahmed Mohamed Hassan, "Exclusive: Qatar Seeking Israel-Hamas Deal to Free 50 Hostages and 3-Day-Truce," *Reuters*, November 15, 2023, https://www.reuters.com/world/middle-east/qatar-seeking-israel-hamas-deal-release-50-hostages-3-day-truce-sources-say-2023-11-15/.

Mosaic, "The Arab Press Blames Iran Rather Than Israel for Gaza's Woes," *Mosaic*, August 10, 2022, https://mosaicmagazine.com/picks/israel-zionism/2022/08/the-arab-press-blames-iran-rather-than-israel-for-gazas-woes/.

Muasher, Marwan, "The Two-State Lie," Carnegie Middle East Center, July 22, 2022, https://carnegie-mec.org/diwan/87558.

Nagarajan, Nithya, "Development Under Colonialism?" in *Critical Readings of Development under Colonialism: Toward a Political Economy for Liberation in the Occupied Palestinian Territories* (Ramallah and Birzeit: Rosa Luxemburg Stiftung and Center for Development Studies, Birzeit University, 2015), 67–87.

Najib, Mohammed, "Poll Shows Decline in Popularity of Fatah Movement," *Arab News*, June 29, 2022, https://www.arabnews.com/node/2113551/middle-east.

Palestinian Center for Survey and Policy Research, "Public Opinion Poll No (85)," September 13–17, 2022, https://pcpsr.org/en/node/920.

Pamuk, Humeyra, "Qatar Open to Reconsidering Hamas Presence in Qatar, US Official Says," *Reuters*, October 27, 2023, https://www.reuters.com/world/middle-east/qatar-told-us-it-is-open-reconsidering-hamas-presence-us-official-says-2023-10-27/.

Rabbani, Mouin, "Qatar and the Palestinians," P*erspectives: Political Analysis and Commentary from the Middle East & North Africa,* 4 (2012): 42–45.

Rabi, Uzi, "Qatar's Relations with Israel: Challenging Arab and Gulf Norms," *Middle East Journal,* 63(3) (2009): 443–459.

Robinson, Glenn, "The Death of the Two-State Solution: Israel, the Palestinians, and the Arab World in the Age of Netanyahu," in *Israel Under Netanyahu: Domestic Politics and Foreign Policy*, ed. Robert Freedoman (Abingdon: Routledge, 2020), 176–196.

Rosman-Stollman, Elisheva, "Balancing Acts: The Gulf States and Israel," *Middle Eastern Studies,* 40(4) (2004): 185–208.

Segal, Jerome, "The Gulf War and the Israeli-Palestinian Conflict," *World Policy Journal,* 8(2) (1991): 351–362.

Siegel, Tobias, "Comparing Muslim Deaths to Holocaust, UAE Royal Suggests Jews are Hung Up on Shoah," *The Times of Israel*, August 7, 2022, https://www.timesofisrael.com/comparing-muslim-deaths-to-holocaust-uae-royal-suggests-jews-are-hung-up-on-shoah/.

"UAE Said to Warn Hamas Planned Gaza Infrastructure Projects Are in Danger," *The Times of Israel,* May 15, 2021, https://www.timesofisrael.com/uae-said-to-warn-hamas-planned-gaza-infrastructure-projects-are-in-danger/.

Ulrichsen, Kristian Coates, *Qatar and the Arab Spring* (Oxford: Oxford University Press, 2014).

Wechsler, William, "Dispatch from Abu Dhabi: Do the Israelis know about the Basus War?," *Atlantic Council*, October 18, 2023, https://www.atlanticcouncil.org/blogs/new-atlanticist/dispatch-from-abu-dhabi-do-the-israelis-know-about-the-basus-war/.

Zanotti, Jim, *US Foreign Aid to the Palestinians* (Washington, DC: Congressional Research Service Report, 2018).

Chapter 4

The UAE and Israel

Economic Diversification, Security, and Geopolitics

Robert Mason

The United Arab Emirates (UAE), a tribal and constitutional monarchy comprising a federation of seven emirates (Abu Dhabi, the capital, and Ajman, Dubai, Fujairah, Ras Al Khaimah, Sharjah, and Umm Al Quwain), has undergone a dramatic shift in recent years in terms of its foreign policy orientation. After 9/11, it became apprehensive over Islamic extremist movements shaping in its emirates that had remained politically and socially conservative federations, and determined to minimize extremist influences.[1] Consequently, it built up its military in part by cooperating with the North Atlantic Treaty Organization (NATO) missions in Afghanistan in 2001 and Libya in 2011, earning it the honorific of "Little Sparta."[2] The motivation for this shift in foreign policy was rooted in the UAE being a small state with limited manpower, and seeking to find security solutions to regional predicaments. By being seen as an indispensable ally of western military partners, it also guaranteed a degree of protection should the UAE come under threat. The more security relationships it could foster, the more the UAE weaved a web of mutual security interdependence and protection, predominantly with western powers.

Former president Khalifa bin Zayed Al Nahyan who worked with emirate-level partners, such as Dubai's Sheikh Mohammed bin Rashid Al Maktoum, launched UAE Vision 2021 in 2010 and built UAE soft power influence regionally and internationally. In tandem, through implementing this and other economic plans such as UAE Centennial 2071, the country has moved at a brisk pace toward economic diversification and modernity. The non-oil sector contributed 72.3 percent to the country's GDP in 2021.[3]

In such circumstances, the UAE defies easy classification. Hill notes that the category of "small states" is generally problematic.[4] The size of a country's military, territory, and economy are often used as metrics to assess state power and yet Middle Eastern sources of state power have been rather diffuse. Lustick notes that no state has been able to dominate the Middle East since the fall of the Ottoman Empire, a point made clear after the Arab Spring.[5] Saouli writes that states aiming for middle powerhood require the intention, strategy, and capacity to project power into the region, the ideological and cultural means to influence, and an ability to enable or disrupt international powers in the region.[6]

What the Arab Spring did, through the political instability caused by popular uprisings that undermined the regime security of allies such as Egypt, was create a new impetus for those with the power to intervene to cushion against ontological threats from Islamist groups. Such threats go beyond physical security to include issues related to identity and national narratives that influence citizens into modes of thinking about governance and political participation.[7] State response(s) can help boost prospects toward middle powerhood, and gain ground over regional adversaries, whether on the battlefield or in competition with states in opposition such as pro-Islamist Qatar.[8] Central to its hedging strategy, defined by a "national security or alignment strategy, undertaken by one state towards another, featuring a mix of cooperative and confrontational elements," is the UAE's maintenance and enhancement of a series of bilateral relationships.[9] Traditionally allied with the United States, the UAE has developed its economic relations with other non-western states such as China and continues to exert economic influence (economic statecraft) over states involved in its Comprehensive Economic Partnership Agreements (CEPAs). Increasingly these overlap in multilateral forums to which the UAE is a member, such as the BRICS. Such a strategy ensures a pool of potential allies continues to exist in the international community, especially allies which can contribute to Emirati security and defense.

The UAE has never been at war with Israel, which has provided a more pliable strategic context in which to explore new opportunities. There have been high-level UAE-Israeli contacts for years, at least since 2009 when UAE foreign minister, Sheikh Abdullah bin Zayed, had a good personal rapport with his Israeli opposite number, Tzipi Livni. Despite strong pro-Palestinian sympathies among the general population, the role of pan-Arabism has diminished over time, and the UAE elite pursued normalized relations with Israel for a range of pragmatic reasons. These include acknowledging the special relationship between the United States and Israel which is important to UAE's commercial and defense interests vis-à-vis the United States. Gaining greater congressional support became a real issue for the UAE during the Dubai Ports World (DP World) bid to run six major US ports in 2006, a bid that became mired in congressional disapproval. Indeed, on March 8, 2006, the US House Committee on Appropriations voted 62-2 to block the deal until DP World announced that they would drop the deal and transfer operations to a US entity.

UAE cooperation with Israel is also conducted with knowledge of Israel's concern about Iran's nuclear program and Iranian support for allied non-state actors even if there exist some differences over how hawkish state policy should be in tackling these challenges.[10] Israel maintains surveillance of Iran and military capabilities which chime with its own threat perception. Although the Oslo Accords could have represented a strategic opening for diplomatic relations in the early 1990s, the peace process stalled, making it difficult to advance relations with Israel. However, the JCPOA in 2015 set in motion closer UAE-Israel contact, whereby a nuclear deal could have opened up greater economic resources for Iran to benefit from. Instead, the Trump administration's unilateral withdrawal from the JCPOA encouraged Iran to further develop its nuclear program and channel support to surrogates, such as the Houthis in Yemen, undermining UAE national security interests. UAE calculations about cooperation with Israel were also reinforced by an escalation in the Gulf during the Iranian-sponsored attacks on Abqaiq and Khurais in 2019, attacks on shipping and Houthi attacks on the UAE itself. The lack of UAE strategic depth makes effective security and defensive partnerships particularly urgent. Should nuclear negotiations with Iran break down again and escalatory activities resume in the Gulf, the UAE has the opportunity to work with Israel, one of the region's most formidable militaries while also potentially benefitting from Israel's nuclear deterrent. Close cooperation between Israel and UAE has been apparent on multiple occasions during the Iran nuclear talks, including after the International Atomic Energy Agency (IAEA) criticized Iran in 2022 after Iran barred some UN inspectors from monitoring its nuclear program.[11]

The chapter asserts that Emirati foreign policy modus operandi provides a rationale for enhanced links with Israel, including the UAE's status as a dealing making entrepôt, search for international allies, investment, and expatriate labor based on religious tolerance. These aspects support its economic requirements on the road to rapid diversification. Ties with Israel replicate Egyptian and Jordanian peace deals while serving the UAE government's broader Middle East agenda vis-à-vis tackling the threat from Islamist groups such as Hamas and other branches of the Muslim Brotherhood, and specifically engaging with Egypt and Israel to roll back their influence.

This chapter accounts for the myriad of ways in which economic, geostrategic, and ideological interests accumulated and intersected up to and beyond the Abraham Accords in 2020, and after the first UAE ambassador arrived in Israel in March 2021, and Israel's first ambassador arrived in the UAE in October 2021. UAE-Israeli relations serve UAE state interests across a range of domains: in the Gulf, Middle East, and beyond. Meanwhile, it is being supported by a growing socioeconomic and geostrategic dimension which will multiply shared interests. This is important for the UAE which has urgent and ongoing needs to generate strategic depth and project influence, diversify its economy, and roll back Islamist groups.

The following sections incorporate the conditioning role of the United States on UAE-Israel relations, socioeconomic relations, security and defense ties, the impact of leadership changes in the UAE and Israel countries, and the impact of terror attacks and continued Israeli-Palestinian clashes along with wider regional and interregional influences. The penultimate section deals with UAE's normative influence as a first mover in this area. The conclusion summarizes the key issues and trends.

CONDITIONING ROLE OF THE UNITED STATES ON UAE-ISRAEL RELATIONS

US policy has been a growing point of contention for the GCC states over the past two decades. From the G. W. Bush administration's decision to lead the invasion of Iraq in 2003 to the Obama administration's policy on the Arab Spring, notably on Egypt, Syria, and Iran, Saudi Arabia and the UAE have engaged in pushback. The lack of US consultation with the GCC states and the outcome, the narrow parameters of the JCPOA in 2015 (which ignored Iranian missile development and regional activities), have perhaps been the most consequential to the threat perception felt by states such as Saudi Arabia and the UAE. The extent to which the UAE felt affected by the JCPOA is evident from a secret UAE and Israeli meeting in Cyprus in 2015, supposed to have involved Crown Prince Mohammad bin Zayed, which focused on how to counter the Iran nuclear deal.[12]

The Saudi-led intervention in Yemen in 2015 also indirectly created favorable conditions for the UAE to focus on Israel, in terms of deflecting criticism for its UAE policies toward Islamist actors in Yemen and Libya, and what Israel could offer in terms of missile defense. The UAE has transitioned from being a key ally in the Saudi-led coalition until it withdrew in 2019 amid concerns about its international standing, some differences with the Saudi kingdom over the mission in Yemen, and concerns about homeland security during a period of growing escalation between the United States and Iran. But since its reversion back to a more regular regional footprint, albeit one in an expansive mode in terms of economic statecraft, UAE territory has experienced a number of aerial attacks carried out by the Houthis. Developments in other parts of the region, such as the Iranian attacks on Abqaiq and Khurais oil installations in Saudi Arabia in 2019 without an immediate and correlated response, also sounded the alarm about an indecisive US in retreat. The chaotic US withdrawal from Afghanistan in 2021 confirmed these suspicions. The need was therefore to diversify security relations and bolster a comprehensive missile defense system beyond the combination of US-built Terminal High Altitude Area Defense, Patriot PAC-3, and Russian-built medium-range Pantsir-S1s, all of which makes UAE missile defense world-class.

The UAE is also building relations with the United States and Israel in more subtle ways. With a view to attracting international talent and boosting its credentials as a country of religious and ethnic tolerance, the UAE announced the Abrahamic Family House built in Abu Dhabi in 2019. Designed by David Adjaye, who also designed the National Museum of African American History and Culture in Washington D.C., this compound houses a mosque, church, and synagogue.[13] Appealing to Christians as well as Jews visiting or residing in the UAE, the project inserts and extends Emirati influence into new and important spheres of political dynamics affecting US and Israeli governance. This was especially the case during the Trump administration which received significant support from conservative Christian constituencies in the Southern states of the United States. The Trump administration vigorously promoted Israel and the Abraham Accords, and the impact of support from these constituencies could have been, and could yet be, an important factor in US support for the UAE and its policies should President Trump win another term in office from 2025.[14]

Although the Bill Clinton, G. W. Bush, and Obama administrations paid lip service to moving the US embassy to Jerusalem, it was the Trump administration that followed through by beginning to implement the move in May 2018, thereby controversially recognizing Jerusalem as the capital of Israel. This decision supported then-Israeli prime minister Netanyahu in challenging the two-state solution to the point that it is no longer seriously talked about in Israeli policy circles. In an attempt to balance out this departure from the peace process, the so-called Peace to Prosperity plan launched in September 2019, worth $50 billion, put investment before politics.[15] In other words, it was done without any immediate and clear political framework and then in direct contravention of established parameters of the two-state solution such as the Clinton Parameters from the 2000 Camp David Summit, including support for Palestinian refugees' right of return, Palestinian sovereignty over East Jerusalem, and withdrawal of Israeli Defense Forces. Thus, Prime Minister Netanyahu had a free reign, without US policy constraints, to implement his annexation plan for around 30 percent of the West Bank on 28 May 2020 without worrying about political fallout in the United States. He only suspended the plan as part of diplomatic normalization with Bahrain and the UAE. The circumstances surrounding the Abraham Accords have come under increasing scrutiny since 2020 with further evidence showing the Trump administration's intent was on using the accords to further isolate Iran.[16]

The UAE has looked to the US-brokered Middle East Peace Process and peace treaties signed between Israel and Egypt in 1979 and between Israel and Jordan in 1994, seeing an opportunity to extend its own influence and become an interlocutor in the Middle East Peace Process.[17] Often small states seek to influence through mediation roles between great or regional powers, giving them relevance and influence over theatres, issues, and outcomes they would otherwise be excluded from. Although diplomatic relations are a sine qua non for conflict resolution, in the advent of the Naftali Bennett premiership (June 13, 2021–June 30, 2022, and as third alternate prime minister from July 1 to November 8, 2022), Israeli annexation has continued. UAE's pressure to advance stability and the two-state solution is bound to be modest.

Another dimension of the Abraham Accords for the UAE is the tangible effect it had on fast-tracking the UAE's purchase of fifty F-35s from the United States which could be interpreted as threatening Israel's Qualitative Military Edge. Martin Indyk, former US special envoy for Israeli-Palestinian negotiations from 2013 to 2014, tweeted in 2020:

> Bibi just can't admit what everybody knows: that his deal with the UAE was not "peace for peace" but "peace for F35s and no annexation." It's a good deal for Israel. Why continue to lie about something of which he should be proud?[18]

US policy toward the GCC states and Israel has had a major bearing on the scope, timing, and enthusiasm of these parties to generate multifaceted relations while they also attempt to deepen relations with the United States to gain maximum relative autonomy and extend new modes of influence. These are not always assured, as the F-35 deal with the US attests (the F-35 deal was canceled in December 2021 due to the UAE being unwilling to cease 5G cooperation with China). However, since then the UAE and the United States appear to have changed tracks somewhat, with UAE economic relations with China continuing but more sensitive aspects being revised. In return, UAE company G42 and Microsoft developed a joint cloud and AI offering in September 2023, with Microsoft taking a minority stake in G42 for $1.5 billion in April 2024.[19] The overall impact on UAE national security interests looks to be favorable given Microsoft's leadership in cyber.

The UAE has found balancing between Iran and Israel more problematic: In 2023, the UAE stopped taking part in the US-led task force (Combined Maritime Forces) protecting Gulf shipping given renewed tanker seizures by Iran, although it remains a partner working on security, counterterrorism, and counter-piracy in the Gulf and Red Sea.[20] The risk of tension or confrontation with Iran in the Persian Gulf was just too high for Abu Dhabi and runs against the UAE's new mode of "zero problems" and de-escalation in the region. The move may reflect the fact that CENTCOM and the IDF completed the largest US-Israeli military exercise in their history on January 26, 2023, *Juniper Oak 23.2*. It integrated US and Israeli's fifth-generation fighters, as well as the USS George H. W. Bush, UAVs, and other aerial assets. Some military planners were advocating for the inclusion of the UAE and Bahrain in future, clearly unaware of the diplomatic fallout this could cause.[21] The UAE also had to postpone a visit from Israeli prime minister Netanyahu in 2023 over the timing of it—coming so soon after the far-right minister Itamar Ben-Gvir visited Temple Mount/Haram al-Sahrif which led to condemnation from Arab countries and Iran.[22] The Gaza War significantly raises the risks of the Abraham Accords for the UAE. Lana Nusseibeh, UAE Ambassador to the UN, has been at the forefront of calls for a humanitarian ceasefire and for "irreversible" progress toward Palestinian statehood for Gaza reconstruction.[23] However, as of April 2024, the prospects look set to get worse for regional conflagration as Israel and Iran engage in reciprocal drone and air strikes.

EMIRATI-ISRAELI SOCIOECONOMIC RELATIONS

In 2013, Israel launched @IsraelintheGulf on Twitter in Arabic, but stopped in 2014, and then relaunched in 2019 as diplomatic activity between Israel and the Gulf increased in the lead-up to the announcement of the Abraham Accords in August 2020. Before the accords, there were limited but notable people-to-people connections between the UAE and Israel. For instance, an Israeli judo sportsman took part in an international contest in Abu Dhabi in 2017 but was not allowed to fly the Israeli flag. Emirati teams took part in the Giro d'Italia cycling race; the first leg began in Israel in May 2018. During another judo competition which took place in the UAE in October 2018, the UAE authorities allowed the Israeli national anthem to be played. It was an event which attracted the attendance of the then-Israeli minister of culture and sport, Miri Regev.

Israel was represented in a pavilion at Expo 2020. However, in light of the accords signed in 2020, the BDS campaign appealed to its supporters in the UAE to boycott any Israeli presence in the country and not to engage either the Israeli embassy or institutions associated with Israel's official actions. At the same time, it appealed to Arabs more generally to boycott "all activities, festivals and projects sponsored by the UAE, including the Dubai EXPO, the Dubai Shopping Festival, as well as sports, cultural and economic/financial festivals and conferences." Finally, it aims to boycott and divest "from any Emirati or other corporation that becomes complicit in implementing this normalization agreement with Israel" and to refrain "from travel to present-day

Israel and the OPT, including the Al-Aqsa mosque, under this unethical agreement."[24] Soon after, more than eighty Arab artists, musicians, cinematographers, and cultural organizations signed a statement saying they would not participate in any UAE-sponsored events or organizations that supported normalization.[25]

In February 2022, an MoU was signed between the UAE and Israel covering measures to "encourage and promote" tourism.[26] Israeli tourists and Israelis traveling to the UAE on business will not need visas to enter the country. Many Israeli tourists are interested in visiting the UAE, and by some estimates, the country ranks second only to Egypt as a regional destination of interest. By October 2021, 250,000 Israeli tourists had already visited the Emirates since the Abraham Accords was signed.[27] El Al, Israir, and Arkia airlines encountered possible difficulty in being able to fly into Dubai International Airport in February 2022 due to the short timeframe and differences that emerged between Israel's Shin Bet security service and their Dubai counterparts.[28] In the worst-case scenario of not finalizing details in time in future, these airlines could simply be rerouted to Abu Dhabi, but the chances are that these preliminary issues will not emerge again without good reason. The UAE tourism ministry's twenty-nine-page Hebrew language advisory, published in 2020, draws attention to Israeli tourism in the UAE remaining susceptible to potentially negative impacts from Israelis discussing with UAE residents topics such as democracy, the UAE royal families, local politics, or state policy toward foreign workers.[29] This will also be an issue for visiting exchange students following the signing of the joint education agreement in November 2021.

However, there appears to be some leniency or a "special gesture" after President Herzog asked his counterpart Mohammed bin Zayed (MBZ) to pardon an Israeli woman who was arrested in April 2021 and convicted for possession of cannabis and cocaine. She faced life in prison but was released in March 2023.[30] Cooperation on education has continued into 2023 when the UAE government confirmed that it would include the Holocaust in the curriculum of its primary and secondary schools.[31]

Joint or combined sporting events have continued apace. Israeli and Emirati rugby teams played in Dubai in March 2021. A one-day Abraham Accords festival in March 2022 included a football game between a combined UAE, Bahrain, Morocco, and Israel squad versus another squad formed of international football stars.[32] However, in July 2022, noted Emirati professor of political science, Abdulkhaleq Abdulla, tweeted that as far as he knew no Emirati has visited Israel for tourism or did so secretly, and that 71 percent of Emiratis had negative or very negative impressions about the UAE relationship with Israel.[33] Indeed, Emiratis which viewed the Abraham Accords as having "a positive effect on the region" has dipped from 40 percent when the accords were signed to just 20 percent in a 2023 survey, although 40 percent still approve of contact.[34] Certainly, UAE tourists are visiting Israel, but the security situation in Israel has already had a knock-on effect on UAE tourism as two Emiratis were mistakenly arrested after an attempted mob hit in Tel Aviv.[35]

The most substantial aspects of UAE-Israel cooperation have been economic and energy-based. They have been reinforced by the visit of Israel's Minister of Energy and Water Resources, Silvan Shalom, to the UAE in 2014. Burgeoning cooperation in this area is also evident in the high number of business-related visits between the two countries, although Israelis don't necessarily travel on their own country's passports. Israel has stationed a permanent diplomat, Rami Hatan, in Abu Dhabi since 2015. He was accredited to IRENA but not at the time to the UAE.[36] His position was filled by Ambassador Dan Shaham who arrived in 2019 and went on to oversee burgeoning relations with the UAE. Then, Eitan Na'eh took over in January 2021. In July 2021, Amir Hayek, with a background in economics and tourism, became the first permanent ambassador to the UAE.[37] Just prior, in February 2021, Mohamed Al Khaja became the first United Arab Emirates ambassador to Israel based in the UAE embassy in Tel Aviv.[38]

Pre-normalization economic cooperation has been in agriculture, including irrigation supplies, homeland security-related products, medical technology, the diamond industry, and computer systems, including cyber security.[39] Critical infrastructure protection is also in demand for Emirati oil and gas installations, as the $816 million contract signed between Abu Dhabi's Critical National Infrastructure Authority (CNIA) and AGT International in 2008 shows.[40] Trade continued to be discreet, often with imports from Israel via Cyprus, Jordan, or Palestine. Israeli trade with its Arab neighbors, estimated to be around $1 billion in 2018, was found by the Tony Blair Institute for Global Change to have the potential to reach $25 billion.[41] That figure appears to be somewhat of an understatement since UAE-Israeli trade already reached $1 billion at the end of 2021, not including tourism and investment. By 2023, the UAE embassy in Washington put bilateral trade at $6.5 billion and drew attention to further agreements on energy and artificial intelligence cooperation.[42] A free trade pact was signed in March 2023 and UAE officials have, perhaps somewhat optimistically, envisioned $1 trillion of bilateral trade over the next decade.[43] Labor shortages in Israel are said to be driving fintech companies such as Rapyd to open offices in the UAE, while venture capital company Our Crowd announced that it was opening in Abu Dhabi Global Marketplace (ADGM).[44] Other agreements have been signed in areas such as health, AI, and finance. The growth in deals has had some sticking points, with some Israeli officials uneasy at a deal granting Abu Dhabi government-backed ADQ Developmental Holding Company a 25 percent controlling part of Israel's Phoenix insurance company including pensions and savings of hundreds of thousands of Israelis.[45] Concerns are said to be related to corruption and the use of sensitive customer data.[46]

For many years, Israel and the UAE have been cooperating on cyber. For example, AGT International has been linked to UAE companies in Abu Dhabi for an emirate-wide surveillance system called Falcon Eye.[47] Cyber cooperation has come under intense scrutiny as GCC states such as Saudi Arabia, Bahrain, and the UAE were found to be making use of Israeli software to hack cell phones used by journalists, activists, and US officials.[48] The Israeli Ministry of Defense has since cut down its cyber export list, including the removal of the UAE.[49] NSO Group, an Israeli company, was added to the US Commerce Department's "entity list," effectively blacklisting it in November 2021 for malicious cyber activity and the company has since blocked the use of its software against US or UK telephone numbers. While drawing attention to such covert activity and raising awareness among potential targets, many similar companies continue to operate.

Pegasus, another Israeli spyware firm, has been implicated in UAE attempts to hack into a UK official's phone who was working for Prime Minister Boris Johnson in Number 10 Downing Street at the time.[50] While surveillance has been targeted against UAE adversaries such as Qatar and as part of the UAE's global intelligence gathering effort, it could equally be used to monitor and control domestic dissent, including those against UAE normalization with Israel. Given that many UAE media outlets are owned or part-owned by the UAE government or the ruling families closely aligned with the government and there are heavy penalties for criticizing the government or rulers of the UAE, harming state interests or security, or criticizing friendly foreign states, any domestic opposition is unlikely to be expressed openly through the media.

The UAE, as in many other regions, has benefited from first mover advantage in its relations with Israel, over regional competitors such as Saudi Arabia.[51] The Abraham Accords give the UAE more trade and investment possibilities in a period of increasing economic pressure to diversify, secure water and food supplies, and address climate and health challenges such as COVID-19. G42 was the first UAE business to open an office in Israel. The company, which has links to the UAE government through UAE national security advisor, Sheikh Tahnoon, seeks to replicate the Israeli Defense Forces (IDF) incubation of tech companies which work closely with the defense industry.[52] The UAE-Israel Business Council was set up to build ties that "promote trade, innovation and cooperation."[53] The UAE has also proposed the "Silicon Wadi" project in East Jerusalem in August 2020.

Such a high concentration of high-technology companies creates a great demand for investment, which the UAE is ideally suited to meet.[54] Indeed, in

March 2021, the UAE set up a \$10-billion fund to invest in Israel.[55] According to a report by Israel's IVC Research Center, Israeli tech start-ups raised \$17.8 billion in the first three quarters of 2021, almost double the 2020 total amount of funding.[56] Israel and the UAE have sought to capitalize on this opportunity expressly through a new initiative called Synaptech Capital which was launched in March 2022. It aims to raise \$100 million to support Israeli and UAE start-ups.[57] However, "Silicon Wadi" may lead to commercial development on private Palestinian land and further complicate the UAE's position as a guarantor of no further Israeli settlement activity.[58] The project also looks to have been suspended pending the restoration of calm after IDF-Palestinian clashes in 2021–2022.

In November 2021, the UAE, Israel, and Jordan signed a groundbreaking energy deal. Supported by then US climate envoy John Kerry, the project involved the UAE building a massive solar farm in Jordan to supply electricity to Israel, and Israel in turn building a desalination plant to provide water to Jordan.[59] Amman later said it was pulling out of the deal due to the Gaza War. UAE state company, Mubadala, completed its \$1 billion stake in Israel's Tamar gas field in December 2021, its largest investment in Israel to date. The Israel Diamond Exchange opened an office in the UAE in February 2022 and the diamond sectors pledged to do more business in future. Israel and the UAE also signed a free trade agreement in 2022 to support a burgeoning commercial relationship. Due to a large proportion of UAE economic activity being state-led or at least hybridized and coupled with a new nationalism "displacing Arab and Islamic solidarities,"[60] the UAE remains relatively insulated from the fallout of further Israeli-Palestinian violence or calls for an Israeli boycott.

UAE-ISRAELI SECURITY AND DEFENSE TIES

At the onset of Netanyahu's second period of premiership (2009–2021), the Israeli Ministry of Defense refused to approve a multimillion-dollar drone deal with the UAE in 2009. The deal, which was refused at a late stage due to concerns about the transfer of sensitive technology and due to some US reservations, is said to have caused difficulties in the bilateral relationship for the following two years.[61] This was coupled with the assassination of a Hamas operative in Dubai in 2010 by a group of Israeli agents traveling on bogus passports. The UAE responded by temporarily banning any Israeli citizen from entering the country. Although the Israeli government did not take official responsibility for the assassination, the crisis in bilateral relations ended with assurances that Israel would not conduct assassinations in the UAE again. A partial reimbursement and offset program for Israeli military hardware was established in lieu of the failed drone deal, and an enhanced security and intelligence dialogue took place. This was targeted toward Iran and extremist groups especially. In 2011, CNIA agreed to purchase Unmanned Aerial Vehicles (UAVs) from Israel's Aeronautics Defense Systems (ADS).[62] But again the Israeli Ministry of Defense refused the sale due to a combination of selling sensitive technology to the UAE and due to US reservations.

In December 2013, Israeli president Shimon Peres spoke via video link to twenty-nine foreign ministers from the Muslim world attending the Gulf Security Conference in Abu Dhabi. The UAE and Israel have since been involved in joint military exercises, including training exercises in 2016 in the United States. In 2017, they held additional exercises with the United States, Italy, and Greece, and in 2018 a UAE military official may have visited an Israeli military base to study the F-35 which the UAE was considering to purchase from the United States at the time. Security cooperation continues to center around the Israeli supply of drones, Israeli surveillance of Iran, and UAE access to Israel's Eros B satellite and imagery.[63] Bilateral cooperation is also flexible in supporting US objectives, such as IsraAID working with the UAE to evacuate forty-one Afghans from Kabul via Tajikistan to the UAE in 2021, including human rights activists and members of a girls' cycling and robotic teams.[64]

Part of the Israeli Iron Dome technology, including warning and interception equipment, was always an attractive feature when considering UAE-Israeli ties. Although delays and uncertainty surrounding any deal meant the UAE had to develop its own short-range counter-rocket, artillery, and mortar (C-RAM) technology. SkyKnight manufactured by Halcon, which is part of the EDGE Group, sold its first rockets to Rheinmetall's Oerlikon Sykynex air defense system in 2021, which was announced at IDEX Abu Dhabi the same year.[65] By potentially integrating the UAE into the Iron Dome missile defense system, there is the possibility that missile defense cooperation could be extended back to Israel in terms of better early warning of missiles launched from Iran. In September 2022, Israel agreed to supply the UAE with an unknown number of Rafael-made SPYDER mobile interceptors, which can be attached to the back of vehicles to defend against short and long-range threats.[66] The need is clearly apparent, as the Houthis had stepped up drone and missile attacks on Saudi Arabia and the UAE in early 2022.

In January 2022, Elbit Systems Emirates Limited signed a $53 million deal to supply airborne infrared counterattack measures for the A380 tanker aircraft. Israel Aerospace Industries (IAI) is working with EDGE on counter-drone technology, and Rafael Advanced Defense Systems has set up a joint venture with G42 focused on AI.[67] UAE-Israel security relations have a wider bearing on Gulf security as the UAE already provides some aerial defense coverage for other GCC states such as parts of Saudi Arabia. However, these are tempered by the fact that the UAE, like most GCC states, has implemented a global search for economic and security-related partners and is also looking to buttress its missile defenses with purchases from South Korea and France. Israel is just one of many UAE defense partners, including the United States, the UK, France, South Korea, Turkey, and China. The UAE also works with Cyprus, Greece, and Egypt in the Eastern Mediterranean. The imperatives of small states to maintain diverse partnerships and stability and eventually rely on the development of its own military-industrial complex are the main reasons why relations with Israel will not become strategic or constitute an alliance. But they will remain important in a number of spheres to further UAE state objectives.

The evolving security situation in the Gulf continues to support relations with Israel. For example, the UAE's counterattack against the Houthi missile launch sites in January 2022 after three people were killed on tankers in Abu Dhabi, may be due to tactical intelligence received from Israel's network of infrared nanosatellites, which can detect missile effluxes.[68] In contrast to the slow US response to the event, Israel is said to have sent intelligence officials and a shipment of batteries from the SPYDER defense system to the UAE.[69]

IMPACT OF LEADERSHIP CHANGES IN
THE UAE AND ISRAEL

Sheikh Mohammad bin Zayed has been the de-facto ruler of Abu Dhabi and the UAE since 2014 when his half-brother, Khalifa bin Zayed Al Nahyan, was incapacitated by a stroke. MBZ, as he is known, then acceded to the presidency in May 2022. In doing so, he has cemented the leadership position and interests of Al Nahyan and Abu Dhabi over the other emirates, especially Al Maktoum and the interests of Dubai, which has a settled Iranian community and a different threat perception vis-à-vis Iran. In reality, this transition was in train as far back as 2009 when Abu Dhabi bailed out Dubai during the financial crash, to the tune of $10 billion. From inter-emirate rivalries that have existed since the formation of the UAE, certain tensions still exist within the wider Emirati nation-building project, including Sharjah's distinct identity and differentiation from the other emirates.

MBZ set the UAE on a more assertive foreign policy course in the context of the perceived Islamist threat domestically and later, the Arab Spring, in answer to and in competition with Qatar's independent and divergent foreign policy.[70] Part of the rivalry is based on the fact that as a constitutional monarchy, the UAE leadership abhors democratization in the Middle East and Islamist activism, the latter supported by Doha, which both threaten the dominant political model in the Arab Gulf. The UAE requires domestic stability as a prerequisite in order to advance its economic interests, including as a hub in an interconnected world, spanning sports, transport, logistics, trade and investment, and new industrial and employment projects which aim to prepare the UAE for post-rentier status. In a speech, he said: "In 50 years, when we might have the last barrel of oil, the question is: when it is shipped abroad, will we be sad? If we are investing today in the right sectors, I can tell you we will celebrate at that moment."[71] The UAE has therefore pursued a range of international partnerships to grow its economy and service its security needs.

Relations with Israel fit this monarchy's threat perception and search for potential military partners even at a time when the UAE was also seeking to de-escalate tensions by engaging in diplomacy with Iran. Israel offers dual-use value-added high-technology goods as well as missile defense possibilities. Benjamin Netanyahu's annexation plan and US policy have facilitated relations which the UAE said were in the offing anyhow. The enthusiasm with which Prime Minister Naftali Bennett embraced the Abraham Accords was clear and offered consistency with the policies of his predecessor. Bennett praised the "new and groundbreaking chapter in the history of peace in the Middle East" and promised to "develop, deepen and expand relations between the [Abraham Accord] countries, as well as work to develop relations with other countries in the region."[72] However, in 2020, Bennett, a former leader of the pro-settler party Yamina, said then-Israeli prime minister "Netanyahu missed a once-in-a-century opportunity to extend Israeli sovereignty over the Jordan Valley . . . and the rest of Israeli settlements [in the West Bank]."[73]

The Israeli leadership and its domestic/Palestine policy is almost irrelevant in an era when Palestine has been subordinated to other UAE national interests. That subordination is due to not only a combination of regional developments but also Palestinian political ruptures which have attracted UAE attempts at leverage for monarchical stability. The UAE is a major aid donor to the Palestinian cause, both through multilateral and bilateral mechanisms. For example, the UAE contributes $500,000 each year to the UN Relief and Works Agency for Palestine Refugees in the Near East (UNRWA) and paid the same amount in October 2000 through the Sheikh Zayed Charitable Foundation to the UN High Commission for Refugees.[74] An additional $25 million (part of a $50 million commitment) was paid to UNRWA in 2019, taking total UAE contributions to more than $203 million from 2014 to 2019.[75] The UAE also transferred aid to Palestine through the UN Educational, Scientific and Cultural Organization (UNESCO) and the UN International Children's Emergency Fund (UNICEF). The UAE also donates to the Arab Fund for Economic and Social Development, the Arab Monetary Fund, and the Arab Gulf Program for United Nations Development. The war in Gaza created significant humanitarian need and the UAE responded by allocating $20 million for humanitarian assistance and $5 million to support UNRWA in its reconstruction efforts in Gaza in 2024.[76] The UAE has also given $15 million via the Amalthea Fund which coordinates the flow of aid arriving in Gaza and through other public fundraising efforts, especially during Ramadan.[77]

The UAE has a representative office in Ramallah, and Palestine has an embassy in Abu Dhabi. Despite this overt support, the UAE is said to be attempting to use Mohammed Dahlan, a former Palestinian official turned critic of President Mahmoud Abbas, as its Palestine fix-it person, especially with reference to his experience in Gaza, past election to the Central Committee of the Palestinian Authority in the West Bank and links to Israel.[78] While UAE-PLO ties go back years, there is a growing frustration with PA leadership which may have impacted UAE decision-making on normalization with Israel. The loss of Gaza to Hamas since June 2007, an Islamist group proscribed as a terror group by the Arab League in 2021, weighs on UAE influence in Palestine, especially given the group's alignment with the UAE's pro-Islamist competitors such as Qatar and Turkey. Influence over Hamas also serves UAE interest vis-à-vis Egypt, and its security and diplomatic influence during periods of Israel-Hamas conflict. While the UAE could have attempted to leverage aid and infrastructure investment in Gaza for relative stability and wrestle back influence from regional competitors, it is not clear how effective such a policy will now be. Already amid Israeli settlement expansion in November 2022, Abdulkhaleq Abdulla, an outspoken UAE academic, noted on Twitter (now X) that the Abraham Accords should be temporarily frozen.[79] Now the UAE focus looks set to be on a political transition in Gaza. In an interview with the Economist in October 2023, Mr. Dahlan promoted the idea of first unifying Gaza and the West Bank under a technocratic administration for up to two years, and then holding democratic elections in Gaza, including Hamas, but shifting toward a parliamentary system that would do away with Mahmoud Abbas, the PA's aging and contentious president.[80] The general view of senior PLO officials so far appears to be that the UAE is "selling out" the Palestinians. Furthermore, the PA is said to have attempted to limit Dahlan and UAE influence through Fatah parliamentarians and PA security officers, as well as websites and foundations operating in the West Bank linked to Dahlan or the UAE.[81] UAE influence and relations with Fatah look set to be dependent on internally or externally induced machinations in Ramallah or other favorable changes conducive to extending UAE influence.

As a member of the Supreme Council of Economic Affairs since December 2020, and named crown prince on 29 March 2023, Khaled bin Mohammed bin Zayed al-Nahyan, the son of Mohammed bin Zayed, is set to have significant contact with various branches of the Israeli government. However, Ebtesam Al-Ketbi, founder of the Emirates Policy Center, had already noted that the UAE was "embarrassed" by the right-wing Netanyahu government in May 2023 and predicted no more Arab states would normalize ties with Israel.[82] During the Gaza War, the UAE has articulated its "red lines" being "that Israel does not undermine the interests of Jordan and Egypt, does not modify the status quo of the Holy sites in Jerusalem and finally we oppose any military escalation by Israel on Iran and we have made it clear that it's not in our interest."[83] The bombing of the Iranian embassy in Damascus on April 1, 2024, was clearly one such breach, turning years-old shadow war into open conflict. Iran responded with a volley of drones and missiles most of which were successfully intercepted. At the time of writing, Israel was plotting its response.

The 2023 Israel-Hamas war further underscores the risks to the UAE and raises more questions about sustaining bilateral relations going forward. Although the UAE has noted it is not changing its position and does not mix trade with politics,[84] that position hinges on Israel-Iran attacks coming under control and a break in the cycle of violence.[85] Jordan, on the other hand, which had an energy and water exchange deal with the UAE and Israel, has canceled the ratification of the deal that was expected to happen at the end of October 2023. A top Jordanian diplomat said Amman's priority was to end "Israel's barbarism in Gaza."[86] While not, so far, devastating to UAE's regional policy, it is certainly a blow to Emirati attempts to use the Abraham Accords to build greater stability and win-win solution through joint energy deals. The low-hanging fruit that appeared after the accords has disappeared in a new environment of conflict.

TERROR ATTACKS, ISRAELI-PALESTINIAN CLASHES, AND SUSTAINABILITY OF UAE-ISRAELI NORMALIZATION IN REGIONAL CONTEXT

The normalization of the UAE-Israel relationship has so far survived a series of turbulent events, including some of the worst fighting between Hamas and Israel in 2021 since the 2014 Gaza War. Lana Nusseibeh, UAE ambassador to the UN, noted on May 23, 2021, that "the ongoing violence of the past two weeks and the growing number of civilian casualties indicate that we must redouble international efforts to find a just, comprehensive, and lasting peaceful solution to the Palestinian issue consistent with relevant Security Council and General Assembly resolutions."[87]

Following the 2021 Israel-Palestine crisis, the UAE showed a brief but rare interest in engaging Hamas in Gaza. But Hamas put out a statement that "we don't think the Emirates have anything real to offer."[88] Ismail Haniyeh, a senior leader in the Hamas political wing, went on to note in December 2021 that "we must have an integrated plan to bring down normalization, which, unfortunately has taken the character of military and security alliances with some countries."[89]

Turkey was the first Muslim country to recognize Israel in 1948. But President Erdogan said in August 2020 that he may suspend ties with the UAE over the deal with Israel, and withdraw Turkey's ambassador.[90] While improved UAE-Iran relations may undercut some of the rationale of the Abraham Accords, more cordial UAE-Turkey relations could sustain it. In a period of economic decline, Turkey is attempting to rebuild bridges back to the Gulf and warm up relations with the UAE. The expansion of the relationship appears to be more fruitful, at least in the short term, in areas such as trade and investment, construction, energy, and tourism. With the logic and imperative of economic diversification, relations such as those with Israel will be increasingly valuable to multiply bilateral gains into subregional development, especially if bilateral trade and investment figures match political aspirations.

Qatar, which also has a stake in aid and development to Gaza initially, has ruled out an Arab-Israeli normalization calculus for an Arab-Israeli peace. In October 2021, Qatari foreign minister Sheikh Mohammed bin Abdulrahman Al Thani said, "We should not focus on economic normalization and forget the (Israeli) occupation of Arab lands."[91] It shows the extent to which the regional outlook for Qatar and the UAE, even after the apparent rapprochement at the GCC Summit in Al Ula in January 2021, remains almost diametrically opposed.

Given the continuing challenges to expanding spheres of UAE activity and influence, relations with Egypt are of great consequence in sustaining UAE interests and influence in North Africa and the Levant. First, like Abu Dhabi, the military regime in Egypt considers the Muslim Brotherhood to be a threat, as was clear in the forced removal of President Morsi from power in 2013 and some of the so-called "13 points," raised by the Quartet (Saudi Arabia, UAE, Egypt, and Bahrain) and communicated to Qatar in 2017, which specifically included reference to the Muslim Brotherhood.[92] The UAE, along with Saudi Arabia and Kuwait, considers Egypt to be an important and traditional pillar of the Arab security system. Its influence can be felt in the Middle East and Africa, and as a mediator in the Israel-Palestine conflict. Egypt also represents much-needed manpower and an investment opportunity for the UAE. To get to an Arab version of NATO, some analysts believe that Israel, Saudi Arabia, the UAE, Jordan, and Egypt will need to be involved, with Iraq possibly at the margins.[93] The UAE, Saudi Arabia, and other Gulf States have serious issues with Iran, but the UAE is said to prefer diplomacy, and there is a need to find a process.[94]

On March 22, 2022, the leaders of Israel, Egypt, and the UAE were in Sharm El Sheikh to discuss the Iran nuclear talks, the war in Ukraine, and its effects on the global energy market and food security. Just days later, the foreign ministers of the UAE, Bahrain, Morocco, Egypt, Israel, and the United States attended the Negev Summit, aimed at consolidating the Abraham Accords and deterring Iran. Terror attacks in Israel during the summit led the chairman of the Defense Affairs, Interior and Foreign Affairs Committee of the UAE Federal National Council to state that "the holy month of Ramadan is a month of worship and reflection, but the terrorists always choose Ramadan to kill innocent people. We as Muslim[s] should take a firm action against these terrorists."[95]

Beyond the March 2022 terror attacks in Israel, Israel-Palestine tensions have continued to escalate after a series of Israeli raids and clashes. These have been ongoing since tensions flared after the eviction of Palestinian families from Sheikh Jarrah in January 2022. Violence during Ramadan was expected as has been the case in previous years, and the rare convergence of Ramadan, Passover, and Easter also raised fears of tensions and violence. Tensions inevitably escalated after Israeli police entered the Muslim holy site of Al-Aqsa Mosque in April 2022, quickly followed by more rocket attacks from Hamas in Gaza. Young Israeli ultranationalists chanted "death to Arabs" in Jerusalem.[96]

As the new far-right dominated government took office under Prime Minister Netanyahu in 2023, the visit of Israel's national security minister, Itamar Ben-Gvir, to the Temple Mount/Haram al-Sharif on January 3, 2023, had the potential to once again trigger escalation and potentially another Intifada. The UAE, Saudi Arabia, Jordan, Turkey, and Qatar quickly condemned the move, with the UAE stating that he was "storming" the area.[97] As a non-permanent member of the UN Security from 2022 to 2023, the UAE was instrumental, with China, in bringing the matter before the council.[98] The UAE even went so far as to draft a UN Security Council resolution calling on Israel to immediately cease all settlement activity. However, possibly after the Biden administration exerted pressure on Israel and Palestine to engage in talks, the UAE has instead opted for a formal statement, known as a presidential statement in the UN Security Council to be agreed to by consensus.[99] The move has been a useful ploy for the Biden administration to avoid uncomfortable contrasts in the way it treats Russian policy toward Ukraine and the way it treats Israeli policy toward Palestine.

Prime Minister Netanyahu was forced to postpone his impending visit to the UAE and instead MBZ met with former Israeli prime minister Naftali Bennett in Abu Dhabi on March 27, 2023. His expected anti-Iranian rhetoric on UAE territory would also not have played well in light of the UAE's attempts to reduce tensions with Iran. The UAE will continue to navigate treacherous waters by maintaining a pragmatic stance. However, should escalation lead to a third Intifada and lacking a peace process since 2014, it is difficult to see how its chosen policy could be sustained amid such extreme circumstances.

UAE AND ISRAEL IN A NEW QUAD ("QUAD 2.0") IN THE INDO-PACIFIC

A new Quad involving the UAE, Israel, India, and the United States was announced in October 2021. Focused primarily on technology, infrastructure, and trade finance—as well as important arms sales links between Israel, the UAE, and India—it recognizes growing inter-regional competition and is a natural progression from the Abraham Accords. These quadrilateral relations are still in their infancy, and with other more geo-strategic Quads being developed (e.g., the UAE, Saudi Arabia, Bahrain, and Egypt; the United States, Japan, Australia, and India) or trilateral security pacts with the potential to expand (e.g., AUKUS), there is a significant degree of uncertainty as to how the UAE will engage. But having had a close working relationship with President Widodo of Indonesia,[100] including having signed a Comprehensive Economic Partnership Agreement (CEPA) on July 1, 2022, and in the process of concluding another CEPA with Malaysia in 2024, perhaps spurred on by attempting to block or contain the repercussions of any new Hamas base in Malaysia and/or the rise of other political Islamist groups.[101]

This is within the context of US-China tensions, particularly over Taiwan, India's working relationship with Russia, as well as US-GCC tensions during the onset of the Russian invasion of Ukraine in 2022, when Saudi Arabia and the UAE resisted President Biden's overtures concerning energy policy. UAE's inclusion into a Quad initially signifies the Emirates' rising importance in the Indo-Pacific, especially as an important economic partner as part of its accelerated economic diversification process, which could lead to the development of more strategic cooperation going forward.

UAE'S DIPLOMATIC AND NORMATIVE INFLUENCE ON WIDER REGION

The ambition and speed of UAE's foreign and economic policy maneuvres often mean that it has the first mover advantage. The Abraham Accords are no exception. UAE's normative influence over other target states for Israel to normalize with, in the Gulf, wider Middle East, and Africa, is therefore an important factor to consider when thinking through the trajectory and sustainability of the Abraham Accords. Sudan, for example, which moved firmly into the Saudi and UAE camps post-2016, normalized relations with Israel in

October 2020. Khartoum negotiated a package of measures with the Trump administration including $335 million paid to the victims of the 1998 bombings of the US embassies in Kenya and Tanzania, as well as the bombing in 2000 of the USS Cole off the coast of Yemen. The UAE helped facilitate talks in September 2020 and may have been involved in pledges amounting to $2 billion with the United States, and possibly other actors such as Saudi Arabia.[102] However, with civil war having ravished the country since 2023, the future of Sudan's policy toward Israel is unknown.

After relations with Iran became more complex over the last decade, Mauritania has also looked to the UAE-Israel deal and said it trusts the "wisdom and good judgement of" the UAE leadership in signing the agreement.[103] Mauritania is the only Arab country to have previously formalized relations with Israel under another US-brokered diplomatic accord led by then-secretary of state, Madeline Albright. She hailed the deal in 1999 as a "force for regional reconciliation and peace" only for it to be overtaken by Israel's Operation Cast Lead in 2008–2009 which led to frozen ties in 2010.[104] The war in Gaza has once again raised the point that internal Israeli political and security dynamics are the impediment to sustaining regional relations. At a time of rising violence with the potential for regional escalation, the benefits of any state facilitating further accords would be questionable. The same can be said for the Israel-Morocco agreement, facilitated by the Trump administration by recognizing Morocco's sovereignty over Western Sahara in December 2020,[105] in effect deepening a crisis in one region to advance a deal in another region and in the end achieving very little.

CONCLUSION

The motivations behind the UAE entering into the Abraham Accords are becoming clearer after an interim period has elapsed from 2020 to 2022. The UAE entered the agreement as part of a clear-eyed strategy to advance military-industrial relations with Israel (missile defense, intelligence vis-à-vis Iran, and surveillance technology which can be deployed internally and globally). This could become vital should Iran become more belligerent which may occur if a new nuclear agreement is unforthcoming, during a period of internal revolt, or, as looks to be the case, during heightened tensions with Israel. The Abraham Accords also play into advancing UAE relations with the United States and sustaining influence in Washington as the UAE deepens relations with the BRICS. Whether dealing with Prime Minister Netanyahu or the former far-right prime minister Naftali Bennett, the UAE's core and long-term national security imperatives that drive its relations with Israel remain intact.

While socioeconomic relations with Israel support the UAE's attempts to transition to a post-rentier economy within a generation, they do not generally appear to enjoy widespread Emirati public support or Israeli support in areas of economic sensitivity. There remains a great degree of uncertainty as to how UAE foreign policy tools can solve the intractable political problem of Israeli annexation and build relations with the PA. Although there have been cross-currents of Emirati public anger expressed over the Israel government's continued annexation policy, it doesn't look set to threaten UAE-Israel relations writ large. The only time when MBZ has apparently been furious is due to interrupted arms sales from Israel, and an assassination conducted on UAE soil, issues that affect UAE security and sovereignty.

Notwithstanding the expansion of the Abraham Accords to include Morocco and Sudan, this was always going to be an entrepreneurial but risky undertaking, as the Mauritania case shows. But for a small state such as the UAE, such risks dovetail within its overall hedging strategy and its ability to lead change and build influence through normative and diplomatic mechanisms. The UAE and Israel have been quick to extend their bilateral relations into new theatres. The United States, Israel, the UAE, and India are developing a new trade-based Quad in West Asia, not only increasing their overall competitiveness but also increasing their sources of leverage and other strategic options available to them. For the UAE and Israel which are becoming more heavily engaged with China, managing US-China tensions and challenges to globalization is especially important since changes and risks in West Asia could disproportionately affect their development, growth, and stability. As they enter their fourth year of normalization, both sides remain committed to the status quo, but they are certainly entering a more challenging period.

NOTES

1. Michele J. Sison, "UAE Minimizing Influence of Islamic Extremists," November 10, 2004, https://wikileaks.org/plusd/cables/04ABUDHABI4061_a.html.

2. "Little Sparta" is a term attributed to General James Mattis, President Trump's first secretary of defense, to describe the UAE's military experience and ability to punch above its weight. Rajiv Chandrasekaran, "In the UAE, the United States has a Quiet, Potent Ally Nicknamed 'Little Sparta,'" *The Washington Post*, November 9, 2014, https://www.washingtonpost.com/world/national-security/in-the-uae-the-united-states-has-a-quiet-potent-ally-nicknamed-little-sparta/2014/11/08/3fc6a50c-643a-11e4-836c-83bc4f26eb67_story.html.

3. Adam Lucente, "UAE Reports Slight Growth of Non-Oil GDP," *Al-Monitor*, April 20, 2022, https://www.al-monitor.com/originals/2022/04/uae-reports-slight

-growth-non-oil-gdp#:~:text=The%20non%2Doil%20sector%20contribution,Emir-ates%20News%20Agency%20reported%20Tuesday.

4. Christopher Hill, "Foreign Policy in International Relations," in *Foreign Policy in the Twenty-First Century* (New York: Palgrave Macmillan, 2016), 15.

5. Ian S. Lustick, "The Absence of Middle Eastern Great Powers: Political 'Backwardness' in Historical Perspective," *International Organization*, 51(4) (Autumn 1997): 657.

6. Adham Saouli, "Middling or Meddling? Origins and Constraints of External Influence in the Middle East," in *Unfulfilled Aspirations: Middle Power Politics in the Middle East*, ed. Adham Saouli (New York: Oxford University Press, 2020), 1–10.

7. David Roberts, "Ontological Security and the Gulf Crisis," *Journal of Arabian Studies*, 10(2) (2021): 221–237.

8. Robert Mason, "Small State Aspirations to Middle Powerhood: The Cases of Qatar and the UAE," in *Unfulfilled Aspirations: Middle Power Politics in the Middle East*, ed. Adham Saouli (London: Hurst/Oxford University Press: 2020), 157–183.

9. John D. Ciorciari and Jürgen Haacke, "Hedging in International Relations: An Introduction," *International Relations of the Asia-Pacific*, 19(3) (September 2019): 367–374.

10. See comment made by H.E. Ambassador Shaika Najla Mohammad Salem Al Qasimi, former UAE ambassador to Sweden, Denmark, Finland, and Portugal in a presentation made to the International Institute for Strategic Studies, "Understanding GCC Policy: Perspectives on the US Strategic Partnership," September 13, 2022, https://www.youtube.com/watch?v=PISmbQ9V7uA&list=PL06gBmITAMbcSm Zjs3BKkEPxEWfX_J8pt&index=5.

11. Rina Bassist, "After IAEA Criticizes Iran, Israeli Prime Minister Meets with Emirati Leader," *Al-Monitor*, June 9, 2022, https://www.al-monitor.com/originals /2022/06/after-iaea-criticizes-iran-israeli-prime-minister-meets-emirati-leader.

12. Adam Entous, "Donald Trump's New World Order," *The New Yorker*, June 11, 2018, https://www.newyorker.com/magazine/2018/06/18/donald-trumps-new -world-order.

13. Lizzie Crook, "David Adjaye Designs Trio of Multifaith Temples in Abu Dhabi," *Dezeen*, September 26, 2019, https://www.dezeen.com/2019/09/26/david -adjaye-the-abrahamic-family-house-temples-abu-dhabi-architecture/.

14. Boris Heersink and Jeffrey A. Jenkins, "The Republican Party is White and Southern. How Did That Happen?," *The Washington Post,* February 7, 2020, https:// www.washingtonpost.com/politics/2020/02/07/republican-party-is-white-southern -how-did-that-happen/.

15. Trump White House, "Peace to Prosperity: A Vision to Improve the Lives of the Palestinian and Israeli People," January 2020, https://trumpwhitehouse.archives .gov/wp-content/uploads/2020/01/Peace-to-Prosperity-0120.pdf.

16. Joost Hilterman, "Is the Middle East's Makeover a Mirage?" *Foreign Affairs,* August 1, 2023, https://www.foreignaffairs.com/united-states/middle-easts-makeover -mirage.

17. Being an interlocutor in the Israel-Palestine conflict was mentioned as one of the motivating factors for the UAE joining the Abraham Accords. Discussion with a senior UAE official who asked not to be named, January 19, 2021.

18. Martin Indyk, *Twitter*, October 24, 2020, https://twitter.com/Martin_Indyk/status/1320072707833270274.

19. "Microsoft Invests $1.5 Billion in UAE's G42 for Minority Stake," *Wamda*, April 16, 2024, https://www.wamda.com/2024/04/microsoft-invests-1-5-billion-uaes -g42-minority-stake.

20. Lisa Barrington, "UAE Says it Has Stopped Taking Part in US-led Maritime Coalition," *Reuters*, May 31, 2023, https://www.reuters.com/world/middle-east/uae -says-it-withdrew-us-led-maritime-coalition-two-months-ago-2023-05-31/#.

21. US-UAE Business Council Report, "An Enduring Partnership: The US-UAE Defense and Security Relationship," February 2023, p. 11, https://usuaebusiness.org/ wp-content/uploads/2023/02/Final-Defense-Report-2023.pdf.

22. Barak Ravid, "Scoop: The Real Reason Netanyahu Didn't go to the UAE in January," *Axios*, March 1, 2023, https://www.axios.com/2023/03/01/reason-netan-yahu-uae-visit-postponed.

23. "UAE Diplomat Says 'Irreversible' Progress to Palestinian State Needed for Gaza Reconstruction," *Reuters*, February 12, 2024, https://www.reuters.com/world /middle-east/uae-diplomat-says-irreversible-progress-palestinian-state-needed-gaza -2024-02-12/.

24. "UAE Dictatorship Sells Out Palestinian Rights Through Agreement with Israel," August 14, 2020, https://bdsmovement.net/news/uae-dictatorship-sells-out -palestinian-rights-through-agreement-with-israel.

25. Hakim Bishara, "Dozens of Arab Artists Boycott UAE for Normalization Deal With Israeli Government," September 22, 2020, https://hyperallergic.com /588922/uae-israel-normalization-open-letter-boycott/.

26. Nerea Belmonte, "UAE and Israel Sign "Historic" Tourism Agreement," *Atalayar*, February 11, 2022, https://atalayar.com/en/content/uae-and-israel-sign-historic -tourism-agreement.

27. Josh Corder, "250,000 Israel Tourists Visit UAE Since Abraham Accords," *Hotelier*, October 17, 2021, https://www.hoteliermiddleeast.com/news/250000-israel -tourists-visit-uae-since-abraham-accords.

28. "Israel May Halt Flights to Dubai Over Security Arrangements," *Reuters*, February 6, 2022, https://www.reuters.com/world/middle-east/israel-may-halt-flights -dubai-over-security-arrangements-2022-02-06/.

29. Daniel Estrin, "Israeli Tourism Ministry Warns Against Discussing Sensitive Topics with UAE Citizens," *NPR*, November 30, 2020, https://www.npr.org/2020 /11/30/940122963/israeli-tourism-ministry-warns-against-discussing-sensitive-topics -with-uae-citi.

30. "UAE Pardons Israeli Woman Who Faced Life in Prison," *BBC*, March 26, 2023, https://www.bbc.com/news/world-middle-east-65080918.

31. Marita Kassis, "UAE Schools Will Now Teach Holocaust in National Curriculum," *Al-Monitor*, January 9, 2023, https://www.al-monitor.com/originals/2023 /01/uae-schools-will-now-teach-holocaust-national-curriculum?amp.

32. Sue Surkes, "Abraham Accords Nations Get Battered – in a Friendly Soccer Game," *Times of Israel*, March 30, 2022, https://www.timesofisrael.com/abraham-accords-nations-get-battered-in-a-friendly-soccer-game/.

33. Abdulkhaleq Abdulla, *Twitter*, July 25, 2022, https://twitter.com/Abdulkhaleq_UAE/status/1551617228822515715.

34. David Pollock, "Forty Percent of Saudis and Emiratis Still Accept Israeli Contacts, Even Under Netanyahu," T*he Washington Institute for Near East Policy, Fikra Forum*, January 19, 2023, https://www.washingtoninstitute.org/policy-analysis/forty-percent-saudis-and-emiratis-still-accept-israeli-contacts-even-under.

35. "Two Tourists from UAE Mistakenly Arrested After Attempted Mob Hit in Tel Aviv," *The Times of Israel*, August 3, 2022, https://www.timesofisrael.com/liveblog_entry/two-tourists-from-uae-mistakenly-arrested-after-attempted-mob-hit-in-tel-aviv/.

36. Ali Younes, "Israel to Open Office for Renewable Energy in Abu Dhabi," *Al Jazeera*, November 27, 2015, https://www.aljazeera.com/news/2015/11/27/israel-to-open-office-for-renewable-energy-in-abu-dhabi.

37. Taylor Heyman, "Amir Hayek Appointed Israel's First Permanent Ambassador to the UAE," *The National*, July 25, 2021, https://www.thenationalnews.com/mena/2021/07/25/amir-hayek-appointed-israels-first-ambassador-to-the-uae/.

38. Shireena Al Nowais, "Who is Mohamed Al Khaja, the UAE's First Ambassador to Israel?," *The National*, February 15, 2021, https://www.thenationalnews.com/uae/government/who-is-mohamed-al-khaja-the-u-a-e-s-first-ambassador-to-israel-1.1166426.

39. Ian Black, "Just Below the Surface: Israel, the Arab Gulf States and the Limits of Cooperation," LSE Middle East Center, p. 13, http://eprints.lse.ac.uk/100313/7/JustBelowtheSurface.pdf.

40. Kristian Coates-Ulrichsen, *Israel and the Arab Gulf States: Drivers and Directions of Change. Rice University's Baker Institute for Public Policy.* https://scholarship.rice.edu/handle/1911/92693

41. Tony Blair Institute for Global Change, "Assessing Israel's Trade with its Arab Neighbors," August 2018, https://institute.global/advisory/assessing-israels-trade-its-arab-neighbours.

42. "The UAE and Israel: A Warm Peace", April 2022, https://www.uae-embassy.org/sites/default/files/inline-files/UAE%20Embassy_Abraham%20Accords_April%202022.pdf.

43. Katherine Bauer, "Israeli – UAE Economic Cooperation Has Deep Roots and Broad Dividends," *Caravan, The Washington Institute for Near East Policy*, March 8, 2022, https://www.washingtoninstitute.org/policy-analysis/israel-uae-economic-cooperation-has-deep-roots-and-broad-dividends.

44. Ibid.

45. Mazal Mualem, "Israel Uneasy with a Deal Granting UAE Control Over Pensions," *Al-Monitor*, December 16, 2022, https://www.al-monitor.com/originals/2022/12/israel-uneasy-deal-granting-uae-control-over-pensions.

46. Ibid.

47. Rori Donaghy, "Falcon Eye: The Israeli-Installed Mass Civil Surveillance System of Abu Dhabi," *Middle East Eye*, February 28, 2015, https://www.middleeasteye.net/news/falcon-eye-israeli-installed-mass-civil-surveillance-system-abu-dhabi.

48. Dana Priest, Craig Timberg, and Souad Mekhennet, "Private Israeli Spyware Used to Hack Cell Phones of Journalists, Activists Worldwide," *The Washington Post*, July 18, 2021, https://www.washingtonpost.com/investigations/interactive/2021/nso-spyware-pegasus-cellphones/.

49. "Israel Defense Ministry Slashes Cyber Export List, Drops Saudi Arabia, UAE," *CTech*, November 25, 2021, https://www.calcalistech.com/ctech/articles/0,7340,L-3923361,00.html.

50. Mario Ledwith and Oliver Wright, "Agents Sweep Boris Johnson's Phone After 'Hack on No 10'," *The Times*, April 19, 2022, https://www.thetimes.co.uk/article/boris-johnsons-phone-is-checked-after-downing-street-targeted-by-hackers-d79xzgjh2.

51. Robert Mason, *Foreign Policy in Saudi Arabia and the United Arab Emirates: Foreign Policy and Strategic Alliances in an Uncertain World* (Manchester: Manchester University Press, 2023).

52. Andrew England and Simeon Kerr, "The Abu Dhabi Royal at the Heart of UAE Business and National Security," *Financial Times*, January 25, 2021, https://www.ft.com/content/ce09911b-041d-4651-9bbb-d2a16d39ede7.

53. UAE – Israel Business Council, https://www.uaeisraelbusiness.com/.

54. Hadeel Al Sayegh and Steven Scheer, "Israeli Tech's 'Thirst' for UAE Cash Must Overcome Old Enmity," *Reuters*, August 27, 2020, https://www.reuters.com/article/us-israel-emirates-investment-idUSKBN25N0PN.

55. "UAE Sets up $10 Billion Fund to Invest in Israel," *Arab News*, March 11, 2021, https://www.arabnews.com/node/1823961/middle-east.

56. Eyal Bino, "Is Israel the Next Silicon Valley," *Forbes*, October 21, 2021, https://www.forbes.com/sites/eyalbino/2021/10/21/is-israel-the-next-silicon-valley/?sh=5c93e46177f8.

57. Ismail Sebugwaawo, "New Initiative to Raise $100 Million for Startups in UAE, Israel," *Khaleej Times*, March 25, 2022, https://www.khaleejtimes.com/uae/new-initiative-to-raise-100-million-for-startups-in-uae-israel.

58. Salim Tamari, "Israel to Advance Four Annexation Schemes, Possible UAE Funding for 'Silicon Wadi,'" Institute for Palestinian Studies, January 28, 2021, https://www.palestine-studies.org/en/node/1650952.

59. Barak Ravid, "Scoop: Saudis Tried to Stop UAE-Israel-Jordan Solar Energy Deal," *Axios*, November 24, 2021, https://www.axios.com/saudis-uae-solar-farm-israel-d836a165-b901-4cc7-a929-377555784ec6.html.

60. Kristin Smith Diwan, "Abraham Accords Face Early Test," Arab Gulf States Institute in Washington, May 24, 2021, https://agsiw.org/abraham-accords-face-early-test/.

61. Barak Ravid, "Exclusive: The Secret Drone Deal That Created an Israel-UAE Rift," *Axios*, February 12, 2019, https://www.axios.com/secret-drone-deal-israel-uae-iran-netanyahu-mbz-48caa235-1ed8-45fe-b691-b9bd41223ebb.html.

62. "Emirates has Security Links with Israel," UPI, January 27, 2012, https://www.upi.com/Defense-News/2012/01/27/Emirates-has-security-links-with-Israel/73471327687767/#:~:text=Jan.%2027%2C%202012%20%2F%201%3A09%20PM%20Emirates%20%27has,Israel%20to%20protect%20its%20oil%20fields%20and%20borders.

63. Black, "Just Below the Surface: Israel, The Arab Gulf States and the Limits of Cooperation," 13.

64. James Rothwell, "Dozens of Afghan Women Rescued from Kabul in First Ever Israeli-Emirati Aid Mission," *The Telegraph*, September 16, 2021, https://www.telegraph.co.uk/world-news/2021/09/16/dozens-afghan-women-rescued-kabul-first-ever-israeli-emirati/.

65. Chyrine Mezher, "UAE's First Air Defense Missile to be Used on German Oerlikon Skynex," *Breaking Defense*, February 24, 2021, https://breakingdefense.com/2021/02/uaes-first-air-defense-missile-to-be-used-on-german-oerlikon-skynex/.

66. Alexander Cornwell and John Irish, "Exclusive: Israel to Sell Air Defence System to United Arab Emirates," *Reuters*, September 23, 2022, https://www.reuters.com/world/middle-east/exclusive-israel-sell-air-defence-system-united-arab-emirates-sources-say-2022-09-22/.

67. "An Enduring Partnership: The US-UAE Defense and Security Relationship," 5–6.

68. "Israel Offers UAE Security, Intelligence Support After Deadly Houthi Attack," *Reuters*, January 18, 2022, https://www.reuters.com/world/middle-east/israel-offers-uae-security-intelligence-support-after-deadly-houthi-attack-2022-01-18/.

69. Jacob Magid, "How Israel Came to the UAE's Aid After 2022 Houthi Missile Strikes," *The Times of Israel*, May 9, 2023, https://www.timesofisrael.com/how-israel-came-to-the-uaes-aid-after-the-2022-houthi-missile-strikes.

70. Rory Miller and Harry Verhoeven, "Overcoming Smallness: Qatar, the United Arab Emirates and Strategic Realignment in the Gulf," *International Politics*, 57 (2020): 1–20.

71. "Sheikh Mohammed bin Zayed's Inspirational Vision for a Post-Oil UAE," *The National*, 2022, https://www.thenationalnews.com/opinion/sheikh-mohammed-bin-zayed-s-inspirational-vision-for-a-post-oil-uae-1.8710.

72. "Bennett Cheers 'Groundbreaking' Abraham Accords on 1-Year Anniversary," September 17, 2021, https://www.timesofisrael.com/bennett-cheers-groundbreaking-abraham-accords-on-1-year-anniversary/.

73. Hagar Shezaf and Noa Landau, "Netanyahu 'Betrayed Our Trust': Settler Leaders Criticize UAE Deal Blocking Annexation," *Haaretz*, August 13, 2020, https://www.haaretz.com/israel-news/.premium-netanyahu-betrayed-us-settler-leaders-criticize-uae-deal-blocking-annexation-1.9071007.

74. Khalid S. Almezaini, "UAE Aid to Palestine," in *The UAE and Foreign Policy: Foreign Aid, Identities and Interests* (London: Routledge, 2012), 128.

75. "The UAE Makes Additional Contribution of AED 95 Million to UNRWA, Fulfilling its Pledge of AED 184 Million for 2019," *UNRWA, Reliefweb*, December 19, 2019, https://reliefweb.int/report/occupied-palestinian-territory/uae-makes-additional-contribution-aed-95-million-unrwa#:~:text=The%20United%20Arab%20Emirates%20(UAE,the%20Near%20East%20(UNRWA).

76. United Nations Relief and Works Agency for Palestine Refugees in the Near East, "The United Arab Emirates Generously Heeds UNRWA's Call for Urgent Support: US $20 Million for the Humanitarian Response in Gaza," October 15, 2023, https://www.unrwa.org/newsroom/news-releases/united-arab-emirates-generously-heeds-unrwa%E2%80%99s-call-urgent-support; Agencies, "UAE Allocates $5 Million to Support UNRWA's Gaza Reconstruction Efforts," *Times of Israel*, February 3,

2024, https://www.timesofisrael.com/liveblog_entry/uae-allocates-5-million-to-support-unrwas-gaza-reconstruction-efforts/.

77. Khiam Al Amir, "UAE Supports 'Amalthea Fund' for Humanitarian Response in Gaza with $15 Million," *Gulf News*, April 10, 2024, https://gulfnews.com/uae/government/uae-supports-amalthea-fund-for-humanitarian-response-in-gaza-with-15-million-1.1712778405371.

78. Neri Zilber, "The Talented Mr Dahlan," *New Lines Magazine*, November 11, 2020, https://newlinesmag.com/reportage/the-talented-mr-dahlan/.

79. Abdulkhaleq Abdulla, November 3, 2022, https://twitter.com/abdulkhaleq_uae/status/1588215615323623430?s=43&t=V-WhbgQRPFyDPt5Vw2c71w.

80. The Economist, "A Vision for the Palestinians After the War," October 30, 2023, https://www.economist.com/middle-east-and-africa/2023/10/30/a-vision-for-the-palestinians-after-the-war.

81. Ibid; Jack Khoury and Noa Landau, "Palestinians Slam 'Betrayal' by UAE in Deal with Israel: 'Reward of the Occupation's Crimes,'" *Haaretz*, August 13, 2020, https://www.haaretz.com/israel-news/.premium-plo-official-lashes-out-at-uae-for-selling-out-palestinians-in-israel-agreement-1.9071095.

82. Jonathan Shamir, "No More Arab States Will Normalize Ties with Israel, Netanyahu Gov't 'Embarrassed' UAE, Emirati Analyst Warns," *Haaretz*, May 22, 2023, https://www.haaretz.com/israel-news/2023-05-22/ty-article/.premium/netanyahu-govt-hampering-arab-normalization-efforts-emirati-analyst-says/00000188-4408-dc2a-a798-f59b9cb50000.

83. Georges Malbrunot reporting via Twitter, August 1, 2023, https://twitter.com/Malbrunot/status/1686361848646430720.

84. Rachna Uppal, "UAE, After Israel-Gaza Conflict, Says it Does Not Mix Trade with Politics," *Reuters*, October 10, 2023, https://www.reuters.com/world/middle-east/uae-after-israel-gaza-conflict-says-it-does-not-mix-trade-with-politics-2023-10-10/.

85. William Wechsler, "Dispatch from Abu Dhabi: Do the Israelis Know About the Basus War?," *Atlantic Council*, October 18, 2023, https://www.atlanticcouncil.org/blogs/new-atlanticist/dispatch-from-abu-dhabi-do-the-israelis-know-about-the-basus-war/.

86. Al Jazeera, "Jordan Says it Won't Sign Energy and Water Exchange Deal with Israel," *Al Jazeera,* November 16, 2023, https://www.aljazeera.com/amp/news/2023/11/16/jordan-says-it-will-not-sign-energy-and-water-exchange-deal-with-israel.

87. Rebecca Anne Proctor, "UAE Ramps Up Diplomacy Following Israel-Hamas Conflict," *Al-Monitor*, May 27, 2021, https://www.al-monitor.com/originals/2021/05/uae-ramps-diplomacy-following-israel-hamas-conflict.

88. Hussain Abdul-Hussain, "Blinken Should Invite Kuwait to Join Abraham Accords," *The National Interest*, July 28, 2021, https://nationalinterest.org/blog/buzz/blinken-should-invite-kuwait-join-abraham-accords-190652.

89. "Hamas Calls for 'Plan' to Undermine Israel's Abraham Accords," *I24 News*, December 2, 2021, https://www.i24news.tv/en/news/middle-east/palestinian-territories/1638469206-hamas-calls-for-plan-to-undermine-israel-s-abraham-accords.

90. Daren Butler and Tuvan Gumrukcu, "Turkey May Suspend Ties with UAE Over Israel Deal, Erdogan Says," *Reuters*, August 14, 2020, https://www.reuters.com/article/us-israel-emirates-turkey-idUSKCN25A0ON.

91. John Mason, "Qatar Continues its Principled Rejection of the Abraham Accords as Anti-Palestinian," *Arab America,* October 20, 2021, https://www.arabamerica.com/qatar-continues-its-principled-rejection-of-the-abraham-accords-as-anti-palestinian/.

92. AP, "What are the 13 Demands Given to Qatar?," *Gulf News,* June 23, 2017, https://gulfnews.com/world/gulf/qatar/what-are-the-13-demands-given-to-qatar-1.2048118.

93. Interview with Michael Knights, Jill and Jay Bernstein Fellow of the Washington Institute for Near East Policy, May 25, 2021.

94. Discussion with a senior UAE official who asked not to be named, January 19, 2021.

95. Omri Nahmias and Aaron Reich, "Bahrain, UAE Condemn 'Terrorist Operation' Shooting in Tel Aviv," *The Jerusalem Post*, April 8, 2022, https://www.jpost.com/breaking-news/article-703585.

96. "Several Attacked as Jerusalem Mob Chants 'Death to Arabs', 6 Arrested," *The Times of Israel*, April 20, 2022, https://www.timesofisrael.com/police-arrest-6-in-jerusalem-on-assault-charges-mob-chants-death-to-arabs/.

97. Adam Lucente, "UAE, Saudi, Others Condemn Israeli Minister's Visit to Jerusalem Holy Site," *Al-Monitor*, January 3, 2023, https://www.al-monitor.com/originals/2023/01/uae-saudi-others-condemn-israeli-ministers-visit-jerusalem-holy-site.

98. Jacob Magid, "UN Security Council Slated to Meet on Widely Decried Temple Mount Visit by Ben Gvir," *The Times of Israel*, January 4, 2023, https://www.timesofisrael.com/un-security-council-slated-to-meet-on-widely-decried-temple-mount-visit-by-ben-gvir/.

99. Michelle Nichols, "No UN Vote Monday on Israel Settlements, Diplomats Say," *Reuters*, February 19, 2023, https://www.reuters.com/world/middle-east/no-un-vote-monday-israel-settlements-diplomats-2023-02-19/.

100. Robert Mason, "Revitalized Interactions Between the Gulf and Indonesia," *Middle East Institute*, February 10, 2022, https://www.mei.edu/publications/revitalized-interactions-between-gulf-and-indonesia.

101. Adnan Abu Amer, "How Malaysia is Becoming Hamas' Gateway to Asia," *Al-Monitor*, December 18, 2019, https://www.al-monitor.com/originals/2019/12/kuala-lumpur-summit-hamas-diplomatic-ties.html.

102. Magdi El-Gizouli, "Sudan's Normalization with Israel: In Whose Interests?," *Arab Reform Initiative*, August 17, 2021, https://www.arab-reform.net/publication/sudans-normalization-with-israel-in-whose-interests/.

103. Rina Bassist, "Is Oman Next in Line to Normalize Relations with Israel?," *Al-Monitor,* August 17, 2020, https://www.al-monitor.com/originals/2020/08/israel-united-arab-emirates-oman-bahrain-mauritania-sudan.html.

104. "Islamic Republic of Mauritania and Israel," GlobalSecurity.org, https://www.globalsecurity.org/military/world/africa/mr-forrel-is.htm.

105. The White House, "Proclamation on Recignizing The Sovereignty of the Kingdom of Morocco Over The Western Sahara," December 10, 2020, https://trump-whitehouse.archives.gov/presidential-actions/proclamation-recognizing-sovereignty -kingdom-morocco-western-sahara/.

REFERENCES

Abdul-Hussain, Hussain, "Blinken Should Invite Kuwait to Join Abraham Accords," *The National Interest*, July 28, 2021, https://nationalinterest.org/blog/buzz/blinken -should-invite-kuwait-join-abraham-accords-190652.

Abdulla, Abdulkhaleq, *Twitter*, July 25, 2022, https://twitter.com/Abdulkhaleq_UAE /status/1551617228822515715.

Abdulla, Abdulkhaleq, *Twitter*, November 3, 2022, https://twitter.com/abdulkhaleq _uae/status/1588215615323623430?s=43&t=V-WhbgQRPFyDPt5Vw2c71w.

Abu Amer, Adnan, "How Malaysia is Becoming Hamas' Gateway to Asia," *Al-Monitor*, December 18, 2019, https://www.al-monitor.com/originals/2019/12/ kuala-lumpur-summit-hamas-diplomatic-ties.html.

Agencies, "UAE Allocates $5 Million to Support UNRWA's Gaza Reconstruction Efforts," *Times of Israel*, February 3, 2024, https://www.timesofisrael.com/liveblog _entry/uae-allocates-5-million-to-support-unrwas-gaza-reconstruction-efforts/.

Al Amir, Khiam. "UAE Supports 'Amalthea Fund' for Humanitarian Response in Gaza with $15 Million," *Gulf News*, April 10, 2024, https://gulfnews.com/uae/ government/uae-supports-amalthea-fund-for-humanitarian-response-in-gaza-with -15-million-1.1712778405371.

Al Jazeera, "Jordan Says it Won't Sign Energy and Water Exchange Deal with Israel," *Al Jazeera*, November 16, 2023, https://www.aljazeera.com/amp/news/2023/11/16 /jordan-says-it-will-not-sign-energy-and-water-exchange-deal-with-israel.

Almezaini, Khalid S., "UAE Aid to Palestine," in *The UAE and Foreign Policy: Foreign Aid, Identities and Interests* (London: Routledge, 2012), 116–138.

Al Nowais, Shireena, "Who is Mohamed Al Khaja, the UAE's First Ambassador to Israel?," *The National*, February 15, 2021, https://www.thenationalnews.com/ uae/government/who-is-mohamed-al-khaja-the-uae-s-first-ambassador-to-israel-1 .1166426.

Al Sayegh, Hadeel, and Steven Scheer, "Israeli Tech's 'Thirst' for UAE Cash Must Overcome Old Enmity," *Reuters*, August 27, 2020, https://www.reuters.com/ article/us-israel-emirates-investment-idUSKBN25N0PN.

AP, "What are the 13 Demands Given to Qatar?," *Gulf News*, June 23, 2017, https://gulfnews.com/world/gulf/qatar/what-are-the-13-demands-given-to-qatar-1 .2048118.

Arab News, "UAE Sets up $10 Billion Fund to Invest in Israel," *Arab News*, March 11, 2021, https://www.arabnews.com/node/1823961/middle-east.

Barrington, Lisa, "UAE Says it Has Stopped Taking Part in US-led Maritime Coalition," *Reuters*, May 31, 2023, https://www.reuters.com/world/middle-east/uae -says-it-withdrew-us-led-maritime-coalition-two-months-ago-2023-05-31/#.

Bassist, Rina, "After IAEA Criticizes Iran, Israeli Prime Minister Meets with Emirati Leader," *Al-Monitor*, June 9, 2022, https://www.al-monitor.com/originals/2022/06/after-iaea-criticizes-iran-israeli-prime-minister-meets-emirati-leader.

Bassist, Rina, "Is Oman Next in Line to Normalize Relations with Israel?," *Al-Monitor*, August 17, 2020, https://www.al-monitor.com/originals/2020/08/israel-united-arab-emirates-oman-bahrain-mauritania-sudan.html.

Bauer, Katherine, "Israeli – UAE Economic Cooperation Has Deep Roots and Broad Dividends," *Caravan, The Washington Institute for Near East Policy*, March 8, 2022, https://www.washingtoninstitute.org/policy-analysis/israel-uae-economic-cooperation-has-deep-roots-and-broad-dividends.

BBC News, "UAE Pardons Israeli Woman Who Faced Life in Prison," *BBC News*, March 26, 2023, https://www.bbc.com/news/world-middle-east-65080918.

BDS National Committee, "UAE Dictatorship Sells Out Palestinian Rights Through Agreement with Israel," August 14, 2020, https://bdsmovement.net/news/uae-dictatorship-sells-out-palestinian-rights-through-agreement-with-israel.

Belmonte, Nerea, "UAE and Israel Sign "Historic" Tourism Agreement," *Atalayar*, February 11, 2022, https://atalayar.com/en/content/uae-and-israel-sign-historic-tourism-agreement.

"Bennett Cheers 'Groundbreaking' Abraham Accords on 1-Year Anniversary," *The Times of Israel*, September 17, 2021, https://www.timesofisrael.com/bennett-cheers-groundbreaking-abraham-accords-on-1-year-anniversary/.

Bino, Eyal, "Is Israel the Next Silicon Valley," *Forbes*, October 21, 2021, https://www.forbes.com/sites/eyalbino/2021/10/21/is-israel-the-next-silicon-valley/?sh=5c93e46177f8.

Bishara, Hakim, "Dozens of Arab Artists Boycott UAE for Normalization Deal With Israeli Government," September 22, 2020, https://hyperallergic.com/588922/uae-israel-normalization-open-letter-boycot/.

Black, Ian, "Just Below the Surface: Israel, the Arab Gulf States and the Limits of Cooperation," LSE Middle East Center, p. 13, http://eprints.lse.ac.uk/100313/7/JustBelowtheSurface.pdf.

Butler, Daren, and Tuvan Gumrukcu, "Turkey May Suspend Ties with UAE Over Israel Deal, Erdogan Says," *Reuters*, August 14, 2020, https://www.reuters.com/article/us-israel-emirates-turkey-idUSKCN25A0ON.

Chandrasekaran, Rajiv, "In the UAE, the United States has a Quiet, Potent Ally Nicknamed "Little Sparta"," *The Washington Post*, November 9, 2014, https://www.washingtonpost.com/world/national-security/in-the-uae-the-united-states-has-a-quiet-potent-ally-nicknamed-little-sparta/2014/11/08/3fc6a50c-643a-11e4-836c-83bc4f26eb67_story.html.

Ciorciari, John D., and Jürgen Haacke, "Hedging in International Relations: An Introduction," *International Relations of the Asia-Pacific*, 19(3) (September 2019): 367–374.

Kristian Coates-Ulrichsen, *Israel and the Arab Gulf States: Drivers and Directions of Change. Rice University's Baker Institute for Public Policy. https://scholarship.rice.edu/handle/1911/92693*

Corder, Josh, "250,000 Israel Tourists Visit UAE Since Abraham Accords," *Hotelier*, October 17, 2021, https://www.hoteliermiddleeast.com/news/250000-israel-tourists-visit-uae-since-abraham-accords.

Cornwell, Alexander, and John Irish, "Exclusive: Israel to Sell Air Defence System to United Arab Emirates," *Reuters*, September 23, 2022, https://www.reuters.com /world/middle-east/exclusive-israel-sell-air-defence-system-united-arab-emirates -sources-say-2022-09-22/.

Crook, Lizzie, "David Adjaye Designs Trio of Multifaith Temples in Abu Dhabi," *Dezeen*, September 26, 2019, https://www.dezeen.com/2019/09/26/david-adjaye -the-abrahamic-family-house-temples-abu-dhabi-architecture/.

CTech, "Israel Defense Ministry Slashes Cyber Export List, Drops Saudi Arabia, UAE," *CTech*, November 25, 2021, https://www.calcalistech.com/ctech/articles/0 ,7340,L-3923361,00.html.

Diwan, Kristin Smith, "Abraham Accords Face Early Test," *Arab Gulf States Institute in Washington*, May 24, 2021, https://agsiw.org/abraham-accords-face-early-test/.

Donaghy, Rori, "Falcon Eye: The Israeli-Installed Mass Civil Surveillance System of Abu Dhabi," *Middle East Eye*, February 28, 2015.

The Economist, "A Vision for the Palestinians After the War," October 30, 2023, https://www.economist.com/middle-east-and-africa/2023/10/30/a-vision-for-the -palestinians-after-the-war.

El-Gizouli, Magdi, "Sudan's Normalization with Israel: In Whose Interests?," *Arab Reform Initiative*, August 17, 2021, https://www.arab-reform.net/publication/ sudans-normalization-with-israel-in-whose-interests/.

"Emirates has Security Links with Israel," *UPI*, January 27, 2012, https://www .upi.com/Defense-News/2012/01/27/Emirates-has-security-links-with-Israel /73471327687767/#:~:text=Jan.%2027%2C%202012%20%2F%201%3A09 %20PM%20Emirates%20%27has,Israel%20to%20protect%20its%20oil%20fields %20and%20borders.

England, Andrew, and Simeon Kerr, "The Abu Dhabi Royal at the Heart of UAE Business and National Security," *Financial Times*, January 25, 2021, https://www .ft.com/content/ce09911b-041d-4651-9bbb-d2a16d39ede7.

Entous, Adam, "Donald Trump's New World Order," *The New Yorker*, June 11, 2018, https://www.newyorker.com/magazine/2018/06/18/donald-trumps-new -world-order.

Estrin, Daniel, "Israeli Tourism Ministry Warns Against Discussing Sensitive Topics with UAE Citizens," *NPR*, November 30, 2020, https://www.npr.org/2020/11 /30/940122963/israeli-tourism-ministry-warns-against-discussing-sensitive-topics -with-uae-citi.

Heersink, Boris, and Jeffrey A. Jenkins, "The Republican Party is White and Southern. How Did That Happen?," *The Washington Post*, February 7, 2020, https:// www.washingtonpost.com/politics/2020/02/07/republican-party-is-white-southern -how-did-that-happen/.

Heyman, Taylor, "Amir Hayek Appointed Israel's First Permanent Ambassador to the UAE," *The National*, July 25, 2021, https://www.thenationalnews.com/mena /2021/07/25/amir-hayek-appointed-israels-first-ambassador-to-the-uae/.

Hill, Christopher, "Foreign Policy in International Relations," *Foreign Policy in the Twenty-First Century* (New York: Palgrave Macmillan, 2016).

Hilterman, Joost, "Is the Middle East's Makeover a Mirage?," *Foreign Affairs*, August 1, 2023, https://www.foreignaffairs.com/united-states/middle-easts-makeover-mirage.

"Hamas Calls for 'Plan' to Undermine Israel's Abraham Accords," *I24 News*, December 2, 2021, https://www.i24news.tv/en/news/middle-east/palestinian-territories/1638469206-hamas-calls-for-plan-to-undermine-israel-s-abraham-accords.

Indyk, Martin, *Twitter*, October 24, 2020, https://twitter.com/Martin_Indyk/status /1320072707833270274.

International Institute for Strategic Studies, "Understanding GCC Policy: Perspectives on the US Strategic Partnership," September 13, 2022, https://www.youtube .com/watch?v=PISmbQ9V7uA&list=PL06gBmITAMbcSmZjs3BKkEPxEWfX _J8pt&index=5.

"Islamic Republic of Mauritania and Israel," GlobalSecurity.org, https://www.globalsecurity.org/military/world/africa/mr-forrel-is.htm.

Kassis, Marita, "UAE Schools Will Now Teach Holocaust in National Curriculum," *Al-Monitor*, January 9, 2023, https://www.al-monitor.com/originals/2023/01/uae -schools-will-now-teach-holocaust-national-curriculum?amp.

Khoury, Jack, and Noa Landau, "Palestinians Slam 'Betrayal' by UAE in Deal with Israel: 'Reward of the Occupation's Crimes,'" *Haaretz*, August 13, 2020, https:// www.haaretz.com/israel-news/.premium-plo-official-lashes-out-at-uae-for-selling -out-palestinians-in-israel-agreement-1.9071095.

Ledwith, Mario, and Oliver Wright, "Agents Sweep Boris Johnson's Phone After 'Hack on No 10,'" *The Times*, April 19, 2022, https://www.thetimes.co.uk/article/boris-johnsons-phone-is-checked-after-downing-street-targeted-by-hackers-d79xzgjh2.

Lucente, Adam, "UAE Reports Slight Growth of Non-Oil GDP," *Al-Monitor*, April 20, 2022, https://www.al-monitor.com/originals/2022/04/uae-reports-slight -growth-non-oil-gdp#:~:text=The%20non%2Doil%20sector%20contribution ,Emirates%20News%20Agency%20reported%20Tuesday.

Lucente, Adam, "UAE, Saudi, Others Condemn Israeli Minister's Visit to Jerusalem Holy Site," *Al-Monitor*, January 3, 2023, https://www.al-monitor.com/originals /2023/01/uae-saudi-others-condemn-israeli-ministers-visit-jerusalem-holy-site.

Lustick, Ian S., "The Absence of Middle Eastern Great Powers: Political 'Backwardness' in Historical Perspective," *International Organization*, 51(4) (Autumn 1997): 653–683.

Magid, Jacob, "How Israel Came to the UAE's Aid After 2022 Houthi Missile Strikes," *The Times of Israel*, May 9, 2023, https://www.timesofisrael.com/how -israel-came-to-the-uaes-aid-after-the-2022-houthi-missile-strikes.

Magid, Jacob, "UN Security Council Slated to Meet on Widely Decried Temple Mount Visit by Ben Gvir," *The Times of Israel*, January 4, 2023, https://www .timesofisrael.com/un-security-council-slated-to-meet-on-widely-decried-temple -mount-visit-by-ben-gvir/.

Malbrunot, Georges, reporting via Twitter, August 1, 2023, https://twitter.com/Malbrunot/status/1686361848646430720.

Mason, John, "Qatar Continues its Principled Rejection of the Abraham Accords as Anti-Palestinian," *Arab America*, October 20, 2021, https://www.arabamerica.com/ qatar-continues-its-principled-rejection-of-the-abraham-accords-as-anti-palestinian/.

Mason, Robert, *Foreign Policy in Saudi Arabia and the United Arab Emirates: Foreign Policy and Strategic Alliances in an Uncertain World* (Manchester: Manchester University Press, 2023).

Mason, Robert, "Revitalized Interactions Between the Gulf and Indonesia," *Middle East Institute*, February 10, 2022, https://www.mei.edu/publications/revitalized -interactions-between-gulf-and-indonesia.

Mason, Robert, "Small State Aspirations to Middle Powerhood: The Cases of Qatar and the UAE," in *Unfulfilled Aspirations: Middle Power Politics in the Middle East*, ed. Adham Saouli (London: Hurst/Oxford University Press, 2020), 157–183.

Mezher, Chyrine, "UAE's First Air Defense Missile to be Used on German Oerlikon Skynex," *Breaking Defense*, February 24, 2021, https://breakingdefense.com/2021 /02/uaes-first-air-defense-missile-to-be-used-on-german-oerlikon-skynex/.

Miller, Rory, and Harry Verhoeven, "Overcoming Smallness: Qatar, the United Arab Emirates and Strategic Realignment in the Gulf," *International Politics*, 57 (2020): 1–20.

Mualem, Mazal, "Israel Uneasy with a Deal Granting UAE Control Over Pensions," *Al-Monitor*, December 16, 2022, https://www.al-monitor.com/originals/2022/12/ israel-uneasy-deal-granting-uae-control-over-pensions.

Nahmias, Omri, and Aaron Reich, "Bahrain, UAE Condemn 'Terrorist Operation' Shooting in Tel Aviv," *The Jerusalem Post*, April 8, 2022, https://www.jpost.com /breaking-news/article-703585.

Nichols, Michelle, "No UN Vote Monday on Israel Settlements, Diplomats Say," *Reuters*, February 19, 2023, https://www.reuters.com/world/middle-east/no-un -vote-monday-israel-settlements-diplomats-2023-02-19/.

Pollock, David, "Forty Percent of Saudis and Emiratis Still Accept Israeli Contacts, Even Under Netanyahu," *The Washington Institute for Near East Policy, Fikra Forum*, January 19, 2023, https://www.washingtoninstitute.org/policy-analysis/ forty-percent-saudis-and-emiratis-still-accept-israeli-contacts-even-under.

Priest, Dana, Craig Timberg and Souad Mekhennet, "Private Israeli Spyware Used to Hack Cell Phones of Journalists, Activists Worldwide," *The Washington Post*, July 18, 2021, https://www.washingtonpost.com/investigations/interactive/2021/ nso-spyware-pegasus-cellphones/.

Proctor, Rebecca Anne, "UAE Ramps Up Diplomacy Following Israel-Hamas Con-flict," *Al-Monitor*, May 27, 2021, https://www.al-monitor.com/originals/2021/05/ uae-ramps-diplomacy-following-israel-hamas-conflict.

Ravid, Barak, "Exclusive: The Secret Drone Deal That Created an Israel-UAE Rift," *Axios*, February 12, 2019, https://www.axios.com/secret-drone-deal-israel-uae-iran -netanyahu-mbz-48caa235-1ed8-45fe-b691-b9bd41223ebb.html.

Ravid, Barak, "Scoop: The Real Reason Netanyahu didn't go to the UAE in Janu-ary," *Axios*, March 1, 2023, https://www.axios.com/2023/03/01/reason-netanyahu -uae-visit-postponed.

Ravid, Barak, "Scoop: Saudis Tried to Stop UAE-Israel-Jordan Solar Energy Deal," *Axios*, November 24, 2021, https://www.axios.com/saudis-uae-solar-farm-israel -d836a165-b901-4cc7-a929-377555784ec6.html.

Reuters, "Israel May Halt Flights to Dubai Over Security Arrangements," *Reuters*, February 6, 2022, https://www.reuters.com/world/middle-east/israel-may-halt -flights-dubai-over-security-arrangements-2022-02-06/.

Reuters, "Israel Offers UAE Security, Intelligence Support After Deadly Houthi Attack," *Reuters*, January 18, 2022, https://www.reuters.com/world/middle-east/israel-offers-uae-security-intelligence-support-after-deadly-houthi-attack-2022-01-18/.

Roberts, David, "Ontological Security and the Gulf Crisis," *Journal of Arabian Studies*, 10(2) (2021): 221–237.

Rothwell, James, "Dozens of Afghan Women Rescued from Kabul in First Ever Israeli-Emirati Aid Mission," *The Telegraph*, September 16, 2021, https://www.telegraph.co.uk/world-news/2021/09/16/dozens-afghan-women-rescued-kabul-first-ever-israeli-emirati/.

Saouli, Adham, "Middling or Meddling? Origins and Constraints of External Influence in the Middle East," in *Unfulfilled Aspirations: Middle Power Politics in the Middle East*, ed. Adham Saouli (New York: Oxford University Press, 2020).

Sebugwaawo, Ismail, "New Initiative to Raise $100 Million for Startups in UAE, Israel," *Khaleej Times*, March 25, 2022, https://www.khaleejtimes.com/uae/new-initiative-to-raise-100-million-for-startups-in-uae-israel.

"Several Attacked as Jerusalem Mob Chants 'Death to Arabs', 6 Arrested," *The Times of Israel*, April 20, 2022, https://www.timesofisrael.com/police-arrest-6-in-jerusalem-on-assault-charges-mob-chants-death-to-arabs/.

Shamir, Jonathan, "No More Arab States Will Normalize Ties with Israel, Netanyahu Gov't 'Embarrassed' UAE, Emirati Analyst Warns," *Haaretz*, May 22, 2023, https://www.haaretz.com/israel-news/2023-05-22/ty-article/.premium/netanyahu-govt-hampering-arab-normalization-efforts-emirati-analyst-says/00000188-4408-dc2a-a798-f59b9cb50000.

"Sheikh Mohammed bin Zayed's Inspirational Vision for a Post-Oil UAE," *The National*, 2022, https://www.thenationalnews.com/opinion/sheikh-mohammed-bin-zayed-s-inspirational-vision-for-a-post-oil-uae-1.8710.

Shezaf, Hagar, and Noa Landau, "Netanyahu 'Betrayed Our Trust': Settler Leaders Criticize UAE Deal Blocking Annexation," Haaretz, August 13, 2020, https://www.haaretz.com/israel-news/.premium-netanyahu-betrayed-us-settler-leaders-criticize-uae-deal-blocking-annexation-1.9071007.

Sison, Michele J., "UAE Minimizing Influence of Islamic Extremists," November 10, 2004, https://wikileaks.org/plusd/cables/04ABUDHABI4061_a.html.

Surkes, Sue, "Abraham Accords Nations Get Battered – in a Friendly Soccer Game," *Times of Israel*, March 30, 2022, https://www.timesofisrael.com/abraham-accords-nations-get-battered-in-a-friendly-soccer-game/.

Tamari, Salim, "Israel to Advance Four Annexation Schemes, Possible UAE Funding for 'Silicon Wadi'," *Institute for Palestinian Studies*, January 28, 2021, https://www.palestine-studies.org/en/node/1650952.

Tony Blair Institute for Global Change, "Assessing Israel's Trade with its Arab Neighbors," August 2018, https://institute.global/advisory/assessing-israels-trade-its-arab-neighbours.

Trump White House, "Peace to Prosperity: A Vision to Improve the Lives of the Palestinian and Israeli People," January 2020, https://trumpwhitehouse.archives.gov/wp-content/uploads/2020/01/Peace-to-Prosperity-0120.pdf.

"Two Tourists from UAE Mistakenly Arrested After Attempted Mob Hit in Tel Aviv," *The Times of Israel*, August 3, 2022, https://www.timesofisrael.com/live-blog_entry/two-tourists-from-uae-mistakenly-arrested-after-attempted-mob-hit-in -tel-aviv/.

"The UAE and Israel: A Warm Peace," April 2022, https://www.uae-embassy .org/sites/default/files/inline-files/UAE%20Embassy_Abraham%20Accords_April %202022.pdf.

"The UAE Makes Additional Contribution of AED 95 Million to UNRWA, Fulfilling its Pledge of AED 184 Million for 2019," *UNRWA, Reliefweb*, December 19, 2019, https://reliefweb.int/report/occupied-palestinian-territory/uae-makes-additional -contribution-aed-95-million-unrwa#:~:text=The%20United%20Arab%20Emir-ates%20(UAE,the%20Near%20East%20(UNRWA).

"UAE Diplomat Says 'Irreversible' Progress to Palestinian State Needed for Gaza Reconstruction," *Reuters*, February 12, 2024, https://www.reuters.com/world/ middle-east/uae-diplomat-says-irreversible-progress-palestinian-state-needed-gaza -2024-02-12/.

UAE – Israel Business Council, https://www.uaeisraelbusiness.com/.

United Nations Relief and Works Agency for Palestine Refugees in the Near East, "The United Arab Emirates Generously Heeds UNRWA's Call for Urgent Support: US $20 Million for the Humanitarian Response in Gaza," October 15, 2023, https:// www.unrwa.org/newsroom/news-releases/united-arab-emirates-generously-heeds -unrwa%E2%80%99s-call-urgent-support.

Uppal, Rachna, "UAE, After Israel-Gaza Conflict, Says it Does Not Mix Trade with Politics," *Reuters*, October 10, 2023, https://www.reuters.com/world/middle-east /uae-after-israel-gaza-conflict-says-it-does-not-mix-trade-with-politics-2023-10 -10/.

US-UAE Business Council Report, "An Enduring Partnership: The US-UAE Defense and Security Relationship," February 2023, https://usuaebusiness.org/wp-content/ uploads/2023/02/Final-Defense-Report-2023.pdf.

Wamda, "Microsoft Invests $1.5 Billion in UAE's G42 for Minority Stake," April 16, 2024, https://www.wamda.com/2024/04/microsoft-invests-1-5-billion-uaes -g42-minority-stake.

Wechsler, William, "Dispatch from Abu Dhabi: Do the Israelis know about the Basus War?," *Atlantic Council*, October 18, 2023, https://www.atlanticcouncil.org/blogs /new-atlanticist/dispatch-from-abu-dhabi-do-the-israelis-know-about-the-basus -war/.

The White House, "Proclamation on Recignizing The Sovereignty of the Kingdom of Morocco Over The Western Sahara," December 10, 2020, https://trumpwhitehouse .archives.gov/presidential-actions/proclamation-recognizing-sovereignty-kingdom -morocco-western-sahara/.

Younes, Ali, "Israel to Open Office for Renewable Energy in Abu Dhabi," *Al Jazeera*, November 27, 2015, https://www.aljazeera.com/news/2015/11/27/israel-to-open -office-for-renewable-energy-in-abu-dhabi.

Zilber, Neri, "The Talented Mr Dahlan," *New Lines Magazine*, November 11, 2020, https://newlinesmag.com/reportage/the-talented-mr-dahlan/.

Chapter 5

Bahrain and Israel

Elusive Amity

Banafsheh Keynoush

The Abraham Accords signed at the White House on September 15, 2020, enabled the Kingdom of Bahrain to extend a hand of friendship to the State of Israel. But large segments of Bahraini society did not support the accords, and attempts to characterize it as a treaty of amity were challenging from the start. Normalization between Bahrain and Israel, it was soon clear, was an elusive amity despite the two countries' efforts to encourage people-to-people and inter-governmental contacts.[1]

Above all, the Bahraini-Israeli normalization process encouraged an "economy first" model to help the two sides monetize their budding relations. This model enabled Bahrain to maintain a generally quietist political stance on the Palestinian-Israeli conflict despite being a member of the Arab League, a body that frequently denounced Israel over its treatment of Palestinians. Bahrain's stance made it a participant in pan-Arab initiatives in Palestine without having to disturb Manama's ties with Israel.

CONDITIONING FACTORS IN BAHRAINI-ISRAELI NORMALIZATION

Prior to the signing of the Abraham Accords, by supporting a pan-Arab discourse on Palestine in the Arab League as well as through the Gulf Cooperation Council (GCC), Bahrain appeased public opinion at home that might have otherwise renounced the Al Khalifa over a friendship with Israel. The Al Khalifa, the Sunni founding fathers of modern Bahrain, ruled over a by-and-large pro-Palestinian population and faced opposition from Bahrain's majority Shia population which along with segments of Bahrain's Sunni community opposed the normalization with Israel.

Due to its polarized society, Bahrain was profoundly impacted by Saudi Arabia's failed attempts to advance three Arab-Israeli peace initiatives that attempted to restore the full rights of Palestinians, that is, the 1981 Fahd Plan, the 1989 Ta'if Agreement, and the 2002 Arab Peace Initiative (also known as the Arab Peace Plan or the Abdullah Plan). These initiatives came with the possibility that Arab states might recognize Israel. But when the Fahd Plan and Ta'if Agreement collapsed, two major Palestinian uprisings or Intifadas ensued in the early 1990s. Bahrain's next steps to appease its population failed, including a 2001 National Action Charter to end popular uprisings stemming partly from the Arab-Israeli tensions.

Bahrain slowly opened up to the idea of publicly working with Israel, and joining the Abraham Accords, after Israel and the United Arab Emirates (UAE) first normalized their ties. Before then, Manama took its lead from the Kingdom of Saudi Arabia on the issue of Israel. Riyadh meanwhile, having failed to advance peace for the Palestinians, welcomed increased US commitment to building security in the Middle East region which ultimately led to more GCC engagement with Israel and the Abraham Accords.

A speedy exchange of ambassadors between Bahrain and Israel after the Abraham Accords spoke of a spirit of amity that emerged between the two countries and which came through a partnership that evolved in public sight. At the people-to-people level, polls showed signs of a modest opening to the idea of normalization in Bahraini society by 2021, although some 62 percent of the population disagreed with the notion that doing business with Israel was justifiable. The polls showed a public desire to resolve the Palestinian conflict as well.[2] Support for the normalization of ties with Israel remained low in Bahrain, according to the Arab Barometer of 2022.[3] Other polls in 2022 showed that only 23 percent of Bahrainis believed the accords had a positive impact on the region of the Middle East.[4]

Whether Bahrain received Saudi Arabia's blessing to formalize its ties with Israel was not publicly known at the time of the signing of the accords. Riyadh's support for Manama joining the accords may have been forthcoming to the extent that it helped Bahrain to ensure its survival as a small Gulf state in a volatile region by cooperating with Israel in the security sphere and to keep up with the UAE which quickly embraced ties with Israel. Through Bahrain, Saudi Arabia could then indirectly have a say in the direction that the accords took. Meanwhile, Israeli officials publicly expressed a desire to build an open partnership with Saudi Arabia as well.[5]

Manama's modest security impact on Gulf regional affairs, and a reputation as a facilitator of regional security rather than as an agitator, suggested that it could safely join the Abraham Accords without inviting conflict. By joining the accords, Bahrain boosted its economic interests, expanded its regional investment center capacity, and became a security hub through critical partnerships with Saudi Arabia, Israel, and the United States. Meanwhile, the normalization of relations between Bahrain and Israel entailed stronger defense, military, and intelligence cooperation between the two states, although Manama continued to stress the "economy first" aspect of the ties irrespective of new security deals. Bahrain's delicate internal balancing act to boost state security internally by adopting a bandwagon policy through an intelligence partnership with Israel helped boost its standing as a small state with strong foreign partners.[6]

But whether a deep paradigm shift occurred in Bahraini society toward embracing Israel was debatable, and Manama's quick decision to condemn Hamas for attacking Israel on October 7, 2023 (October War), and also to sever economic ties with Israel after the subsequent outbreak of the conflict into Gaza, pointed to the fragility of the Abraham Accords. Moreover, tensions in Manama's ties with Iran challenged the notion that the Abraham Accords could bring about a regional paradigm shift to fully boost Bahrain's security. More specifically, Manama's perception of threat from Iran required that it contain sectarian trends internally in the wake of the accords, and more so following the October War when anti-Israeli protests spread across the Arab world. To ease the impact of potential sectarian divides inside Bahrain due to tensions with Iran and in Gaza, Manama had to weigh how well it could in fact reap the economic benefits of the Abraham Accords in order to ease a hefty public debt, one of the highest in the Gulf region, and generate wealth. Failing to obtain optimal economic results from the accords, and in light of the war in Gaza, segments of the Bahraini population remained restive.[7]

The economic and defense-layered security partnerships that Manama openly built through the Abraham Accords, however, served to advance Arab coexistence with Jews, boost Israel's influence in the Persian Gulf waterway and the Indian Ocean, and enable better protection against Iranian threats. But these partnerships triggered Iran to continually threaten navigation in the Gulf waterway. They may have also inadvertently encouraged some de-escalation to happen in the region, including the resumption of diplomatic relations with Tehran by Riyadh after they broke off in 2016. The renewed Saudi-Iranian relations served to signal to Iran that the GCC including Bahrain was not seeking escalation. Iran's actions to challenge the accords and safe navigation meanwhile stalled the emergence of a strong geopolitical paradigm shift in the form of a permanent alignment against it by Bahrain and Israel.

Meanwhile, the Abraham Accords fell into the bracket of the classic security dilemma. By joining the Abraham Accords, Bahrain risked losing the very security it achieved by remaining relatively neutral in regional conflicts. Neutrality in international relations generally offered small states a survival option, and Bahrain's departure from it posed an existential threat to the kingdom if the accords were to be seriously challenged down the road by Iran or an Iranian-backed internal Bahraini opposition, or due to an unresolvable war in Gaza. The fact that Bahrain joined the accords meant that it was betting on building amity with Israel as a better alternative to the practice of political quietism toward the issue of ties with the Jewish state, despite the many ambiguities generated by joining the accords. But Bahrain faced more risks than it could readily address, by embracing a stronger US-Israeli security paradigm for the Gulf region through the accords while Manama itself failed to fully contain Iranian threats or contribute to an end to the war in Gaza.[8]

Taken in this context, Bahrain's elusive amity with Israel within the framework of the Abraham Accords was a critical option but not without its challenges. To start with, the accords emphasized state-centric security, premised on realist theory that carries a bias against small states like Bahrain and instead looks at how to grant key regional roles only to middle powers including Iran and Israel and to major powers such as the United States.[9] More importantly, to the extent that realistic idealism defined the emerging relations between Bahrain and Israel, by aiming to bridge two cultures and people, the ideational power required to build such cultural ties seemed to lag behind the material power that was leading to stronger security contacts between the two countries. In Bahrain, speaking about the Abraham Accords was frowned upon in the public sphere, despite the fact that a core leadership philosophy encouraged the pragmatic aspect of normalized ties with Israel including enhanced security for the Gulf state.[10]

Against this backdrop, applying the Aberystwyth or Welsh School to the evolving Israeli-Bahraini ties proved challenging. The school, a component of critical security studies, calls for the overhaul of international relations theory to include social transformation. Manama's difficult ties with Sunni Islamist groups and its majority Shia population, and the split loyalty among members of this latter community between Bahrain and a transnational Shia community, meant that the accords could not be used by them to build sufficient social capital to ensure a smoother Israeli-Bahraini partnership. Rather, it appeared that Bahrain could not part from state-centric realist calculations that plainly focused on building security through a partnership with Israel. At best, the Bahraini government could hold on to the elusive hope that through this partnership it might eventually alleviate the human and sectarian dimension of its security concerns resulting from a decision to normalize the ties with Israel.[11]

A critical securitization theory could therefore only go so far by way of problem-solving for Bahrain and the prospects for its relations with Israel. Critical theories assess how existing social institutions build security. This reality in turn necessitates a factual definition of the meaning of the Abraham

Accords for Bahrain and Israel. The two countries' relations evolved mainly along realist lines to build joint Bahraini and Israeli offensive and defensive capabilities as realism in international relations theory would prescribe for nations, in order to prepare for a changing world order while the United States planned to reduce its presence in the Middle East during and after the Obama administration. But with the social component of the Bahraini-Israeli ties challenged, the Welsh School would criticize realism for its traditional state-centric security approach if Manama deprived the same security that it sought by working with Israel for others, including not only the disgruntled Bahraini Shias but also Palestinians and their Bahraini Sunni patrons.[12]

Because the Abraham Accords emphasize building people-to-people relations, a new framework of analysis for security is needed to examine the Bahraini-Israeli ties, one that retains a state-centric security focus through the prism of realist theory without precluding critical theory's focus on the social fabric of security. Otherwise, the mere absence of segments of a population or their opposition to the accords could pose challenges to normalized ties between Bahrain and Israel. The more marginalized these groups of Bahraini society are, the harder Bahrain's ruling elite has to work to perpetuate and sustain the momentum of the accords.

Herein rests the puzzle of Bahrain's attempt to build up its security through the accords. Bahrain opted to sustain its survival in a volatile region through the Abraham Accords rather than accumulate power on its own, which as a small state it did not possess the capability for in a manner to be able to compete with larger regional powers like Iran. As such, any security that Bahrain aimed to achieve by normalizing its ties with Israel remained a variable of the larger regional trends that would be shaped by the rivalries among the Gulf's middle regional powers, including Israel and Iran, and external powers such as the United States.

Bahrain's gradual mastery of its imperfect but constant internal and external balancing act since the Arab Spring suggested that shifting regional geopolitical trends would not pose an immediate challenge to the country. However, this prediction could fail to materialize if Bahrain's security rested on external protection without a strong security base at home. Bahrain's relatively fragmented social fabric, a mosaic of locally marginalized communities, could in fact disturb the country's internal security in the face of a powerful region-wide security challenge. The prospect of this potential security meltdown for Bahrain, premised in part on the idea of 'consequentialism', meant that the country's security could then depend on the consequences of the steps it took to securitize the Bahraini political and societal landscape. Furthermore, it could also depend on Bahrain's ability to ease tight security measures internally through a series of de-securitization and democratization policies, the outcomes of which could be affected by internal opposition to an Israeli-Bahraini partnership. This in turn could yield better or worse security results for Bahrain depending on the state of the Gulf region's volatile environment and how well this small Gulf state, being a beneficiary of the securitization induced by the accords, could then ensure internal security.[13]

Translated into a wider sphere of staggered practice by Manama to engage with marginalized communities in Bahrain, especially after the Arab Spring, security for this Gulf Arab state was not possible by entirely precluding Shias or Sunni Islamists from the accords. Such preclusion could only add to the problem of the Bahraini elite seeking security simply to identify and manage existing threats, without necessarily mitigating the problem unless through state-centric security practices that could divide its population. The Paris School of security studies, which insisted that new security challenges would emerge by precluding others, therefore applied to the case study of Bahrain and the normalization of its ties with Israel.[14]

If the Abraham Accords were to carry clear security guarantees for Bahrain and Israel, both countries would be required to engage with the uncomfortable contradictions and moral dilemmas of their choices in the security sphere, and only then could real amity between them emerge. The following sections examine and assess how well they fared in this regard since the Arab Spring, to build and ensure security, promote socioeconomic policies, and strengthen leadership to sustain the accords, following a brief introductory history.

BAHRAINI-ISRAELI RELATIONS BEFORE THE ARAB SPRING

Bahraini Jews constitute one of the smallest communities in the world. In the twelfth century, the Jewish adventurer Benjamin Tatlili mentioned some 500 Jews living in a location by the name of Gheis and another 5,000 in Al Qatif, modern-day Saudi Arabia, running the area's pearl industry. In the nineteenth century, around 1880, there are recorded histories of Jewish traders from Iraq, Fars, and India visiting Bahrain in search of economic opportunities. A smaller number of Jews settled in Bahrain from Iran around the same period, as Bahrain under the Al Khalifa fell under British protectorate territories and separated from Iran between 1868 and 1892.[15]

The formation of an independent Jewish state in 1948 led to anti-Semitic riots in Bahrain. On December 5, 1948, the outbreak of violence in Palestine led to a public backlash against the Jewish community in Bahrain, leading some to leave for Bombay (now Mumbai) and then for Israel, and only less than 300 Jews remained in the country according to a census in 1950. The Arab-Israeli wars of 1956 and 1967 (which led Bahrain to back an Arab oil embargo on Israel), and the September 1978 Camp David Accords signed between Egypt and Israel, did little to change hearts toward Israel in Bahrain. Meanwhile, the Bahraini Jewish population had declined to about 50 Jews when Bahrain (known as Mishmahig or the fourteenth Province in Iran) remained an administrative division of Iran until 1971. But Bahrain kept a Jewish cemetery, and it rebuilt its standing synagogue in the 1980s. The synagogue opened to welcome the Abraham Accords, as did public Jewish worshipping ceremonies. The Bahraini Jews remained financially successful, and they were represented as religious minorities in 2001 and onward in the National Assembly's upper house of the Consultative or Shura Council which was established in the 1930s.[16]

Before the accords, Bahrain was impacted by Saudi Arabia's failed attempts to advance three Arab-Israeli peace initiatives that could restore the full rights of Palestinians, that is, the 1981 Fahd Plan, the 1989 Ta'if Agreement, and the 2002 Arab Peace Initiative (also known as the Arab Peace Plan or the Abdullah Plan). As Israeli-Palestinian tensions mounted in the early 1990s, leading to two major Palestinian uprisings or Intifadas, unrest brewed in Bahrain. Manama had revisited its position on Israel in November 1989 in order to improve ties with the Jewish state, during the time that Saudi Arabia helped Lebanon end its civil war (from 1975 to 1990) and finalize the Ta'if Agreement. Bahrain, along with Saudi Arabia, may have hoped that the Ta'if Agreement would potentially lead to Arab recognition of Israel if Palestinian rights were restored. The agreement demanded that Israel return Arab-occupied lands in southern Lebanon it had infringed to contain military operations of the Palestinian Liberation Organization in 1977–1978. In a second full invasion of southern Lebanon in 1982, Israel carried out plans leading to the occupation of entire areas in southern Lebanon by 1985. However, it refused to return the occupied lands, and Washington refused to help uphold the Ta'if Agreement.

Manama could not expect to normalize ties with Israel and simultaneously appease Bahrain's vocal pro-Palestinian Sunni dissidents and its majority Shia population. The breakdown of the Ta'if Agreement, in fact, led to the violent eruption of sect-based conflicts in southern Lebanon that triggered numerous other forms of unrest across the Arab world. Both Riyadh and Manama viewed these developments with trepidation because of their struggles to control Saudi and Bahraini Shias and dissident Sunnis.

Iraq's invasion of Kuwait in late 1990 polarized the Arab world once again. Some Palestinians may have briefly hoped that the Iraqi dictator Saddam Hussein would reemerge as a potential strong leader for the Arab world, especially after the Iraqi army launched missiles at Israel. The US-led and Saudi-funded coalition to end the Gulf War in 1991, however, quickly repelled Iraqi troops from Kuwait, and it would eventually build international momentum to end the Israeli-Palestinian conflict at the Madrid Conference held late in the year. The two main sides to the conflict, that is, the Israelis and Palestinians, agreed to maintain a dialogue that finally led to the Oslo Accords in 1993. This dialogue led to the creation of the Palestinian National Authority (PA) to conduct limited self-governance over the West Bank and the Gaza Strip, which received Gulf financial aid. Bahraini societies and religious groups offered financial donations that PA said it could not take at times especially as tensions with Hamas brewed in Gaza, but direct or under-the-radar financial flows from private Gulf citizens to Palestinians may have continued. This financial assistance was probably significant. In 2019, Hamas which moved to control Gaza in 2007 publicly hailed the people of Bahrain for this support.[17]

Meanwhile, between 1993 and 2019, Israel set up new settlements despite accepting peace with Palestinian factions. Mindful of the tensions this course of action caused in Bahraini society, Manama built a heavily centralized system of governance in order to promote top-down inclusivity and discourage divisive protests in a politicized society. Simultaneously, Manama embraced new opportunities to build up its regional ties and security. The rushed Israeli-Jordanian peace treaty and normalization in October 1994, promising both parties mutual prosperity through cooperation, led Bahrain to openly align its policies with the United States which happened to be a key broker of the latest regional peace agreement. The momentous partnership with Washington enabled Manama to boost its regional standing quickly. In 1995, the US Fifth Fleet and US Naval Forces Central Command (NAVCENT) took control of the command of US afloat units that deployed to the Gulf for extended periods following the Gulf War, based from Bahrain, while extending maritime operations to the Sea of Oman, the Gulf of Aden, and the Red Sea.

The US Navy presence in Bahrain, in place since Bahraini independence in 1971, had already turned the small country into a US military hub, making Manama's security vital to Washington. For example, it enabled Bahrain to assist US military strategy in the Gulf War (1990–1991) when Iraq invaded Kuwait, and in the Iraq War in 2003 which toppled Saddam Hussein. Saddam's ouster from power ended his divisive influence over the region and boosted Israel's regional security in which Bahrain played a part by hosting the US Fifth Fleet. Earlier, the end of the Gulf War propelled Bahrain and Israel to start a dialogue on environmental issues by 1994.[18]

The rise to power of Bahrain's new leader Hamad bin Isa Al Khalifa in 1999 occurred shortly before the 2000 Camp David Summit that brought together Israeli and Palestinian leaders, briefly offering another opening to Manama to boost its own ties with Israel, despite an ensuing Palestinian uprising known as the second Intifada. Bahrain proceeded to back the Saudi-led 2002 Arab Peace Initiative with Israel. Bahrain's crown prince, Salman bin Hamad Al Khalifa, met with Israeli officials during the World Economic

Forum in 2000 and 2003. President George W. Bush's call on Palestinians to elect new leaders and for a roadmap for Arab-Israeli peace eased contacts between Bahrain and Israel. In 2005, Bahrain ended the boycott of Israeli goods to comply with a free trade agreement with the United States.[19]

Hezbollah and Iran's Islamic Revolutionary Guards Corps (IRGC) attempted to stir unrest among dissident Bahrainis in the course of the ensuing Lebanese-Israeli War of 2006. In 2007, on the heels of the Annapolis Conference to normalize Arab-Israeli ties, Israeli and Bahraini delegates reportedly met during the annual gathering of the United Nations General Assembly. An official Bahraini delegation traveled to Israel that same year to return pro-Palestinian Bahraini activists held in custody after the Israeli navy seized a ship heading for the Gaza Strip despite a blockade on Hamas. In 2009, Bahrain's parliament rejected outreach to Israel. But in April, King Hamad bin Isa Al Khalifa showed support for Bahrain's Jewish community, months after the breakdown of the Arab support for Hamas and a special summit to address an Israeli offensive in Gaza. Some twenty-two members of the Arab League withdrew support for the summit that was to be held in Qatar, leaving the forum short of the required fifteen-member quorum to officially endorse the event. In 2010, Prince Salman bin Hamad Al Khalifa shook hands with Israeli president Shimon Peres at the Clinton Global Initiative in New York.[20]

BAHRAINI-ISRAELI RELATIONS AFTER ARAB SPRING

The collapse of the 2001 National Action Charter, which had aimed to strengthen constitutional rule by holding a referendum for reforms, left Bahrain with fewer options to balance its internal threats. Bahrain's Arab Spring led to a violent Day of Rage calling for reforms on February 14, 2011, pushing the island nation along with its partners Saudi Arabia and the United States to view Iran's influence in the Arab world with trepidation, sentiments that Israel shared and which drew it closer to Bahrain. On March 14, a month after the massive protests in Bahrain erupted, the country invoked a GCC security clause to invite Saudi and GCC forces to restore order under the aegis of the Peninsula Shield Force (PSF).

Meanwhile, Bahrain distributed financial payments to citizens, promoted non-sectarian policies, and introduced parliamentary political representation. But the country's fierce sectarian tensions continued until 2014. To contain this upheaval, Manama encouraged a common national identity and a collective ethos to control violence resulting from sectarian imbalances. Its security forces were deployed to preserve the public order, contain sectarian protests, and monitor potential sectarian spillover to neighboring Saudi Arabia. Iran's provocations aiming to shape the Arab Spring came through statements that aimed to boost the status of the Arab Shias in Bahrain, but it increased Bahraini-Saudi collaboration to curb the Arab Spring. For Israel, meanwhile, any major shift in the regional status quo that increased Iran's influence and ability to shape the Arab Spring was undesirable, irrespective of a brief shift in US foreign policy under the Obama administration to support the Arab Spring in Egypt.

Bahrain remained a prime target for Iran in the following years. Tehran attempted to influence the Bahraini Arab Spring through provocative statements of support for Bahraini opposition groups. The main opposition group, the Shia-led Al Wefaq, and its leader Ayatollah Isa Qasim, emerged as leaders of the Bahraini Arab Spring. The Iranian-backed Lebanese Hezbollah, meanwhile, influenced events in Bahrain by winning followers through its news networks. The IRGC and its paramilitary group, the Quds Force, operated across the Gulf region in this period to challenge the Al Khalifa.

But Hezbollah denied involvement in the Bahraini Arab Spring, although Manama charged that some leaders of the uprising had intelligence contacts with the group. Manama would proceed to deport Lebanese citizens with alleged ties to Hezbollah.[21] Iran-based media, academics, and IRGC-linked websites, meanwhile, claimed that Bahrain's uprising proved that its people did not want the Al Khalifas but wanted to be part of Iran, a pointed reminder to Manama that Bahrain had gained its full independence only after a UN referendum in 1971, prior to which it was regarded as an administrative part of Iran.[22]

Although the PSF contained the Bahraini uprising and prevented its spillover into the Shia-dominated region of the Saudi Eastern Province, it was forced to lay out new foundations for GCC security, involving unified laws and a fresh approach to emerging threats from Iran. Tehran denied being directly involved in the Bahraini Arab Spring, but the GCC proceeded to appoint a joint command staff in November 2018 and enhanced the power of its Unified Military Command.[23]

The quest for a GCC security structure reinforced a tilt among the bloc's member states (i.e., Saudi Arabia, Bahrain, Kuwait, Oman, Qatar, and the UAE) toward Israel as a potential security partner, in light of Israel's previous outreach to bloc members to contain Hezbollah prior to, during, and after the Lebanese-Israeli War.[24] Bahrain's sectarian approach to handling its internal security led to the enforcement of laws that subordinated the opposition but aimed to promote cross-sectarian and inter-faith moderation. This approach enabled Manama to keep a door open to embrace the ties with the Jewish state.

The suspension of the Shia Al Wefaq political party in 2016 made Bahrain's reconciliation with Iran challenging, after the two severed relations early that year. This in turn accelerated Bahrain's transition from a relatively marginal GCC state to one aiming to build superior capabilities by initiating ties with Israel. Unlike Qatar, which enjoyed substantial natural wealth from its abundant gas resources, Bahrain's meager natural resources and economic codependency on the GCC may have prompted Manama's decision to engage with Israel, in order to attract new economic and investment opportunities. Additionally, an opening with Israel carried the advantage of allowing Manama to expand its security posture vis-à-vis Iran. Iran's interference in Iraqi, Syrian, and Yemeni affairs after the Arab Spring, along with its support for Hamas and the Muslim Brotherhood, served to remind Manama of the need to encourage the tilt toward Israel.

BAHRAINI-ISRAELI SECURITY RELATIONS

Following the Abraham Accords, Tehran condemned Bahrain's normalization with Israel, insisting that no good would come of it by way of enhancing Gulf security or protecting Bahraini sovereignty while vowing that Bahrain would bear the consequence of the normalization deal. The IRGC directly condemned Bahrain's normalization with Israel and threatened the Bahraini monarchy which it said should await a "hard revenge" from the Quds Force, a branch of the IRGC.[25] Bahrain's Shia leaders expressed outrage over the Abraham Accords, including Ayatollah Isa Qasim's representative in Iran, Abdullah Al Daqqaq, who condemned the normalization, Abdullah Al Saleh of the Islamic Action Society (Al Amal) who spoke of popular resistance against Bahrain's decision, and a member of the Haq Movement for Liberty and Democracy, Abdul Ghani Al Khanjar, who issued warnings that the monarchy in Bahrain would collapse.[26]

Manama seemingly remained unfazed by Iranian provocations and allowed Israel overflight rights in September 2020, shortly before a bilateral steering committee meeting between Bahrain and Israel in August.[27] But to contain Tehran's exploitation of the Palestinian issue, it continued to stress that the resolution of the Israeli-Palestinian conflict along with Palestinian statehood remained key to the success of the Abraham Accords. Manama also condemned Israeli actions when violence broke out with the Palestinian protestors in the Al-Aqsa compound in April through June 2021, but remained more quietist over similar violent confrontations between Israel and Hamas that Egypt tried to put an end to in May.

Earlier in February 2021, Israel's defense minister Benjamin Gantz visited Bahrain, to sign a memorandum of understanding for intelligence and defense cooperation. In late March, Israel hosted the Negev Summit that aimed to turn into a permanent security and economic cooperation forum for Israel, Egypt,

Bahrain, Morocco, the UAE, and the United States and bring more countries on board.[28] Tehran denounced Bahrain, the UAE, Morocco, Egypt, and Israel, by calling the summit an "evil meeting."[29]

Israel's maritime projection in the Gulf waterway and the Red Sea, in collaboration with Bahrain and the UAE, remained another source of agitation between Manama and Tehran in 2021 and 2022. In August 2021, NAVCENT embarked on a multilateral maritime security operation exercise in the Red Sea along with Bahrain, Israel, and the UAE, which Israeli sources confirmed would help counter Iranian power projections in the vital waterway.[30] Israel participated in a Red Sea maritime drill alongside dozens of countries including Bahrain, the UAE, Saudi Arabia, and Oman in February 2022. The drills could help prevent the flow of Iranian arms and goods as well as oil on the high seas, thereby strangling the Iranian economy. Israel's visits to the US Fifth Fleet Headquarters in Bahrain spoke of expanded cooperation with the GCC to contain potential Iranian threats, after Iranian drone activities picked up in the Gulf waterway.[31]

In February 2022, a subsidiary of Israel Aerospace Industries known as BATS said it would sell radars and anti-drone systems to Bahrain.[32] That same month, senior Bahraini diplomat Abdullah bin Ahmed Al Khalifa confirmed at the Munich Security Conference that the Israeli intelligence agency Mossad was active in Bahrain.[33] The statement endorsed what Iran feared, that Israel was advancing its intelligence operations in the Gulf region and closer to Iranian borders.

In July 2022, Israel again said that it would sell anti-drone systems to Bahrain, according to reports, helping the Gulf state embark on a new phase of security as the Iranian drone technology rapidly expanded.[34] On July 15, Prince Salman bin Hamad took part in the Jeddah Security and Development Summit, a gathering of the GCC along with Egypt, Iraq, and the United States. Israeli drones were simultaneously seen flying over the Bahraini airspace, while Israel's Shin Bet internal security services reportedly trained Bahraini intelligence officers as the Biden administration forwarded a Middle East Air Defense plan with Israel and Saudi Arabia, highlighting some 150 meetings between Israeli defense officials and their Arab counterparts since the signing of the Abraham Accords.[35] The meetings were expected to help integrate Bahrain's air defense system with Israel's Iron Dome anti-missile system, after Bahrain applied to buy the system from its new partner in March 2022, which along with the Green Pine radar system and Arrow system could defend against ballistic missiles that Iran was rapidly developing.[36]

In addition, Bahrain bought F-16 airplanes from the United States that it would receive by 2024. In October 2022, Israeli paratroopers and soldiers from Bahrain, the UAE, and the United States held a joint jump over in the island nation.[37] In December, Bahrain's new foreign minister, Abdul Latef Al

Zayani, insisted that his country would look forward to working with Netanyahu after his reelection as prime minister.[38] Israel and Bahrain extended their discussions to include cooperation in cyber security and the defense industries. Manama's Cyber Leaders Forum held in December was preceded by measures to enable Israel's defense industries to operate in Bahrain. The discussions involved creating a "cyber Iron Dome" after Iranian hackers leaked the personal details of more than 300,000 Israeli travelers.[39]

ECONOMIC DRIVERS OF
BAHRAINI-ISRAELI RELATIONS

The idea of building strong economic ties between the Gulf region and Israel was explored in the 1990s, with a series of international peace initiatives aimed at normalizing Arab-Israeli relations. But trade missions were controlled, and they shut down after the Palestinian Intifada, although a level of indirect trade took place that helped build early contacts in the technology sector. Israel's interest in the high-return markets of the Gulf region, where Bahrain served as an investment hub, and possible gas exports from Israel to the Gulf aimed to strengthen these initiatives.

To speed up normalization after the Abraham Accords, Israel's minister of economy and industry Eli Cohen was invited to the Entrepreneurship Congress and the Startup Nations Ministerial Conference in Bahrain in April 2019. But leaked information covering private discussions, and security concerns after an outcry in Bahrain against Israeli participation, led Israel to cancel the visit.[40] In 2020, Israel announced a $220 million trade goal with Bahrain in the non-defense sectors.[41] However, efforts by Israel's Embassy in Manama to grow business contacts were stalled due to local opposition to the accords, despite outreach efforts to prominent Bahraini business communities and traders, and other measures to encourage Israeli-Palestinians to engage in entrepreneurial initiatives in Bahrain.[42]

In February 2022, Bahrain and Israel signed a technology and science cooperation agreement, followed by a deal on health and medical innovation and research. In August, Bahraini and Israeli organizations signed an agreement for cooperation in fintech.[43] But a new economic pole shaping between Bahrain and Israel was still to come as a result of the Abraham Accords. The BDS movement, founded in 2005, and its Gulf Group condemned Bahrain's willingness to import goods from Israeli settlements built on Palestinian lands in December 2020 and expressed confidence that Bahraini citizens would not purchase such products.[44]

Meanwhile, the trade volume between Bahrain and Israel stood at approximately less than US$7.5 million in 2021.[45] Israel exported US$3.81 million to Bahrain in 2021. Bahrain exported US$3.5 million to Israel.[46] While levels of optimal regional trade were yet to be achieved, liberalization patterns encouraging free trade promised the transformation of Bahrain's markets. In February 2022, Prime Minister Naftali Bennett visited Bahrain to agree on a ten-year plan dubbed "The Joint Warm Peace Strategy" aiming to expand bilateral relations in innovation, food and water security, healthcare, trade and investment, and education. In June, Israeli Foreign Ministry director general Alon Ushpiz traveled to Manama to initiate the warm peace strategy.[47]

Bahrain's economic diversification to scale down the share of oil and gas from more than 40 percent to less than 20 percent of revenues meant that manufacturing, financial service, and tourism sectors had to thrive through partnerships with Israel. As a producer of raw aluminum and iron ore, the industrial sector received US$4.3 billion in foreign direct investment, and, through the Negev Summit of June 2022, Bahrain said it would build joint industrial projects to generate employment and protect against volatile international markets.[48]

In 2022, talks to build a new free trade deal promised to facilitate commerce between Bahrain and Israel.[49] In October, the two signed a deal on agriculture, livestock, and food production.[50] Israel helped Start-Up Nation Central in Bahrain spur business ties. Finance Minister Avigdor Lieberman and Minister of Commerce and Industry Zayed Al Zayani worked jointly to build new economic deals.[51] These steps kept the Abraham Accords on track despite political concerns in Bahrain over its ties with Israel and the receding popularity of the accords. According to polls, the popularity of the accords stood at 20 percent in March 2022, compared to 45 percent in November 2020.[52]

Bahrain took additional steps to support Back 2 Business meetings for trade and industrial cooperation, when minister of trade Al Zayani traveled to Israel in October 2022. That same month, the two countries discussed cooperation in petrochemicals. A water sustainability project shaped to help Bahrain's loss of its treasured water resources and to boost the potential for collaboration and rehabilitation projects on both sides. A desalination deal to this end was helping supply Bahrain with needed water and expanding ocean and marine conservation water management.

Bahrain merged its economic interests with other emerging trade blocs in the wake of the accords, by connecting to the US-backed Israel, India, and the UAE West Asia Quad trade and investment source that served as an alternative to the China Belt and Road Initiative. Aided by tourism and flights to and from Bahrain and Israel, an emerging Indian-Arabian-Mediterranean trade route would serve to connect Bahrain to wider markets.[53] In April 2022, India and the GCC had exchanged trade data and explored concluding a trade pact. In September, Saudi Arabia and India discussed a rupee-riyal trade to boost economic ties, which could facilitate commerce with Bahrain where the Saudi riyal was readily exchanged into dinar.[54]

A visit by President Isaac Herzog to Bahrain in December 2022 led to discussions about aiding Bahrain's growing economy, and meetings with the Bahraini public sector, business communities, and the Economic Development Board. Bahrain's subsidized and low-cost operational business capacity attracted Israeli startups and tech companies, financial technologies, information and communication technologies, and manufacturing.[55] In March 2023, Bahrain and Israel signed an agreement to develop human capital and exchanged views in a Connect2Innovate forum in Manama.

LEADERSHIP AND SOCIAL FACTORS IMPACTING BAHRAINI-ISRAELI RELATIONS

Before the Abraham Accords, Manama relied on numerous grassroots societies to support its policies. The Abraham Accords, however, aligned many Bahraini groups in voicing opposition to the normalization of ties with Israel. This is at least according to information that websites claiming to oppose the accords provide, but official Bahraini government news sites generally do not discuss. As a result, this author could not find a credible way to independently verify information collected on numerous websites, except to collect as many sources as possible to show some of the debates shaping among Bahrainis against the accords.

A few facts emerged showing that opposition to the accords was widespread among social groups. These included members of the Bahraini Muslim Brotherhood (some of whom may have retained ties with Hamas), founded in 1941 and renamed Jamiyaat al-Islah or Reform Society in 1948, which helped consolidate central power in Manama by often criticizing overt manifestations of non-Bahraini identities by the Bahraini Shias or Arab nationalists. In 2002, it set up its political wing known as the Jamiyyat al-Minbar al-Watani al-Islami (al-Minbar National Islamic Society, or al-Minbar), mainly representing the Hawala tribe of elite merchants. Al-Minbar engaged in political activities and was represented in the Bahraini parliament, supporting Manama and its regional security outlook well through the Arab Spring. But the Bahraini parliament's inclusive representation eroded following the Arab Spring. Meanwhile, the political wing of al-Minbar was marginalized in Bahrain's parliamentary elections after 2014, making room for Bahrain's al-Asalah al-Islamiyya (Al-Asalah Islamic Society), a Salafi organization set up in 2002 that attracted support from poorer communities and conservative Sunni tribes from Muharraq and Riffa and naturalized Bahrainis, and which was linked with the Saudi quietist Salafis who avoided challenging government policies. In so doing, the society stood opposed to the Bahraini Shia Al Wefaq National Islamic Society, although it would at times join forces with it in demanding social reforms.[56]

Meanwhile, Bahraini Shias led the public opposition to Bahrain's normalization of ties with Israel. At the public level, there was no strong momentum for the ties, it being questioned frequently by Bahrainis including government employees. Al Wefaq questioned the legitimacy of the Al Khalifa and Israel, and its leader Ayatollah Isa Qasim warned Bahrainis against a Judaization plot.[57] As sporadic protests erupted in Bahrain to oppose the accords, more than 240 Bahraini Shia clerics signed a statement rejecting the normalization of ties with the "Zionist enemy" in reference to Israel. Al-Asalah and al-Minbar, as well as Bahrain's National Unity Coalition, expressed outrage when Israel opened its embassy in Manama in September 2021.[58]

Bahrain's revolutionary youth coalition insisted that the Al Khalifa did not constitute the nation of Bahrain, while hashtags circulated for Bahrainis against normalization. The Islamic Amal of Bahrain called the Abraham Accords a betrayal. The Bahraini Society Against Normalization with the Zionist Enemy, founded in 2001, expressed surprise when it learned about the accords, and the absence of state-civil society debates over the issue of normalization. In September 2022, the society's General Assembly postponed its meeting until further notice, following government orders, after expressing doubt that the accords could help advance Bahraini security and backing the twenty-four-member organizations constituting the Bahraini National Initiative Against Normalization in forwarding demands that Israel's ambassador be expelled. The initiative represented a host of civil society and professional groups opposed to the accords.[59]

The Society Against Normalization with Zionist Enemy condemned the accords and called for a stop to the annexation of Palestinian territories, and noted that the policy of Judaizing Palestinian territories and expelling residents from their homes increased after the normalization, while insisting that the people of Bahrain continued to support Palestinian resistance until the liberation of their entire national territory.[60]

Bahrain's tensions with Iran over the Abraham Accords directly affected Bahraini society. Tehran claimed that to silence dissent against the Abraham Accords, Bahrain, and the United States frequently hyped the Iranian threat, which Manama would then use to silence dissidents but with great difficulty and at great risk to its own security. In December 2020, the US State Department designated one of many Iranian-backed Bahraini Shia groups, the Saraya Al Mokhtar, a terrorist organization. At least three members of the group had died at sea attempting to travel to Iran in 2018. As early as 2014, the group had posted a vague threat on social media to attack US military personnel in Bahrain.[61] In 2019, the Katibat Al Haydariyah with links to Iran reemerged on social media to threaten new attacks in Bahrain. The group may have served as an alias for the Saraya Al Ashtar or Al Ashtar Brigades, the Iranian-backed Shia opposition movement inside Bahrain that used the alias name Saraya Waad Allah which threatened to attack a meeting between an Israeli delegation and Bahrainis, forcing the latter to cancel the event in return for a secret gathering. Washington would proceed to sanction individuals for supporting the Al Ashtar Brigades in March 2024.[62]

Iranian financial operations in Bahrain were also of concern. In August 2021, for example, Iran denounced Bahrain's Higher Criminal Court ruling against Iranian banks, to control the flow of money between Iran and the Gulf state, after the court charged the Central Bank of Iran and other Iranian banks of money laundering and fining them 19 million Bahraini Dinars, while confiscating an approximate sum of $1.3 billion it claimed was laundered money.[63] This latest move, labeled by Bahrain as the country's biggest money laundering bust, came on the heels of similar cases that revealed close commercial, trade, social, and political connections between Iran and Bahraini citizens and opposition networks. Still, Iran claimed its assets were being unlawfully taken. In July 2022, an international tribunal using UNCITRAL (United Nations Commission on International Trade Law) arbitration rules awarded EUR 243 million plus interest to the Bank Melli Iran and Bank Saderat Iran by finding Bahrain in breach of its obligations against unlawful expropriation under an agreement with Iran on the reciprocal promotion and protection of investments that dated back to October 2002.[64]

Bahrain meanwhile remained cautious so as not to be seen by Tehran as plotting against it with Israel. In November 2020, Bahrain condemned the killing of chief Iranian nuclear scientist Mohsen Fakhrizadeh, which Tehran blamed on Israel. Manama urged all sides to show restraint, in an effort to prevent the breakout of conflict in the region in which it would inevitably be squared in.[65] But that same month, Manama also proceeded to sentence fifty-one people linked to IRGC terror plots against the Gulf state.[66]

To control the internal opposition to the Abraham Accords, in November 2021, Bahrain arrested several militants ahead of an attack, carrying weapons that had come from Iran. Tehran denied involvement with the militants, despite the fact that neighboring Kuwait had also just arrested eighteen people on charges of providing financial support to Hezbollah.[67] Meanwhile, Manama issued a royal decree on October 23, 2022, amending the internal regulation of the Bahraini Council of Representatives to reduce the powers of the members of parliament and their potential opposition to the accords. Bahrain's forty-member Majlis Al Nuwab (Council of Representatives) parliamentary elections of November 2022 were hailed by its monarchy for marking a 70 percent turnout, but rights groups criticized it for barring the outlawed Al Wefaq and the leftist National Democratic Action Society

(Waad), both of which were dissolved in 2017, from nominating candidates to participate.[68]

In addition, Bahrain vowed to build up its partnership with Israel following Netanyahu's electoral victory in November 2022, despite Israel's embrace of its most right-wing government.[69] In response, and in exile, Ayatollah Isa Qasim retained his clerical networks inside Iran and Iraq, condemned Manama's outreach to Israel, expressed concern about attempts to turn Bahrain into an Israeli outpost, and continued to issue provocative statements to mark the February 14 uprising of Bahrainis in 2011.[70]

Clearly, the definition of security for Bahrain following the Abraham Accords extended to citizen-level debates about its ties with Iran. At the grassroots level, the two countries were culturally and linguistically connected. Hence, a campaign was shaping on both sides of the Gulf in Bahrain and Iran to compromise the security of the other through social pressure after the Abraham Accords. This was an area that Israel had far less control over, except perhaps through intelligence gathering that it could potentially offer Manama in order to help it guide the national Bahraini dialogue in favor of normalization.

For its part, Iran keenly exploited Bahraini vulnerabilities, by offering refuge to Bahraini Shias stripped of their citizenships. Since many Bahrainis left their homeland without passports or identifications to enter Iran and reside in the country, the exact number of those working with Tehran was unknown, although the Israeli Pegasus spyware developed by the NSO Group was reportedly used in Bahrain in the past several years to hack conversations and monitor citizens. Meanwhile, Iran's positions on Israel and the Iranian pro-Hamas stance pressured Bahrain which in turn advanced a dialogue forum for coexistence that involved collaboration with the UAE to fight terrorism under the GCC umbrella.

Iran repeatedly reacted to Bahrain promoting positions against it and attempts to frame Iranian provocations as acts of terrorism, and said it was an excuse Manama exploited in order to build up its ties with Israel. As in the past, Bahrain was careful not to invite Iran's anger, this time over the issue of terrorism, by appearing one-sided in its condemnation of terrorist acts. In October 2022, for example, Manama condemned a terrorist attack targeting an Iranian religious shrine in Shiraz, which took place in the midst of nationwide anti-government protests in Iran.[71]

Deemed an attraction for Bahraini Shia tourists, Iranian shrines and their protection remained a sensitive topic in Manama as it attempted to appease Shia dissent inside Bahrain. Mindful of Bahraini sensitivities to this issue, Iran pointed out the importance of Manama holding an inclusive national dialogue that would entail restoring damaged religious sites in the Gulf state. According to Tehran, the destruction of these sites by Manama happened as a result of an ongoing Bahraini revolution that had lasted eleven years since the Arab Spring and forced dissidents into silence.[72]

To retaliate against these Iranian provocations, anonymous online groups launched campaigns to support the latest anti-government protests in Iran that shaped in September 2022 after the death of an Iranian-Kurdish woman, Mahsa Amini, in police custody. These campaigns encouraged Iranian dissidents to cooperate with countries like Bahrain and Saudi Arabia through shared grievance groups such as the Citizens for Bahrain, arguing that condemnation of Iranian crackdown was not enough and more needed to be done to topple the Iranian regime.[73]

On both sides, it was clear that Iran and Bahrain were keen to encourage a Spring, an Arab Spring and a Persian-style Spring respectively, and it was a matter of time which happened sooner and in whose favor. Israel's role in this social web was crucial, as it not only helped boost Bahraini security but also sabotaged Iranian security infrastructure and backed anti-regime protests against Tehran. Bahrain's insistence on upholding Palestinian rights helped protect the island nation against Iran as well, which charged the Gulf Arab state of failing to protect the Palestinians. Israel's willingness to ignore Bahrain's refusal to fully abandon the Palestinian cause meant that the issue was not a defining point in the accords, as Iran may have hoped. Rather, Israel believed that the security and economic dialogue generated by the Abraham Accords was enough to justify the normalization of ties with Bahrain.

Meanwhile, the mutual hatred and paranoia that Manama and Tehran bred at the grassroots level exacerbated numerous unresolved conflicts between them. Iranian websites claimed that Bahraini Shias had friendly ties with Sunni Bahrainis except those that followed the Wahhabi sect, and that friendly Sunnis participated in Shia ceremonies, suggesting that opposition to Manama and its pro-Israeli policies was on a much wider scale that transcended the sect. This opposition seemed to brew in a large network of groupings with names borrowed from similar opposition movements in the Middle East that Iran backed and which highlighted the transnational nature of the Bahraini opposition.

Some of these Bahraini Shia groups—such as the Hezbollah of Bahrain, Islamic Front for the Liberation of Bahrain IFLB (dismantled after a Shia uprising in the 1990s), and Sacred Defense Bahrain or the al jibha al islamiya altahrir al Bahrain that started operating following the Iranian Islamic Revolution of 1979—aimed to overthrow the Al Khalifa. Other groupings included the military wing of Hezbollah Bahrain joined by several others like the February 14 Youth Coalition and Saraya al Ashtar (SaA), or the jamiyat al islamiy that receives backing from Sunnis, and the hizb al dawa al islamiya or even the Saudi Islamic Umma Party that formed in response to the Arab Spring, or the Front for Islamic Salvation of Bahrain and Hezbollah of Bahrain, all of which are seen as political organizations that include the Al Wefaq. Meanwhile, the Shia-dominated Bahraini villages of Sanabis, Sitra Island, Diraz, Al Daih, and Bani Jamra showed festering tension and conflict with Manama despite a desire by all sides to find space for dialogue.[74] In addition, a new generation of SaA directly being trained in Iran and Iraq, and organized by the Popular Mobilization Units set up by the IRGC in Iraq and other places like Yemen was reactivating cells in Bahrain.[75] Bahrain's Gulf waterway access to Iran and Iraq facilitated the regular exchange, as a result of which the Bahraini-Israeli security agreement signed in early 2022 was expected to support future military and intelligence cooperation that could potentially help contain these groups.

Irrespective of the challenges posed by these groups, however, Bahrain and Israel advanced their ties, and a Knesset delegation traveled to Manama in March 2023. The exchanges that followed aimed to ease tensions on Israel in the Middle East committee of the Inter-Parliamentary Union (IPU) that convened in Manama and was expected to condemn the anti-Palestinian decisions of the right-wing government of Prime Minister Netanyahu. It also enabled Bahrain to show its own citizens that it remained a staunch advocate for Palestinian rights. Simultaneously, the IPU was called on by the international community to urge Bahrain to protect the human rights of its citizens, especially after Manama dissolved the two main opposition groups of Al Wefaq and Wa'ad in 2016 and 2017. A visit by Israeli Foreign Ministry cadets led to meetings with Bahraini civil society groups in February 2023, in an attempt to help Manama build social connections needed to boost support for the Abraham Accords, as negative reports surfaced that Bahrain may have sold an island in the Gulf to an Israeli company and before the island nation proceeded to recall its ambassador from Israel after the October War.

CONCLUSION

Political anarchy in the Middle East resulting from the Palestinian conflict, Iranian provocations, and the Arab Spring enabled Bahrain and Israel to carve out a new path to cooperate and translate a heavily securitized outlook on their relations into practical measures aimed at building an emerging partnership. Bahrain's efforts to use the Abraham Accords to build statecraft also aimed to reduce domestic conflicts. However, by precluding opposition figures and Shias in boosting the Abraham Accords, Bahrain faced problems in its quest for security and a new form of inclusive identity. Consequently, Bahrain constantly managed existing threats and identified new ones in the course of the normalization of its ties with Israel, which the Paris School of security studies would argue resulted in non-inclusive or inadequate policies.

On the other side, Israel insisted that ties with Bahrain remained stable after the October War. But Israel had to embrace continual dialogue and normalization with Bahrain to sustain its cooperation and help advance US interests in the Middle East as well. These measures involved building up Gulf security while containing Iran. From Iran's perspective, the Abraham Accords were a failed attempt to hijack Gulf politics by the United States, with Israeli assistance, in order to tip the regional balance of power against Tehran. The October War was a turning point to help Tehran assert its regional influence through Hamas. As a result, as far as Tehran was concerned, Bahrain meanwhile deluded itself into thinking that its ties with Israel could sustain American commitment to Gulf security and to the Arab monarchies in the longer haul.

In fact, an emerging order that the accords were expected to build in the Gulf region could also be hijacked by Iran as a result of its persistent hostility with the United States and Israel, causing deeper cleavages in the existing security system that had helped ensure relative peace and security for the region and Bahrain. The 2023 Israel-Hamas War, in which Tehran was accused of backing the Palestinian group, was one indicator of how Iran could manipulate the regional security architecture. As a result, the lack of cohesion and absence of a shared outlook among the various actors in the Gulf on the issue of the Bahraini-Israeli normalization meant that part of the region's security structures would constantly aim at dominating other parts, thereby intensifying a segregated and fragmented regional foreign policy that could potentially fuel more dissent and conflict inside Bahrain.

NOTES

1. On the relevance of amity in international relations theory, see Yves Viltard "What to Do with the Rhetoric of Amity in International Relations?," *Raisons Politiques*, 33(1) (2009): 127–147, https://www.cairn-int.info/article-E_RAI_033_0127--what-to-do-with-the-rhetoric-of-amity.htm.

2. Henry Petrillo and David Pollock, "Bahrainis Support Internal Political Focus, but Differ Somewhat on Foreign Policy Priorities," Washington Institute, September 9, 2021, https://www.washingtoninstitute.org/policy-analysis/bahrainis-support-internal-political-focus-differ-somewhat-foreign-policy.

3. "Presenting the Findings From the 2022 Arab Barometer Report: Attitudes Toward International Relations," Middle East Institute, September 15, 2022, https://www.mei.edu/events/presenting-findings-2022-arab-barometer-report-attitudes-toward-international-relations.

4. David Pollock, "Bahrain Opinion Poll Confirms Sectarian Split on Iran, but Not on US or Israel," The Washington Institute, September 9, 2022, https://www.washingtoninstitute.org/policy-analysis/bahrain-opinion-poll-confirms-sectarian-split-iran-not-us-or-israel.

5. Felix Pope, "Israel and Saudi Arabia Deal Expected 'Within a Year' Says Top Israeli Diplomat," *The JC*, December 8, 2022, https://www.thejc.com/news/israel /israel-and-saudi-arabia-deal-expected-within-a-year-says-top-israeli-diplomat-KgL L8HcFQtnzmcjaGrVaf.

6. See Ceren Altinecekic on Kenneth Waltz, "Summary of "Theory of International Politics"" *Beyond Intractability*, https://www.beyondintractability.org/bksum /waltz-theory; Randall L. Schweller, "Bandwagoning for Profit: Bringing the Revisionist State Back In," *International Security*, 19(1) (Summer 1994): 72–107, https:// www.jstor.org/stable/2539149.

7. "Bahrain Says Pays \$2.6 Million Compensation Over Uprising Deaths," *Reuters*, June 26, 2012, https://www.reuters.com/article/us-bahrain-compensation -deaths/bahrain-says-pays-2-6-million-compensation-over-uprising-deaths-idU SBRE85P0J020120626; Yasmina Abouzzohour, "Heavy Lies the Crown: The Survival of Arab Monarchies, 10 Years After the Arab Spring," *Brookings*, March 8, 2021, https://www.brookings.edu/blog/order-from-chaos/2021/03/08/heavy-lies-the -crown-the-survival-of-arab-monarchies-10-years-after-the-arab-spring/.

8. See Archie W. Simpson, "Realism Small States and Neutrality," *E-International Relations*, February 5, 2018, https://www.e-ir.info/2018/02/05/realism-small -states-and-neutrality/.

9. Ibid.

10. Author's discussions with Bahraini and Arab scholars working on the Abraham Accords, August 2022; also see "Difference Between Idealism and Realism," http://www.differencebetween.net/miscellaneous/difference-between-idealism-and -realism/.

11. See R. Floyd, "Toward a Consequentialist Evaluation of Security: Bringing Together the Copenhagen and Welsh Schools of Security Studies," *Review of International Studies*, 33 (2007): 335–337; Securitization theory was originally developed by Ole Wæver, see O. Wæver, "Securitization and Desecuritization," in *On Security*, ed. Ronnie D. Lipschutz (New York: Columbia University Press, 1995), 29.

12. See Floyd, "Toward a Consequentialist Evaluation of Security: Bringing Together the Copenhagen and Welsh Schools of Security Studies"; Wæver, "Securitization and Desecuritization."

13. Ibid.

14. Ibid; see also R. Floyd, "Can Securitization Theory be Used in Normative Analysis," *Security Dialogue*, 42 (2011): 428, 431; D. Bigo and A. Tsoukala, "Understanding (in)security," in D. Bigo and A. Tsoukala (eds.) *Terror, Insecurity and Liberty: Illiberal Practices of Liberal Regimes After 9/11* (Oxon: Routledge, 2008), 4–5.

15. Walter Fischel, "Bahrain," in *Encyclopedia Judaica 3*, ed. Michael Berenbaum, 2nd ed. (Jerusalem: Keter Publishing House Ltd), 64; Burhanadldeen Delew and Nancy Elly Khedouri, *From Our Beginning to Present Day* (Bahrain: Al Manar Press, 2007); Josefin Dolsten, "Jews Have Lived in Bahrain for 140 Years; The Israel Deal Changes Their Lives," *The Times of Israel*, September 16, 2020, https://www .timesofisrael.com/jews-have-lived-in-bahrain-for-140-years-the-israel-deal-changes -their-lives/; "Bahrain: History & Background," *Education Encyclopedia*, https://edu-cation.stateuniversity.com/pages/107/Bahrain-HISTORY-BACKGROUND.html;

"Mishmahig Islands (Bahrain)," Iran Chamber Society, based on excerpts by Piruz Mojtahedzadeh, "Bahrain: The Land of Political Movements," *Rahavard,* XI(39) (1995), https://www.iranchamber.com/geography/articles/mishmahig_islands_bahrain.php; Nissan Ratzlav-Katz, "The King of Bahrain Wants the Jews Back," *Israel National News,* August 14, 2008, https://www.israelnationalnews.com/news/127201.

16. Dolsten, "Jews Have Lived in Bahrain for 140 Years; The Israel Deal Changes Their Lives"; Amy Spiro, "The Bahraini Jewish Family Making Waves Around the World," *Jewish Insider,* September 17, 2020, https://jewishinsider.com/2020/09/the-bahraini-jewish-family-making-waves-around-the-world/; "Bahrain's Jews Worship in Public for First Time in Decades," *France 24,* September 14, 2021, https://www.france24.com/en/live-news/20210914-bahrain-s-jews-worship-in-public-for-first-time-in-decades.

17. Nour Abu Aisha, "Hamas Hails Bahraini People's Support for Palestine," *Anadolu Agency (AA),* June 27, 2019, https://www.aa.com.tr/en/middle-east/hamas-hails-bahraini-people-s-support-for-palestine/1517321.

18. "Middle East Monitor: Bahrain-Israel Links Go Back to 1994," *Bahrain Mirror,* October 11, 2017, http://bahrainmirror.com/en/news/41466.html.

19. "Arab Support Slips for Doha Summit on Gaza," *Reuters,* January 15, 2009, https://www.reuters.com/article/us-palestinians-israel-summit-support-sb/arab-support-slips-for-doha-summit-on-gaza-idUKTRE50E3P920090115; "In a Landscape of Tension, Bahrain Embraces Its Jews. All 36 of Them," *The New York Times,* April 5, 2009, https://www.nytimes.com/2009/04/06/world/middleeast/06bahrain.html; "Bahrain Ends Boycott of Israeli Goods," *AlJazeera,* September 23, 2005, https://www.aljazeera.com/news/2005/9/23/bahrain-ends-boycott-of-israeli-goods; "Bahrain-Israel: From Discreet to Public," *Kuwait Times,* December 9, 2020, https://www.kuwaittimes.com/bahrain-israel-from-discreet-to-public/.

20. Ibid.

21. Andrew Hammond, "Bahrain Court Upholds Sentences on Uprising Leaders," *Reuters,* September 4, 2012, https://www.reuters.com/article/uk-bahrain-leaders/bahrain-court-upholds-sentences-on-uprising-leaders-idUKBRE8830CM20120904; "Bahrain Detains Activist Zinab al-Khawaja and Her One-Year-Old-Son," *The Guardian,* March 14, 2016, https://www.theguardian.com/world/2016/mar/14/bahrain-detains-activist-zainab-al-khawaja-and-one-year-old-son.

22. Ali Alfoneh, "Iran Chooses a Harsher Tone as it Reacts to the Bahrain-Israel Rapprochement," Arab Gulf States Institute in Washington, September 16, 2020, https://agsiw.org/iran-chooses-a-harsher-tone-as-it-reacts-to-the-bahrain-israel-rapprochement/.

23. Abdel Aziz Aluwaisheg, "GCC Summit Stresses Gulf Security Through Integration," *Arab News,* December 17, 2019, https://www.arabnews.com/node/1600236.

24. Author's discussion with a senior Israeli diplomat who traveled to the GCC capitals before, during and after Lebanon's 2006 war with Israel, Los Angeles, CA, June 6, 2008.

25. "Iran Says UAE, Bahrain Will Bear 'Consequences' of Israel Deals," *Ahram Online,* September 16, 2020, https://english.ahram.org.eg/WorldCup/News/383199.aspx;

"IRGC Condemns Bahrain-Israeli Tie Normalization," *Mehr News Agency,* September 12, 2020, https://en.mehrnews.com/news/163425/IRGC-condemns-Bahrain-Israeli-tie-normalization.

26. Alfoneh, "Iran Chooses a Harsher Tone as it Reacts to the Bahrain-Israel Rapprochement."

27. Lazar Berman, "Israeli Team Heads to Bahrain for Talks on Bilateral Ties," *The Times of Israel,* June 1, 2022, https://www.timesofisrael.com/israeli-team-heads-to-bahrain-for-talks-on-bilateral-ties/.

28. Ibid.

29. Maryam Sinaee, "Iran Condemns the Negev Summit as 'An Evil Meeting'," *Iran International,* March 28, 2022, https://www.iranintl.com/en/202203280307.

30. "UAE, Bahrain, Israel and US Forces in First Joint Naval Drill," *Reuters,* November 11, 2021, https://www.reuters.com/world/middle-east/uae-bahrain-israel-us-forces-conduct-red-sea-military-exercise-2021-11-11/.

31. Lisa Barrington, "Israel Participates in Huge US Mideast Naval Exercise Alongside Saudi, Oman," *Reuters,* February 2, 2022, https://www.reuters.com/world/middle-east/israel-participates-huge-us-gulf-naval-exercise-alongside-saudi-oman-2022-02-02/.

32. "Bahrain Buys Israel Radars, Anti-Drone Systems," *Middle East Monitor,* February 10, 2022, https://www.middleeastmonitor.com/20220210-bahrain-buys-israel-radars-anti-drone-systems/.

33. "Senior Bahraini Diplomat Says Mossad Active in His Country, Boosting Security," *The Times of Israel,* February 21, 2022, https://www.timesofisrael.com/senior-bahraini-diplomat-says-mossad-active-in-his-country/.

34. "Israel Sells Drone, Anti-Drone System to Bahrain," *Middle East Monitor,* July 13, 2022, https://www.middleeastmonitor.com/20220713-israel-sells-drones-anti-drone-system-to-bahrain/; "Bahrain Buys Israel Radars, Anti-Drone Systems."

35. "Iran Emphasizes Inclusive National Dialogues in Bahrain," *Iran Press,* November 7, 2022, https://iranpress.com/content/69343/iran-emphasises-inclusive-national-dialogues-bahrain.

36. "UAE, Bahrain, Morocco Apply to Buy Israel's Iron Dome Missile Defense System," *Middle East Monitor,* March 30, 2022, https://www.middleeastmonitor.com/20220330-uae-bahrain-morocco-apply-to-buy-israels-iron-dome-missile-defence-system/.

37. "Netanyahu Speaks to Bahrain Crown Prince of 'Great Opportunities' for Cooperation," *The Times of Israel,* November 13, 2022, https://www.timesofisrael.com/netanyahu-speaks-to-bahrain-crown-prince-of-great-opportunities-for-cooperation/.

38. Lazar Berman, "Bahrain: Netanyahu Believes in Peace, We Look Forward to Working with Him," *The Times of Israel,* December 4, 2022, https://www.timesofisrael.com/bahrain-netanyahu-believes-in-peace-we-look-forward-to-working-with-him/.

39. Ariel Grossman, "Israel Discusses 'Cyber Iron Dome' With UAE, Bahrain, Morocco," *No Camels,* December 19, 2022, https://nocamels.com/2022/12/israel-discusses-cyber-iron-dome-with-uae-bahrain-morocco/.

40. "Israeli Minister Says Bahrain Invitation Proof of Growing Arab Relations," *Middle East Eye,* November 26, 2018, https://www.middleeasteye.net/fr/news/israeli
-minister-says-bahrain-invitation-proof-growing-arab-relations-867764361.

41. "Israel Expects $220 Million in Non-Defense Trade with Bahrain in 2021," *Reuters,* December 2, 2020, https://www.reuters.com/article/us-israel-bahrain/israel
-expects-220-million-in-non-defence-trade-with-bahrain-in-2021-idUSKBN28C1WB.

42. "What to Know About Second Most Important Figure in Israeli Embassy in Manama," *Bahrain Mirror,* October 27, 2022, http://bahrainmirror.com/en/news
/62001.html.

43. "Netanyahu Speaks to Bahrain Crown Prince of 'Great Opportunities' for Cooperation," *The Times of Israel*, November 13, 2022, https://www.timesofisrael
.com/netanyahu-speaks-to-bahrain-crown-prince-of-great-opportunities-for-coop-
eration/#:~:text=According%20to%20the%20statement%2C%20Netanyahu,Israel
%20soon%2C%20his%20office%20said.

44. "BDS Slams Bahrain's Recognition of Israel Settlement Goods," *Middle East Monitor,* December 5, 2022, https://www.middleeastmonitor.com/20201205-bds
-slams-bahrains-recognition-of-israel-settlement-goods/.

45. Zain Khalil, "Israel, Bahrain Eye to Sign Free Trade Deal by Year-End," *AA,* October 31, 2022, https://www.aa.com.tr/en/economy/israel-bahrain-eye-to-sign-free
-trade-deal-by-year-end/2725783.

46. "Israel Exports to Bahrain," *Trading Economics,* https://tradingeconomics
.com/israel/exports/bahrain; "Israel, Bahrain 'Successfully' Complete First Round of Free Trade Talks," *I24,* November 20, 2022, https://www.i24news.tv/en/news/middle
-east/economy/1669017410-israel-bahrain-successfully-complete-first-round-of-free
-trade-talks.

47. Lazar Berman, "Israel Team Heads to Bahrain for Talks on Bilateral Ties," *The Times of Israel,* June 1, 2022, https://www.timesofisrael.com/israeli-team-heads
-to-bahrain-for-talks-on-bilateral-ties/

48. Seth J. Frantzman, "Huge Industrial Partnership Links Bahrain, UAE, Egypt and Jordan," *The Jerusalem Post,* July 26, 2022, https://m.jpost.com/middle-east/
article-713056/amp.

49. "Israel, Bahrain Hope to Seal Free Trade Deal by End of Year," *Reuters,* October 31, 2022, https://www.reuters.com/world/middle-east/israel-bahrain-hope
-seal-free-trade-deal-by-end-year-2022-10-31/.

50. "Israel and Bahrain Sign Agriculture Cooperation Agreement," *Middle East Monitor,* October 21, 2022, https://www.middleeastmonitor.com/20221021-israel
-and-bahrain-sign-agriculture-cooperation-agreement/.

51. "Israel, Bahrain Discuss Strengthening Economic Ties," *Xinhua,* November 11, 2022, https://english.news.cn/20221101/bb7b393cc9b64f10a46fe401d02c5351/c.html.

52. Lazar Berman, "With Doubts Rising in Bahrain, Herzog Seeks to Get Abraham Accords Back on Track," *The Times of Israel,* December 8, 2022, https://
www.timesofisrael.com/with-doubts-rising-in-bahrain-herzog-seeks-to-get-abraham
-accords-back-on-track/.

53. "Israel Expects $220 Million in Non-Defense Trade with Bahrain in 2021," *Reuters*, December 2, 2020, https://www.arabnews.com/node/1771531/business-economy.

54. Shreya Nandi, "India Now Sets Sights on Free Trade Agreement with Gulf Countries," *Business Standard,* April 6, 2022, https://www.business-standard.com /article/economy-policy/india-now-sets-sights-on-free-trade-agreement-with-gulf -countries-122040501480_1.html; Nidhi Verma, "India, Saudi Arabia Discuss Start-ing Rupee-Riyal Trade," *Nasdaq,* September 19, 2022, https://www.nasdaq.com/ articles/india-saudi-arabia-discuss-starting-rupee-riyal-trade.

55. Avi Hasson, "Israel's President Visited Bahrain This Week. This is Why It's Important," *North Jersey,* December 7, 2022, https://www.northjersey.com/story/ opinion/2022/12/07/improving-israels-ties-to-bahrain-continues-this-is-why-it-mat-ters/69708870007/.

56. See Courtney Freer, "Challenges to Sunni Islamism in Bahrain Since 2011," *Malcolm H. Kerr Carnegie Middle East Center*, March 6, 2019, https://carnegie-mec .org/2019/03/06/challenges-to-sunni-islamism-in-bahrain-since-2011-pub-78510.

57. "Sheikh Issa Qassem Warns Bahrainis Against Judaization Scheme," *Iran Press,* September 4, 2022, https://iranpress.com/content/66096/sheikh-issa-qassem -warns-bahrainis-against-judaization-scheme.

58. "#BahrainRejectsZionists: Protestors Slam Opening of Israeli Embassy in Manama," *The New Arab,* September 30, 2021, https://english.alaraby.co.uk/news/bah-raini-protesters-slam-israeli-embassy-manama; Aziz El Yaakoubi and Lisa Barrington, "In US Ally Bahrain, Israel Deal Rallies a Weakened Opposition," *Reuters,* Septem-ber 17, 2020, https://www.reuters.com/article/israel-gulf-usa-bahrain-int/in-u-s-ally -bahrain-israel-deal-rallies-a-weakened-opposition-idUSKBN2682MC; Emile Nakhleh, "Despite Official Celebrations, Arab Street Resents the Abraham Accords," *Responsible Statecraft,* October 13, 2021, https://responsiblestatecraft.org/2021/10/13/despite-offi-cial-celebrations-arab-publics-still-resent-the-abraham-accords/; "Government Orders Postpone General Assembly Meeting of Bahraini Society Against Normalization," *Bahrain Mirror,* September 24, 2022, http://bahrainmirror.com/en/news/61914.html; "Bahraini Society Against Normalization with Zionist Enemy: Signing Security Agree-ments with Zionist Entity Threatens Bahrain's Stability," *Bahrain Mirror,* February 11, 2022, http://bahrainmirror.com/en/news/61099.html; "24 Organizations Call on Bahrain Gov't to Expel Zionist Enemy's Ambassador, End Normalization Agreement," *Bahrain Mirror,* May 13, 2021, http://bahrainmirror.com/en/news/59636.html.

59. Ibid.

60. "Bahraini Society Against Normalization with Zionist Enemy: Signing Secu-rity Agreements with Zionist Entity Threatens Bahrain's Stability."

61. Caleb Weiss, "State Department Designated Iranian-Backed Bahraini Militia," *FDD's Long War Journal,* December 15, 2020, https://www.longwarjournal.org/ archives/2020/12/state-department-designates-iranian-backed-bahraini-militia.php.

62. Caleb Weiss, "Bahraini Militia Re-emerges to Threaten New Attacks," *FDD's Long War Journal,* November 3, 2019, https://www.longwarjournal.org/archives /2019/11/bahraini-militia-reemerges.php.

63. "Khatibzadeh Denounces Bahraini Court's Ruling Against Iran Central Bank," *MENA Affairs,* August 3, 2021, https://menaaffairs.com/khatibzadeh-denounces-bah-raini-courts-ruling-against-iran-central-bank/.

64. "Bahrain Found Liable for Indirect Expropriation for Putting Iranian-Controlled Future Bank Under Administration," *Investment Treaty News,* July 4, 2022, https://www.iisd.org/itn/en/2022/07/04/bahrain-found-liable-for-indirect-expropria-tion-for-putting-iranian-controlled-future-bank-under-administration/.

65. "Bahrain Condemns Killing of Iranian Nuclear Scientist Fakhrizadeh," *Reuters,* November 30, 2020, https://www.reuters.com/article/iran-nuclear-scientist-israel-bahrain-in/bahrain-condemns-killing-of-iranian-nuclear-scientist-fakhrizadeh-idUSKBN28A2G6.

66. "Bahrain Sentences 51 Accused of Iran-Linked Terror Plots," *Al-Monitor,* November 3, 2020, https://www.al-monitor.com/originals/2020/11/bahrain-terrorism-iran-irgc-convict-high-criminal-court-jail.html.

67. "Iran Rejects Connction to "Terrorist Operations" Plot in Bahrain," *Radio Farda,* Azar 4, 1400, https://www.radiofarda.com/a/iran-foreign-ministry-bahrain-terrorist/31578193.html.

68. "Another Shura Council in Bahrain: King Takes Over What's Left of Constitution and Parliament," *Bahrain Mirror,* October 27, 2022, http://bahrainmirror.com/en/news/62003.html.

69. "After Netanyahu's Win, Bahrain Pledges to 'Continue Building' Israel Partnership," *The Times of Israel,* November 6, 2022, https://www.timesofisrael.com/after-netanyahus-win-bahrain-pledges-to-continue-building-israel-partnership/.

70. "Sheikh 'Isa Qasim' Calls for Resistance Against Compromise with Zionists," *IRNA,* February 25, 1400, https://www.irna.ir/news/84650341/%D8%B4%DB%8C%D8%AE-%D8%B9%DB%8C%D8%B3%DB%8C-%D9%82%D8%A7%D8%B3%D9%85-%D8%AE%D9%88%D8%A7%D8%B3%D8%AA%D8%A7%D8%B1-%D9%85%D9%82%D8%A7%D9%88%D9%85%D8%AA-%D8%AF%D8%B1-%D9%85%D9%82%D8%A7%D8%A8%D9%84-%D8%B3%D8%A7%D8%B2%D8%B4-%D8%A8%D8%A7-%D8%B5%D9%87%DB%8C%D9%88%D9%86%DB%8C%D8%B3%D8%AA-%D9%87%D8%A7-%D8%B4%D8%AF.

71. "Bahrain Strongly Condemns Shrine Terrorist Attack in Iran," *Bahrain News Agency,* October 27, 2022, https://www.bna.bh/en/news?cms=q8FmFJgiscL2f-wIzON1%2BDo284XzT3kd9O0q5owQFES0%3D.

72. "Iran Emphasizes Inclusive National Dialogues in Bahrain."

73. See, for example, the website Citizens of Bahrain that says it represents young and moderate Bahrainis seeking to promote collective engagement in their country regardless of sect while encouraging Iranian protestors, https://www.citizensfor-bahrain.com/2022/10/06/beginning-of-the-end-for-the-ayatollahs-bahraini-views-on-irans-revolution%EF%BF%BC/.

74. Fatemeh Ebadi Niyk, "A Look at the Status of Shias in Bahrain," http://intjz.net/maqalat/sh-bahrein.htm.

75. Mitchell Belfer and Khalid Alshaikh, "Iran's Clandestine War on the Kingdom of Bahrain: Saraya al Ashtar and the Military Wing of Hezbollah Bahrain," *Dirasat,* KFCRIS, January 2019, https://www.kfcris.com/pdf/09677d7a8899e33b05594dd8c0c433975d69199a5cf98.pdf.

REFERENCES

Abouzzohour, Yasmina, "Heavy Lies the Crown: The Survival of Arab Monarchies, 10 Years After the Arab Spring," *Brookings*, March 8, 2021, https://www.brookings.edu/blog/order-from-chaos/2021/03/08/heavy-lies-the-crown-the-survival-of-arab-monarchies-10-years-after-the-arab-spring/.

Abu Aisha, Nour, "Hamas Hails Bahraini People's Support for Palestine," *Anadolu Agency (AA),* June 27, 2019, https://www.aa.com.tr/en/middle-east/hamas-hails-bahraini-people-s-support-for-palestine/1517321.

"After Netanyahu's Win, Bahrain Pledges to 'Continue Building' Israel Partnership," *The Times of Israel,* November 6, 2022, https://www.timesofisrael.com/after-netanyahus-win-bahrain-pledges-to-continue-building-israel-partnership/.

Alfoneh, Ali, "Iran Chooses a Harsher Tone as it Reacts to the Bahrain-Israel Rapprochement," Arab Gulf States Institute in Washington, September 16, 2020, https://agsiw.org/iran-chooses-a-harsher-tone-as-it-reacts-to-the-bahrain-israel-rapprochement/.

Altinecekic, Ceren, "Summary of "Theory of International Politics," *Beyond Intractability,* https://www.beyondintractability.org/bksum/waltz-theory.

Aluwaisheg, Abdel Aziz, "GCC Summit Stresses Gulf Security Through Integration," *Arab News,* December 17, 2019, https://www.arabnews.com/node/1600236.

"Another Shura Council in Bahrain: King Takes Over What's Left of Constitution and Parliament," *Bahrain Mirror,* October 27, 2022, http://bahrainmirror.com/en/news/62003.html.

"Arab Support Slips for Doha Summit on Gaza," *Reuters,* January 15, 2009, https://www.reuters.com/article/us-palestinians-israel-summit-support-sb/arab-support-slips-for-doha-summit-on-gaza-idUKTRE50E3P920090115.

"Bahrain Buys Israel Radars, Anti-Drone Systems," *Middle East Monitor,* February 10, 2022, https://www.middleeastmonitor.com/20220210-bahrain-buys-israel-radars-anti-drone-systems/.

"Bahrain Condemns Killing of Iranian Nuclear Scientist Fakhrizadeh," *Reuters,* November 30, 2020, https://www.reuters.com/article/iran-nuclear-scientist-israel-bahrain-in/bahrain-condemns-killing-of-iranian-nuclear-scientist-fakhrizadeh-idUSKBN28A2G6.

"Bahrain Detains Activist Zinab al-Khawaja and Her One-Year-Old-Son," *The Guardian,* March 14, 2016, https://www.theguardian.com/world/2016/mar/14/bahrain-detains-activist-zainab-al-khawaja-and-one-year-old-son.

"Bahrain Ends Boycott of Israeli Goods," *Al Jazeera,* September 23, 2005, https://www.aljazeera.com/news/2005/9/23/bahrain-ends-boycott-of-israeli-goods.

"Bahrain Found Liable for Indirect Expropriation for Putting Iranian-Controlled Future Bank Under Administration," *Investment Treaty News,* July 4, 2022, https://www.iisd.org/itn/en/2022/07/04/bahrain-found-liable-for-indirect-expropriation-for-putting-iranian-controlled-future-bank-under-administration/.

"Bahrain: History & Background," *Education Encyclopedia,* https://education.stateuniversity.com/pages/107/Bahrain-HISTORY-BACKGROUND.html.

"Bahrain-Israel: From Discreet to Public," *Kuwait Times,* December 9, 2020, https://www.kuwaittimes.com/bahrain-israel-from-discreet-to-public/.

"#BahrainRejectsZionists: Protestors Slam Opening of Israeli Embassy in Manama," *The New Arab,* September 30, 2021, https://english.alaraby.co.uk/news/bahraini-protesters-slam-israeli-embassy-manama.

"Bahrain Says Pays $2.6 Million Compensation Over Uprising Deaths," *Reuters,* June 26, 2012, https://www.reuters.com/article/us-bahrain-compensation-deaths/bahrain-says-pays-2-6-million-compensation-over-uprising-deaths-idUSBRE85P0J020120626.

"Bahrain Sentences 51 Accused of Iran-Linked Terror Plots," *Al-Monitor,* November 3, 2020, https://www.al-monitor.com/originals/2020/11/bahrain-terrorism-iran-irgc-convict-high-criminal-court-jail.html.

"Bahrain Strongly Condemns Shrine Terrorist Attack in Iran," *Bahrain News Agency,* October 27, 2022, https://www.bna.bh/en/news?cms=q8FmFJgiscL2fwIzON1%2BDo284XzT3kd9O0q5owQFES0%3D.

"Bahrain's Jews Worship in Public for First Time in Decades," *France 24,* September 14, 2021, https://www.france24.com/en/live-news/20210914-bahrain-s-jews-worship-in-public-for-first-time-in-decades.

"Bahraini Society Against Normalization with Zionist Enemy: Signing Security Agreements with Zionist Entity Threatens Bahrain's Stability," *Bahrain Mirror,* February 11, 2022, http://bahrainmirror.com/en/news/61099.html.

Barrington, Lisa, "Israel Participates in Huge US Mideast Naval Exercise Alongside Saudi, Oman," *Reuters,* February 2, 2022, https://www.reuters.com/world/middle-east/israel-participates-huge-us-gulf-naval-exercise-alongside-saudi-oman-2022-02-02/.

"BDS Slams Bahrain's Recognition of Israel Settlement Goods," *Middle East Monitor,* December 5, 2022, https://www.middleeastmonitor.com/20201205-bds-slams-bahrains-recognition-of-israel-settlement-goods/.

Belfer, Mitchell, and Khalid Alshaikh, "Iran's Clandestine War on the Kingdom of Bahrain: Saraya al Ashtar and the Military Wing of Hezbollah Bahrain," *Dirasat,* KFCRIS, January 2019, https://www.kfcris.com/pdf/09677d7a8899e33b05594dd8c0c433975d69199a5cf98.pdf.

Berman, Lazar, "Bahrain: Netanyahu Believes in Peace, We Look Forward to Working with Him," *The Times of Israel,* December 4, 2022, https://www.timesofisrael.com/bahrain-netanyahu-believes-in-peace-we-look-forward-to-working-with-him/.

Berman, Lazar, "Israeli Team Heads to Bahrain for Talks on Bilateral Ties," *The Times of Israel,* June 1, 2022, https://www.timesofisrael.com/israeli-team-heads-to-bahrain-for-talks-on-bilateral-ties/.

Berman, Lazar, "With Doubts Rising in Bahrain, Herzog Seeks to Get Abraham Accords Back on Track," *The Times of Israel,* December 8, 2022, https://www.timesofisrael.com/with-doubts-rising-in-bahrain-herzog-seeks-to-get-abraham-accords-back-on-track/.

Bigo, Didier, and Anastassia Tsoukala, "Understanding (in)security," in Bigo, Didier, and Anastassia Tsoukala (eds.), *Terror, Insecurity and Liberty: Illiberal Practices of Liberal Regimes After 9/11* (Oxon: Routledge, 2008), 1–9.

Delew, Burhanadldeen, and Nancy Elly Khedouri, *From Our Beginning to Present Day* (Bahrain: Al Manar Press, 2007).

"Difference Between Idealism and Realism," http://www.differencebetween.net/miscellaneous/difference-between-idealism-and-realism/.

Dolsten, Josefin, "Jews Have Lived in Bahrain for 140 Years: The Israel Deal Changes Their Lives," *The Times of Israel,* September 16, 2020, https://www.timesofisrael.com/jews-have-lived-in-bahrain-for-140-years-the-israel-deal-changes-their-lives/.

El Yaakoubi, Aziz, and Lisa Barrington, "In US Ally Bahrain, Israel Deal Rallies a Weakened Opposition," *Reuters,* September 17, 2020, https://www.reuters.com/article/israel-gulf-usa-bahrain-int/in-u-s-ally-bahrain-israel-deal-rallies-a-weakened-opposition-idUSKBN2682MC.

Frantzman, Seth J., "Huge Industrial Partnership Links Bahrain, UAE, Egypt and Jordan," *The Jerusalem Post,* July 26, 2022, https://m.jpost.com/middle-east/article-713056/amp.

Fischel, Walter, "Bahrain," in *Encyclopedia Judaica 3,* ed. Michael Berenbaum, 2nd ed. (Jerusalem: Keter Publishing House Ltd).

Floyd, R., "Can Securitization Theory be Used in Normative Analysis," *Security Dialogue,* 42 (2011): 427–439.

Floyd, R., "Toward a Consequentialist Evaluation of Security: Bringing Together the Copenhagen and Welsh Schools of Security Studies," *Review of International Studies*, 33 (2007): 335–337.

Freer, Courtney, "Challenges to Sunni Islamism in Bahrain Since 2011," Malcolm H. Kerr Carnegie Middle East Center, March 6, 2019, https://carnegie-mec.org/2019/03/06/challenges-to-sunni-islamism-in-bahrain-since-2011-pub-78510.

"Government Orders Postpone General Assembly Meeting of Bahraini Society Against Normalization," *Bahrain Mirror,* September 24, 2022, http://bahrainmirror.com/en/news/61914.html.

Grossman, Ariel, "Israel Discusses 'Cyber Iron Dome' With UAE, Bahrain, Morocco," *No Camels,* December 19, 2022, https://nocamels.com/2022/12/israel-discusses-cyber-iron-dome-with-uae-bahrain-morocco/.

Hammond, Andrew, "Bahrain Court Upholds Sentences on Uprising Leaders," *Reuters,* September 4, 2012, https://www.reuters.com/article/uk-bahrain-leaders/bahrain-court-upholds-sentences-on-uprising-leaders-idUKBRE8830CM20120904.

Hasson, Avi, "Israel's President Visited Bahrain This Week. This is Why It's Important," *North Jersey,* December 7, 2022, https://www.northjersey.com/story/opinion/2022/12/07/improving-israels-ties-to-bahrain-continues-this-is-why-it-matters/69708870007/.

"In a Landscape of Tension, Bahrain Embraces Its Jews. All 36 of Them," *The New York Times,* April 5, 2009, https://www.nytimes.com/2009/04/06/world/middleeast/06bahrain.html.

"Iran Emphasizes Inclusive National Dialogues in Bahrain," *Iran Press,* November 7, 2022, https://iranpress.com/content/69343/iran-emphasises-inclusive-national-dialogues-bahrain.

"Iran Rejects Connection to "Terrorist Operations" Plot in Bahrain," *Radio Farda,* Azar 4, 1400, https://www.radiofarda.com/a/iran-foreign-ministry-bahrain-terror-ist/31578193.html.

"Iran Says UAE, Bahrain Will Bear 'Consequences' of Israel Deals," *Ahram Online,* September 16, 2020, https://english.ahram.org.eg/WorldCup/News/383199.aspx.

"IRGC Condemns Bahrain-Israeli Tie Normalization," *Mehr News Agency,* September 12, 2020, https://en.mehrnews.com/news/163425/IRGC-condemns-Bahrain-Israeli-tie-normalization.

"Israel and Bahrain Sign Agriculture Cooperation Agreement," *Middle East Monitor,* October 21, 2022, https://www.middleeastmonitor.com/20221021-israel-and-bahrain-sign-agriculture-cooperation-agreement/.

"Israel, Bahrain Discuss Strengthening Economic Ties," *Xinhua,* November 11, 2022, https://english.news.cn/20221101/bb7b393cc9b64f10a46fe401d02c5351/c.html.

"Israel, Bahrain Hope to Seal Free Trade Deal by End of Year," *Reuters,* October 31, 2022, https://www.reuters.com/world/middle-east/israel-bahrain-hope-seal-free-trade-deal-by-end-year-2022-10-31/.

"Israel, Bahrain 'Successfully' Complete First Round of Free Trade Talks," *I24,* November 20, 2022, https://www.i24news.tv/en/news/middle-east/economy/1669017410-israel-bahrain-successfully-complete-first-round-of-free-trade-talks.

"Israel Expects $220 Million in Non-Defense Trade with Bahrain in 2021," *Reuters,* December 2, 2020, https://www.reuters.com/article/us-israel-bahrain/israel-expects-220-million-in-non-defence-trade-with-bahrain-in-2021-idUSKBN28C1WB.

"Israeli Minister Says Bahrain Invitation Proof of Growing Arab Relations," *Middle East Eye,* November 26, 2018, https://www.middleeasteye.net/fr/news/israeli-min-ister-says-bahrain-invitation-proof-growing-arab-relations-867764361.

"Israel Sells Drone, Anti-Drone System to Bahrain," *Middle East Monitor,* July 13, 2022, https://www.middleeastmonitor.com/20220713-israel-sells-drones-anti-drone-system-to-bahrain/.

Khalil, Zain, "Israel, Bahrain Eye to Sign Free Trade Deal by Year-End," *AA,* October 31, 2022, https://www.aa.com.tr/en/economy/israel-bahrain-eye-to-sign-free-trade-deal-by-year-end/2725783.

"Khatibzadeh Denounces Bahraini Court's Ruling Against Iran Central Bank," *MENA Affairs,* August 3, 2021, https://menaaffairs.com/khatibzadeh-denounces-bahraini-courts-ruling-against-iran-central-bank/.

"Middle East Monitor: Bahrain-Israel Links Go Back to 1994," *Bahrain Mirror,* October 11, 2017, http://bahrainmirror.com/en/news/41466.html.

"Mishmahig Islands (Bahrain)," Iran Chamber Society, based on excerpts by Piruz Mojtahedzadeh, "Bahrain: The Land of Political Movements," *Rahavard,* XI(39) (1995), https://www.iranchamber.com/geography/articles/mishmahig_islands_bahrain.php.

Nakhleh, Emile, "Despite Official Celebrations, Arab Street Resents the Abraham Accords," *Responsible Statecraft,* October 13, 2021, https://responsiblestatecraft.org/2021/10/13/despite-official-celebrations-arab-publics-still-resent-the-abraham-accords/.

Nandi, Shreya, "India Now Sets Sights on Free Trade Agreement with Gulf Countries," *Business Standard,* April 6, 2022, https://www.business-standard.com /article/economy-policy/india-now-sets-sights-on-free-trade-agreement-with-gulf -countries-122040501480_1.html.

"Netanyahu Speaks to Bahrain Crown Prince of 'Great Opportunities' for Cooperation," *The Times of Israel,* November 13, 2022, https://www.timesofisrael.com/netanyahu-speaks-to-bahrain-crown-prince-of-great-opportunities-for -cooperation/.

Niyk, Fatemeh Ebadi, "A Look at the Status of Shias in Bahrain," http://intjz.net/ maqalat/sh-bahrein.htm.

Petrillo, Henry, and David Pollock, "Bahrainis Support Internal Political Focus, but Differ Somewhat on Foreign Policy Priorities," Washington Institute, September 9, 2021, https://www.washingtoninstitute.org/policy-analysis/bahrainis-support -internal-political-focus-differ-somewhat-foreign-policy.

Pollock, David, "Bahrain Opinion Poll Confirms Sectarian Split on Iran, but Not on US or Israel," The Washington Institute, September 9, 2022, https://www.washingtoninstitute.org/policy-analysis/bahrain-opinion-poll-confirms-sectarian-split-iran -not-us-or-israel.

Pope, Felix, "Israel and Saudi Arabia Deal Expected 'Within a Year' Says Top Israeli Diplomat," *The JC*, December 8, 2022, https://www.thejc.com/news/israel/israel -and-saudi-arabia-deal-expected-within-a-year-says-top-israeli-diplomat-KgL L8HcFQtnzmcjaGrVaf.

"Presenting the Findings From the 2022 Arab Barometer Report: Attitudes Toward International Relations," Middle East Institute, September 15, 2022, https://www .mei.edu/events/presenting-findings-2022-arab-barometer-report-attitudes-toward -international-relations.

Ratzlav-Katz, Nissan, "The King of Bahrain Wants the Jews Back," *Israel National News,* August 14, 2008, https://www.israelnationalnews.com/news/127201.

Schweller, Randall L., "Bandwagoning for Profit: Bringing the Revisionist State Back In," *International Security,* 19(1) (Summer 1994): 72–107, https://www.jstor.org/ stable/2539149.

"Senior Bahraini Diplomat Says Mossad Active in His Country, Boosting Security," *The Times of Israel,* February 21, 2022, https://www.timesofisrael.com/senior-bahraini-diplomat-says-mossad-active-in-his-country/.

"Sheikh "Isa Qasim" Calls for Resistance Against Compromise with Zionists," *IRNA,* Bahman 25, 1400, https://www.irna.ir/news/84650341/%D8%B4%DB %8C%D8%AE-%D8%B9%DB%8C%D8%B3%DB%8C-%D9%82%D8%A7 %D8%B3%D9%85-%D8%AE%D9%88%D8%A7%D8%B3%D8%AA%D8%A7 %D8%B1-%D9%85%D9%82%D8%A7%D9%88%D9%85%D8%AA-%D8%AF %D8%B1-%D9%85%D9%82%D8%A7%D8%A8%D9%84-%D8%B3%D8%A7 %D8%B2%D8%B4-%D8%A8%D8%A7-%D8%B5%D9%87%DB%8C%D9 %88%D9%86%DB%8C%D8%B3%D8%AA-%D9%87%D8%A7-%D8%B4 %D8%AF.

"Sheikh Issa Qassem Warns Bahrainis Against Judaization Scheme," *Iran Press,* September 4, 2022, https://iranpress.com/content/66096/sheikh-issa-qassem-warns -bahrainis-against-judaization-scheme.

Simpson, Archie W., "Realism Small States and Neutrality," *E-International Relations*, February 5, 2018, https://www.e-ir.info/2018/02/05/realism-small-states-and -neutrality/.

"24 Organizations Call on Bahrain Gov't to Expel Zionist Enemy's Ambassador, End Normalization Agreement," *Bahrain Mirror,* May 13, 2021, http://bahrainmirror .com/en/news/59636.html.

Verma, Nidhi, "India, Saudi Arabia Discuss Starting Rupee-Riyal Trade," *Nasdaq,* September 19, 2022, https://www.nasdaq.com/articles/india-saudi-arabia-discuss -starting-rupee-riyal-trade.

Viltard, Yves, "What to Do with the Rhetoric of Amity in International Relations?" *Raisons Politiques,* 33(1) (2009): 127–147, https://www.cairn-int.info/article-E _RAI_033_0127--what-to-do-with-the-rhetoric-of-amity.htm.

Wæver, Ole, "Securitization and Desecuritization," in *On Security*, ed. Ronnie D. Lipschutz (New York: Columbia University Press, 1995), 46–87.

Weiss, Caleb, "State Department Designated Iranian-Backed Bahraini Militia," *FDD's Long War Journal,* December 15, 2020, https://www.longwarjournal .org/archives/2020/12/state-department-designates-iranian-backed-bahraini-militia .php.

Weiss, Caleb, "Bahraini Militia Re-emerges to Threaten New Attacks," *FDD's Long War Journal,* November 3, 2019, https://www.longwarjournal.org/archives/2019 /11/bahraini-militia-reemerges.php.

"What to Know About Second Most Important Figure in Israeli Embassy in Manama," *Bahrain Mirror,* October 27, 2022, http://bahrainmirror.com/en/news/62001.html.

Chapter 6

Qatar, Israel, and the Palestinians

Ambiguous Engagement

Guy Burton

Qatar's relationship with both Israel and the Palestinians is an ambiguous one. On one side, it rejects any normalization without an end to the occupation, a resolution of Israel's conflict with the Palestinians and the creation of a Palestinian state. On the other side, it has also been among the most pragmatic of GCC (Gulf Cooperation Council) states to engage Israel, even before the Abraham Accords. It was one of the first GCC states to allow Israel to set up a mission within its borders, and its leaders regularly met with Israeli officials during the 1990s. Subsequently, it became interested in the opportunities presented by Israeli technological know-how, including in the fields of cybersecurity and surveillance technologies. Although not widely or publicly discussed, a number of Israeli security firms have worked with and in Qatar over the years despite Qatari criticism of it and its treatment of the Palestinians.

Yet Qatar has been more critical of Israel while maintaining a dialogue. Between 2009 and 2022, it donated a total of $861.97 million in humanitarian and development assistance around the world, of which $76.83 million (8.9 percent) went to the occupied Palestinian territory.[1] Over the past decade it has become a key provider of humanitarian assistance to Hamas-controlled Gaza, a relationship that can only be possible with Israel's acquiescence and which by some estimates, has totaled more than $1 billion.[2] That aid has generated tensions in Qatar's other relations with the Palestinians, including with Hamas's principal rival, Fatah, which dominates the Palestinian Authority (PA) and the West Bank.

Qatar's ability to straddle different positions reflects its wider foreign policy behavior, which this chapter delves into. It highlights Qatar's peripheral status in the Gulf and its willingness to engage with parties on opposing sides, including Saudi Arabia, the UAE, and Iran. This "hedging" behavior, along with outreach to important external actors like the United States, is the way that Qatar has sought to protect itself from potential threats. It has resulted in an ambiguous and adventurist foreign policy, in which it has sought to project itself beyond its immediate neighborhood. It has done this by portraying itself as a conflict mediator across the Middle East, including both between the Palestinians and Israel and between the principal Palestinian factions, Hamas, and Fatah.[3]

While conflict mediation has been an important feature of Qatar's projection of itself, it is not the only one. It has also sought to do so through the use of soft power persuasion through its successful bid to host the 2022 football World Cup and as host to the Al Jazeera media network. Formed in 1996, Al Jazeera captured attention across the Arab world during the Second Intifada between Israel and the Palestinians and then the Arab Spring.

Qatar's willingness to pursue these efforts at home and abroad could not have been possible without important domestic factors. As the chapter will show, a settled internal political scene in which there is a virtual absence of social conflict and strife has helped the leadership become more adventurous abroad, along with the country's immense wealth. Qatar's vast natural gas deposits, production, and export have helped make its citizens among the richest on the planet in per capita terms.

QATAR'S FOREIGN POLICY: AN OUTSIDER AND MEDIATOR

Qatar is perhaps best understood as a more contrary actor among the Arab Gulf states. Of the six GCC states it has challenged the more dominant Saudi and Emirati actors the most, and their opposition toward Iran and the Muslim Brotherhood. Qatar's greater accommodation for these two actors has prompted wariness and distrust by Saudi Arabia, the UAE, and Israel who see Doha as unreliable. However, much of the reason for this perception is due to the overall approach toward foreign policy.

In particular, Qatar's adoption of this apparent unreliability reflects its leadership's perception that this best ensures both the regime's and state's security and survival. Doha sees the Gulf region as volatile and has sought to maximize opportunities where possible while diminishing risk. Toward that end, it has adopted a "hedging" strategy between the region's two major powers, Saudi Arabia and Iran, while prioritizing the United States as its principal security provider.[4]

Here hedging has a particular meaning. Hedging involves not taking sides between a state or group of states and instead adopting a position of strategic ambiguity toward them.[5] Such stances are more viable in uncertain international environments and where a hegemonic actor is lacking. At the same time, hedging may also be understood as neither balancing nor band-wagoning, in that it neither resists other actors directly nor joins with them to ensure its security, respectively. Instead, it is a midpoint between the two.[6]

Qatar's differences with Saudi Arabia are long-standing and the result of structural and ideological factors. According to Kamrava, Saudi Arabia, and Qatar occupy contrary positions.[7] Saudi Arabia is a dominant state in the region and aspires to regional hegemony. For smaller states, the options available to them are either to accept such demands or—as in Qatar's case—to resist it. That structural difference is also arguably apparent in an ideological manner as well. While both Saudi and Qatari leaderships subscribe to the Wahhabi school of Islam (including support for authoritarian and dynastic rule), the Qatari version is perceived to be more tolerant than the Saudi version; this is reflected in Doha's greater tolerance of other strains of Islam, including the Shia (the majority faith in Iran) and groups like the Muslim Brotherhood.[8]

The difference between Saudi Arabia and Qatar has been felt in various ways since Qatar gained independence form the British. They have included territorial disputes between the two countries while more recently it has been Qatar's active and unaligned foreign policy that has irritated Riyadh. Especially problematic for Saudi Arabia (and also Israel) is Qatar's willingness to engage in dialogue with Iran. While some in Riyadh and Jerusalem would prefer that the Qataris not do so, that is not an option for Doha. Qatar and Iran share the world's largest known gas field, which is the basis of Qatar's present wealth and power.[9] Therefore, it has to maintain cordial relations with Tehran to ensure its continuing prosperity.

Even if the GCC states and Israel were to acknowledge that necessity, they believe Doha has gone further than it should. In 2010, for example, Doha signed a defense cooperation pact with Tehran.[10] Yet even if Doha's outreach to Iran is more than its Arab neighbors and Israel would like, there are limits. Like other GCC states, Qatar is wary of Iran's nuclear ambitions, especially if it becomes militarized, even as it opposes any particular Israeli attempt to disarm Iran.[11]

In sum then, Qatar's hedging strategy means that its foreign policy is quite distinct from other GCC states. Within the Gulf, Qatar is similar to Saudi Arabia, the UAE, and Kuwait as being the most generous and involved GCC donors and investors. At the same time, it stands out from its neighbors in having a more engaged relationship with Iran (especially when compared to the rivalry between Iran and Saudi Arabia and the territorial tensions between Iran and Bahrain and the UAE).[12]

Qatar's willingness to stand out has also been felt further afield, through its efforts as a conflict mediator around the wider Middle East.[13] The purposes of these efforts have been to portray itself as an important and indispensable state actor that others can call on. While useful in its presentation as a benevolent actor, there is an important element of self-interest too. Involvement in mediation can also limit and contain any conflicts that it addresses, thereby preventing blowback. From the early 2000s, Qatar began to develop this approach by engaging some of the conflict parties associated with Iran, including Hezbollah in Lebanon, Hamas in Palestine, and the Houthis in Yemen. Such relations were unsettling for Saudi Arabia since it entailed dialogue with Iran and its proxies and undermined its own pursuit of regional leadership.

THE UNITED STATES IN QATARI CALCULATIONS

While Qatar's status in the Gulf has largely been that of an outsider, of being outside the tent, it has sought to avoid that perception with its principal ally, the United States. Although Qatar's accommodation of Iran has generated suspicion among the Saudis, Emiratis, and Israel, its outreach toward Iran does not mean that it is pursuing equidistance in all its foreign relations. When it comes to choosing between Washington and Tehran, Doha's inclination is toward the former. Indeed, notwithstanding Qatar's outreach toward Iran, it has presented itself as a useful partner for the United States through its capacity as a third-party mediator that can tackle issues that the United States cannot, for example, with Hamas in Gaza or the Taliban in Afghanistan.[14] In both cases, it has hosted them in Doha, thereby having direct access to them and being able to serve as intermediaries for those opposed to them, like the United States.[15]

That Qatar's mediation efforts can support American interests belies the transformation in relations between the two countries. Although the United States established an embassy in Doha in 1973, relations between the two were fraught during the first two decades. During the 1980s the United States and Qatar were caught in a dispute over Qatar's black-market acquisition of US-made Stinger anti-aircraft missiles. The tension between the two limited cooperation and prompted Congress to vote for a ban on arms sales to Qatar. It also led to Qatari criticism of American military actions in the Gulf and Washington's concern at Qatari support for "terrorist" groups.[16]

Relations improved with the 1990 Gulf crisis and Qatar's contribution of troops during the first Gulf War in 1991. In 1992, Qatar signed a defense cooperation agreement with the United States, which heralded the current state of the relationship. During the 1990s, Washington placed its regional military command, CENTCOM (the US Central Command), in the emirate. In 2003, the Americans moved their air operations center from Saudi Arabia to the Al Udeid airbase in Qatar and Doha contributed $400 million to construct and upgrade the facilities there.[17] Doha's willingness to invest in the base rather than have the Americans pay for it may be seen as an indication that it wants Washington to base itself permanently in the country.[18]

The closeness of the Qatar-US relationship transcends Qatar's more fraught relationship with its Arab neighbors and rejection of normalization with Israel. The Saudis' and Emiratis' persuasion of President Donald Trump that Qatar was an unreliable partner and supporter of both terrorism and Iran helped discredit Doha and initiate the two countries' blockade of Qatar in mid-2017. But further American backing was not forthcoming, owing to push back from within the American political system as well as Qatar's own efforts at persuasion. In 2017, for instance, Qatar tripled its spending on lobbying activities in Washington to $13 million and keeping it at over $10 million each year thereafter.[19]

It helped that the importance of Qatar to American interests was widely recognized beyond the Trump administration. American officials have been willing to give Qatar some latitude in its actions, including its engagement of actors that the United States finds problematic, like Hezbollah in Lebanon and Hamas in Gaza. Indeed, some sources in Qatar have suggested that Hamas's political office was set up in Doha in coordination with the United States as a way of enabling "indirect lines of communication."[20] That Qatar would do this may have been motivated by self-interest and intended to avoid blowback, as the US ambassador to Qatar in 2008–2011, Joseph LeBaron, observed when he wrote that "we do believe Qatar has been reluctant to combat the financing of terrorist groups and activities in part because it does not want to invite an attack by antagonizing terrorist groups."[21]

In February 2022, Washington granted Qatar the status of "major non-NATO ally," a legal definition that the United States has given to twenty other countries, including Australia, Israel, Japan, and Brazil. That recognition places it ahead of other and more prominent regional powers like Saudi Arabia and the UAE.[22] Among the reasons put forward to explain its elevated status are Qatar's role in mediating with the Taliban in Afghanistan and in becoming a key source of natural gas for the West in the wake of Russia's invasion of Ukraine.[23]

The closeness of the United States and Qatar alliance transcends Qatar's differences with Israel and the Abraham Accords. Despite Qatar's criticism of current moves toward normalization, it has had to accommodate Israel's presence through its American ally. Following the upgrade in Qatar-American relations, in March 2022, Qatari military officials joined their counterparts from Saudi Arabia, the UAE, Egypt, Jordan, the United States, and Israel to discuss a plan for joint missile defense. Then in July, it was reported that Israeli military officials had traveled to Qatar, ostensibly to meet American military officials at CENTCOM. Although officials from Qatar were reticent to state how many Israelis were present in the country, the move was a consequence of the Americans' reorganization of their regional security arrangements following normalization, which brought Israel into CENTCOM.[24]

In sum then, Qatar's significance to the United States means that its past and present behavior as an "awkward" actor in the Gulf has and can be over-looked. Moreover, it would appear that Qatar's contribution toward American objectives means that Washington is willing to accept its ambiguous stance toward Israel and its aid to Gaza. Indeed, it seems to have done so for much the same reasons as the Israelis see it: as a way of ensuring a degree of stability and order in the territory.

QATAR'S POLITICAL TIES WITH ISRAEL
AND THE PALESTINIANS

The Abraham Accords are but the latest expression of normalization between the Arab world and Israel. Earlier efforts included the Camp David agreement between Israel and Egypt in 1979 and the Israel-Jordan peace agreement in the wake of the Oslo Accords, in 1994. Beyond these two most formal expressions, there have been others, including the attempt at the Madrid conference in 1991 and in the subsequent multilateral talks which took place the following year.

Qatar was among the first Arab states to embrace the opportunity. Qatar supported the GCC's observer status at Madrid. Later, following the Oslo Accords, Qatar and Oman were the two GCC states which most actively pursued normalization with Israel.[25] Qatar's steps were initially tentative, reflecting the nature of Sheikh Khalifa Al-Thani, the country's then leader, or Emir. But in 1995, his son, Sheikh Hamad bin Khalifa Al-Thani, seized power, and outreach toward Israel became more substantive. It was during this time that the Israelis opened a trade office in Doha, one of the first in the Gulf. There were also talks about the possibility of Israel being supplied with Qatari gas. Qatar sent representatives to assassinated prime minister Rabin's funeral and also hosted Shimon Peres, his successor, in 1996.[26]

Even as Qatar and Israel explored possibilities, Doha did not discount the Palestinians. Sheikh Hamad made several visits to the occupied territory and met with the Palestinian leader, Yasser Arafat. Officially, it adhered to the Arab consensus that a resolution of the conflict required a Palestinian state.

Qatar's attempts to have it both ways faced growing difficulties, especially following Likud's election in 1996. The new government, led by Benjamin Netanyahu, was less enthusiastic about the Oslo process. A consequence of this was that Israel's previously encouraging relations with the Gulf countries began to cool. The exception to this, however, was Qatar.

Through the 1990s, Qatar continued to explore dialogue with Israel. Israeli ministers were invited to participate in the 1997 Fourth Economic Conference of MENA Countries in Doha and despite Gulf pressure on Qatar to withdraw the offer and public opposition. Several countries, including Saudi Arabia, the UAE, Egypt, Morocco, the PA, Syria, and Lebanon, all boycotted the event.[27]

Following Ehud Barak's victory in the 1999 election, Qatar's leaders were more optimistic that the new prime minister would re-energize the peace process. However, Barak and the Emir had a difficult meeting on the side of the UN Millennium Summit in New York in 2000, soon after the Second Intifada broke out, subsuming earlier efforts at engagement. Qatar allowed protests against Israel to take place and the Emir refused to meet with Barak at the latter's request.[28]

Qatar initially resisted pressure from other Arab states to break relations with Israel when the Second Intifada began. Saudi Arabia threatened to boycott the Organization of Islamic Cooperation conference that was scheduled to take place in Doha. Eventually the pressure proved too great and Israel's trade mission was temporarily expelled. However, clandestine contact continued, including several meetings between high-level representatives between 2000 and 2003.[29]

Notwithstanding these visits, relations between Qatar and Israel remained at a low ebb during the early 2000s. This continued after the Second Intifada and the Second Lebanon War both ended. But whereas Qatar had previously been conciliatory and discreet toward Israel in the 1990s, now it was more confrontational and vocal after 2006. It criticized Israel for what it saw as "disproportionate" attacks on Lebanon that went beyond its rivalry with Hezbollah to inflame the whole country. In part, Qatar's greater antagonism coincided with the country's higher international profile as a temporary member of the United Nations Security Council. Qatar also offered to send peacekeepers to the region.[30]

Beyond the fiery rhetoric, however, contact between Israel and Qatar continued. It included a visit between Prime Minister Shimon Peres and the emir in 2007. Yet despite this, relations between Qatar and Israel were not especially warm, and Qatari appeals to restart the peace process was complicated by Israel's rejection of any Hamas involvement.[31] Instead, they deteriorated following Israel's military action in Gaza in 2008–2009. Israel's trade office was closed again, relations were frozen, and Qatar advised other Arab states to do the same.[32] Soon after, Qatar hosted an emergency summit in Doha, but only more radical groups like Hamas, Palestinian Islamic Jihad, and the Popular Front for the Liberation of Palestine attended; PA and

Fatah leader Abbas did not, along with Egypt, Saudi Arabia, and the other GCC states.[33]

By now the distance between Israel and Qatar looked wide. In March 2011, Israel broke its last remaining ties with Qatar, which included banning Qatari passport holders from visiting the West Bank and ending the "discreet" cooperation between the two countries' security sectors.[34]

As relations between Israel and Qatar worsened, Doha looked to reconcile the growing differences between the two main Palestinian factions. Those had become more acute in 2006–2007 following Hamas's election victory, short-lived government, and fighting with Fatah which split the occupied territory between Fatah's control of the West Bank and Hamas's of Gaza.

Qatari efforts began in late 2006 when it hosted talks between the two sides. Those efforts were subsequently overshadowed by the Saudi effort in 2007, which brought the two sides together in the short-lived Mecca Agreement in March 2007.[35] Then in February 2012, Qatar invited the Fatah and Hamas factions again for reconciliation talks. The two agreed to establish a national unity government pending elections. A lack of sufficient compromise by the two parties, an absence of guarantees to enforce the Doha Agreement and the non-involvement of more influential Arab mediators like Egypt, meant it did not last. It was soon succeeded by a Cairo Agreement in May, but like the previous effort, the partnership did not hold and elections did not happen.[36] Later, following fighting between Israel and Hamas in 2014, Qatar also played an important backstage role in enabling indirect dialogue between Israel and Hamas, which contributed to the Egypt-led ceasefire in August.[37]

Qatar's attempts at Palestinian reconciliation were not only the result of its mediation-driven foreign policy after 2000 but were also helped by its greater access to Hamas—a stance that has been less available to other GCC states. Indeed, Qatar's connections to Hamas reflect its own, earlier links to the Muslim Brotherhood, from which Hamas emerged. Beginning in the 1950s, Doha hosted growing numbers of Brothers to help staff its educational system. Their presence served a mutual purpose: for the Muslim Brotherhood, Qatar was a refuge, especially given the persecution they faced from Arab nationalist leaderships elsewhere, especially in Egypt. For Doha, it provided a means to distinguish itself from its Saudi neighbor, who both shared the Wahhabist creed and viewed Qatar as part of their territorial and religio-ideological domain. What made the Muslim Brothers' presence in Qatar different from that in Saudi Arabia were the limits they faced: as well as providing an alternative source of instructors to Saudi educators, they did not become entrenched in the Qatari state or society and acquire ideological power as happened in Saudi Arabia. This meant there was no similar reckoning in Qatar between the leadership and the Brothers as there was in Saudi Arabia in the 1990s when the royal family eventually turned against them.[38]

The Brothers' arrival in Qatar coincided with that of other exiles, including Palestinians. Throughout the 1950s and 1960s, they came in growing numbers, rivaling Kuwait in terms of the size of the diaspora. Among their number included Mahmoud Abbas, who worked in the education ministry between 1957 and 1969. He and other like-minded individuals, including Shaker Al Natshah and Hani Hassan would contribute to the building of the Palestinian Liberation Organisation, taking on leadership roles in later decades.[39]

The presence of outsiders like the Brothers and Palestinians did not challenge Qatar's leadership. Whereas the Brotherhood was able to build public support elsewhere through its involvement in the community, running schools and hospitals, it was unable to do so in Qatar. Certainly the Brothers had been able to work within Qatar's education system and even set up educational establishments, but their actions in the country were politically and ideologically circumscribed. There were few institutional opportunities for religious scholars and a prohibition of proselytization. This limited space for them to build up domestic influence, promoting to project their efforts outward, beyond the country's borders, which Qatari rulers could accept.[40]

Alongside the constraints that the Brothers faced, the Qatari leadership was also active in building up its own legitimacy. In particular, this was achieved through the generation of rents from the country's massive gas reserves, which provided the resources necessary for the Al-Thanis to build a welfare state that met citizens' demands and needs while undermining the influence of others.[41]

The relative weakness of Islamists like the Muslim Brotherhood inside Qatar has meant that the country's leadership has since gained the confidence to host an assortment of other exiles. They have included potentially useful political figures like the Palestinian Christian pan-Arabist and former Knesset member, Azmi Bishara as well as Hamas's Ahmed Meshal, who moved to Doha following the closure of the Hamas office in Jordan in 1999. Beyond these Palestinians, Qatar has also played host to other Arab visitors: these have included the Tunisian Ennahda leader Raschid Ghannouchi, the former Algerian Islamist leader Abbasi Madani, the Libyan cleric Ali Al Sallabi and the former Mauritanian president, Maaouya Ould Sid Ahmed Taya. To their number may also include the prominent Egyptian cleric and Brother, Yusuf Al Qaradawi, who acquired a reputation as a prominent and influential religious scholar disseminating Brotherhood thinking across the Middle East, owing in part to his "Sharia and Life" talk show on the Al Jazeera network since the mid-1990s. In addition to Al Qaradawi, Qatar became home to other, less politically useful characters like Omar bin Laden, a son of Osama bin Laden.[42] Qatar's preparedness to allow these dissidents in may also have contributed to the suspicion and distrust that others in the Gulf, like the

Saudis and Emiratis, have for Doha, adding to their perception of the emirate as unreliable.

QATAR'S ECONOMIC RELATIONS WITH ISRAEL AND THE PALESTINIANS

The 1990s was the heyday for the Oslo process. During this time, Qatar was one of the few places in the Gulf where Israel had an official mission, in the form of a trade office. But from 2000, the relationship between Qatar and Israel became more strained, owing at first to the Second Intifada and then after, the Second Lebanese War. Yet even as differences between them arose, the trade office remained an important point of contact. Only in 2009, following Israel's military action against Hamas in Gaza in Operation Cast Lead, was it finally closed at Qatar's request.

Despite the differences between the two, in 2010, the then-Israeli industry, trade, and labor minister visited Doha. Soon after Qatar offered to reestablish relations with Israel, which also included reopening its trade office. At the same time, it offered to finance reconstruction work in Gaza. However, the offer went nowhere. For one, there were machinations by Egypt's then leader, Hosni Mubarak, who resented Sheikh Hamad's seizure of power from his father while he was visiting Cairo and then Europe in 1995 followed his suspicion that Qatar was subsequently behind Palestinian pressure to overrun Egypt's border checkpoint with Gaza in 2009.[43] At the same time, Israel was suspicious of Qatari ties with both Iran and Hamas: Prime Minister Netanyahu claimed that construction materials could be used by Hamas to build bunkers and rocket launchers which could then be used against Israel.[44]

Despite his suspicions, Netanyahu went ahead with meeting Qatar's prime minister in Paris that year. Later, in May 2013, an Israeli trade delegation visited Doha, which generated speculation about potential Qatari investment in Israel's high-tech sector.[45] Details of what this and other exchanges in the sector entailed have been scant, owing to the sensitive nature of such ties alongside Doha's public position vis-à-vis Israel and the Palestinians. What is known is that Israeli firms have done business with and in Qatar. The Sdema Group, for instance, supplied the emirate with physical and cybersecurity services during the 2022 football World Cup. The NSO Group (named after its founders: Niv, Shalev, and Omri) and Gamma Group indicated interest in pursuing opportunities in Qatar, and there were suggestions that Qatar showed interest in Israeli surveillance technology, including investment by some minority shareholders linked to Qatar in Israel's Candiru company.[46]

Beyond the interest in high-tech and surveillance technologies, Israel and Qatar have also managed to make other economic sectors work between them. One notable example came months after the Abraham Accords when the two reached an agreement in relation to the diamond market in 2021. The deal allowed Qatar to join the international list of countries allowed to trade in diamonds and Israeli merchants to enter the country without obstruction and establish a formal presence if necessary. Qatar's involvement had been blocked in part by the UAE, which following the end of the intra-Gulf crisis, withdrew its objections toward Qatar. However, while the deal was important for Qataris and Israelis working in the diamond market, it is not apparent that this will have a spillover effect on further commercial interaction between the two.[47]

If current economic exchanges between Qatar and Israel are both limited and opaque, they have been more visible and important with the Palestinians, particularly Hamas in Gaza.

Qatar's first direct financial assistance to Hamas was in 2006. After Hamas won the elections that year and took over the PA, its funds were frozen by Israel, the United States, and the European Union. Qatar responded by donating $22 million to help cover civil servants' salaries.[48] Later, Qatar's contributions rose to $50 million when Doha met Hamas officials to help reconciliation between it and their Fatah rivals.[49]

Later, following Qatar's offer to help rebuild Gaza in 2010, Sheikh Hamad paid a visit to the territory in 2012. The visit was notable for being the first by a head of state after Hamas had taken control. Sheikh Hamad again repeated the offer he had made a few years earlier, declaring his intention to spend $400 million to help rebuild roads and houses.[50]

Again, the proposal faced opposition. In Israel, the Netanyahu government feared that the money would not reach the poor who needed it, but be taken up by Hamas to finance its operations against Israel.[51] In the West Bank, Fatah opposed it on the grounds that it undermined Palestinian political unity (and its own status as the principal Palestinian political actor) by tacitly recognizing Hamas's control of Gaza. Yet regardless of the opposition, Doha pressed ahead while claiming that its assistance would be systematic and transparent and not trigger Israeli prohibitions on dual-use equipment. Toward that end then, it made use of both bank transfers and cash. Qatar used bank transfers as a way to track money and ensure that it did not end up in Hamas's pockets.[52] At the same time, Qatar also made use of cash to pay for the building of infrastructure, education, and medical projects in the territory, as well as to families directly, to ensure they had some income.[53]

Qatar's offer to finance Gazan reconstruction set it apart from other GCC states, as one of the most generous. After the 2014 Israel-Hamas war it pledged up to $1 billion at the donors' conference in Cairo.[54] Over time Qatar's contributions became regularized, and from 2018 Qatar was supplying a monthly grant of $30 million to support salaries and provide subsidies to the local population.[55]

Yet even if Qatar has gained a prominent status as a donor to the Palestinians, it is worth noting several aspects of Qatari assistance. One is that Qatar's pledges and disbursements have not always matched up. Although this is a common feature of most states, Zureik notes that by 2016 Qatar had only disbursed 19 percent of its pledged amount, against 23 percent by Saudi Arabia.[56] Drawing on newspaper sources and official accounts, Zureik calculated that Qatar's contribution to Palestine has been less than promised, at around $800 million. Notwithstanding the lower amounts, it does appear that the bulk of Qatari assistance has been concentrated on essential needs like housing, health, education, and poverty alleviation.

QATAR'S SECURITY CONSIDERATIONS OVER ISRAEL/PALESTINE

Qatar's differences between Israel and Fatah on one side and growing involvement with Gaza and Hamas on the other occurred in the wake of the Arab Spring. Those mobilizations put into chain a series of political upheavals across the region, many of which are still playing out today.

That change challenged Qatar's foreign policy activism and conflict mediation. Before 2011, Qatar's pursuit of a more prominent role for itself had occurred in a regional system that was largely stable at both the international level and between states and their societies. By contrast, after 2011, Qatar had to deal with a wider context that included a relative decline in American hegemony and the emergence of other, outside powers like China and Russia. Within the region, Qatar and other GCC states had to deal with the consequence of fracturing societies from Libya to Syria and Yemen. Even Bahrain looked at risk, prompting the Saudis to lead a force across the causeway to contain the protests and provide backing to the leadership there—a move that Qatar quietly concurred with.

The backlash in Bahrain contrasted with earlier Qatari activism elsewhere. Qatar had backed the 2011 Arab Spring uprisings from the start, a position that was amplified by the Al Jazeera media network that had been based in Doha since 1996. Qatar threw support behind opposition groups in Libya and Syria, supplying them with military and financial assistance.[57] Yet even as it did so in this early period, Qatar was not unique: in Libya, for instance, its more aggressive stance was broadly in line with wider Arab opinion, where it joined other states in what was a critical Arab League stance against Gaddafi. Similarly, in Syria, other states, like Turkey and Iran, were also actively acquiring clients to sponsor.

Even as Qatar supported the changes taking place, it also tried to manage them. It tried to adopt the same path it had taken over the previous decade and engage as many different groups and partners as possible. In part that was done so as to ensure that no one group felt ignored and prompt them to hold a grudge against Doha. But there was a flipside to this stance: it also meant engaging radical Islamists, which set Qatar against other regional regimes who were suspicious of such groups and their Qatari backer.[58] It is in this light that Qatar's donations to Gaza may also partly be understood. Although Sheikh Hamad's offer predated the uprisings, the bulk of Qatari assistance has taken place since then.

Despite its initial reservations about Qatar's aid to Gaza, Israel subsequently came around to see its value. Israeli leaders condoned Qatar's involvement because the funds helped to limit tensions and offered a degree of stability. Additionally, Israel saw Qatar as a more reliable partner than the Fatah-led PA, whose influence and authority were being eroded by Israeli intransigence on the peace process and hostile action against Palestinians.[59]

Qatar's presence in Gaza arguably gave it greater access to Hamas. That may have given Doha an expectation that it should be an important party to any reconciliation talks, whether between the Palestinian factions themselves or between the Palestinians and Israel.[60] Indeed, after 2011, Qatar's leadership appealed to Israel to restart negotiations with the Palestinians. To support this position, Doha pointed to the changes taking place, including Mubarak's fall and Israel's apparent isolation in the Middle East[61]—a position that was ironically undermined after 2017 when Qatar itself faced isolation at the hands of the Saudis and Emiratis and Israel extended its contacts wider in the Gulf, culminating in the Abraham Accords.

Even if some in Israel welcomed the Saudi and UAE-led blockade of Qatar in 2017, others viewed it with concern. Although Riyadh's and Abu Dhabi's intentions were focused on curbing Qatari outreach to Iran and limiting Tehran's influence in the Gulf, it had potential repercussions in Gaza. While Israeli leaders shared Saudi and Emirati sentiment toward Iran, the blockade threatened to limit Qatar's involvement and finance in Gaza. Because Qatar had to divert funds to boost domestic production and redirect supply routes, that risked reducing the transfers to Gaza. That could have undermined the stability that had been built up via Qatari payments. For thoughtful Israeli observers, were Hamas to find itself in a financial crisis as a result of the Saudi/UAE blockade of Qatar, it might look toward Iran as an alternative sponsor.[62]

That Iran might advance in Gaza at the expense of Qatar was anathema to Israeli leaders. One response then was for Israel to encourage alternate involvement and assistance from the other Arab Gulf states to Gaza despite their own aversion to Hamas.[63] This became amplified in the wake of the

Abraham Accords when Israel wanted to encourage more involvement by its new UAE partner in relation to the Palestinians. But while Abu Dhabi indicated some interest, it was unable to move forward significantly, because Qatar continued to remain the preeminent Arab Gulf state actor in Gaza.[64]

Yet even if Qatar remains ahead of the UAE as a partner in Gaza, its position as a vital party to the Palestinian question and mediation is by no means assured. While the principal Palestinian political axis has and remains that between Fatah and Hamas, there are signs that the two parties' positions and authority are being eroded by developments on the ground. Not only has there been a growing disconnect between the two parties and wider Palestinian society over the years, but most recently a number of armed groups have emerged or grown in influence in recent years in both the West Bank and Gaza, from the Lion's Den and Jenin Brigades in the former to Islamic Jihad in the latter.[65] While such groups are far from challenging Fatah's or Hamas's current dominance, they do represent separate voices which Qatar does not yet (publicly) acknowledge or engage.

Additionally, Qatar's position as the principal Gulf partner in Gaza may not survive the Israel-Hamas war that began in October 2023 and followed a surprise attack by the group in southern Israel and the taking of over 200 Israeli hostages into Gaza. The reaction by Israel's leadership and public has been more existential than it has hitherto been following previous Hamas attacks. The government declared its determination to eliminate Hamas and mounted a military campaign whose impact may well upend previous arrangements.[66] This has presented Qatar with both an opportunity and a challenge. On the one hand, Qatar's links with Hamas have made it a key party to talks over freeing the hostages and establishing a ceasefire following Israel's subsequent invasion and destruction of the territory, its infrastructure, and its people. On the other hand, Israel's public rejection to allow Hamas to remain in Gaza threatens Qatar's status in Gaza. Indeed, some in Israel want to go further and call Qatar an "enemy state" for hosting Hamas leaders and financing the group.[67]

LEADERSHIP AND CHANGE IN QATAR

Qatar's foreign policy in general and in relation to Israel and the Palestinians has operated under a relatively stable leadership at home, and one which looks set to continue. Qatar is ruled by the Al Thani family, whose dominance has meant very little space for others, whether in the form of civil or political rights. The country is categorized as "not free" by Freedom House, with a ranking of 5.5 out of a total average of 7 over most of the past two decades.

Despite Qatar's low ranking, however, it is comparatively more free than other GCC countries, with the exception of Kuwait.[68]

Since independence in 1971, Qatar has experienced only three changes of power. The first, several months after the British left, took place when Sheikh Khalifa Al-Thani, who had previously served as prime minister and finance minister in the 1960s, overthrew his cousin, Sheikh Ahmad Al-Thani. Sheikh Khalifa stayed in power until 1995, when he was similarly deposed by his son, Sheikh Hamad, in a palace coup. Sheikh Hamad ruled until 2013 when he abdicated in favor of his son, Sheikh Tamim.

In each case, the incoming ruler had prior administrative experience. That meant there was a degree of overlap from one ruler to the next, even when the transition was confrontational and abrupt, as in 1972 and 1995. Sheikh Hamad, for instance, had control over the country's oil and gas industry during his father's reign. Sheikh Tamim, similarly, had a similar background in the economic sphere, along with key security portfolios during the decade before he took over. At the time of his accession, it was unclear why Sheikh Hamad chose to hand over to Sheikh Tamim when he did, not least because it coincided with a reversal in Qatar's fortunes, when the Muslim Brotherhood presidency of Mohamed Morsi was overthrown in Egypt. Although the timing was unfortunate, it has been speculated that Hamad's health had begun to fail.[69]

In general, the transition from one ruler to the next has not led to a substantial change in Qatar's foreign policy. Instead, it has been one of style. For example, Sheikh Tamim was expected to keep much of Sheikh Hamad's activist foreign policy and efforts to be a conflict mediator in place, even if it was also assumed that he would present himself as less confrontational or contentious toward his neighbors.[70]

Indeed, Sheikh Tamim appeared to live up to prior expectations. Soon after taking over, he refused to align with a common GCC position in the region, which set him against several of his neighbors, including the Saudis and Emiratis. That resulted in a brief, nine-month diplomatic boycott in 2014 when Saudi, UAE, and Bahraini ambassadors were withdrawn.[71] Yet even though the ambassadors returned at the end of the year, the consensus at the time was that the underlying differences between Qatar and its regional neighbors had not been fully resolved.[72] Those differences would remain dormant until they burst into life once again in mid-2017, when the Saudis and Emiratis imposed a diplomatic and economic blockade against the country.

On the Israeli-Palestinian file, Sheikh Tamim continued the course already set. Qatar continued to be critical of Israeli behavior and reiterated the need for a resolution that included a Palestinian state. Doha also continued to send assistance to Gaza and even reorganized it from early 2018, when aid was delivered on a monthly basis. That Sheikh Tamim was able to follow his father's lead was helped greatly by the domestic environment. Despite the lack of freedom, Qatar's political system is extremely stable, a development that was helped by the highly homogenous and cohesive nature of Qatar's national population in ethnic and religious terms.[73] Stability has been helped by Qatar's immense wealth, which enabled it to sustain its adventurist foreign policy, in particular the second hydrocarbon boom which took place after 2000 (the first having taken place during the 1970s).

During the second boom, oil and gas producers kept hold of the massive rents generated by hydrocarbon production and sale. The revenues were plowed into national sovereign wealth funds and used by states to increase their influence externally.[74] Perhaps with that in mind, Doha took a forward-thinking decision when it established the Qatar Investment Agency in 2005. Today the fund is estimated as being worth $450 billion. That money has been used by Qatar to diversify the country's economic prospects as well as risks—and was significant in sustaining the country during the Gulf blockade between 2017 and 2021 by helping boost local production and import substi-tution policies while also realigning its trade routes and partners.

QATAR-ISRAEL TIES SINCE THE ABRAHAM ACCORDS

Following the UAE's announcement that it would normalize relations with Israel and the later Abraham Accords, Qatar has stated its unwillingness to do the same. In February 2022, for instance, the foreign minister Sheikh Mohammed bin Abdulrahman al-Thani said that this would remain the case "in the absence of [Israel's] real commitment to a two-state solution."[75]

Yet even though Qatar will not recognize Israel, a tacit relationship exists between them. That was not only illustrated by Qatar's agreeing to allow tem-porary flights between Tel Aviv and Doha during the World Cup and allow up to 30,000 Israelis to visit the country during the tournament—a decision that prompted a small-scale protest in the emirate by an anti-normalization group. Even though a Qatari official claimed that it did not constitute a change in the country's position vis-à-vis Israel, the exchange did extend to a phone call between Israel's acting prime minister, Yair Lapid, and Qatar's foreign minister.[76] Since then, Qatari and Israeli officials have been in further direct contact; following the outbreak of the Israel-Hamas war in October 2023, Qatari officials have allegedly worked with Mossad and intelligence delegations hosted in Israel to find ways to free the Israeli hostages taken into Gaza.[77]

That Qatar maintains a formal connection with Israel may perhaps be lost on many Palestinians and their supporters, who presume that Qatar's stance portrays a hard-line position vis-à-vis Israel and that it is unwilling to abandon them.[78] Certainly, so long as Qatar continues to maintain its current line—that normalization with Israel cannot come before a resolution of the Palestinian-Israeli conflict and a peace agreement—then the Palestinians may argue that they continue to have an element of relevance in the Gulf.[79] At the same time, Qatar's current solidarity with the Palestinians may only be politically expedient; should the advantages of normalization with Israel become more appealing and outweigh the value of the Palestinians to Qatari foreign policy, then that could herald a shift in behavior.[80] For example, Qatar's contacts with Hamas have meant that it was able to lead negotiations for the return of some of the Israeli hostages taken after Hamas's surprise attack on Israel on October 7, 2023. At the same time, it has faced pressure to review its willingness to host Hamas leaders in the country[81]—a position that it could follow through should it judge it to be in its interests. At the time of writing, it is uncertain what will happen in this regard. As for October 2023, Qatar's star was high among some Palestinians—especially those in Gaza and by Hamas. By contrast, Qatar's relations with the Fatah-led PA were less robust in comparison; Qatar's involvement in Gaza constituted an effective recognition of Hamas, its main rival.[82]

Regardless of the difference in warmth between Qatar's ties to Hamas and Fatah, on the big issue of the Israeli-Palestinian conflict, Doha faced less complications than some of its neighbors have had since the Abraham Accords. This came to a head in May–June 2021, when violence erupted between Israelis and Palestinians, not just between Israel and Hamas but also in Jerusalem and in several cities across Israel, where Jews and Palestinians clashed.

During the fighting between Israel and Hamas, Qatari financial assistance was suspended. Once the violence ended, they resumed, but this time in different format. The new Israeli government was opposed to any funding that might directly benefit Hamas and its officials. Consequently, an agreement was reached in October 2021 whereby Qatar's money would be used to buy fuel and construction materials from Egypt. These would be transferred to Gaza and sold by Hamas, the revenue being used to support civil servants' salaries.[83]

Also in this period, Qatar offered a larger sum of $500 million to help with Gaza's economic recovery. The amount, which was offered in summer 2021, was matched by Egypt—although it was suggested that the amount might have actually been UAE money. As for whether this UAE/Egyptian money would make a difference, both in terms of financing reconstruction and in challenging Qatar's influence in the territory, was unclear; in contrast to the UAE, Qatar's presence in Gaza was established for longer and was perceived as a more reliable partner by Hamas.[84]

During the first half of 2022, attacks on Israelis prompted a heavier Israeli response, including raids against armed groups in the West Bank and killing of civilians that also included the journalist Shireen Abu Akleh. Among Israel's targets were leaders of Islamic Jihad, which eventually led to airstrikes against the group in Gaza in August. Over three days nearly fifty Palestinians were killed, including seventeen children. The attacks were condemned across the Arab world, with Qatar issuing "strong condemnation and denunciation" toward Israel and repeating its commitment toward the Palestinians and an independent Palestinian state.[85] Soon after, the Qatar Red Crescent Society announced a $1.1 million humanitarian package to cover food support, medical support, and rehabilitation of both damaged homes and water and sewage systems. The support was welcomed by the Hamas government, even as it noted that the territory required $3 billion to fulfill its development and reconstruction needs.[86]

At the same time, however, relations between Qatar and Hamas were not as positive as they were often portrayed. This was most visible in August 2023, two months before the surprise Hamas attack on southern Israel. Then the Administrative Committee of the Gaza Strip declared that employees' salaries were being cut by 5 percent, a step which followed other austerity measures also taken by the Hamas leadership. A cut in Qatari assistance was suspected to be behind the development, although other suggestions were also put forward, including possible US or Saudi pressure on Qatar and Israel allowing more Egyptian goods and fuel to enter the territory and squeeze the availability of money. To these was also a suggestion that Qatar had taken exception to the Hamas leadership's improving relationship with both Iran and Syria, especially following a visit by a delegation from the group to Damascus in October 2022.[87]

CONCLUSION

This chapter has highlighted the ambiguous nature of Qatar's foreign policy, not only in the Gulf but also in relation to Israel and the Palestinians. Within the Gulf, it sets itself at odds with the regional hegemon, Saudi Arabia and its UAE partner, by engaging with Iran. That behavior aroused suspicion within Israel, which also shared that wariness with Qatar's larger neighbors. Moreover, Israeli guardedness was compounded further by Qatari humanitarian and reconstruction assistance to Gaza, which served only to entrench its rival, Hamas.

At the same time, however, Israel's distaste was tempered by the fact that Qatari assistance discharged Israel from its responsibility as an occupying power and paying for its siege of Gaza. In addition, it provided a modicum of sustenance to the Gaza population which ensured stability until October 2023 and kept Hamas in power. Although Hamas remained in control until then and constituted a danger to Israel, it was judged to be a known threat. As a result, Qatar was useful to Israel, even as it remains outside the circle of normalizing countries.

Qatar's strong and critical stance on Israel toward the Palestinians must also be viewed with some caution. While Qatari aid to Palestine—and specifically Gaza—was a prominent feature of Qatar's foreign policy over the past decade, this must be set against the fact that Qatar was historically one of the GCC states closest to achieving a normalization with Israel during the highpoint of the Oslo period. Indeed, Qatar was among the last to retreat from normalization following the outbreak of the Second Intifada; but even then, the break was never complete, as dialogue continued thereafter.

In essence, Qatar's behavior toward Israel and the Palestinians suggested that while it was cloaked in principle, it remained highly pragmatic. That was evident not just in its approach toward Israel and the Palestinians and among the Palestinians but through its wider regional and foreign policy more generally, in particular the use of hedging. Even as it berated Israel, it held an olive branch toward it, just as its aid to Gaza did not seem intended to replace one Palestinian faction with another. Similarly, even as it sought to evade Saudi pressure and engage with Iran, it did so on its own terms and without ever forgetting its primary partnership with the United States. Indeed, that relationship with the United States not only led to dividends, in the form of it being recognized as a non-NATO ally, but also meant that compromises had to be sought, through the presence of Israeli military officials based in their country.

For Qatar, such trade-offs were judged as a price worth paying. Its foreign policy behavior was adventurist, which also included wider efforts at conflict mediation and dialogue with different groups. Those efforts constituted very self-interested activity by a small state with substantial material resources to boost its regional importance (and necessity) and in so doing, insulated itself from potential threats, especially by its neighbors. At the same time, its leadership shows a degree of realism regarding the scope of its influence; in January 2024 Qatar's prime minister Sheikh Mohammad bin Abdulrahman bin Jassim Al-Thani claimed that its leverage over Hamas in its fight with Israel since October 2023 was largely one of "words and proposals for solutions" when it came to tackling the hostage crisis and a ceasefire in Gaza: "We don't see that Qatar is a superpower that can impose something."[88]

Looking ahead, should current circumstances change—and this is a strong possibility given Israeli calculations regarding its previous accommodation of Hamas in Gaza after October 2023—then it is highly likely that so will Qatari calculations will also have to change. One might be whether Saudi Arabia was to join the UAE and Bahrain in eventually recognizing Israel and formalizing relations. Were that to happen, Doha would have a choice to make: whether to accept the direction that Arab Gulf relations are heading with Israel and also do the same. Then the prospects for the Palestinians would become even gloomier than they currently are. They would find themselves sidelined by the richest and politically influential Arab states in the Middle East, which could result in them receiving less attention to their plight and potentially a loss of financial aid.

By contrast, Doha might find it in its interest to maintain its current stance, especially if the Saudis did recognize Israel. Doing so would help it stand apart from other Arab Gulf states and boost its status as the most prominent backer of Palestinian rights. Yet even this may not be enough to improve the Palestinians' status either in the Gulf or in their dealings with Israel. As this chapter has shown, although Qatar has sought to stand apart from Israel on the Palestinian issue, it has also engaged in forms of informal and discreet normalization that can only have adverse effects on Palestine and the Palestinians.

NOTES

1. OCHA Services, "Humanitarian Aid Contributions," Financial Tracking Services, https://fts.unocha.org/.
2. Intelligence Online, "Doha, like Abu Dhabi, also Hooked on Israeli Technology," August 26, 2020, https://www.intelligenceonline.com/government-intelligence/2020/08/26/doha-like-abu-dhabi-also-hooked-on-israeli-technology,109602026-evg; Stuart Winer, "Qatar Gave Over $1.1 billion to Gaza Strip from 2012-18, Ministers Told," *The Times of Israel*, February 11, 2019, https://www.timesofisrael.com/qatar-gave-over-1-1-billion-to-gaza-strip-over-six-years-report/.
3. See Mehran Kamrava, *Qatar: Small State, Big Politics* (Ithaca, NY: Cornell University Press, 2013); Mehran Kamrava, "The Foreign Policy of Qatar," in *The Foreign Policies of Middle East States*, eds. Raymond Hinnebusch and Anoushiravan Ehteshami (Boulder, CO: Lynne Rienner, 2014), 157–183; Kristian Coates Ulrichsen, *Qatar and the Arab Spring* (Oxford: Oxford University Press, 2014).
4. Kamrava, *Qatar: Small State, Big Politics*; Kamrava "The Foreign Policy of Qatar;" Lina Khatib, "Qatar's Foreign Policy," *International Affairs,* 89(2) (2013): 417–431.
5. Kei Koga, "The Concept of "Hedging" Revisited: The Case of Japan's Foreign Policy Strategy in East Asia's power Shift," *International Studies Review,* 20(4) (2018): 633–660.
6. Cheng-Chwee Kuik and Gilbert Rozman, "Light or Heavy Hedging: Positioning Between China and the US," in *Joint US-Korea Academic Studies 2015*, ed. Gilbert Rozman (Washington, DC: Korea Economic Institute of America, 2015), 1–9,

http://www.keia.org/sites/default/files/publications/introduction_-_light_or_heavy_hedging.pdf.

7. Kamrava, *Qatar: Small State, Big Politics*, 28.

8. Engin Yüksel and Haşhim Tekineş, *Turkey's Love in with Qatar: A Marriage of Convenience* (The Hague: Clingendael, 2021), https://www.clingendael.org/pub/2021/drivers-of-turkish-qatari-relations/.

9. Guido Steinberg, *Regional Power United Arab Emirates: Abu Dhabi is no Longer Saudi Arabia's Junior Partner*, SWP Research Paper 10/2020 (Berlin: Stiftung Wissenschaft und Politik), 27.

10. Christopher Blanchard, "Qatar: Background and US Relations," May 2010 (Washington, DC: Congressional Research Service), 1.

11. Yoel Guzansky, "Israel and the Arab Gulf States: From Tacit Cooperation to Reconciliation?," *Israel Affairs,* 21(1) (2015): 131–147; Uzi Rabi, "Qatar's Relations with Israel: Challenging Arab and Gulf Norms," *Middle East Journal,* 63(3) (2009): 443–459.

12. Steven Wright, "Foreign Policy in the GCC States," in *The International Politics of the Persian Gulf*, ed. Mehran Kamrava (Syracuse, NY: Syracuse University Press, 2011), 86, 89.

13. Kamrava, "The Foreign Policy of Qatar"; Dania Akkad, "How Qatar Became the US-Taliban Mediator: And What Happens Next," *Middle East Eye*, September 13, 2021, https://www.middleeasteye.net/news/qatar-us-taliban-how-became-mediator-talks.

14. Kamrava, "The Foreign Policy of Qatar," 167.

15. Akkad, "How Qatar Became the US-Taliban Mediator."

16. Blanchard, "Qatar," 12–13.

17. Ibid, 14.

18. Akkad, "How Qatar Became the US-Taliban Mediator."

19. Ibid.

20. Aya Batrawy, "Freeing Hostages, Hosting Hamas: Qatar's Influence in Israel-Hamas War, Explained," *NPR*, November 2, 2023, https://www.npr.org/2023/11/02/1210110109/qatar-israel-gaza-hamas-war.

21. Michael Quentin Morton, *Masters of the Pearl: A History of Qatar* (London: Reaktion Books, 2020), 192.

22. R. Clarke Cooper, "As Qatar Becomes a Non-NATO Ally, Greater Responsibility Conveys the Status," *Atlantic Council*, March 3, 2022, https://www.atlanticcouncil.org/blogs/menasource/as-qatar-becomes-a-non-nato-ally-greater-responsibility-coveys-with-the-status/; Neville Teller, "Qatar: The US's New Non-NATO Ally – Opinion," *Jerusalem Post*, March 22, 2022, https://www.jpost.com/opinion/article-701948.

23. Teller, "Qatar."

24. Sean Mathews, "Israeli Military Officials Sent to Qatar as US Works to Bolster Security Cooperation," *Middle East Eye*, July 8, 2022, https://www.middleeasteye.net/news/qatar-israel-military-officials-dispatched-amid-us-efforts-bolster-security.

25. Guzansky, "Israel and the Arab Gulf States."

26. Ibid.

27. Federica D'Acunto, "The Brand of Peace: The Relations Between Qatar, Palestine and Israel," MA Dissertation (Venice: Università Ca'Foscari, 2016): 88–89; Rabi, "Qatar's Relations with Israel."

28. Ibid, 89–90; Rabi, "Qatar's Relations with Israel."

29. Guzansky, "Israel and the Arab Gulf states"; Rabi, "Qatar's Relations with Israel."

30. Ibid; Guzansky, "Israel and the Arab Gulf states"; D'Acunto, "The Brand of Peace," 92.

31. D'Acunto, *"The Brand of Peace,"* 94.

32. Guzansky, "Israel and the Arab Gulf States."

33. Morton, *Masters of the Pearl,* 190.

34. Guzansky, "Israel and the Arab Gulf States"; Robert Blecher and Ofer Zalzberg, "A Changing Region: Israel's Islamist Dilemma," *World Politics Review*, December 18, 2012, https://www.worldpoliticsreview.com/a-changing-region-israels-islamist-dilemma/.

35. Ulrichsen, *Qatar and the Arab Spring,* 70.

36. D'Acunto, "The Brand of Peace," 64–65.

37. Ibid, 63.

38. David Roberts, "Qatar and the Muslim Brotherhood: Pragmatism or Preference?," *Middle East Policy*, 21(3) (2014): 84–94; Stéphane Lacroix, "Saudi Arabia's Muslim Brotherhood predicament," in *The Qatar Crisis*, POMEPS Briefing 31 (October 2017), 51–53, https://pomeps.org/wp-content/uploads/2017/10/POMEPS_GCC_Qatar-Crisis.pdf; David Roberts, "Qatar, the Ikhwan, and transnational relations in the Gulf," in *The Qatar Crisis*, POMEPS Briefing 31 (October 2017): 54–59, https://pomeps.org/wp-content/uploads/2017/10/POMEPS_GCC_Qatar-Crisis.pdf.

39. Roberts, "Qatar and the Muslim Brotherhood."

40. Roberts, "Qatar, the Ikhwan, and Transnational Relations in the Gulf."

41. Ibid.

42. Ibid.

43. *Al Arabiyah*, "WATCH: What Mubarak Said About Qatar and its Role in the Region," June 10, 2017, https://english.alarabiya.net/features/2017/06/10/Watch-What-Mubarak-said-about-Qatar-and-its-role-in-the-region.

44. Debra Kamin, "Can Israel and Qatar Learn to be Friends Again?," *The Times of Israel*, December 9, 2013, https://www.timesofisrael.com/can-israel-and-qatar-learn-to-be-friends-again/.

45. Ulrichsen, *Qatar and the Arab Spring,* 76.

46. "Candiru Receives Boost from Investors Linked to Qatar," *Intelligence Online*, August 26, 2020, https://www.intelligenceonline.com/corporate-intelligence/2020/08/26/candiru-receives-boost-from-investors-linked-to-qatar,109602043-art; "Doha, like Abu Dhabi, also hooked on Israeli technology," *Intelligence Online*, August 26, 2020, https://www.intelligenceonline.com/government-intelligence/2020/08/26/doha-like-abu-dhabi-also-hooked-on-israeli-technology,109602026-evg.

47. Danny Zaken, "Qatar, Israel Reach Agreement on Diamond Trade," *Al-Monitor*, December 15, 2021, https://www.al-monitor.com/originals/2021/12/qatar-israel-reach-agreement-diamond-trade.

48. D'Acunto, "The Brand of Peace," 68.

49. Blanchard, "Qatar," 21.

50. Guzansky, "Israel and the Arab Gulf States."

51. Morton, *Masters of the Pearl,* 192.

52. D'Acunto, "The Brand of Peace," 68.

53. Winer, "Qatar Gave Over $1.1 Billion to Gaza Strip from 2012-18, Ministers Told"; Tovah Lazaroff and Anna Aronheim, "No More Suitcases of Cash for Hamas in Gaza," *Jerusalem Post,* July 5, 2021, https://www.jpost.com/middle-east/un-to -handle-the-disbursement-of-the-qatari-money-in-gaza-672809.

54. D'Acunto, "The Brand of Peace," 75.

55. Ahmad Abu Amer, "Egypt, Qatar Agreement with Israel, Hamas Provides Boost for Gaza Economy," *Al-Monitor,* November 23, 2021, https://www.al-moni-tor.com/originals/2021/11/egypt-qatar-agreement-israel-hamas-provides-boost-gaza -economy.

56. Elia Zureik, "Qatar's Humanitarian Aid to Palestine," *Third World Quarterly,* 39(4) (2018): 786–798.

57. Khatib, "Qatar's Foreign Policy."

58. Ibid.

59. Yoel Guzansky and Yohanan Tzoroff, "Gaza, Qatar and the UAE: The Abraham Accords After Operation Guardian of the Walls." Fikra Forum, Washington Institute of Near East Policy, June 16, 2021, https://www.washingtoninstitute.org/ policy-analysis/gaza-qatar-and-uae-abraham-accords-after-operation-guardian-walls.

60. Ibid.

61. Guzansky, "Israel and the Arab Gulf States."

62. Kobi Michael and Yoel Guzansky, "Qatar Under Siege: Regional Implications and Ramifications for the Palestinian Arena," Institute for National Securty Studies, Insight No. 935, June 12, 2017, https://www.inss.org.il/publication/qatar-siege -regional-implications-ramifications-palestinian-arena/.

63. Ibid.

64. Guzansky and Tzoroff, "Gaza, Qatar and the UAE"; Kenneth Katzman, "The United Arab Emirates (UAE): Issues for US Policy," October (Washington, DC: Congressional Research Service, 2021), 13.

65. Monir Ghaedi, "What is the Palestinian Islamic Jihad?," *DW,* September 8, 2022, https://www.dw.com/en/what-is-the-palestinian-islamic-jihad/a-62746894; Hani al-Masri, "The Jenin Brigades and the Lion's Den: Palestine's New Resistance," *Middle East Eye,* October 21, 2022, https://www.middleeasteye.net/opinion/phenomenon-jenin -brigades-and-lions-den; Ahmad Melhem, "More Armed Palestinian Groups Emerge in the West Bank," *Al-Monitor,* November 21, 2022, https://www.al-monitor.com/origi-nals/2022/11/more-armed-palestinian-groups-emerge-west-bank?utm_medium=email &utm_campaign=Daily%20Briefing%20November%2021%202022%20300&utm _content=Daily%20Briefing%20November%2021%202022%20300+CID_0bc7e1e b7a9cb787b90b361186e86640&utm_source=campmgr&utm_term=More%20armed %20Palestinian%20groups%20emerge%20in%20West%20Bank.

66. Carrie Keller-Lynn, "Gantz: Israel's War against Hamas is Existential and Carries No Time Limit," *The Times of Israel,* November 8, 2023, https://www

.timesofisrael.com/gantz-israels-war-against-hamas-is-existential-and-carries-no
-time-limit/; International Institute for Middle East and Balkan Studies, "Israel –
Hamas 2023: What Will the Gaza Strip Look Like the Day after the War?" November
6, 2023, https://www.ifimes.org/en/researches/israel-hamas-2023-what-will-the-gaza
-strip-look-like-the-day-after-the-war/5231?#.

67. Yoel Guzansky, "Qatar's Balancing Act in Gaza," *Foreign Affairs*, January 5,
2024, https://www.foreignaffairs.com/israel/qatars-balancing-act-gaza-hamas.

68. Freedom House, "Country and Territory Ratings and Statuses, 1973-2020,"
https://freedomhouse.org/sites/default/files/2020-02/2020_Country_and_Territory
_Ratings_and_Statuses_FIW1973-2020.xlsx.

69. Simon Henderson, "Regime Change in Qatar," *Foreign Policy*, June 14, 2013,
https://foreignpolicy.com/2013/06/14/regime-change-in-qatar/.

70. Kristian Coates Ulrichsen, "Foreign Policy Implications of the New Emir's
Succession in Qatar," Norwegian Peacebuilding Resource Center, August 2013,
https://www.files.ethz.ch/isn/170552/Foreign%20Policy%20Implications%20of
%20the%20New%20Emir%20in%20Qatar.pdf.

71. Jamal Abdullah and Nabil Al-Nasiri, "Qatari Foreign Policy: Carryover or
Redirection," *Al Jazeera* Center for Studies, July 10, 2014, https://studies.aljazeera
.net/en/reports/2014/07/2014710113458205705.html.

72. Islam Khalid Hassan, "GCC's 2014 Crisis: Causes, Issues and Solutions,"
Al Jazeera Center Studies, March 31, 2015, https://studies.aljazeera.net/en/dossiers
/2015/03/201533172623652531.html.

73. Ulrichsen, *Qatar and the Arab Spring*; Kamrava, *Qatar*; Kamrava, "The Foreign Policy of Qatar."

74. Mehran Kamrava, ""Introduction," La Política Exterior de Qatar," *Comillas
Journal of International Relations,* 5 (2016): II–III.

75. "Qatar's Foreign Minister Rules Out Normalisation with Israel," *Middle East
Eye*, February 2, 2022, https://www.middleeasteye.net/news/qatar-foreign-minister
-rules-out-normalisation-israel.

76. Guy Azriel, "Exclusive: Israel's Lapid, Qatari FM Hold Phone Call Ahead of
World Cup," *i24*, November 14, 2022, https://www.i24news.tv/en/news/israel/diplo-
macy/1668445888-israel-s-lapid-qatari-fm-hold-phone-call-ahead-of-world-cup; "Qatari
Activists Criticize Government over Tel Aviv-Doha World Cup Flights," *i24*, November 11, 2022, https://www.i24news.tv/en/news/middle-east/the-gulf/1668199967-qatari
-activists-criticize-government-over-tel-aviv-doha-world-cup-flights.

77. Guzansky, "Qatar's Balancing Act in Gaza."

78. Omar Rahman, "The Emergence of GCC-Israel Relations in a Changing
Middle East," *Brookings*, July 28, 2021, https://www.brookings.edu/research/the
-emergence-of-gcc-israel-relations-in-a-changing-middle-east/.

79. Abigail Ng, "Qatar Unlikely to Establish Ties with Israel Unless Palestinian
Conflict is Resolved, Minister Says," *CNBC*, June 4, 2021, https://www.middleeast-
eye.net/news/qatar-foreign-minister-rules-out-normalisation-israel.

80. Rahman, "The Emergence of GCC-Israel Relations in a Changing Middle
East."

81. Batrawy, "Freeing Hostages, Hosting Hamas: Qatar's Influence in Israel-
Hamas War, Explained"; Humeyra Pamuk, "Qatar Open to Reconsidering Hamas

Presence in Qatar, US Official Says," *Reuters*, October 27, 2023, https://www.reuters
.com/world/middle-east/qatar-told-us-it-is-open-reconsidering-hamas-presence-us
-official-says-2023-10-27/.

82. D'Acunto, "The Brand of Peace"; Mouin Rabbani, "Qatar and the Palestinians," *Perspectives: Politial Analysis and Commentary from the Middle East & North
Africa*, 4 (2012): 42–45.

83. Aaron Boxerman, "Israel to Begin Allowing Qatar-Funded Fuel into Gaza on
Monday," *The Times of Israel*, June 27, 2021, https://www.timesofisrael.com/israel
-to-begin-allowing-qatar-funded-fuel-into-gaza-on-monday/; Abu Amer, "Egypt,
Qatar Agreement With Israel, Hamas Provides Boost for Gaza Economy."

84. Guzansky and Tzoroff, "Gaza, Qatar and the UAE."

85. *Al Jazeera*, "'Restraint and Common Sense': Reaction to Israel's Gaza
Attack," August 5, 2022, https://www.aljazeera.com/news/2022/8/5/restraint-and
-common-sense-reaction-to-israels-gaza-attack.

86. Relief Web, "QRCS Launches $1.1 Million Humanitarian Response to
Gaza War," August 9, 2022, https://reliefweb.int/report/occupied-palestinian-ter-
ritory/qrcs-launches-11-million-humanitarian-response-gaza-war; Jack Khoury,
"Qatar Agrees to Reconstruct Gaza Homes Destroyed by Israeli Occupation,"
Haaretz, August 12, 2022, https://www.haaretz.com/middle-east-news/palestinians
/2022-08-12/ty-article/.premium/qatar-agrees-to-reconstruct-gaza-homes-destroyed
-by-israeli-operation/00000182-9200-d9bc-affb-f39ea1960000; "Palestine Hails
Qatar's Support for Gaza Reconstruction," *The Peninsula*, August 23, 2022, https://
thepeninsulaqatar.com/article/23/08/2022/palestine-hails-qatars-support-for-gaza
-reconstruction.

87. Motasem Dalloul, "Is Qatar Upset with the besieged Gaza Strip?," *Middle
East Monitor*, September 5, 2023, https://www.middleeastmonitor.com/20230905-is
-qatar-upset-with-the-besieged-gaza-strip/; Patrick Wintour, "Qatar's Peacemaking
Ambitions Face Ultimate Test in Crucible of Israel-Hamas War," *Guardian*, October 28, 2023, https://www.theguardian.com/world/2023/oct/28/qatars-peacemaking
-ambitions-face-ultimate-test-in-crucible-of-israel-hamas-war; "Hamas Leaders Meet
Assad in Damascus to 'Turn the Page'," *Reuters*, October 19, 2022, https://www
.reuters.com/world/middle-east/hamas-leaders-meet-assad-damascus-turn-page-2022
-10-19/.

88. Katherine Walla, "Qatar's Prime Minister Sees Progress on Israel-Hamas
Hostage Negotiations–But Warns Regional Tensions are 'Boiling Up,'" *Atlantic
Council*, January 29, 2024, https://www.atlanticcouncil.org/blogs/new-atlanticist/
qatars-prime-minister-sees-progress-on-israel-hamas-hostage-negotiations-but-warns
-regional-tensions-are-boiling-up/.

REFERENCES

Abdullah, Jamal, and Nabil Al-Nasiri, "Qatari Foreign Policy: Carryover or Redirection," *Al Jazeera* Center for Studies, July 10, 2014, https://studies.aljazeera.net/en
/reports/2014/07/2014710113458205705.html.

Abu Amer, Ahmad, "Egypt, Qatar Agreement with Israel, Hamas Provides Boost for Gaza Economy," *Al-Monitor,* November 23, 2021, https://www.al-monitor.com/originals/2021/11/egypt-qatar-agreement-israel-hamas-provides-boost-gaza-economy.

Akkad, Dania, "How Qatar Became the US-Taliban Mediator: And What Happens Next," *Middle East Eye*, September 13, 2021, https://www.middleeasteye.net/news/qatar-us-taliban-how-became-mediator-talks.

Al-Masri, Hani, "The Jenin Brigades and the Lion's Den: Palestine's New Resistance," *Middle East Eye*, October 21, 2022, https://www.middleeasteye.net/opinion/phenomenon-jenin-brigades-and-lions-den.

Azriel, Guy, "Exclusive: Israel's Lapid, Qatari FM Hold Phone Call Ahead of World Cup," *i24*, November 14, 2022, https://www.i24news.tv/en/news/israel/diplomacy/1668445888-israel-s-lapid-qatari-fm-hold-phone-call-ahead-of-world-cup.

Batrawy, Aya, "Freeing Hostages, Hosting Hamas: Qatar's Influence in Israel-Hamas War, Explained," *NPR*, November 2, 2023, https://www.npr.org/2023/11/02/1210110109/qatar-israel-gaza-hamas-war.

Blanchard, Christopher, "Qatar: Background and US Relations" (Washington, DC: Congressional Research Service, May 2010).

Blecher, Robert, and Ofer Zalzberg, "A Changing Region: Israel's Islamist Dilemma," *World Politics Review*, December 18, 2012, https://www.worldpoliticsreview.com/a-changing-region-israels-islamist-dilemma/.

Boxerman, Aaron, "Israel to Begin Allowing Qatar-Funded Fuel into Gaza on Monday," *The Times of Israel*, June 27, 2021, https://www.timesofisrael.com/israel-to-begin-allowing-qatar-funded-fuel-into-gaza-on-monday/.

"Candiru Receives Boost from Investors Linked to Qatar," August 26, 2020, https://www.intelligenceonline.com/corporate-intelligence/2020/08/26/candiru-receives-boost-from-investors-linked-to-qatar,109602043-art.

Cooper, R. Clarke, "As Qatar Becomes a Non-NATO Ally, Greater Responsibility Conveys the Status," *Atlantic Council*, March 3, 2022, https://www.atlanticcouncil.org/blogs/menasource/as-qatar-becomes-a-non-nato-ally-greater-responsibility-coveys-with-the-status/.

D'Acunto, Federica, "The Brand of Peace: The Relations Between Qatar, Palestine and Israel," MA Dissertation (Venice: Università Ca'Foscari, 2016).

Dalloul, Motasem. "Is Qatar upset with the besieged Gaza Strip?" *Middle East Monitor*, September 5, 2023, https://www.middleeastmonitor.com/20230905-is-qatar-upset-with-the-besieged-gaza-strip/.

"Doha, like Abu Dhabi, also Hooked on Israeli Technology," August 26, 2020, https://www.intelligenceonline.com/government-intelligence/2020/08/26/doha-like-abu-dhabi-also-hooked-on-israeli-technology,109602026-evg.

Freedom House, "Country and Territory Ratings and Statuses, 1973-2020," https://freedomhouse.org/sites/default/files/2020-02/2020_Country_and_Territory_Ratings_and_Statuses_FIW1973-2020.xlsx.

Ghaedi, Monir, "What is the Palestinian Islamic Jihad?," *DW*, September 8, 2022, https://www.dw.com/en/what-is-the-palestinian-islamic-jihad/a-62746894.

Guzansky, Yoel, "Israel and the Arab Gulf States: From Tacit Cooperation to Reconciliation?," *Israel Affairs,* 21(1) (2015): 131–147.

"Hamas Leaders Meet Assad in Damascus to 'Turn the Page'," *Reuters*, October 19, 2022, https://www.reuters.com/world/middle-east/hamas-leaders-meet-assad -damascus-turn-page-2022-10-19/.

Hassan, Islam Khalid, "GCC's 2014 Crisis: Causes, Issues and Solutions," *Al Jazeera Center Studies*, March 31, 2015, https://studies.aljazeera.net/en/dossiers/2015/03 /201533172623652531.html.

Henderson, Simon, "Regime Change in Qatar," *Foreign Policy*, June 14, 2013, https://foreignpolicy.com/2013/06/14/regime-change-in-qatar/.

International Institute for Middle East and Balkan Studies, "Israel – Hamas 2023: What Will the Gaza Strip Look Like the Day After the War?," November 6, 2023, https://www.ifimes.org/en/researches/israel-hamas-2023-what-will-the-gaza-strip -look-like-the-day-after-the-war/5231?#.

"Light or Heavy Hedging: Positioning Between China and the United States," Joint US-Korea Academic Studies, http://www.keia.org/sites/default/files/publications/ introduction_-_light_or_heavy_hedging.pdf.

Kamin, Debra, "Can Israel and Qatar Learn to be Friends Again?," *The Times of Israel*, December 9, 2013, https://www.timesofisrael.com/can-israel-and-qatar -learn-to-be-friends-again/.

Kamrava, Mehran, ""Introduction," La Política Exterior de Qatar," *Comillas Journal of International Relations*, 5 (2016): II–III.

Kamrava, Mehran, "The Foreign Policy of Qatar," in *The Foreign Policies of Middle East States*, eds. Raymond Hinnebusch and Anoushiravan Ehteshami (Boulder, CO: Lynne Rienner, 2014), 157–183.

Kamrava, Mehran, *Qatar: Small State, Big Politics* (Ithaca, NY: Cornell University Press, 2013).

Katzman, Kenneth, "The United Arab Emirates (UAE): Issues for US Policy," October (Washington, DC: Congressional Research Service, 2021).

Keller-Lynn, Carrie, "Gantz: Israel's War against Hamas is Existential and Carries No Time Limit," *The Times of Israel*, November 8, 2023, https://www.time-sofisrael.com/gantz-israels-war-against-hamas-is-existential-and-carries-no-time -limit/.

Khatib, Lina, "Qatar's Foreign Policy," *International Affairs,* 89(2) (2013): 417–431.

Khoury, Jack, "Qatar Agrees to Reconstruct Gaza Homes Destroyed by Israeli Occupation," *Haaretz*, August 12, 2022, https://www.haaretz.com/middle-east-news /palestinians/2022-08-12/ty-article/.premium/qatar-agrees-to-reconstruct-gaza -homes-destroyed-by-israeli-operation/00000182-9200-d9bc-affb-f39ea1960000.

Koga, Kei, "The Concept of "Hedging" Revisited: The Case of Japan's Foreign Policy Strategy in East Asia's Power Shift," *International Studies Review,* 20(4) (2018): 633–660.

Kuik, Cheng-Chwee, and Gilbert Rozman, "Light or Heavy Hedging: Positioning Between China and the US," in *Joint US-Korea Academic Studies 2015*, ed. Gilbert Rozman (Washington, DC: Korea Economic Institute of America, 2015), 1–9.

Lazaroff, Tovah, and Anna Aronheim, "No More Suitcases of Cash for Hamas in Gaza," *Jerusalem Post*, July 5, 2021, https://www.jpost.com/middle-east/un-to -handle-the-disbursement-of-the-qatari-money-in-gaza-672809.

Mathews, Sean, "Israeli Military Officials Sent to Qatar as US Works to Bolster Security Cooperation," *Middle East Eye*, July 8, 2022, https://www.middleeasteye.net/news/qatar-israel-military-officials-dispatched-amid-us-efforts-bolster-security.

Melhem, Ahmad, "More armed Palestinian Groups Emerge in the West Bank," *Al-Monitor*, November 21, 2022, https://www.al-monitor.com/originals/2022/11/more-armed-palestinian-groups-emerge-west-bank?utm_medium=email&utm_campaign=Daily%20Briefing%20November%2021%202022%20300&utm_content=Daily%20Briefing%20November%2021%202022%20300+CID_0bc7e1eb7a9cb787b90b361186e86640&utm_source=campmgr&utm_term=More%20armed%20Palestinian%20groups%20emerge%20in%20West%20Bank.

Michael, Kobi, and Yoel Guzansky, "Qatar Under Siege: Regional Implications and Ramifications for the Palestinian Arena," Institute for National Securty Studies, Insight No. 935, June 12, 2017, https://www.inss.org.il/publication/qatar-siege-regional-implications-ramifications-palestinian-arena/.

Morton, Michael Quentin, *Masters of the Pearl: A History of Qatar* (London: Reaktion Books, 2020).

Ng, Abigail, "Qatar Unlikely to Establish Ties with Israel Unless Palestinian Conflict is Resolved, Minister Says," *CNBC*, June 4, 2021, https://www.middleeasteye.net/news/qatar-foreign-minister-rules-out-normalisation-israel.

OCHA Services, "Humanitarian Aid Contributions," Financial Tracking Services, https://fts.unocha.org/.

"Palestine Hails Qatar's Support for Gaza Reconstruction," *The Peninsula Qatar,* August 23, 2022, https://thepeninsulaqatar.com/article/23/08/2022/palestine-hails-qatars-support-for-gaza-reconstruction.

Pamuk, Humeyra, "Qatar Open to Reconsidering Hamas Presence in Qatar, US Official Says," *Reuters*, October 27, 2023, https://www.reuters.com/world/middle-east/qatar-told-us-it-is-open-reconsidering-hamas-presence-us-official-says-2023-10-27/.

"Qatar's Foreign Minister Rules Out Normalisation with Israel," *Middle East Eye,* February 2, 2022, https://www.middleeasteye.net/news/qatar-foreign-minister-rules-out-normalisation-israel.

"Qatari Activists Criticize Government over Tel Aviv-Doha World Cup Flights," November 11, 2022, https://www.i24news.tv/en/news/middle-east/the-gulf/1668199967-qatari-activists-criticize-government-over-tel-aviv-doha-world-cup-flights.

Rabbani, Mouin, "Qatar and the Palestinians," *Perspectives: Politial Analysis and Commentary from the Middle East & North Africa* 4 (2012): 42–45.

Rabi, Uzi, "Qatar's Relations with Israel: Challenging Arab and Gulf Norms," *Middle East Journal* 63(3) (2009): 443–459.

Rahman, Omar, "The Emergence of GCC-Israel Relations in a Changing Middle East," *Brookings*, July 28, 2021, https://www.brookings.edu/research/the-emergence-of-gcc-israel-relations-in-a-changing-middle-east/.

Relief Web, "QRCS Launches $1.1 Million Humanitarian Response to Gaza War," August 9, 2022, https://reliefweb.int/report/occupied-palestinian-territory/qrcs-launches-11-million-humanitarian-response-gaza-war.

"'Restraint and Common Sense': Reaction to Israel's Gaza Attack," *Al Jazeera*, August 5, 2022, https://www.aljazeera.com/news/2022/8/5/restraint-and-common -sense-reaction-to-israels-gaza-attack.

Roberts, David, "Qatar and the Muslim Brotherhood: Pragmatism or Preference?," *Middle East Policy*, 21(3) (2014): 84–94.

Steinberg, Guido, *Regional power United Arab Emirates: Abu Dhabi is no Longer Saudi Arabia's Junior Partner*, SWP Research Paper 10/2020 (Berlin: Stiftung Wissenschaft und Politik).

Teller, Neville, "Qatar: The US's New Non-NATO Ally – Opinion," *Jerusalem Post*, March 22, 2022, https://www.jpost.com/opinion/article-701948.

Ulrichsen, Kristian Coates, "Foreign Policy Implications of the New Emir's Succession in Qatar," Norwegian Peacebuilding Resource Center, August 2013, https:// www.files.ethz.ch/isn/170552/Foreign%20Policy%20Implications%20of%20the %20New%20Emir%20in%20Qatar.pdf.

Ulrichsen, Kristian Coates, *Qatar and the Arab Spring* (Oxford: Oxford University Press, 2014).

"WATCH: What Mubarak Said About Qatar and Its Role in the Region," *Al Arabiyah*, June 10, 2017, https://english.alarabiya.net/features/2017/06/10/Watch-What -Mubarak-said-about-Qatar-and-its-role-in-the-region.

Winer, Stuart, "Qatar Gave Over $1.1 Billion to Gaza Strip from 2012-18, Ministers Told," *The Times of Israel*, February 11, 2019, https://www.timesofisrael.com/ qatar-gave-over-1-1-billion-to-gaza-strip-over-six-years-report/.

Wintour, Patrick, "Qatar's Peacemaking Ambitions Face Ultimate Test in Crucible of Israel-Hamas War," *Guardian*, October 28, 2023, https://www.theguardian.com/ world/2023/oct/28/qatars-peacemaking-ambitions-face-ultimate-test-in-crucible-of -israel-hamas-war.

Wright, Steven, "Foreign Policy in the GCC States," in *The International Politics of the Persian Gulf*, ed. Mehran Kamrava (Syracuse, NY: Syracuse University Press, 2011), 72–93.

Yüksel, Engin, and Haşhim Tekineş, *Turkey's Love in with Qatar: A Marriage of Convenience* (The Hague: Clingendael, 2021), https://www.clingendael.org/pub /2021/drivers-of-turkish-qatari-relations/.

Zaken, Danny, "Qatar, Israel Reach Agreement on Diamond Trade," *Al-Monitor*, December 15, 2021, https://www.al-monitor.com/originals/2021/12/qatar-israel -reach-agreement-diamond-trade.

Zureik, Elia, "Qatar's Humanitarian Aid to Palestine," *Third World Quarterly*, 39(4) (2018): 786–798.

Chapter 7

Saudi Arabia and Israel

Exploring Ambivalent Relations

Banafsheh Keynoush

An international gathering in January 2023 in East Jerusalem of the Negev Forum Steering Committee and Working Groups to discuss multi-sector integration among leaders from the Arab world and Israel was fortuitously and momentously preceded almost a week earlier by a visit to the Al-Aqsa Mosque compound in Jerusalem (or the al-Haram al-Sharif, also referred to as the Temple Mount including the Dome of the Rock) by Israel's right-wing national security minister Itamar Ben-Gvir. Leading the condemnation against the visit was the Kingdom of Saudi Arabia which saw it as part of Israel's attempts to change the historical and legal status of Al-Aqsa as a holy Muslim site.[1]

The Al-Aqsa compound, however, had a Jewish heritage. The Jews in Arabia who inhabited Madinah (then known as Yathrib) prayed toward Al-Aqsa shortly before Islam emerged. And they had long anticipated the arrival of a new prophet, but not necessarily an Arab prophet. The Prophet of Islam, Muhammed (Peace Be Upon Him), was a merchant who interacted with this Jewish community, many of whom were also merchants, when he led trade caravans up north from Makkah where he resided. It was on these trips that he visited the Al-Aqsa where it was believed that he once briefly ascended to heaven before returning to earth to carry on his prophecy.[2]

The Prophet Mohammad fought with and eventually ruled over this Jewish community, after migrating to Madinah from Makkah in 622CE. He made the Al-Aqsa temporarily the qibla or the direction in which he and his followers read their prayers. He then returned to conquer Makkah and take over the Holy House of Ka'bah in 629–630 CE, turning it into the new qibla for Muslims. But he failed to convince all the Jews of Madinah to obey his command despite a pact with them. Consequently, Muslims in the Arabian Peninsula were led to believe that the Jews were treacherous and would be

Islam's worst enemies, despite the fact that the descendants of the Prophet Abraham's sons, Ishmael (father of Arabs) and Isaac (progenitor of the biblical Israelites), had both venerated Makkah and the Ka'bah long before Islam emerged.[3]

For decades before 9/11, Saudi schoolbooks taught material promoting hatred for the Jews. Saudi Arabia supported and funded initiatives to preserve the religious and cultural heritage of Al-Aqsa as a holy Muslim site. As the custodian of Islam's two holiest cities Makkah and Madinah in the Hijaz in western Arabia, the kingdom's defense of Al-Aqsa was an integral part of its assertions of leadership in the Muslim world. Based in part on this complex history, the founder of modern Saudi Arabia, King Abd al-Aziz Al Saud, refused to recognize Israel or its assertions of sovereignty over East Jerusalem where Al-Aqsa is located. Saudi Arabia insisted on the Palestinian right to statehood and control of East Jerusalem, and it forwarded several failed Arab-Israeli peace initiatives to resolve the conflict in the Middle East.

When signs emerged that Riyadh could join the Abraham Accords signed between Israel and a number of Arab countries at The White House in 2020, the kingdom had to choose between backing the accords, which the United States encouraged, or displaying its commitment to preserving Al-Aqsa's legacy for Muslims while insisting on the right of Palestinians to statehood. As of the time of this writing, Saudi Arabia took the latter course of action by conditioning normalization with the Jewish state, especially after the outbreak of war in Gaza in October 2023 (October War), to Palestinian statehood.

CONDITIONING FACTORS IN SAUDI-ISRAELI RELATIONS

Iran's 1979 Islamic Revolution ended its strong periphery ties with Israel that had previously bonded the two non-Arab states of the Middle East against the core Arab countries of the region. The revolution's meddling in Arab affairs in the 1980s pushed Saudi Arabia to contain Tehran. The kingdom forwarded several Middle East peace initiatives in exchange for Israel upholding Palestinian rights. The initiatives were expected to isolate Iran, especially if Israel converged its regional policies with the Arab core states of the Gulf Cooperation Council (GCC) led by Saudi Arabia, including the United Arab Emirates, Bahrain, Qatar, Oman, and Kuwait.

Iran condemned the GCC for its outreach to the Jewish state. But Israel contemplated parting ways with its periphery ties with Tehran which had previously allowed the Jewish state to focus on containing immediate security threats from the Arab core. After all, the Arab core and not Iran had fought four wars with Israel, that is, in 1948–1949 (First Arab-Israeli War), 1956

(Suez War), 1967 (Six-Day War), and 1973 (Yom Kippur War). Israel, however, rejected Saudi peace initiatives, including the 1981 Fahd Peace Plan and the 2002 Abdullah Peace Plan, although it quietly worked on building ties with the GCC states. The outbreak of the Lebanon War between Israel and the Iranian-backed Hezbollah in 2006 pushed to the fore Tel Aviv's embrace of stronger ties with the GCC. Israel maintained that the war could dismantle Hezbollah, according to discussions between a senior Israeli diplomat and this author, who confirmed his visit to Riyadh to reinforce the message prior to the outbreak of the war.[4]

Israel's calculations proved wrong, Hezbollah emerged stronger after the war with Iran's help, and the GCC countries were exposed for failure to resolve the conflict through Arab-led peace initiatives. Moreover, the 2011 Arab Spring threatened to topple the status-quo Arab governments of the GCC states. This posed a mutual threat to Saudi Arabia and Israel if events of the Arab Spring helped Iran build up its regional influence. Saudi Arabia was keen to avoid this scenario when US president Barack Obama swiftly supported the Arab Spring in Egypt. But the kingdom could not publicly harmonize its policies to control the events of the Arab Spring with Israel, in light of Arab opposition to the idea of normalization with the Jewish state. It opted instead to end a major popular uprising against the Bahraini Royal Family while taking initial steps to build a stronger Saudi national identity that had previously formed through tight circles of power surrounding the Saudi Royal Family but marginalized large segments of society including the youth and women. This step could in turn discourage an Arab Spring uprising against the Saudi Royal Family.

Reacting to the threat from Iran which aimed to shape the events of the Arab Spring, Riyadh's regional posturing evolved through informal public exchanges between prominent Saudis and Israelis. Saudi Arabia and Israel called for stronger monitoring of the Iranian nuclear enrichment program as well. The program was contained through negotiations between Iran and the world powers that took place in part during the events of the Arab Spring, leading to the conclusion of the 2015 Iran nuclear deal known as the Joint Comprehensive Plan of Action. Iran, however, decided to accelerate its enrichment program when President Donald J. Trump withdrew the United States from the nuclear deal in May 2018, leaving Saudi Arabia and Israel concerned that Tehran might build a nuclear bomb.

Partly to contain the Iranian nuclear threat, under the leadership of Crown Prince Muhammed bin Salman bin Abd al-Aziz Al Saud and his father, King Salman bin Abd al-Aziz Al Saud, who came to power in 2015, Riyadh promoted tolerance toward Israel and the Jewish state through public debates, educational initiatives, and television programs. The Trump-brokered 2020 Abraham Accords, and Washington's commitment under the

Biden administration to strengthen the accords, had Tehran suspecting that Saudi Arabia and Israel planned to establish formal ties. Iranian suspicions grew when Washington delivered Patriot missile systems to Saudi Arabia in March 2022, to intercept missiles launched by the Iranian-backed Houthis in Yemen who threatened Israel and targeted Saudi oil facilities. The administration of President Joseph R. Biden had earlier ignored Riyadh's request for the Patriot missile systems. In September 2021, Washington had even removed the Patriot and Terminal High Altitude Area Defense (THAAD) missile systems from the Prince Sultan Air Base in Saudi Arabia. Its goal then was to encourage the kingdom to end a deadly military conflict in Yemen and make peace with the Houthis.[5]

But Saudi Arabia clearly succeeded in receiving stronger US guarantees of protection. In July 2022, the White House reaffirmed US commitment to help protect the kingdom and defend its territory and people from all external attacks. However, by avoiding direct conflict with Iran, the United States was in no position to offer full protection guarantees to the kingdom if Tehran advanced its nuclear program. Frustrated by lackluster promises of protection from the United States, Saudi Arabia insisted that it had the right to respond to Iranian provocations. However, it refused to join the Abraham Accords partly to avoid provoking Iran which strongly warned Riyadh to avoid normalization with the Jewish state. Instead, the kingdom watched Bahrain and the United Arab Emirates (UAE) join the accords which in turn promised to strengthen Israel's ties with the GCC states.

Riyadh resumed its diplomatic relations with Iran in March 2023, after breaking ties with Tehran in early 2016 when Iranian students stormed the Saudi embassy to protest the kingdom's decision to behead the prominent Saudi Shia cleric Nimr Baqir Al Nimr. This paved the way for Saudi Arabia to have an open dialogue with Iran, which had quietly started since April 2021. Reduced tensions carried the bonus of allowing Riyadh to offer Tehran incentives to enhance cooperation, while the kingdom entertained normalization with Israel. Publicly, however, Riyadh had opposed the 2017 US recognition of Jerusalem as the capital of Israel.[6]

Due to this and other fundamental differences with Israel, Saudi Arabia was unable to normalize its ties with the Jewish state before it resumed diplomatic relations with Iran. Riyadh's decision to diplomatically engage with Israel had in fact only evolved with the Biden administration's restrained response to Iran's enrichment program and the Houthi-led attacks on Saudi Arabia. The Houthis were hitting civilian infrastructure in Saudi Arabia, and they attacked the UAE during a state visit by Israeli president Isaac Herzog in January 2022. When the Biden administration insisted on a short truce with the Houthis by the summer of 2022, Saudi Arabia had to back the idea despite its own hesitations about it, in order to avoid compromising its partnership with Washington. As prospects for a US-Iran nuclear deal diminished, in June 2022, US secretary of state Antony J. Blinken indicated that Saudi Arabia was contemplating ties with Israel, by stating that the kingdom would play a role in expanding the Abraham Accords, thereby indirectly reminding Iran of the dangers to its security if the kingdom and Israel were to align forces.[7]

In response, Iran pursued a dialogue with Saudi Arabia, but it challenged Riyadh's decision to contemplate normalization with Israel without delivering peace to the Palestinians. Tehran also jeopardized navigation in the Persian Gulf and the Bab-el-Mandeb, to remind Saudi Arabia and Israel that if they built an anti-Iran alliance, it could have dangerous regional consequences. This, however, pushed Saudi Arabia and Israel to recognize that while they could not join forces to directly provoke Iran, they had interests that could merge through their expressed opposition to Iran's potential nuclear weaponization, and to encourage the United States to contain the Iranian regional influence while sorting out a resolution to the Palestinian plight.

The Copenhagen School's emphasis on the non-military aspects of problem-solving in the security field suggested, however, that Iran's nuclear program and the Palestinian issue were not enough to justify convergent policies between Saudi Arabia and Israel. The unresolved status of the two issues, and US policy failures to address them, no doubt posed real threats to Saudi Arabia and Israel. However, the issues resulted in part from intersubjective social and discursive interactions between Saudi Arabia and Israel whose definitions of threats were relevant mainly to their own domestic audiences. As a result, neither the Iranian nuclear program nor the Palestinian issue constituted an objective or immediate threat to Saudi Arabia or Israel at all times, considering that the two states had survived the consequences of a broken diplomacy over Iran and Palestine for a considerably lengthy period of time. Rather, it appeared that the Iranian nuclear challenge and the Palestinian conflict were existential threats only when Saudi Arabia and Israel opted to define them as such and selectively converge interests on those issues.[8]

Saudi Arabia's and Israel's visions also diverged over the level of their perceived threat from the Iranian nuclear program and Palestine. The two issues posed a more immediate existential threat to Israel compared to Saudi Arabia. Hence, Saudi and Israeli interests converged only over the need to welcome US diplomatic initiatives to address and resolve the Iranian nuclear crisis as well as the Palestinian crisis. Diplomatically, however, the two issues were mainly state-centric problems. This meant that resolving them required mainly state-level answers and resolutions. But developing cohesive state-level responses to the two problems was impossible mindful of major differences between Iran and Israel, and the US failure to offer solutions to bridge those differences. This meant that there were clear limits to how well the United States could encourage an alliance between Saudi Arabia and

Israel to help them jointly balance against a potential Iranian nuclear threat and the consequences of an unresolved Palestinian crisis.

Furthermore, Saudi Arabia and Israel failed to address the divisive moral and ethical aspects of security on the question of the Iranian nuclear program and the Palestinian issue.[9] In the Arab world, for example, opinions were divided about the threat that Iran's nuclear activities posed, with many believing that Iran had a right to have a strong nuclear program if Israel had one. Several states including Qatar, Kuwait, Oman, and the UAE viewed Iran's nuclear program as a lesser threat than the prospect of an outright military conflict with Iran to curb the program. In general, the Arab world's perceptions about Iran posing an immediate existential nuclear threat were more muted than Israel's. Meanwhile, when Riyadh advocated for a Middle East free of nuclear weapons, Israel did not subscribe to the idea if it meant abandoning its arsenal of nuclear weapons. Similarly, on the issue of Palestine, morally Saudi Arabia supported international policies addressing the human and social aspects of the Palestinian plight, along with the GCC and the Arab League, as did Iran. These policies challenged Israel when its security forces clashed with the Palestinians, but they went only so far in persuading Israel to end the Palestinian plight which Arabs cared deeply about.

Israel preferred accelerated regime change in Iran as a quick fix to regional problems, as did possibly Saudi Arabia. But unlike Israel, Riyadh avoided directly provoking Tehran. After the Saudi-Iranian normalization deal, Riyadh listened to Iranian concerns over difficult regional files through regular diplomatic exchanges. International relations theories on the balance of threat suggested here that as a militarily weaker country compared to Israel and lacking a strong nuclear program of its own, Saudi Arabia preferred not to take direct action to provoke Tehran.[10] Instead, the kingdom frequently preferred to bandwagon with other Arab countries in the GCC and the Arab League to collectively address the Iranian challenge. This approach appeared to uphold Saudi security better, compared to the other option of joining forces with Israel to confront an Iranian challenge, especially when Israel itself faced threats from the Iranian-backed Hamas after the outbreak of the Israeli-Hamas/Gaza war of October 7, 2023.

This suggested that a major security alliance between Saudi Arabia and Israel could only emerge if the Arab core collectively embraced ties with the Jewish state, which was not the case. While support for building Arab ties with Israel was on the rise following the Abraham Accords, public backing for the idea was not extremely high after the October War. In the absence of strong relations with Israel and few US guarantees to address challenges facing Saudi Arabia over the unresolved status of the Iranian nuclear program and the Palestinian plight, identifying the two issues as immediate threats was not justifiable in Riyadh, and this gave more reason to the kingdom to address the issues collectively with other Arab countries which were keen on maintaining a dialogue with Tehran.[11]

Contextually prioritizing different threats emerging from Iran or Palestine became Saudi Arabia's preferred modus operandi, rather than treating the two issues as constant and immediate existential threats, as Israel did. For Saudi Arabia, mitigating adversarial circumstances due to an Iranian regional challenge or the unresolved Palestinian conflict involved a combination of policy options that it could entertain in the future. These included positive balancing, by engaging with the Arab world to advance collective responses to the two issues and negative balancing, that is, to initiate steps to discourage Iranian policies targeting Israel. Iran, for example, supported militant groups such as the Palestinian Islamic Jihad and the Houthis which fired missiles against Israel following the outbreak of the October War.[12]

Meanwhile, the US failure to fully contain the Iranian nuclear program and regional influence suggested that the Saudis and Israelis would likely fail to build an alternative joint security system to protect against acts of regional aggression by Tehran. Furthermore, Israel's conception of its national security involved insisting on securing first and foremost its borders with Gaza and the West Bank. This approach weakened the Saudi leadership role in mobilizing Arab public opinion to support the normalization of ties with Israel, as long as Israeli-Palestinian tensions persisted.

In addition, Israel's nuclear ambiguity which Iran replicated in its drive to obtain the know-how to produce a nuclear bomb introduced what this author terms "fluid nuclear spheres" in the Middle East. In these spheres, Saudi Arabia's future nuclear ambitions served to complicate the Israeli and Iranian nuclear drives. By contemplating normalization with Israel, Saudi Arabia aimed to negotiate a comprehensive deal with Washington to receive advanced nuclear know-how, as well as additional security guarantees and access to advanced weaponry. Extensive diplomatic negotiations between Washington and Riyadh and public debates on these issues, as well as Saudi demands that Israel address Palestinian aspirations to statehood, however, failed to show progress as of the time of this writing.

Within the Copenhagen School, fluid nuclear spheres could lead to and sustain the regional imbalance of power. While containing Iran's nuclear drive constituted a core reason to build up the Saudi-Israeli nuclear partnership, the issue was variable with fluctuating levels of importance against the backdrop of larger forces such as the prospect of unrestrained nuclear proliferation in the Middle East not just by Iran but also by Saudi Arabia.

It was in this context that the Abraham Accords emerged to boost the socioeconomic and leadership aspects of the connections between Israel and Saudi Arabia. The world system theory's focus on wealth distribution supported the strengthening of a Saudi-Israeli partnership through the accords.

But while support for a normalization of ties with Israel to generate wealth was not marginal in Saudi society, with polls showing that about 43 percent of Saudi society backed the idea, other polls indicated that Saudis remained committed to their core Islamic and Arab identities which involved backing Palestine and that 57 percent of them opposed normalization.[13]

Consequently, different strategies and role behaviors emerged in the Saudi-Israeli connection, reflecting Randall S. Schuler's theorizing that strategic international management could shape clusters of interest. Such clustered interests, I argue, prevented Saudi Arabia and Israel from moving ahead with normalization or decidedly moving to build a strong alliance as of the time of this writing, but it encouraged them to embrace issue-based interests such as Iran and Palestine to ensure a progression of alternatives to address the security challenges which they faced. This prospect promised both continuity and disruption in the conduct of the Saudi-Israeli partnership, which only theories of change in international relations could explain, based on an examination of the distribution of power shifts and interests, as well as disruptive and incremental changes occurring in the Middle East region.[14]

OVERVIEW OF SAUDI-ISRAELI RELATIONS

According to historic documents, Britain had entertained granting King Abd al-Aziz Al Saud a leadership role in the Arab world, and payment of debts to the British government, if he were to recognize the partition of Mandatory Palestine (1920–1948) to create independent Arab and Jewish States by 1942 (the plan for the partition was adopted by the United Nations General Assembly/UNGA in November 1947). Saudi Arabia refused diplomatic relations with Israel, and it rejected the Zionist enterprise, despite a rich history connecting the Jewish people to the Arabian Peninsula. As far as Abd al-Aziz was concerned, there was little evidence of an established Jewish community in his land, and if there was, Riyadh did not publicize it because under Saudi law Islam was the only religion that could be practiced in public.[15]

The birth of Israel prompted Abd al-Aziz to show displeasure with British policies, but the 1948 Arab-Israeli War left him with few options to work out a solution over Palestine. Arab defeat in the war in fact undermined Saudi credentials as a champion of the Palestinian cause. The armistice agreement that followed between Israel and the Arab parties in the war led by Egypt, Jordan, and Syria in 1949 came as a blow to Saudi prestige. It enabled Israel to control more territory and allowed Jordan to annex eastern Palestine, that is, the West Bank. The armistice arrived without sufficient consultation with Riyadh, which had contributed only two small battalions of tribal fighters to the war.[16]

In October 1956, Saudi Arabia supported Egypt against an incursion by Israeli armed forces during the Suez Canal Crisis. The end of the crisis a month later did little to contain tensions with Israel. Earlier in 1952, the Arab League's Damascus-based Central Boycott Office had already boycotted third-country companies with branches in Israel, to hinder the prospects of normalized Arab-Israeli ties. Saudi Arabia adhered to the boycott, and its regional standing in the Arab world improved.

In June 1967, in response to the six-day Arab-Israeli War, Saudi Arabia led a brief and symbolic oil embargo on the West that lasted through September. Riyadh viewed with apprehension Israel's occupation of the Gaza Strip, the Sinai Peninsula, the Golan Heights, and the West Bank, and it urged Washington not to confuse its Arab Middle East policy with Israel's interests, bearing in mind that Saudi Arabia would push for Israeli withdrawal from the occupied territories, aided by the rise in oil prices after the war.

In October 1973, Egypt and Syria attacked Israel to end the occupation of the Sinai and Golan Heights. Saudi Arabia imposed an oil embargo against the West, despite reported threats from the Nixon administration that the United States would consider using force against the kingdom for imposing the embargo on countries supporting Israel.[17] Riyadh insisted on the embargo which lasted until Israel signed a peace agreement with Egypt and Syria, and in so doing, helped Jordan quell a Palestinian Liberation Organization (PLO) uprising in which some 700,000 resident Palestinians threatened to drag the country into civil war. Since Jordan was the custodian of Al-Aqsa per an earlier 1924 deal with the Supreme Muslim Council in Mandatory Palestine, the move enabled Saudi Arabia to exert its financial influence to preserve the site's Islamic heritage.[18]

By 1981, an Arab summit in Fez endorsed Crown Prince Fahd bin Sultan bin Abd al-Aziz Al Saud's proposal for a two-state solution to the Palestinian-Israeli conflict, and for the first time, Arab states officially called for the withdrawal of Israel from its pre-1967 borders. But Likud Party leader and prime minister, Menachem Begin, opposed the Saudi initiative to advance peace, due to Riyadh's earlier calls for a Palestinian uprising against Israel. Washington sided with Begin by overlooking new Israeli settlements on land seized after that period. The move challenged Saudi-Syrian relations when Damascus tried to reclaim the Golan Heights. As a result, Syria drew closer to revolutionary Iran. Meanwhile, Saudi Arabia found it harder to restore peace in southern Lebanon after Israel's 1982 invasion to curb Syria's influence over Beirut and quell a rebellion in Palestinian refugee camps led by the PLO. Prince Bandar bin Sultan bin Abd al-Aziz Al Saud, who began serving as the Saudi ambassador in Washington in 1983, was tasked to convince Syria to accept a peace agreement with Israel. Yet, despite a Reagan administration 1982 plan to resolve the Palestinian-Israeli conflict, Washington rejected any

Saudi peace proposal—including holding direct talks with Syria, resettling Palestinian refugees in Arab states, or recognizing the PLO.[19]

When US casualties in Lebanon mounted due to Iranian-led attacks on US military sites, Washington pulled American forces out of Lebanon, and Saudi Arabia was left with the impossible task of ending the tensions on the ground.[20]

By the fall of 1989, Riyadh had negotiated the terms of the Ta'if Agreement to help set up a new cabinet in Lebanon and ensure there would be no political vacuum in the country for Iran to exploit. When Washington pushed for a Syrian withdrawal from Lebanon, Damascus worked with Riyadh to try to negotiate a peace deal over the Golan Heights.[21] The PLO's backing of Iraq's invasion of Kuwait during the Second Gulf War (1990–1991), however, forced Riyadh to withdraw peace initiatives between the group and Israel. But the October 1991 Madrid Peace Conference tried to resolve Arab-Israeli tensions, and it led to the decline of the Arab boycott against Israel. Saudi Arabia played a marginal role at the conference, but it sent Prince Bandar to represent the kingdom. In the lead-up to the conference, the United States backed initiatives to advance election rights for Palestinians in East Jerusalem and a five-year process to resolve the Israeli-Palestinian conflict.[22] According to reports, Prince Bandar met with Jewish leaders, prime ministers, and Mossad chiefs to advance peace proposals.[23] Saudi sources did not verify such claims, including reports that Israelis met with the Saudis as early as 1991 and during the premiership of Yitzhak Shamir.[24]

The 1993 Oslo Accords may have revived the behind-the-scenes contacts between Saudi Arabia and Israel.[25] Saudi Arabia saw its role as a mediator of the Israeli-Palestinian conflict and a coordinator of Arab initiatives to support and fund the newly established Palestinian National Authority (PA). The accords granted a self-governing arrangement to Palestinians in Gaza in addition to Israeli recognition of the PLO, enabled ongoing GCC-Hamas contacts. Saudi Arabia considered its options on a broader scale, by entertaining the possibility of normalized ties with Israel. This far-reaching accord, however, did not stand the test of time. Israel failed to abide by any prescribed settlement arrangements and expansion, and Palestinians rejected any deal that would end up robbing them of statehood and control over their territories.

In 1997, Saudi Arabia refused to participate in a Middle East economic summit in Qatar, despite US urging, in which Israel was present. But to manage Pan-Arab trends, and to offer selective financial pledges that would ensure inter-Arab unity over the Palestinian issue, the kingdom remained engaged in the Israeli-Palestinian issues. When Benjamin Netanyahu assumed power in 1996, his policies to advance Israeli settlements and open an entrance into the Western Wall Tunnel within the Muslim Quarter of Jerusalem derailed the 1993 peace process. Saudi criticism of Israel therefore remained conditioned to Egyptian measures to moderate Arab outreach to the Palestinians, using money collected in the GCC.

Riyadh saw its evolving ties with Hamas in this period as a step to discourage the group from promoting extremism in the region and turning to Iran for help. The Hamas Charter, which demanded that Arab countries open their borders for the group's operation, led to the emergence of a Palestinian-style Muslim Brotherhood movement across the region. Reports of Saudi engagements with Hamas had emerged prior to the 1991 Gulf War, but contacts were lukewarm due to Hamas's opposition to US military engagement in the war. In February 1998, Hamas spiritual leader Ahmad Yassin (who was killed in an Israeli strike in 2004) made a tour of the Arab states including Saudi Arabia. A year after when Jordan expelled the director of the Politics Section of Hamas, Khalid Mashal, official Saudi financial help went to the PA through United Nations channels.[26]

In 2002, former Saudi leader, King Abdullah bin Abd al-Aziz Al Saud, advanced the Abdullah Peace Plan to recognize Israel in exchange for its commitment to Palestinian rights. Saudi Arabia funded Hamas between 2000 and 2004 but scaled back the support due to US pressures.[27] The plan did not materialize; Israel refused to recognize a Hamas victory in the legislative elections in the West Bank in early 2006, and it brought pressure on the Arab states to halt payment of funds to the Palestinian government to administer the West Bank and the Gaza Strip, pushing Hamas to break away and declare its own administration in Gaza.

Then on July 12, 2006, the Israeli army entered Lebanon to defeat Hezbollah. Both sides charged each other with provocations that led to the conflict. Iran reached out to Saudi Arabia to build a consensus through the Arab League to end the war. As casualties in Lebanon multiplied, Saudi Arabia called on Syria to use its influence over Hezbollah to bring the war to an end. King Abdullah then dispatched Prince Bandar to Tehran to help negotiate an end to the conflict. On July 26, Saudi foreign minister Saud al-Faisal bin Abd al-Aziz Al Saud delivered a letter to The White House urging for a ceasefire, which Washington maintained would not last. , , .

The war came to an end after twenty-six days, but it was followed by a large-scale conflict between Israel and Hamas in Gaza in 2008–2009. Saudi Arabia tried to encourage international donations to the PA in this period, although Saudi public opinion at times sided with the resistance that Hamas put up against Israel. Consequently, Riyadh's foreign policy was shaped to advance international consensus regarding the Palestinian-Israeli conflict, and it maintained an uneasy relationship with Hamas.

In 2011, in the aftermath of the Arab Spring, Saudi Arabia turned against Syrian president Bashar al-Assad, as Israel monitored the Golan Heights to ensure that Iranian and Syrian militias would not attack its positions in the area. Qatar, meanwhile, sided with Muslim Brotherhood (which Saudi Arabia designated a terrorist organization in 2014) groups in Syria while Riyadh reportedly may have backed anti-Assad rebel groups including the Free Syrian Army and the Syrian Democratic Forces. In response, Iran aided Assad and courted Hamas which was aligned with the Syrian Muslim Brotherhood, to help ease the brotherhood's tensions with the Syrian president. But Hamas, which disliked Iranian meddling in the Arab Spring, abandoned its headquarters in Damascus to relocate to Qatar, and it backed the Syrian opposition, which helped restore the group's relations with Saudi Arabia. Subsequently, Hamas political bureau chief Ismail Haniyeh publicly called on Riyadh to support the new Intifada in Jerusalem that started in late 2015.[28]

Hamas's outreach to Saudi Arabia picked up pace only after Iran suspended its military assistance to the group in 2015. The Iranian shift was viewed as resulting from efforts by Hamas's diplomatic and military wings to engage with Israel toward building a permanent ceasefire in Gaza. But the military wing of Hamas dominated the debate and controlled administrative decisions in Gaza where the group remained largely unpopular, thereby making it difficult for the kingdom to contemplate offering its full backing to Hamas.[29] Nonetheless, in July 2015, a Hamas delegation led by Khaled Mashal traveled to Makkah. The trip was termed as a religious trip by Saudi officials, but private talks may have been held to resolve tensions.[30] Signs of a resolution emerged publicly in 2016, when Al Arabiya columnist Abdulrahman Al-Rashed who was seen as a voice of political reform in the Middle East under the leadership of Crown Prince Muhammed bin Salman suggested that the time may have arrived for Arabs and Israelis to build ties through an interim plan that would enable official Saudi-Israeli relations.[31]

Meanwhile, Hamas members were able to reside in the kingdom. By early 2016, however, Hamas was working hard not to get caught in the fray of Saudi-Iranian tensions over Syria, after Tehran and Riyadh broke off ties when the Jaysh al-Islam commander Zahran Alloush was killed in Syria by pro-Assad forces and the Shia cleric Sheikh Nimr al-Nimr was beheaded by Saudi authorities. In May, the former Saudi intelligence chief, Prince Turki Al-Faisal bin Abd al-Aziz Al Saud, met with Prime Minister Benjamin Netanyahu's former national security adviser Major General Yaakov Amidror at the Washington Institute, a think tank in the US capital. Despite Turki Al-Faisal's position as a non-official member of the Royal Family and his insistence that Israel should understand the importance of endorsing the 2002 Saudi Peace Plan, the meeting was seen as a signal of evolving clandestine Saudi-Israeli ties and was denounced by numerous Arab news websites and coalitions. Nonetheless, Turki al-Faisal would continue to publicly meet with Israelis in different fora but also serve as a voice to highlight the Saudi position that rejects violence against Palestinians and normalization, enabling the kingdom to explain its array of concerns over the future of Palestine.

In 2017, Crown Prince Muhammad bin Salman decided to pressure the PA to accept a US deal for peace, which fell through. By May 2018, Hamas warmed up to Iran again after the United States pulled out of the nuclear deal with Tehran that same month, while Saudi Arabia backed Trump administration initiatives to contain Iran. In response, and to appease Hamas, in a column in the Saudi paper *Arab News*, Al-Rashed argued that a five-year peace deal between Hamas and Israel would prevent the group's strangulation, help it emerge stronger and mindful of the aging Fatah movement that constitutes the core of the PA, and possibly lead to Israeli recognition of Hamas as a legitimate Palestinian entity.[32]

With the prospects of peace in Palestine looking dim, however, Saudi-Hamas ties rapidly deteriorated. In 2018, Riyadh deposited US$80 million in aid to the PA to help restore its budget, representing a monthly contribution by the kingdom.[33] In early 2019, Saudi Arabia arrested Hamas supporters and detained Hamas representative Mohammed al Khodary who had helped retain the group's contacts with the kingdom for two decades. Hamas went public with the arrests of its members in Saudi Arabia, but it was soon cornered after tensions in Palestine mounted amid the group's growing unpopularity, and by the Saudi alignment with the United States as it moved to help normalize Arab ties with Israel during the Trump presidency. In May 2019, Saudi media listed forty Islamic figures around the world believed to be terrorists influenced by the Muslim Brotherhood, including top-tier Hamas leaders Khaled Mashal and Ismail Haniyeh and military commanders Mohammad al-Deif and Yahya al-Sinwar. When Israel launched an offensive on Gaza that same month, Saudis wrote Tweets expressing solidarity with the Jewish state and accusing Hamas of working with Iran, calling the group terrorist and murderous. Inside Israel, the comments were welcomed.[34]

Meanwhile, Crown Prince Muhammed bin Salman endorsed the idea of the Israelis and Palestinians having the right to build peaceful nations, and he steadfastly backed the legitimate rights of the Palestinian people to build a state with Jerusalem as its capital.[35] To this end, Riyadh withdrew its financial support to the PA in October 2019, pointing to a declining relationship between the two after President Mahmoud Abbas failed to reconcile with Hamas and pave the way for Palestinian normalization of relations with Israel. The Palestinian rejection of the Abraham Accords in 2020, however, meant that Saudi Arabia could not readily embrace its normalization with Israel. Furthermore, a starting point for a peace deal that stayed on the table was Israel's embrace of the 2002 Saudi-led Peace Plan that called for the establishment of a Palestinian state along the borders of 1967.

Without Israel's full commitment to this plan, Riyadh used its public posturing and policies to indicate its unwavering support for peace. By 2020, Prince Bandar bin Sultan proceeded to publicly accuse Palestinian leaders of betraying their people over decades, after the PA condemned the Abraham Accords.[36] That same year, Saudi Arabia prosecuted seventy people linked with Hamas. Despite Hamas's efforts to end the crisis with the kingdom, Saudi Arabia remained adamant about cutting its links with the group.[37]

In November 2020, reports pointed out that Benjamin Netanyahu may have traveled to the kingdom to discuss developments in the Red Sea region, a partnership, investments, and ways to contain Iran.[38] Saudi Arabia denied that the discussions had taken place.[39] But according to Israeli media sources, senior Israeli officials had already visited Saudi Arabia using executive aircraft with foreign registration and fictitious stopovers in neighboring countries.[40] In December, Israel's defense minister Benny Gantz, who was said to have already met with many Arab leaders, gave an interview to the Saudi Asharq al-Awsat, insisting that Jerusalem would remain under Israeli control with room for a Palestinian capital.[41]

In 2021, the United States Central Command (CENTCOM) absorbed Israel in its area of responsibility, raising concerns in Iran that the move was designed to encourage a Middle East coalition against it. Saudi Arabia meanwhile sought to strengthen its partnerships with local leaders in northern Iraq, as did Israel, thereby causing concerns in Iran about possible threats emerging along its western borders.[42] Saudi Arabia built a border agreement with Azerbaijan (the deal would solidify in 2023) as well, where Israel was advancing its security ties, pushing Tehran to argue that the three countries aimed to contain Iranian power.[43]

In addition, Riyadh condemned Tehran's attacks targeting the Iraqi Kurdistan region where opposition Kurdish groups fought an armed battle against Iranian strongholds. Saudi Arabian and Israeli media outlets spoke in support of the anti-Iranian protests that spread in Iraq in 2022, and emerging divisions among Iraqi Shia groups against Tehran. Other reports claimed that Israel might be helping Saudi Arabia in Yemen, to preserve security in the Bab-el-Mendeb where Netanyahu had said that if Iran blocked the waterway, it would have to face an international coalition inclusive of Israeli army branches.[44] Israel may have also attacked Iranian-backed Houthi strongholds in Yemen during the Israeli military campaign against the Palestinian Islamic Jihad in Gaza in August 2022. According to the chief of the general staff of the Israel Defense Forces Rav-Aluf Aviv Kochavi, Israel carried out a strike in a third country, which may have referred to Yemen.[45]

Meanwhile, a gathering of the CENTCOM summit of chiefs of defense was reportedly held in Sharm el-Sheikh in June 2022, in which Saudi Arabia participated, along with Israel, Qatar, Egypt, Bahrain, Jordan, and the UAE, following which Jordan's King Abdullah announced his country's support for the formation of a Middle East NATO (in reference to the North Atlantic Treaty Organization, and an idea that was first elaborated when President Trump traveled to Saudi Arabia in May 2017).

Present at the summit were Israel's Defense Forces chief of staff Aviv Kohavi and General Fayyadh bin Hamaed Al Ruwaili, the chief of staff of the Saudi armed forces, although no official account of the event was offered by either Israel or Saudi Arabia. According to reports, Israel sought US approval to provide Saudi Arabia with air defense later, to help expand regional cooperation against Iranian drones and missiles. The plan would entail the delivery of the Iron Beam system to the UAE and potentially to Saudi Arabia. The cheaper Israeli Iron Dome air defense system compared to the US anti-ballistic missile defense system known as the THAAD seemed attractive to Saudi Arabia. The latest laser version of the Israeli Iron Beam that was to be developed and procured as of 2022 and designed to destroy an airborne target that could offer further value as CENTCOM finalized the Red Sands Integrated Experimentation Centre in Saudi Arabia to increase regional cooperation in order to counter threats from Iran and its proxies and shoot down their missiles and drones. While financing for the Red Sands was approximately only 20 percent from the United States, other regional countries were expected to fund the initiative.[46]

Saudi Arabia remained one of the world's largest arms purchasers to ensure its security as well as its lobbying influence in Washington's defense quarters, and to facilitate cooperation with the United States over the Iranian nuclear program which could also entail a new era of partnership for the kingdom with Israel. This partnership was critical as Washington downsized its forces in the Middle East from more than 80,000 in 2020 to about 35,000 by mid-2022.[47] Joint air force training and exercises between Israel and its Arab partners, and the expanded sale of Israeli military equipment and technology to Arab countries, all taking place under the umbrella of a Middle East Air Defense Alliance (MEAD) aimed to guarantee more enhanced security for Saudi Arabia. While details about the MEAD initiative remained scant, it was expected to diffuse Iranian attempts to threaten the region.[48] In the Red Sea, Israel already had diplomatic relations with Egypt, and it conducted drills as well with the UAE and Bahrain, operations that indirectly expanded Saudi Arabia's operational theatre in this vital waterway in order to choke Iranian ability to engage in commercial or military activities in Africa, Yemen, and the Mediterranean region.[49]

Meanwhile, Saudi Arabia forwarded the Arab Peace Plan once again during meetings in New York in the summer of 2022, held conjointly with the Arab

League and the European Union, yet another step to expedite a peace process which would potentially also lead to Israeli guarantees of nuclear deterrent support to the GCC and the kingdom mindful of Iran's refusal to finalize a nuclear agreement with the world powers. Saudi Arabia may have also tried to condition recognition for Israel to US support of a strong Saudi nuclear program. By September, Haniyeh was also once again publicly involved in mustering Saudi support for Hamas, and he charged Fatah officials of hindering interfactional Palestinian reconciliation.[50] Saudi Arabia may have helped ease the tensions between the two Palestinian groups. At a summit held with President Biden in Bethlehem in the West Bank in July 2022, President Mahmoud Abbas thanked Saudi Arabia for backing the Palestinian cause and a two-state solution, and he would convey this message to the kingdom when it held a GCC summit in Jeddah in which President Biden was also present. In October, Saudi Arabia released the senior Hamas official, Mohammad Al Khodary, who was detained as a Hamas envoy in the kingdom back in 2019.[51]

The forty-third session of the GCC Supreme Council in Riyadh in December 2022 reaffirmed the important partnership between the United States, the GCC, Jordan, and Egypt resulting from Security and Development Summit held in Jeddah back in July. The summit's discussions tacitly endorsed the need to unite forces if Saudi Arabia were to embrace the ties with Israel, mindful that the United States aimed to encourage normalization between the two Middle Eastern states in an effort to expand its security umbrella through them in the region. The GCC Supreme Council stressed the need for Palestinians to obtain sovereignty over all their territories since June 1967, the establishment of a Palestinian state in East Jerusalem as its capital, and rejected any intention to annex West Bank settlements to Israel as a clear violation of the UN Charter, despite Prime Minister Netanyahu's position that those annexations were Israel's right. Finally, it reiterated the importance of GCC assistance to the UN Relief and Works Agency for Palestine Refugees in the Near East (UNRWA), founded in 1949 to aid Palestinian refugees.[52]

But despite these unfolding regional events, neither the Saudi Peace Plan nor the Abraham Accords were advancing at a pace that could provide permanent guarantees of security against Iran to Saudi Arabia mindful of rising tensions in Israel with the Palestinians after Prime Minister Netanyahu assumed power again in December 2022. At the same time, heavy Saudi defense spending may have been of concern to Israel, as was the Saudi drive to develop an arms-manufacturing industry using US and Israeli technical help. Meanwhile, in 2023, Riyadh insisted that the formation of an independent Palestinian state was key to having ties with Israel. Without Palestinian statehood, Saudi Arabia would be challenged by its own expatriate Palestinian community and many other Muslim countries if it were to normalize ties with Israel. But Prime Minister Netanyahu insisted on keeping Jerusalem under Israeli control, while also making it his goal to embrace Saudi Arabia through the Abraham Accords.[53]

The Saudi crown prince may have welcomed this embrace when he publicly spoke of Riyadh's ties with Israel in September 2023 and offered hope that they could improve. The statement suggested that the kingdom neither flirted with nor waltzed around the idea of normalizing ties with Israel. According to numerous reports, serious and substantial discussions on this issue ensued between senior Saudi, American, and Israeli officials in 2023. The extent of real progress made in these discussions was unclear, but a number of media reports suggested that normalization was imminent, while Saudi officials either rejected the idea or offered narratives conditioning it to a dual-state solution. Other reports said that there was no support in either the United States or Israel on what the kingdom was seeking as the price for normalization, including a strong Saudi nuclear program. According to discussions this author had with senior Saudi policy officials, it appeared that after the October War, Riyadh was clear that it could not expect to receive the massive American and Israeli security support that it had asked for if normalization remained a distant goal due to the conflict, and would therefore proceed to prioritize its ties with Iran including a dialog over Gaza until better options became available. Meanwhile, during frequent visits to Riyadh, senior US officials continued to offer commitment to a Palestinian state in return for a resolution to the war in Gaza that could ensure Israel's security and a Saudi-Israeli normalization.

ECONOMIC DRIVERS OF SAUDI-PALESTINIAN-ISRAELI RELATIONS

Historically, the volume of bilateral trade between Saudi Arabia and Israel was insignificant. This trade picked up in recent years. However, over the years prior to this period, Saudi Arabia has offered the bulk of its financial support to Palestinian groups through the Popular Committee for Assisting Palestinian Mujahideen and the Support Committee for the Al-Quds Intifada (a Saudi-proposed fund in 2000 to assist families of Palestinian martyrs in reference to those killed by Israelis), and the Al-Aqsa Fund (also a Saudi-recommended fund to finance projects to preserve the Arab and Islamic features of Jerusalem and help with the cause of Palestinian liberation)—groups that may have channeled some US$4 billion in pledges to Palestinians. In addition, Saudi funds for the Palestinian Authority Treasury Department came through the Jeddah-based Islamic Development Bank, at least in the periods reported in official Saudi news websites and archived by the Jewish Virtual Library for the period 1998–2003.[54]

In 2004, Riyadh offered US$92 million, according to the PA data, to help the PA in the West Bank. In 2005, unexpectedly high oil revenues led Saudi Arabia to repledge funds to Palestinians during a conference dedicated to garnering financial support for the PA, organized by then British prime minister Tony Blair in London. But Riyadh made it clear that it saw the Israeli-Palestinian conflict as a long chain of broken and unfulfilled promises that placed the burden on countries like the kingdom to help fix, while London was clear that a key goal of the event was to discourage public or private Arab funding for potential terrorist operations or extremist education and indoctrinations in Palestine.[55]

Through 2010, Palestinian officials received aid from Saudi Arabia, to stabilize the political situation in the West Bank and ease an embargo imposed by Israel and the western powers in 2006–2007. This assistance enabled the PA to run its operations and bar Hamas's influence over Palestinian affairs after the group broke away from the dominant party Fatah in the West Bank following a Hamas legislative election victory in 2006. The United States was unwilling to accept this election result, a move which radicalized Hamas, and despite Saudi urging for moderation by all sides, the kingdom could only hope that it would receive US assurances that it would not penalize foreign banks making the transfers of money to Palestinian officials.[56]

In 2011, Saudi Arabia announced that it would donate US$200 million to the PA.[57] The announcement arrived months after Hamas and Fatah agreed to form an interim government and hold elections. But future pledges of unity among the two main Palestinian groups failed to lead to concrete results, adding to the unstable stature of the PA in the West Bank that could in turn derail Saudi revenues that might otherwise allow for the functioning of Palestinian jurisdiction over the area since the Oslo Accords. In 2020, the kingdom set out to reduce funding for the PA, leading to a drastic decrease in total revenues from foreign aid by 84.9 percent that year. Government funding from Arab countries dropped to $40 million, compared to $265.5 million in 2019. Riyadh cut back $174.7 million to Palestine to $32.5 million, in the midst of a global pandemic due to the coronavirus. The cuts arrived after the signing of the Abraham Accords to normalize Arab-Israeli relations.[58]

The kingdom did not directly renege on its obligation to the Palestinian people. Rather it complied with an economic siege that Palestinians believed the United States was placing on them to push for peace with Israel. Saudi support for UNRWA (which has protected Palestinian refugees mainly through western financing sources, with the United States as a chief contributor) and the United States' calls to cease funding to it remained sources of friction. While the European Union remained the biggest donor to the Palestinians, Israeli clearance of the funds was turning into an important concern. Finally, the United States targeting of Hamas investment and finance networks in May 2022, just as the group's popularity increased in both the West Bank and Gaza following an upsurge in tensions with Israel a year earlier, led to an investigation on how the group amassed millions in its secret investment portfolio and operated companies across the Middle East and North Africa, thereby complicating Saudi financial backing for Palestine.[59]

Saudi support for Palestinians and UNRWA continued through 2022 when the kingdom contributed US$27 million to the UN body. According to Saudi Arabia, its total support to Palestine since 1999 amounted to more than US$5.2 billion, including support to the PA budget and direct support to different sectors to develop infrastructure, food, and agricultural security, and build Palestinian government and civil society and water management systems and environmental reforms. Saudi Arabia renewed its commitment to UNRWA in 2023, amid growing tensions in the West Bank and the fragility on the ground. In addition, it explored ways to help Saudi entities empower Palestinian youth and generate employment for them, in line with the kingdom's Vision 2030 developments goals, in the lead up to a Riyadh International Humanitarian Forum in February 2023.[60]

These measures enabled Saudi Arabia to justify and gradually embrace trade and commercial ties with Israel on a more public scale. In 2005, Saudi Arabia ended its ban on Israeli goods and services, after applying to the World Trade Organization (WTO) that bars a member country from enforcing a total trade ban on another member country. In return, the United States and Israel agreed to support the Saudi application to the WTO, despite Saudi measures to host boycott conferences through the Organization of Islamic Cooperation and the Arab League and prohibit Israeli-made goods in the following years. Riyadh stated that it had lifted second- and third-tier boycotts that respectively prohibited business worldwide with entities that did business with Israel and also banned Arab League members and nationals from business with blacklisted companies over their dealings with Israel, but a first-degree boycott remained in place to prohibit citizens of the Arab League countries from buying from, selling to, or entering into a business contract with either the Israeli government or an Israeli citizen.[61] By 2008, Israeli news sources reported that products made in Israel were sold in Saudi Arabia, through clandestine business partnerships.[62]

In the following years, the US Office of Anti-Boycott Compliance reported activities to force US firms to comply with trade regulations with Israel, helping to ease trade ties between Saudi commercial entities and Israel. Most of this trade between the kingdom and Israel's technology firms reportedly happened quietly, but the economic incentives for trade remained strong.[63] In addition, Saudi Arabia received Israeli agricultural and technological products through the West Bank, Jordan, and Cyprus.[64]

According to figures, Saudi Arabia may have exported less than a million dollars of products to Israel in 2013, and its exports increased over a period of seventeen years before then at an annual rate of 5.17 percent.[65] By 2017, Crown Prince Muhammad bin Salman had launched a "Smart City" plan, known as NEOM, only a few miles away from the Israeli port city of Eilat, to build a joint economic zone with Jordan and Egypt. Amid reports that he may have visited Israel, Israeli companies stepped in to negotiate with the Saudi Public Investment Fund to develop the plan, although the kingdom preferred to work with venture capital firms and private sector funds, rather than publicize any partnership with Israel.[66]

In 2020, it was reported that the Israeli security firm NSO Group Technologies may have sold hacking technology to the kingdom.[67] Other reports pointed out that Israeli engineering and software firms including Qualitest, which was brought by international investors in 2019, sold products to other companies that were then used in Saudi Arabia. The Mithaq Capital SPC, linked with the Al Rajhi family of bankers and based in Riyadh, may also have held stakes in Israeli companies Otonomo Technologies and Tremor International Ltd.[68]

In November 2021, Saudi Arabia reportedly tried to encourage Abu Dhabi to reject the first major and largest cooperation deal that it helped broker between Israel and Jordan, to construct a solar power plant in Jordan to supply power for an Israeli desalination plant that would then send water to Jordanians. According to some reports, Riyadh was unaware of the deal until it emerged in the news, but Israeli, Emirati, and Saudi officials declined to comment.[69] Amman meanwhile proceeded to adhere to the late king Abdullah's description of Arab ties with Israel as a cold peace, but by May 2022, the Saudi crown prince was ready to stress that Israel could be a potential ally.[70]

In 2022, reports also emerged that Israelis were building deals with Saudi Arabia to expand trade and economic relations including desert farming and promoting direct flights with the GCC to lead to unconstrained and formal diplomatic arrangements. Saudi businesses were keen to visit and explore business opportunities, especially as the kingdom tried to rapidly expand NEOM and complete the transfer of the sovereignty of the Red Sea islands of Tiran and Sanafir from Egypt to Saudi Arabia.[71] Future Gig, launched by an American-Jewish businessman Brice Gorvin was keen to explore this market potential, by connecting Israeli startups with Saudi markets, despite the absence of official commercial relations.[72] Asher Bennet, the brother of former Israeli prime minister and founder of the London-based e-truck maker Tevva Motors, sought to offer his products to Saudi Arabia's emerging green markets that same year. To build up these markets, the kingdom allowed top Israeli technology executives to enter Saudi Arabia without holding a second nationality passport, some of whom took part in the Davos in the Desert forum.[73] Meanwhile, following the October War, Saudi media aired views that encouraged sustained economic ties with Israel to incentivize the Jewish state to change course over Palestine and build peace. Saudi officials did not publicly endorse these views, but they continued to express interest in an Israel normalization deal after the war and said it was close.[74]

LEADERSHIP FACTORS IN SAUDI-ISRAELI RELATIONS

Under King Salman, Saudi Arabia delayed making a commitment to join the Abraham Accords, partly because it aimed first to resolve the Palestinian crisis before outreach to Israel, and partly to uphold the king's standing as a leader of the Arab and Muslim world and a supporter of the Palestinian cause. Public pronouncements about Saudi policy toward Israel came from the crown prince who was expected to embark on normalization with new narratives that offered a more critical analysis of seeking peace for Palestinians through a wider dialogue with Israel.

Crown Prince Muhammed bin Salman aimed to expand the Saudi regional influence by accepting emerging political, social, and economic trends designed to bring Arab countries and Israel closer. The soft arm of the US government was also inclined to promote awareness about the leadership aspects of life in Saudi Arabia under the crown prince, which could pave the way for better relations with Israel. In Israel, the ascendency to power of the crown prince overlapped with calls led by former Mossad chief Shabtai Shavit and backed by a coalition of former senior members of the Israel Defense Forces, Shin Bet security service, Mossad, and the police who supported a two-state solution, and the Saudi-led Arab Peace Initiative.[75]

But Riyadh's decision to join the Abraham Accords remained a variable of multiple factors that shaped the Saudi-Israeli relations and which were highlighted in this chapter's earlier sections. Hence, diverging messaging on the issue emerged when, for example, Prince Turki Al-Faisal and Foreign Minister Faisal bin Farhan rejected the idea of normalized ties with Israel, with the former even saying that Palestinians saw Israel as a "western colonizing power," while also welcoming the prospect of better relations should the Palestinian crisis be resolved.[76] The statements were designed to signal to Israel that without some compromise with the Palestinians over settlements and their territories, which could entail an independent Palestinian state, normalization would slow down.

Mohammad Al-Khodari's detention in Saudi Arabia in 2019, a figurehead who first received support to represent Hamas in the kingdom through unverified reports that pointed to an understanding between him and Prince

Turki Al-Faisal in 1993, was a case that spoke of the delicate balancing act that the Royal Family performed to monitor Hamas while paving the way for any normalization trend with Israel. Hamas would proceed to disclose details of this understanding.[77] In October 2022, when reports emerged that Saudi authorities would release Al-Khodari and deport him to Amman, having earlier deported his wife, schisms between Hamas and the Saudi leadership became public knowledge.[78] Another case that pointed to the delicate position in which Saudi Arabia was regarding normalization emerged in March 2020, when the Yemeni Houthis offered to release two Saudi pilots in exchange for the release of Hamas members detained in the kingdom, an issue over which Riyadh remained silent.[79]

Meanwhile, right-wing provocations in Israeli politics, anti-Arab religious Zionism, and public warning in Qatar and Iran over the expansion of Israeli settlements challenged the prospects of normalized ties between Saudi Arabia and Israel. Prime Minister Netanyahu insisted on maintaining Jewish holy sites in lands that the Arabs believed were occupied, and he called the Judea and Samaria encompassing the entire West Bank not settlements but suburbs of Israel and its administrative divisions. He also stressed that it was unrealistic to assume that he would dismantle half of Jerusalem and its suburbs and turn it into a capital for Palestine, an idea that he saw as a Middle East peace fantasy.[80]

Nonetheless, Netanyahu's new government was as fractured as ever in recent Israeli history in its ability to deliver peace, despite his insistence that he intended to build peace with Saudi Arabia so the kingdom could then help contain Hezbollah, secure Syria's borders with Israel, control terrorism led by extremist Islamic groups across the Middle East, and deliver stability in Lebanon.[81] In September 2023, the crown prince offered support for the idea of drawing closer to Israel. Riyadh also withheld funds to Palestinian groups to encourage a new roadmap to peace with Israel, without entirely alienating Palestinians in the face of Netanyahu's decision to control the civilian administration of the West Bank and expand settlements, and later on to take over the administration of Gaza in 2023.

SOCIAL FACTORS IN SAUDI-ISRAELI RELATIONS

Historically, Saudi Arabia's extremely conservative society stood ideologically opposed to the State of Israel. Not surprisingly, Saudi Arabia's opening to Israel triggered unease in communities opposed to normalization. Therefore, the challenge to the Saudi Royal Family was serious if it were to build diplomatic relations with Israel. To address this challenge, Riyadh mobilized clerics to shift the discourse in Saudi Arabia toward building an interfaith understanding with the Jewish people. In 2018, the head of the Muslim World League (MWL) Mohammed bin Abdul Karim al-Issa called for an interfaith peace trip to Jerusalem to promote understanding among the Abrahamic religions. Al-Issa visited the US Holocaust Memorial Museum and declared Holocaust denial a crime against Islam. In April 2019, MWL and the American Jewish Committee agreed to a historic visit to Auschwitz, to promote Muslim-Jewish understanding and launch cooperative projects. In 2022, Al-Issa read the Arafat Day haj sermon, a platform that Saudi Arabia uses annually to delineate the major religious trends shaping inside the kingdom, causing a social media stir over his friendliness toward Israel.[82]

Saudi Arabia also introduced religious reforms and restructured religious institutions. Major institutions linked to religious reforms included the Council of Senior Scholars, the Majlis Shura Council, the Ministry of Islamic Affairs and Dawah and Guidance, the Ministry of Justice, the Ministry of Education as well as bodies that regulated Islamic charitable entities. The Ministry of Islamic Affairs also controlled narratives of reform and promoted apolitical Wahhabism. According to the US Commission on International Religious Freedom report for 2022, power shifts from the Saudi religious establishment to the ruling Royal Family created opportunities for certain reforms including in textbooks and social policies which impacted religious freedom and led to altering texts that previously promoted hatred for Jews.

With warnings from the US Department of Homeland Security that the Abraham Accords could increase the risk of terrorism perpetrated by foreign terrorist organizations, controlling dissent was critical to an unfolding partnership between Saudi Arabia and Israel. This meant changing attitudes in Saudi Arabia toward political Zionism (to maintain a Jewish nation in Palestine in order to pressure all nations to secure protection for Jews in all lands) and religious Zionism (advocating the belief that Jews are God's chosen people and that a messiah will arrive to redeem Israel), sensitive topics that were not publicly raised much beyond the need to promote interfaith tolerance. Although the kingdom removed anti-Semitic and anti-Zionist references from its textbooks in 2020, there were reservations about the actions of orthodox and right-wing Jews to reinterpret political Zionism in order to retake Palestinian lands in the West Bank.

Saudi statements supporting the Jews took place while debates were forming inside Israel of the need to appease Palestinians and even allow them a level of control over East Jerusalem, and in favor of rapid normalization with the Arab world.[83] The narratives forwarded by Riyadh to counter anti-Israeli sentiments in this period expressed public disenchantment in the kingdom over the Palestinian leadership's lack of resolve to build peace with Israel. Simultaneously, Riyadh kept the historic Islamic pillars of propagation through local mosques in place, to promote state views on the issue of Palestine and Israel, even by senior clerics who in the past were known to propagate radical policies against Israel. A number of clerics promoted concepts such as the need to respect the national interest under the supervision of the Ministry of Islamic Affairs. Clerics also increased their verbal attacks on Iran and Hamas, both of which were seen as enemies of the Jewish people. In 2016, following the breakup of ties between Riyadh and Tehran, the Mufti of Saudi Arabia Abd al-Aziz Al Sheikh had called Iranians non-Muslims.[84] In 2017, when the Trump administration forwarded plans to work with Saudi Arabia and Israel, the mufti called Hamas a terror organization and issued a fatwa banning the fight against the Jews and forbidding the killing of Jews.[85] The dislike of the Muslim Brotherhood further helped advance debates over the need to be less supportive of Hamas.

Simultaneously, social and cultural entertainment programs were designed to build tolerance for other faiths. Israelis could travel to Saudi Arabia using third-country passports, and the same could apply to Saudi citizens. In 2019, a Saudi blogger visited the Al-Aqsa but was attacked by Palestinians. A rare Saudi television series, Exit 7, sparked debates about the issue of Saudi ties with Israel, in an attempt to break taboos on the subject, after it was aired during the month of Ramadan in 2020.[86] Saudi Arabia hosted Jewish rabbis to promote interfaith dialog. The MWL hosted World Jewish Congress head Ronald Lauder in a second annual conference for cultural rapprochement between the United States and the Muslim world in New York, in October 2019.[87] In May 2022, a gathering of faith leaders in Saudi Arabia included twelve rabbis.[88] At the summit between President Biden and Muhammed bin Salman in July 2022, many Jews visited Jeddah, and Saudi Arabia's self-proclaimed Rabbi Jacob Herzog confirmed that many came for work and tourism. Jewish visitors to the kingdom included arms sellers, Hasidic Jews, sports travelers, and car exhibition visitors, among others. In June, an Israeli Jew sneaked into Makkah, a city that only Muslims can visit for pilgrimage purposes.[89]

Before the latest crises in Israel which began to transpire in late 2022, and involved the ascendency of a far-right government, the Saudi daily Arab News offered a social media spin to normalization by altering its Twitter banner briefly to welcome the Jewish New Year with a Shana Tovah message in September 2020. A year earlier, the Saudi ambassador to the United States, Reema bint Bandar bin Sultan sent her greetings marking the occasion of Rosh Hashanah. Yet these subtle messages of embrace for the Jewish people also had to contend with opposition among Saudis to the idea of normalization. In 2011, the Saudi cleric Awad al-Qarni offered cash for the kidnapping of an Israeli soldier in response to a similar award that was promised by an Israeli family for catching a person who killed one of its members in 1998.[90] Saudi cleric Salih bin Abdallah Al-Humayd, a prominent imam of the Grand

Mosque in Makkah, had reportedly called for the annihilation of the occupying Jewish state.[91]

Other Saudis including Shias with extremist views and held in prison were unable to publicly voice positions on normalization with Israel. There was no doubt that to contain Iranian meddling in Saudi affairs, Riyadh was keen to monitor attempts that could mobilize these Shias against the government and to take additional steps to contain emerging pockets of Shia unrest inside the kingdom. Some Saudi Shias could oppose ties with Israel, thereby promoting a position that Iran advocated.[92] Meanwhile, the kingdom's dissident views among both its Sunni and Shia communities on the issue of normalization were yet to be measured.[93] Saudis who harbored religious or political beliefs that were deemed sensitive served to remind political observers of the fragile internal balancing act that the state had to undertake in order to manage potential public mobilization around religious themes. Due to the sensitivity of these topics, the Islamic scholar and talk-show personality who discussed politics and other religions, Ali al-Omari, was detained in 2017 and charged with forming a terrorist youth organization. The cleric Salman al-Awdah who once preached for a brotherhood-inspired Sahwa movement following the Arab Spring was detained in 2017. Sulaiman al-Dowaish was arrested a year earlier in 2016, after criticizing the Saudi Royal Family for its policies.[94]

Additionally, a large number of religious students and scholars worked in Saudi Arabia or engaged in covert religious activities that were difficult to monitor, including in Makkah and Madinah, where pilgrims gathered and stayed on to study different versions of the Islamic faith, at times undermining the overriding Hanbali faith that Saudi Arabia was trying to reform. Some of these students and scholars had misled Saudi authorities about their underground activities while appearing to be accommodating toward their Saudi hosts in the kingdom's multiple religious institutions, universities, and educational centers. At times, however, the Saudi state was able to control these groups. In July 2020, for example, ten Egyptian Nubian men were detained in Saudi Arabia after organizing a remembrance event marking the 1973 Arab-Israeli War, and sentenced under the country's counter-terrorism laws on charges of solidarity with the Muslim Brotherhood.[95]

The Khashoggi Ban enforced against Saudis engaged in serious counter-dissident activities and barring them from entering the United States, introduced in February 2021, was a reminder that dissent still brewed inside Saudi Arabia. If Israel were to normalize its ties with Saudi Arabia under these conditions, any acts of terrorism emerging as a result of the normalization could diminish the peace that the Abraham Accords were meant to build.[96] Israel's push for more settlements in the West Bank, its decision to launch a war in Gaza, and the 2023 October war's potentially polarizing impact on Muslims making the pilgrimage and on the hundreds of thousands of Palestinian workers in Saudi Arabia could influence currents of dissent and destabilize the kingdom, if Riyadh were to openly embrace ties with the Jewish state.

Partly because of these challenges, according to the USCIRF Report on Religious Freedom in Saudi Arabia, the US State Department had to redesignate the kingdom as a Country of Particular Concern (CPC) because of arrests and sentencings over religious dissent, and the ability of the Committee for the Promotion of Virtue and the Prevention of Vice to monitor and take action against religious minorities. The US State Department redesignated Saudi Araba as a CPC in 2022 but issued a national security waiver exempting it from punitive actions.[97] Moreover, Israel's right-wing shift left a gap in US policy in terms of justifying how the Abraham Accords promoted moderation, as did the humanitarian crisis in Gaza in 2023–2024, and the Saudi leadership had to fight the subsequent anti-Semitism rising inside the kingdom while avoiding topics such as changing attitudes toward Zionism because the conversation on Israel often remained confined to issues of interfaith tolerance in order to build social capital in support of the Abraham Accords.

There was also a sharp disconnect between the Saudi leadership and other Arab citizens who regarded Iran as a lesser threat than Israel, which in turn presented another challenge to Riyadh in building normalized ties with the Jewish state. In Saudi Arabia, according to the 2022 Arab Opinion Index, only 5 percent of people supported normalization, 38 percent opposed it, and 57 percent did not know or declined to answer.[98] By December 2023, 96 percent of Saudis opposed normalization with Israel.[99] Furthermore, many religious leaders in the GCC countries remained opposed to normalization, including Qatar, Kuwait, and Oman, thus making it harder for Riyadh to publicly justify building strong ties with Israel. In response, members of the Saudi Royal Family such as Prince Turki Al-Faisal discussed prevailing public sentiments about Israel. In 2020, he criticized Israeli policy of grabbing land and said Palestinians were placed in concentration camps, despite Saudi Arabia offering a hand of friendship to the Jewish state.[100] In August 2022, he made a number of public visits to promote the Saudi role in the Jerusalem Empowerment Fund, meeting with the Trustees of the Al-Quds Fund and Endowment, to address developments in Palestine and the status of Jerusalem.[101] In January 2023, a meeting of the Board of Trustees of the Sheikh Sabah Al-Ahmed Al-Jaber Charitable and Development Program was held in the city of Jerusalem via visual technology, with the participation of Prince Turki Al-Faisal, where he emphasized the importance of advancing development programs for Jerusalem, to help retain its Arabic culture and heritage.[102]

CONCLUSION

There remained a great deal of skepticism as to whether the Saudis could actually seek normalized ties with Israel in the absence of guarantees of a real partnership in which the upholding of Saudi interests on Palestine would remain a focal point of successive US and Israeli governments, especially after the October War. These Saudi interests entailed an end to the Palestinian conflict and an expedited return of Palestinian refugees to their homeland, as well as a dual-state solution which Israel was prone to reject. Nonetheless, Riyadh remained open to joining the Abraham Accords, and it was likely to step in to fund Gaza's reconstruction after the war in order to expedite normalization.

Against this backdrop, an evolving Saudi-Israeli partnership rested first and foremost on the United States and its ability to work out policies to ease Israeli-Palestinian tensions. Although Washington was increasingly challenged in bringing peace to Israel in a manner that could lead to a formal Saudi-Israeli relationship and a dual-state solution, the Biden administration continued to invest in keeping the option of normalization alive and the idea that a budding Saudi and Israeli partnership by necessity could contain the Iranian regional threat and its support for Palestinian groups such as Hamas and the Islamic Jihad. An enlarged CENTCOM umbrella that aimed to engage Saudi Arabia and Israel in joint security for the Middle East region therefore remained a promising prospect for the United States, although it was unclear if future CENTCOM operations after the outbreak of the October War could entail peace or cause added regional frictions.

A mission statement for a broader security and economic agenda emerging between Saudi Arabia and Israel therefore had to address modes of cooperation during heightened Palestinian-Israeli tensions. Meanwhile, the idea of a warm peace between the people of Saudi Arabia and Israel had shaped, but flipped, after the October War. This suggested that with an American-led viable regional security architecture not yet fully materializing in the Middle East, stakes were high for normalization between Saudi Arabia and Israel even in the cultural and social spheres, although state-level commitments could advance the prospects for normalization.

NOTES

1. Mohammed Najib, "Saudi Arabia Leads Chorus of Condemnation Following Israeli Minister's 'Provocative' Visit to Al-Aqsa," *Arab News,* January 3, 2023, https://www.arabnews.com/node/2225961/amp.

2. Martin Lings, *Muhammad: His Life Based on the Earliest Sources* (Rochester, NY: Inner Traditions International, 1983), 4–7.

3. Ibid.

4. Author's discussion with a senior Israeli diplomat who wished to remain anonymous, Pacific Council, Santa Monica, CA, June 8, 2008.

5. Joe Truzman, "Houthis Warn Israel, Touts Military Training," *FDD's Long War Journal,* March 7, 2022, https://www.longwarjournal.org/archives/2022/03/houthis-warn-israel-touts-military-training.php.

6. "The Kingdom of Saudi Arabia's Statement on Jerusalem," The Embassy of the Kingdom of Saudi Arabia, December 5, 2017, https://www.saudiembassy.net/news/kingdom-saudi-arabias-statement-jerusalem.

7. Gabby Deutch, "Blinken: Saudi Arabia a 'Critical Partner' for US in Expanding Abraham Accords," *Jewish Insider,* June 1, 2022, https://jewishinsider.com/2022/06/tony-blinken-saudi-arabia-israel-normalization-biden-middle-east/.

8. For information on the Copenhagen School, see Ali Diskaya, "Toward a Critical Securitization Theory: The Copenhagen and Aberystwyth Schools of Security," *E-International Relations*, February 1, 2013, https://www.e-ir.info/2013/02/01/towards-a-critical-securitization-theory-the-copenhagen-and-aberystwyth-schools-of-security-studies/; see also, R. Floyd, "Can Securitization Theory be Used in a Normative Analysis? Toward a Just Securitization Theory," *Security Dialogue,* 42 (2011): 427–439.

9. Ibid.

10. See Scott Cooper, "State-Centric Balance-Of-Threat Theory: Explaining the Misunderstood Gulf Cooperation Council," *Security Studies,* 12(2) (2003): 306–349, https://www.tandfonline.com/doi/abs/10.1080/09636410490521181?journalCode=fsst20.

11. See F. Gregory Gause III, "Balancing What? Threat Perception and Alliance Choice in the Gulf," *Security Studies,* 13(2) (2003): 273–305, https://www.tandfonline.com/doi/full/10.1080/09636410490521271?src=recsys.

12. Kai He, "Undermining Adversaries: Unipolarity, Threat Perception, and Negative Balancing Strategies After the Cold War," *Security Studies,* 21(2) (2012): 154–191, https://www.tandfonline.com/doi/full/10.1080/09636412.2012.679201?src=recsys.

13. See "Presenting the Findings From the 2022 Arab Barometer Report: Attitudes Toward International Relations," *Middle East Institute,* September 15, 2022, https://www.mei.edu/events/presenting-findings-2022-arab-barometer-report-attitudes-toward-international-relations; David Pollock, "New Saudi Poll Shows Biden's Visit Barely Budged Skepticism," *The Washington Institute,* August 26, 2022, https://www.washingtoninstitute.org/policy-analysis/new-saudi-poll-shows-bidens-visit-barely-budged-skepticism.

14. Aseema Sinha, "Building a Theory of Change in International Relations: Pathways of Disruptive and Incremental Change in World Politics," *International Studies Review,* 20(2) (June 2018): 195–203, https://academic.oup.com/isr/article-abstract/20/2/195/4998989.

15. Mitchell Bard, "Saudi-Israel Relations," Jewish Virtual Library, https://www.jewishvirtuallibrary.org/saudi-israel-relations.

16. Banafsheh Keynoush, *Saudi Arabia and Iran: Friends or Foes?* (New York: Palgrave Macmillan, 2016), 65.

17. Alexei Vassiliev, *The History of Saudi Arabia* (New York: New York University Press, 2000), 349; Badr Alkhorayef, "King Faisal Stood Firm on Oil Embargo," *Arab News,* May 4, 2008, https://www.arabnews.com/node/311576.

18. Keynoush, *Saudi Arabia and Iran: Friends or Foes?,* 91.

19. Ibid, 118–119.

20. Sonoko Sunayama, *Syria and Saudi Arabia: Contradictions and Conflicts in the Oil Era* (London: Tauris Academic Studies, 2007), 157–158.

21. Keynoush, *Saudi Arabia and Iran: Friends or Foes?,* 125.

22. "Examine the Events Leading Up to the 1991 Madrid Middle East Peace Conference," Center for Israel Education, https://israeled.org/examine-the-events-leading-up-to-the-1991-madrid-middle-east-peace-conference/.

23. Yossi Melman, "The Saudi Spy Chief Who Pioneered Secret Relations with Israel," *Haaretz,* July 12, 2002, https://www.haaretz.com/israel-news/2022-07-12/ty-article-magazine/.highlight/prince-bandar-bin-sultan-architect-of-the-relations-between-israel-and-saudi-arabia/00000181-f2fc-de0f-a58b-f3fed5b50000.

24. "Israeli Document: The Head of the Mossad Met the Leaders of Egypt, Saudi Arabia and Syria in 1991," *The New Khalij,* October 3, 2022, https://thenewkhalij.news/article/278722/othyk-srayly-alsaaody-saat-lttbyaa-alaalakat-kbl-30-aaama.

25. Bruce Riedel, "How to Understand Israel and Saudi Arabia's Secretive Relationship," *Brookings*, July 11, 2022, https://www.brookings.edu/blog/order-from-chaos/2022/07/11/how-to-understand-israel-and-saudi-arabias-secretive-relationship/.

26. Tianshe Chen, "Support or Hostility: The Relationship Between Arab Countries and Hamas," *Journal of Middle Eastern and Islamic Studies (in Asia),* 4(2) (July 2018): 100–120, https://www.tandfonline.com/doi/pdf/10.1080/19370679.2010.12023158.

27. Samuel Ramani, "Hamas's Pivot to Saudi Arabia," Carnegie Endowment for International Peace, September 17, 2015, https://carnegieendowment.org/sada/61315.

28. Adnan Abu Amer, "Why Hamas Hopes to Keep Low Profile in Saudi-Iranian Tensions," *Al-Monitor,* January 25, 2016, https://www.al-monitor.com/originals/2016/01/palestine-hamas-saudi-iran-crisis.html.

29. Ramani, "Hamas's Pivot to Saudi Arabia."

30. "Saudi Arabia Says Relations with Hamas Have Not Changed After Meeting," *Reuters,* July 23, 2015, https://www.reuters.com/article/uk-saudi-palestinians/saudi-arabia-says-relations-with-hamas-have-not-changed-after-meeting-idUKKCN0PX1H120150723.

31. "Saudi Journalist: Arab Israelis Could Help Build Mideast Ties," *The Times of Israel,* December 9, 2016, https://www.timesofisrael.com/saudi-journalist-arab-israelis-could-help-build-mideast-ties/.

32. Abdulrahman Al-Rashed, "Hamas and the Five-Year Truce Deal," *Arab News,* August 10, 2018, https://www.arabnews.com/node/1354186; Joseph Braude, "Saudi Arabia in the Crucible: A Conversation with Abdulrahman Al-Rashed," *Foreign Policy Research Institute,* December 7, 2016, https://www.fpri.org/article/2016/12/saudi-arabia-crucible-conversation-abdulrahman-al-rashed/.

33. "Saudi Arabia Deposits $80 mln to Support Palestinian Authority Budget," *Al Arabiya,* July 27, 2018, https://english.alarabiya.net/News/middle-east/2018/07/27/Saudi-Arabia-deposits-80-mln-to-support-the-Palestinian-Authority.

34. Adnan Abu Amer, "What is Behind the Saudi Campaign Against Hamas?," *AlJazeera,* September 23, 2019, https://www.aljazeera.com/opinions/2019/9/23/what-is-behind-the-saudi-campaign-against-hamas.

35. Jonathan Marcus, "Israel and Saudi Arabia: The Relationship Emerging into the Open," *BBC,* April 3, 2018, https://www.bbc.com/news/world-middle-east-43632905.

36. Isabel Kershner and Ben Hubbard, "Saudi Prince Accuses Palestinian Leaders of Failing Palestinians," *The New York Times,* November 12, 2020, https://www.nytimes.com/2020/10/06/world/middleeast/saudi-arabia-palestinians-israel.html.

37. Adnan Abu Amer, "How Saudi Arabia Turned Against Palestinians in the Kingdom," *Middle East Eye,* March 11, 2020, https://www.middleeasteye.net/opinion/hamas-trials-how-saudi-arabia-turned-against-palestinians.

38. Paul Goldman and Rachel Elbaum, "Israel's Benjamin Netanyahu Visits Saudi Arabia, Official Says," *NBC News,* November 23, 2020, https://www.nbcnews.com/news/world/israel-s-prime-minister-benjamin-netanyahu-secretly-visits-saudi-official-n1248585.

39. "Saudi Arabia Denies Crown Prince Held 'Secret Meeting' With Israeli PM," *BBC,* November 23, 2020, https://www.bbc.com/news/world-middle-east-55042055.

40. Avi Schard, "How Senior Israeli Officials Secretly Fly to Saudi Arabia," *Haaretz,* July 14, 2022, https://www.haaretz.com/israel-news/security-aviation/2022-07-14/ty-article/.premium/israel-senior-officials-secret-flights-to-saudi-arabia/00000181-fde8-d4e2-a193-fffe90fc0000.

41. Mustafa Abu Sneineh, "Israel's Benny Gantz Gives Interview to Saudi Newspaper," *Middle East Eye,* December 17, 2020, https://www.middleeasteye.net/news/israel-saudi-arabia-gantz-interview-jerusalem-palestine-capital.

42. "Saudi Arabia Also Infiltrated Iran's North!," *Etemad Online,* Bahman 11, 1401, https://www.etemadonline.com/%D8%A8%D8%AE%D8%B4-%D8%B3%DB%8C%D8%A7%D8%B3%DB%8C-9/594074-%D8%B9%D8%B1%D8%A8%D8%B3%D8%AA%D8%A7%D9%86-%D8%A2%D8%B0%D8%B1%D8%A8%D8%A7%DB%8C%D8%AC%D8%A7%D9%86.

43. "New War Beyond Middle East between Saudi Arabia and Iran to Gain Influence in Republic of Azerbaijan!" *Tabnak,* December 10, 1396, https://www.tabnak.ir/fa/news/775981/%D8%AC%D9%86%DA%AF-%D8%AC%D8%AF%DB%8C%D8%AF-%D9%81%D8%B1%D8%A7%D8%AE%D8%A7%D9%88%D8%B1%D9%85%DB%8C%D8%A7%D9%86-%D8%A7%DB%8C-%D8%B9%D8%B1%D8%A8%D8%B3%D8%AA%D8%A7%D9%86-%D8%A8%D8%B1%D8%A7%DB%8C-%DA%A9%D8%B3%D8%A8-%D9%86%D9%81%D9%88%D8%B0-%D8%AF%D8%B1-%D8%AC%D9%85%D9%87%D9%88%D8%B1%DB%8C-%D8%A2%D8%B0%D8%B1%D8%A8%D8%A7%DB%8C%D8%AC%D8%A7%D9%86.

44. Zvi Bar'el, "Yemen's War Is a Mercenary Heaven. Are Israelis Reaping the Profits?," *Haaretz,* February 17, 2019, https://www.haaretz.com/2019-02-17/ty-article/.premium/yemens-war-is-a-mercenary-heaven-are-israelis-reaping-the-profits/0000017f-e139-d75c-a7ff-fdbdee4b0000.

45. "Did Israel Attack a Houthi Camp in Yemen During the Gaza Fighting?," *Middle East Eye,* August 18, 2022, https://www.middleeasteye.net/news/israel-gaza -yemen-houthi-camp-attack.

46. "Israel to Ask Biden for Okay to Provide Air Defense Laser to Saudi Ara-bia," *The Times of Israel,* June 28, 2022, https://www.timesofisrael.com/israel-to -ask-biden-for-okay-to-provide-air-defense-laser-to-saudi-arabia-report/; Abigail Ng, "Jordan's King Says He Would Support a Middle East Version of NATO," *CNBC,* June 24, 2022, https://www.cnbc.com/2022/06/24/jordans-king-says-he-would-sup-port-a-middle-east-version-of-nato.html.

47. Courtney Kube, "US Military is Developing Plans to Open a New Testing Facility in Saudi Arabia," *NBC News,* September 2022, https://www.nbcnews.com /politics/national-security/us-military-developing-plans-open-new-testing-facility -saudi-arabia-rcna46343.

48. "Israel's Unexpected Military Alliance in the Gulf," *The Economist,* June 30, 2022, https://www.economist.com/middle-east-and-africa/2022/06/30/israels-unex-pected-military-alliance-in-the-gulf.

49. See Banafsheh Keynoush, "Revolutionary Iran's Africa Policy," *King Faisal Center for Research and Islamic Studies*, June 2021, https://kfcris.com/en/view/ post/343.

50. "Hamas Aims to Restore Saudi Arabia Ties," *Middle East Monitor,* Septem-ber 17, 2022, https://www.middleeastmonitor.com/20220917-hamas-aims-to-restore -saudi-arabia-ties/.

51. "Saudi Arabia Frees Senior Hamas Official," *Reuters,* October 19, 2022, https://www.reuters.com/world/middle-east/saudi-arabia-frees-senior-hamas-official -2022-10-19/.

52. "GCC Supreme Council Releases Final Communique After 43rd Sum-mit," *Saudi Gazette,* December 9, 2022, https://saudigazette.com.sa/article/627828 /SAUDI-ARABIA/GCC-Supreme-Council-releases-final-communique-after-43rd -summit.

53. Neville Teller, "Abraham Accords: Saudi Arabia is Still Not Budging," *The Jerusalem Post,* January 31, 2023, https://www.jpost.com/opinion/article-730098.

54. Steven Stalinsky, "Palestinian Foreign Aid: Saudi Financial Aid," *Jewish Virtual Library,* July 2003, https://www.jewishvirtuallibrary.org/saudi-financial-aid -to-the-palestinian-authority.

55. Simon Henderson, "Supporting the Palestinian Authority: Will the Oil-Rich Arabs Pay Up?," *The Washington Institute for Near East Policy,* February 28, 2005, https://www.washingtoninstitute.org/policy-analysis/supporting-palestinian-author-ity-will-oil-rich-arabs-pay.

56. Alastair Macdonald, "Palestinian Finance Minister Hails New Saudi Cash," *Reuters,* May 1, 2007, https://www.reuters.com/article/idUSMAC149418.

57. "Saudi Arabia Donates $200 Million to PA," *IMEMC,* September 20, 2011, https://imemc.org/article/62063/.

58. Zehra Nur Duz, "Palestinian Funding from Arab States Down 85% in 2020," *Anadolu Agency,* March 3, 2021, https://www.aa.com.tr/en/middle-east/palestinian -funding-from-arab-states-down-85-in-2020/2163509.

59. "Targeting Covert Hamas Investment Network and Hamas Finance Official," US Department of State, May 24, 2022, https://www.state.gov/targeting-covert
-hamas-investment-network-and-hamas-finance-official/.

60. "Saudi Arabia Supports Palestine Refugees with US$27 Million to UNRWA,"
United Nations, October 23, 2022, https://www.un.org/unispal/document/saudi-ara-
bia-supports-palestine-refugees-with-us-12-million-to-unrwa-press-release/; "Saudi
Arabia and UNRWA Renew Commitment to Palestine Refugees and Regional Peace
and Stability," *OCHA Relief Web,* January 31, 2023, https://reliefweb.int/report/
occupied-palestinian-territory/saudi-arabia-and-unrwa-renew-commitment-palestine
-refugees-and-regional-peace-and-stability.

61. "Saudi Arabia Continues Boycott of Israel," Jewish Virtual Library*,* https://
www.jewishvirtuallibrary.org/saudi-arabia-continues-boycott-of-israel.

62. "Made in Israel, Sold in Saudi Arabia," *The Jerusalem Post,* March 21, 2008,
https://www.jpost.com/middle-east/made-in-israel-sold-in-saudi-arabia.

63. Jonathan Ferziger and Peter Waldman, "How Do Israel's Tech Firms Do
Business in Saudi Arabia? Very Quietly," *Bloomberg,* February 1, 2017, https://www
.bloomberg.com/news/features/2017-02-02/how-do-israel-s-tech-firms-do-business
-in-saudi-arabia-very-quietly#xj4y7vzkg.

64. "Geopolitics Reviews Exciting Details About Saudi Arabia's Relationship
with Israel and Expects Normalization Soon," *The New Khalij,* October 8, 2022,
https://thenewkhalij.news/article/279089/alsaaody-ttgh-nho-alslam-maa-srayl.

65. "Saudi Arabia / Israel," https://oec.world/en/profile/bilateral-country/sau/
partner/isr.

66. "Israeli Companies Talking to Saudi Arabia About $500b 'Smart City,'"
The Jerusalem Post, October 25, 2017, https://www.jpost.com/business-and-inno-
vation/israeli-companies-likely-talking-to-saudi-arabia-about-500-bil-smart-city
-508429.

67. "Israeli Cybersecurity Firm Reportedly Sold Hacking Technology to
UAE, Saudi Arabia," *i24,* August 23, 2020, https://www.i24news.tv/en/news/israel
/1598187507-israeli-cybersecurity-firm-reportedly-sold-hacking-tech-to-uae-saudi
-arabia.

68. Vivian Nereim, Daniel Avis, "Israel and Saudi Arabia: No Longer Enemies,
but Not Quite Friends," *Taipei Times,* September 7, 2022, https://www.taipeitimes
.com/News/editorials/archives/2022/09/07/2003784884.

69. "Saudis Attempted to Block UAE-Israel-Jordan Deal on Energy, Water," *The
Times of Israel,* November 25, 2021, https://www.timesofisrael.com/saudis-attempted
-to-block-uae-israel-jordan-deal-on-energy-water-report/.

70. "Senior Israeli Official Visits Saudi Arabia Over Security Cooperation," *i24,*
May 28, 2022, https://www.i24news.tv/en/news/israel/diplomacy/1653721348-report
-senior-israeli-official-visits-saudi-arabia-over-security-cooperation.

71. Danny Zaken, "Al-Monitor: The Israelis Have Started Making Deals in
Saudi Arabia," *Al Mayadeen,* June 3, 2022, https://www.almayadeen.net/press/
%D8%A7%D9%84%D9%85%D9%88%D9%86%D9%8A%D8%AA%D9%88%D8
%B1:-%D8%A7%D9%84%D8%A5%D8%B3%D8%B1%D8%A7%D8%A6%D9
%8A%D9%84%D9%8A%D9%88%D9%86-%D8%A8%D8%AF%D8%A3%D9

%88%D8%A7-%D8%B9%D9%82%D8%AF-%D8%B5%D9%81%D9%82%D8
%A7%D8%AA-%D9%81%D9%8A-%D8%A7%D9%84%D8%B3%D8%B9%D9
%88%D8%AF%D9%8A%D8%A9.

72. "Saudi Arabia and Israel . . . an Economic, Political and Security Rapprochement Despite the Absence of Official Normalization," *The New Khalij,* September 4, 2022, https://thenewkhalij.news/article/276372/alsaaody-osrayl-tkarb-aktsady -osyasy-oamny-yzyl-hal-alaada.

73. Jonathan H. Ferziger, "Israeli Entrepreneur Looks to Sell Electric Trucks in Saudi Arabia," *The Circuit,* October 27, 2022, https://circuit.news/2022/10/27/asher -bennett-israel-saudi-arabia-tevva-motors/.

74. David Gritten, "Saudi Arabia Interested in Israel Normalization Deal After War," *BBC,* January 9, 2024, https://www.bbc.com/news/world-middle -east-67922238; "Saudi Writer: Peace with Israel and Trade Relations with It Will Turn our Commercial Leverage into a Weapon More Effective than Further Rounds of Fighting," MEMRI, February 13, 2024, https://www.memri.org/reports /saudi-writer-peace-israel-and-trade-relations-it-will-turn-our-commercial-leverage -weapon.

75. Odeh Bisharat, "Israel is Tasking Saudi Arabia with Subduing the Palestinians," *Haaretz,* August 8, 2016, https://www.haaretz.com/opinion/2016-08-08 /ty-article/.premium/israel-is-tasking-saudi-arabia-with-subduing-the-palestinians /0000017f-debe-db5a-a57f-defe40610000.

76. See Ariel Kahana, "Prominent Saudi Prince Strongly Criticizes Israel at Bahrain Summit," *Israel Hayom,* July 12, 2020, https://www.israelhayom.com/2020/12 /07/saudi-prince-strongly-criticizes-israel-at-bahrain-summit/.

77. Adnan Abu Amer, "Hamas Reveals the Hidden Aspects of its Relations with Saudi Arabia," *Middle East Monitor,* May 8, 2020, https://www.middleeast-monitor.com/20200508-hamas-reveals-the-hidden-aspects-of-its-relations-with-saudi -arabia/.

78. "Riyadh Will Release Mohamed Al-Khodari and Deport Him to Amman," *Middle East Monitor,* October 17, 2022, https://www.middleeastmonitor.com /20221017-riyadh-will-release-al-khudari-and-deport-him-to-amman/.

79. "Iran-Backed Houthis Offer to Free Saudis in Exchange for Hamas Members," *The Times of Israel,* March 27, 2020, https://www.timesofisrael.com/iran -backed-houthis-offer-to-free-saudis-in-exchange-for-hamas-members/.

80. Rabi Marc Schneier, "Abraham Accords No Escape from Palestinian Question," *Arab News,* January 11, 2023, https://www.arabnews.com/node/2230776; Alex Traiman, "I Intend to Achieve Peace with Saudi Arabia," *Israel Hayom,* October 24, 2022, https://www.israelhayom.com/2022/10/24/i-intend-to-achieve-peace-with -saudi-arabia/.

81. Ibid.

82. "Muslim World League and AJC Agree on Historic Visit to Auschwitz," *AJC Transatlantic Institute,* https://transatlanticinstitute.org/press-releases/muslim-world -league-and-ajc-agree-historic-visit-auschwitz.

83. Traiman, "I Intend to Achieve Peace with Saudi Arabia."

84. "Senior Saudi Cleric Said Iran's Leaders Are Not "Muslims"," *The Times of Israel,* September 7, 2016, https://fa.timesofisrael.com/%D8%B1%D9%88%D8

%AD%D8%A7%D9%86%DB%8C-%D8%A7%D8%B1%D8%B4%D8%AF-%D8
%B3%D8%B9%D9%88%D8%AF%DB%8C-%DA%AF%D9%81%D8%AA-%D8
%B1%D9%87%D8%A8%D8%B1%D8%A7%D9%86-%D8%A7%DB%8C%D8
%B1%D8%A7%D9%86-%D9%85%D8%B3/.

85. "Israel Welcomes Saudi Mufti's Pro-Israel Remarks, Invited Him to Visit the Country," *Andalou Agency,* November 14, 2017, https://www.dailysabah.com/mideast/2017/11/14/israel-welcomes-saudi-muftis-pro-israel-remarks-invites-him-to-visit-the-country.

86. Vivian Nereim, "Saudi TV Series Sparks Rare Ramadan Debate on Ties with Israel," *Bloomberg,* April 29, 2020, https://www.bloomberg.com/news/articles/2020-04-29/saudi-tv-series-sparks-rare-ramadan-debate-on-ties-with-israel#xj4y7vzkg.

87. "Saudi Cleric Calls for Muslim-Christian-Jewish Peace Delegation to Jerusalem," *The Times of Israel,* October 6, 2018, https://www.timesofisrael.com/saudi-cleric-calls-for-interfaith-peace-delegation-to-jerusalem/.

88. "American Jewish Committee Leader Attends Historic Multi-Faith Gathering in Saudi Arabia," *American Jewish Committee*, May 12, 2022, https://www.ajc.org/news/american-jewish-committee-leader-attends-historic-multifaith-gathering-in-saudi-arabia.

89. Zvika Klein, "Meet Jacob Herzog, Saudi Arabia's Self-Proclaimed Chief Rabbi," *The Jerusalem Post,* July 23, 2022, https://www.jpost.com/diaspora/article-712621.

90. "Saudi Cleric Offers Cash for Israel Soldier Kidnap," *Reuters,* October 26, 2011, https://www.reuters.com/article/us-saudi-israel-reward/saudi-cleric-offers-cash-for-israel-soldier-kidnap-idUSTRE79P7HI20111026.

91. "Saudi Cleric Calls to 'Annihilate the Plundering' Jews," *i24,* English, 2022, https://www.youtube.com/watch?v=5gza0-nn5uo.

92. "USCIRF Releases New Report on Religious Freedom in Saudi Arabia," USCIRF, December 28, 2022, https://www.uscirf.gov/release-statements/uscirf-releases-new-report-religious-freedom-saudi-arabia.

93. Yasmin Farouk and Nathan J. Brown, "Saudi Arabia's Religious Reforms Are Touching Nothing but Changing Everything," in *Islamic Institutions in Arab States: Mapping the Dynamics of Control, Co-option, and Contention,* ed. Frederic Wehrey (Carnegie Endowment for International Peace, 2021), https://carnegieendowment.org/files/202106-IslamicInstitutions-final-updated.pdf.

94. Aziz El Yaakoubi, "Relatives of Some Saudi Detainees Anxiously Await Biden Trip," *Reuters,* July 13, 2022, https://www.reuters.com/world/middle-east/relatives-some-saudi-detainees-anxiously-await-biden-trip-2022-07-13/.

95. Author's interview with a Muslim scholar, Princeton University, October 22, 2018; "Saudi Arabia: Quash Sentences for Egyptian Nubians Who Organized Peaceful Remembrance Event," *Amnesty International*, October 11, 2022, https://www.amnesty.org/en/latest/news/2022/10/saudi-arabia-quash-sentences-for-egyptian-nubians-who-organized-peaceful-remembrance-event/#:~:text=The%2010%20detained%20Egyptian%20Nubian,and%20Wael%20Ahmed%20Hassan%20Ishaq.

96. Ken Klippenstein, "Intel Report Warned Abraham Accords Would Fuel Violence," *The Intercept,* June 22, 2022, https://theintercept.com/2022/06/22/abraham-accords-israel-saudi-arabia-biden/.

97. "USCIRF Releases New Report on Religious Freedom in Saudi Arabia," USCIRF, https://www.uscirf.gov/release-statements/uscirf-releases-new-report-religious-freedom-saudi-arabia.

98. Connor Echols, "Surprise! Arab Public Gives Abraham Accords a Big Thumbs Down," *Responsible Statecraft,* January 19, 2023, https://responsible statecraft.org/2023/01/19/surprise-arab-public-gives-abraham-accords-a-big-thumbs-down/.

99. "Poll: 96% of Saudis Oppose Normalization With Israel," *Middle East Monitor*, December 23, 2023, https://www.middleeastmonitor.com/20231223-poll-96-of-saudis-oppose-normalisation-with-israel/.

100. Raphel Ahren, "Saudi Prince: Bully Israel Steals Land, Puts Palestinians in Concentration Camps," *The Times of Israel,* December 6, 2020, https://www.timesofisrael.com/saudi-prince-bully-israel-steals-land-puts-palestinians-in-concentration-camps/.

101. "In the Video . . . 'And Sanctify It.' An Initiative Launched by the Chamber to Support Jerusalem with 10 Million Dinars," *Alanba,* August 25, 2022, https://www.alanba.com.kw/113732.

102. "The Opening of the "Endowment of Sheikh Sabah Al-Ahmad Al-Jaber Al-Sabah" During the Current Year in Jerusalem," *AlQuds,* January 25, 2023, https://www.alquds.com/posts/4c56e4a9-bd31-495d-8daa-f55102c5be8b.

REFERENCES

Abu Amer, Adnan, "Hamas Reveals the Hidden Aspects of its Relations with Saudi Arabia," *Middle East Monitor,* May 8, 2020, https://www.middleeastmonitor.com/20200508-hamas-reveals-the-hidden-aspects-of-its-relations-with-saudi-arabia/.

Abu Amer, Adnan, "How Saudi Arabia Turned Against Palestinians in the Kingdom," *Middle East Eye,* March 11, 2020, https://www.middleeasteye.net/opinion/hamas-trials-how-saudi-arabia-turned-against-palestinians.

Abu Amer, Adnan, "What is Behind the Saudi Campaign Against Hamas?" *AlJazeera,* September 23, 2019, https://www.aljazeera.com/opinions/2019/9/23/what-is-behind-the-saudi-campaign-against-hamas.

Abu Amer, Adnan, "Why Hamas Hopes to Keep Low Profile in Saudi-Iranian Tensions," *Al-Monitor,* January 25, 2016, https://www.al-monitor.com/originals/2016/01/palestine-hamas-saudi-iran-crisis.html.

Abu Sneineh, Mustafa, "Israel's Benny Gantz Gives Interview to Saudi Newspaper," *Middle East Eye,* December 17, 2020, https://www.middleeasteye.net/news/israel-saudi-arabia-gantz-interview-jerusalem-palestine-capital.

Ahren, Raphel, "Saudi Prince: Bully Israel Steals Land, Puts Palestinians in Concentration Camps," *The Times of Israel,* December 6, 2020, https://www.timesofisrael.com/saudi-prince-bully-israel-steals-land-puts-palestinians-in-concentration-camps/.

Al-Rashed, Abdulrahman, "Hamas and the Five-Year Truce Deal," *Arab News,* August 10, 2018, https://www.arabnews.com/node/1354186

Alkhorayef, Badr, "King Faisal Stood Firm on Oil Embargo," *Arab News,* May 4, 2008, https://www.arabnews.com/node/311576.

"American Jewish Committee Leader Attends Historic Multi-faith Gathering in Saudi Arabia," *American Jewish Committee*, May 12, 2022, https://www.ajc.org/news/american-jewish-committee-leader-attends-historic-multifaith-gathering-in-saudi-arabia.

Bar'el, Zvi, "Yemen's War Is a Mercenary Heaven. Are Israelis Reaping the Profits?" *Haaretz,* February 17, 2019, https://www.haaretz.com/2019-02-17/ty-article/.premium/yemens-war-is-a-mercenary-heaven-are-israelis-reaping-the-profits/0000017f-e139-d75c-a7ff-fdbdee4b0000.

Bard, Mitchell, "Saudi-Israel Relations," Jewish Virtual Library, https://www.jewishvirtuallibrary.org/saudi-israel-relations.

Bisharat, Odeh, "Israel is Tasking Saudi Arabia with Subduing the Palestinians," *Haaretz,* August 8, 2016, https://www.haaretz.com/opinion/2016-08-08/ty-article/.premium/israel-is-tasking-saudi-arabia-with-subduing-the-palestinians/0000017f-debe-db5a-a57f-defe40610000.

Braude, Joseph, "Saudi Arabia in the Crucible: A Conversation with Abdulrahman Al-Rashed," Foreign Policy Research Institute, December 7, 2016, https://www.fpri.org/article/2016/12/saudi-arabia-crucible-conversation-abdulrahman-al-rashed/.

Chen, Tianshe, "Support or Hostility: The Relationship Between Arab Countries and Hamas," *Journal of Middle Eastern and Islamic Studies (in Asia),* 4(2) (July 2018): 100–120, https://www.tandfonline.com/doi/pdf/10.1080/19370679.2010.12023158.

Cooper, Scott, "State-Centric Balance-Of-Threat Theory: Explaining the Misunderstood Gulf Cooperation Council," *Security Studies,* 12(2) (2003): 306–349, https://www.tandfonline.com/doi/abs/10.1080/09636410490521181?journalCode=fsst20.

Deutch, Gabby, "Blinken: Saudi Arabia a 'Critical Partner' for US in Expanding Abraham Accords," *Jewish Insider,* June 1, 2022, https://jewishinsider.com/2022/06/tony-blinken-saudi-arabia-israel-normalization-biden-middle-east/.

"Did Israel Attack a Houthi Camp in Yemen During the Gaza Fighting?" *Middle East Eye,* August 18, 2022, https://www.middleeasteye.net/news/israel-gaza-yemen-houthi-camp-attack.

Diskaya, Ali, "Toward a Critical Securitization Theory: The Copenhagen and Aberystwyth Schools of Security," *E-International Relations*, February 1, 2013, https://www.e-ir.info/2013/02/01/towards-a-critical-securitization-theory-the-copenhagen-and-aberystwyth-schools-of-security-studies/.

Duz, Zehra Nur, "Palestinian Funding from Arab States Down 85% in 2020," *Anadolu Agency,* March 3, 2021, https://www.aa.com.tr/en/middle-east/palestinian-funding-from-arab-states-down-85-in-2020/2163509.

Echols, Connor, "Surprise! Arab Public Gives Abraham Accords a Big Thumbs Down," *Responsible Statecraft,* January 19, 2023, https://responsiblestatecraft.org/2023/01/19/surprise-arab-public-gives-abraham-accords-a-big-thumbs-down/.

El Yaakoubi, Aziz, "Relatives of Some Saudi Detainees Anxiously Await Biden Trip," *Reuters,* July 13, 2022, https://www.reuters.com/world/middle-east/relatives -some-saudi-detainees-anxiously-await-biden-trip-2022-07-13/.

"Examine the Events Leading Up to the 1991 Madrid Middle East Peace Conference," Center for Israel Education, https://israeled.org/examine-the-events-leading -up-to-the-1991-madrid-middle-east-peace-conference/.

Farouk, Yasmin, and Nathan J. Brown, "Saudi Arabia's Religious Reforms Are Touching Nothing but Changing Everything," in *Islamic Institutions in Arab States: Mapping the Dynamics of Control, Co-option, and Contention,* ed. Frederic Wehrey (Carnegie Endowment for International Peace, 2021), https://carnegieendowment.org/files/202106-IslamicInstitutions-final-updated.pdf.

Ferziger, Jonathan H., "Israeli Entrepreneur Looks to Sell Electric Trucks in Saudi Arabia," *The Circuit,* October 27, 2022, https://circuit.news/2022/10/27/asher-bennett-israel-saudi-arabia-tevva-motors/.

Ferziger, Jonathan H., and Peter Waldman, "How Do Israel's Tech Firms Do Business in Saudi Arabia? Very Quietly," *Bloomberg,* February 1, 2017, https://www .bloomberg.com/news/features/2017-02-02/how-do-israel-s-tech-firms-do-business-in-saudi-arabia-very-quietly#xj4y7vzkg.

Floyd, Rita, "Can Securitization Theory be Used in a Normative Analysis? Toward a Just Securitization Theory," *Security Dialogue,* 42 (2011): 427–439.

Gause III, F. Gregory, "Balancing What? Threat Perception and Alliance Choice in the Gulf," *Security Studies,* 13(2) (2003): 273–305, https://www.tandfonline.com/ doi/full/10.1080/09636410490521271?src=recsys.

"GCC Supreme Council Releases Final Communique After 43rd Summit," *Saudi Gazette,* December 9, 2022, https://saudigazette.com.sa/article/627828/SAUDI -ARABIA/GCC-Supreme-Council-releases-final-communique-after-43rd -summit.

"Geopolitics Reviews Exciting Details About Saudi Arabia's Relationship with Israel and Expects Normalization Soon," *The New Khalij,* October 8, 2022, https://the-newkhalij.news/article/279089/alsaaody-ttgh-nho-alslam-maa-srayl.

Goldman, Paul, and Rachel Elbaum, "Israel's Benjamin Netanyahu Visits Saudi Arabia, Official Says," *NBC News,* November 23, 2020, https://www.nbcnews.com/ news/world/israel-s-prime-minister-benjamin-netanyahu-secretly-visits-saudi-official-n1248585.

"Hamas Aims to Restore Saudi Arabia Ties," *Middle East Monitor,* September 17, 2022, https://www.middleeastmonitor.com/20220917-hamas-aims-to-restore -saudi-arabia-ties/.

He, Kai, "Undermining Adversaries: Unipolarity, Threat Perception, and Negative Balancing Strategies After the Cold War," *Security Studies,* 21(2) (2012): 154–191, https://www.tandfonline.com/doi/full/10.1080/09636412.2012.679201 ?src=recsys.

Henderson, Simon, "Supporting the Palestinian Authority: Will the Oil-Rich Arabs Pay Up?," *The Washington Institute for Near East Policy,* February 28, 2005, https://www.washingtoninstitute.org/policy-analysis/supporting-palestinian -authority-will-oil-rich-arabs-pay.

"In the Video…"And Sanctify It." An Initiative Launched by the Chamber to Support Jerusalem with 10 Million Dinars," *Alanba,* August 25, 2022, https://www.alanba .com.kw/113732.

"Iran-Backed Houthis Offer to Free Saudis in Exchange for Hamas Members," *The Times of Israel,* March 27, 2020, https://www.timesofisrael.com/iran-backed -houthis-offer-to-free-saudis-in-exchange-for-hamas-members/.

"Israel to Ask Biden for Okay to Provide Air Defense Laser to Saudi Arabia," *The Times of Israel,* June 28, 2022, https://www.timesofisrael.com/israel-to-ask-biden -for-okay-to-provide-air-defense-laser-to-saudi-arabia-report/.

"Israel's Unexpected Military Alliance in the Gulf," *The Economist,* June 30, 2022, https://www.economist.com/middle-east-and-africa/2022/06/30/israels-unex- pected-military-alliance-in-the-gulf.

"Israeli Companies Talking to Saudi Arabia About $500b 'Smart City'," *The Jeru- salem Post,* October 25, 2017, https://www.jpost.com/business-and-innovation/ israeli-companies-likely-talking-to-saudi-arabia-about-500-bil-smart-city-508429.

"Israeli Cybersecurity Firm Reportedly Sold Hacking Technology to UAE, Saudi Arabia," *i24,* August 23, 2020, https://www.i24news.tv/en/news/israel /1598187507-israeli-cybersecurity-firm-reportedly-sold-hacking-tech-to-uae -saudi-arabia.

"Israeli Document: The Head of the Mossad Met the Leaders of Egypt, Saudi Arabia and Syria in 1991," *The New Khalij,* October 3, 2022, https://thenewkhalij.news/ article/278722/othyk-srayly-alsaaody-saat-lttbyaa-alaalakat-kbl-30-aaama.

Kahana, Ariel, "Prominent Saudi Prince Strongly Criticizes Israel at Bahrain Sum- mit," *Israel Hayom,* July 12, 2020, https://www.israelhayom.com/2020/12/07/ saudi-prince-strongly-criticizes-israel-at-bahrain-summit/.

Kershner, Isabel, and Ben Hubbard, "Saudi Prince Accuses Palestinian Leaders of Failing Palestinians," *The New York Times,* November 12, 2020, https://www .nytimes.com/2020/10/06/world/middleeast/saudi-arabia-palestinians-israel.html.

Keynoush, Banafsheh, "Revolutionary Iran's Africa Policy," *King Faisal Center for Research and Islamic Studies*, June 2021, https://kfcris.com/en/view/post/343.

Keynoush, Banafsheh, *Saudi Arabia and Iran: Friends or Foes?* (New York: Pal- grave Macmillan, 2016).

"The Kingdom of Saudi Arabia's Statement on Jerusalem," *The Embassy of the Kingdom of Saudi Arabia*, December 5, 2017, https://www.saudiembassy.net/news /kingdom-saudi-arabias-statement-jerusalem.

Klein, Zvika, "Meet Jacob Herzog, Saudi Arabia's Self-Proclaimed Chief Rabbi," *The Jerusalem Post,* July 23, 2022, https://www.jpost.com/diaspora/article-712621.

Klippenstein, Ken, "Intel Report Warned Abraham Accords Would Fuel Vio- lence," *The Intercept,* June 22, 2022, https://theintercept.com/2022/06/22/abraham -accords-israel-saudi-arabia-biden/.

Kube, Courtney, "US Military is Developing Plans to Open a New Testing Facility in Saudi Arabia," *NBC News,* September 2022, https://www.nbcnews.com/politics /national-security/us-military-developing-plans-open-new-testing-facility-saudi -arabia-rcna46343.

Lings, Martin, *Muhammad: His Life Based on the Earliest Sources* (Rochester, NY: Inner Traditions International, 1983).

Macdonald, Alastair, "Palestinian Finance Minister Hails New Saudi Cash," *Reuters,* May 1, 2007, https://www.reuters.com/article/idUSMAC149418.

"Made in Israel, Sold in Saudi Arabia," *The Jerusalem Post,* March 21, 2008, https://www.jpost.com/middle-east/made-in-israel-sold-in-saudi-arabia.

Marcus, Jonathan, "Israel and Saudi Arabia: The Relationship Emerging into the Open," *BBC News,* April 3, 2018, https://www.bbc.com/news/world-middle-east-43632905.

Melman, Yossi, "The Saudi Spy Chief Who Pioneered Secret Relations with Israel," *Haaretz,* July 12, 2002, https://www.haaretz.com/israel-news/2022-07-12/ty-article-magazine/.highlight/prince-bandar-bin-sultan-architect-of-the-relations-between-israel-and-saudi-arabia/00000181-f2fc-de0f-a58b-f3fed5b50000.

"Muslim World League and AJC Agree on Historic Visit to Auschwitz," *AJC Transatlantic Institute,* https://transatlanticinstitute.org/press-releases/muslim-world-league-and-ajc-agree-historic-visit-auschwitz.

Najib, Mohammed, "Saudi Arabia Leads Chorus of Condemnation Following Israeli Minister's 'Provocative' Visit to Al-Aqsa," *Arab News,* January 3, 2023, https://www.arabnews.com/node/2225961/amp.

Nereim, Vivian, Daniel Avis, "Israel and Saudi Arabia: No Longer Enemies, but Not Quite Friends," *Taipei Times,* September 7, 2022, https://www.taipeitimes.com/News/editorials/archives/2022/09/07/2003784884.Nereim, Vivian, "Saudi TV Series Sparks Rare Ramadan Debate on Ties with Israel," *Bloomberg,* April 29, 2020, https://www.bloomberg.com/news/articles/2020-04-29/saudi-tv-series-sparks-rare-ramadan-debate-on-ties-with-israel#xj4y7vzkg.

"New War Beyond Middle East between Saudi Arabia and Iran to Gain Influence in Republic of Azerbaijan!," *Tabnak,* December 10, 1396, https://www.tabnak.ir/fa/news/775981/%D8%AC%D9%86%DA%AF-%D8%AC%D8%AF%DB%8C%D8%AF-%D9%81%D8%B1%D8%A7%D8%AE%D8%A7%D9%88%D8%B1%D9%85%DB%8C%D8%A7%D9%86%D9%87-%D8%A7%DB%8C-%D8%B9%D8%B1%D8%A8%D8%B3%D8%AA%D8%A7%D9%86-%D8%A8%D8%A7-%D8%A7%DB%8C%D8%B1%D8%A7%D9%86-%D8%A8%D8%B1%D8%A7%DB%8C-%DA%A9%D8%B3%D8%A8-%D9%86%D9%81%D9%88%D8%B0-%D8%AF%D8%B1-%D8%AC%D9%85%D9%87%D9%88%D8%B1%DB%8C-%D8%A2%D8%B0%D8%B1%D8%A8%D8%A7%DB%8C%D8%AC%D8%A7%D9%86.

Ng, Abigail, "Jordan's King Says He Would Support a Middle East Version of NATO," *CNBC,* June 24, 2022, https://www.cnbc.com/2022/06/24/jordans-king-says-he-would-support-a-middle-east-version-of-nato.html.

"The Opening of the "Endowment of Sheikh Sabah Al-Ahmad Al-Jaber Al-Sabah" During the Current Year in Jerusalem," *AlQuds,* January 25, 2023, https://www.alquds.com/posts/4c56e4a9-bd31-495d-8daa-f55102c5be8b.

Pollock, David, "New Saudi Poll Shows Biden's Visit Barely Budged Skepticism," *The Washington Institute,* August 26, 2022, https://www.washingtoninstitute.org/ policy-analysis/new-saudi-poll-shows-bidens-visit-barely-budged-skepticism.

"Presenting the Findings From the 2022 Arab Barometer Report: Attitudes Toward International Relations," *Middle East Institute,* September 15, 2022, https://www .mei.edu/events/presenting-findings-2022-arab-barometer-report-attitudes-toward -international-relations.

Ramani, Samuel, "Hamas's Pivot to Saudi Arabia," Carnegie Endowment for International Peace, September 17, 2015, https://carnegieendowment.org/sada/61315.

Riedel, Bruce, "How to Understand Israel and Saudi Arabia's Secretive Relationship," *Brookings*, July 11, 2022, https://www.brookings.edu/blog/order-from-chaos/2022 /07/11/how-to-understand-israel-and-saudi-arabias-secretive-relationship/.

"Riyadh Will Release Mohamed Al-Khodari and Deport Him to Amman," *Middle East Monitor,* October 17, 2022, https://www.middleeastmonitor.com/20221017 -riyadh-will-release-al-khudari-and-deport-him-to-amman/.

"Saudi Arabia Also Infiltrated Iran's North!" *Etemad Online,* Bahman 11, 1401, https://www.etemadonline.com/%D8%A8%D8%AE%D8%B4-%D8%B3%DB %8C%D8%A7%D8%B3%DB%8C-9/594074-%D8%B9%D8%B1%D8%A8 %D8%B3%D8%AA%D8%A7%D9%86-%D8%A2%D8%B0%D8%B1%D8%A8 %D8%A7%DB%8C%D8%AC%D8%A7%D9%86.

"Saudi Arabia and Israel… an Economic, Political and Security Rapprochement Despite the Absence of Official Normalization," *The New Khalij,* September 4, 2022, https://thenewkhalij.news/article/276372/alsaaody-osrayl-tkarb-aktsady -osyasy-oamny-yzyl-hal-alaada.

"Saudi Arabia and UNRWA Renew Commitment to Palestine Refugees and Regional Peace and Stability," *OCHA Relief Web,* January 31, 2023, https://reliefweb.int/ report/occupied-palestinian-territory/saudi-arabia-and-unrwa-renew-commitment -palestine-refugees-and-regional-peace-and-stability.

"Saudi Arabia Continues Boycott of Israel," *Jewish Virtual Library,* https://www.jew ishvirtuallibrary.org/saudi-arabia-continues-boycott-of-israel.

"Saudi Arabia Denies Crown Prince Held 'Secret Meeting' With Israeli PM," *BBC News,* November 23, 2020, https://www.bbc.com/news/world-middle-east -55042055.

"Saudi Arabia Deposits $80 mln to Support Palestinian Authority Budget," *Al Arabiya,* July 27, 2018, https://english.alarabiya.net/News/middle-east/2018/07/27/ Saudi-Arabia-deposits-80-mln-to-support-the-Palestinian-Authority.

"Saudi Arabia Donates $200 Million to PA," *IMEMC,* September 20, 2011, https:// imemc.org/article/62063/.

"Saudi Arabia Frees Senior Hamas Official," *Reuters,* October 19, 2022, https://www .reuters.com/world/middle-east/saudi-arabia-frees-senior-hamas-official-2022-10 -19/.

"Saudi Arabia / Israel," https://oec.world/en/profile/bilateral-country/sau/partner/isr.

"Saudi Arabia: Quash Sentences for Egyptian Nubians Who Organized Peaceful Remembrance Event," *Amnesty International*, October 11, 2022, https://

www.amnesty.org/en/latest/news/2022/10/saudi-arabia-quash-sentences-for-egyp-
tian-nubians-who-organized-peaceful-remembrance-event/#:~:text=The%2010
%20detained%20Egyptian%20Nubian,and%20Wael%20Ahmed%20Hassan
%20Ishaq.

"Saudi Arabia Says Relations with Hamas Have Not Changed After Meeting,"
Reuters, July 23, 2015, https://www.reuters.com/article/uk-saudi-palestinians
/saudi-arabia-says-relations-with-hamas-have-not-changed-after-meeting-idU
KKCN0PX1H120150723.

"Saudi Arabia Supports Palestine Refugees with US$27 Million to UNRWA," United
Nations, October 23, 2022, https://www.un.org/unispal/document/saudi-arabia
-supports-palestine-refugees-with-us-12-million-to-unrwa-press-release/.

"Saudi Cleric Calls for Muslim-Christian-Jewish Peace Delegation to Jerusalem,"
The Times of Israel, October 6, 2018, https://www.timesofisrael.com/saudi-cleric
-calls-for-interfaith-peace-delegation-to-jerusalem/.

"Saudi Cleric Calls to 'Annihilate the Plundering' Jews," *i24,* English, 2022, https://
www.youtube.com/watch?v=5gza0-nn5uo.

"Saudi Cleric Offers Cash for Israel Soldier Kidnap," *Reuters,* October 26, 2011,
https://www.reuters.com/article/us-saudi-israel-reward/saudi-cleric-offers-cash-for
-israel-soldier-kidnap-idUSTRE79P7HI20111026.

"Saudi Journalist: Arab Israelis Could Help Build Mideast Ties," *The Times of Israel,*
December 9, 2016, https://www.timesofisrael.com/saudi-journalist-arab-israelis
-could-help-build-mideast-ties/.

"Saudis Attempted to Block UAE-Israel-Jordan Deal on Energy, Water," *The Times
of Israel,* November 25, 2021, https://www.timesofisrael.com/saudis-attempted-to
-block-uae-israel-jordan-deal-on-energy-water-report/.

"Senior Israeli Official Visits Saudi Arabia Over Security Cooperation," *i24,* May
28, 2022, https://www.i24news.tv/en/news/israel/diplomacy/1653721348-report
-senior-israeli-official-visits-saudi-arabia-over-security-cooperation.

"Senior Saudi Cleric Said Iran's Leaders Are Not "Muslims"," *The Times of Israel,*
September 7, 2016, https://fa.timesofisrael.com/%D8%B1%D9%88%D8%AD
%D8%A7%D9%86%DB%8C-%D8%A7%D8%B1%D8%B4%D8%AF-%D8
%B3%D8%B9%D9%88%D8%AF%DB%8C-%DA%AF%D9%81%D8%AA-
%D8%B1%D9%87%D8%A8%D8%B1%D8%A7%D9%86-%D8%A7%DB%8C
%D8%B1%D8%A7%D9%86-%D9%85%D8%B3/.

Schard, Avi, "How Senior Israeli Officials Secretly Fly to Saudi Arabia," *Haaretz,*
July 14, 2022, https://www.haaretz.com/israel-news/security-aviation/2022-07-14
/ty-article/.premium/israel-senior-officials-secret-flights-to-saudi-arabia/00000181
-fde8-d4e2-a193-fffe90fc0000.

Schneier, Rabi Marc, "Abraham Accords No Escape from Palestinian Question,"
Arab News, January 11, 2023, https://www.arabnews.com/node/2230776.

Sinha, Aseema, "Building a Theory of Change in International Relations: Pathways
of Disruptive and Incremental Change in World Politics," *International Studies
Review,* 20(2) (June 2018): 195–203, https://academic.oup.com/isr/article-abstract
/20/2/195/4998989.

Stalinsky, Steven, "Palestinian Foreign Aid: Saudi Financial Aid," *Jewish Virtual Library,* July 2003, https://www.jewishvirtuallibrary.org/saudi-financial-aid-to-the -palestinian-authority.

Sunayama, Sonoko, *Syria and Saudi Arabia: Contradictions and Conflicts in the Oil Era* (London: Tauris Academic Studies, 2007).

"Targeting Covert Hamas Investment Network and Hamas Finance Official," US Department of State, May 24, 2022, https://www.state.gov/targeting-covert-hamas -investment-network-and-hamas-finance-official/.

Teller, Neville, "Abraham Accords: Saudi Arabia is Still Not Budging," *The Jerusalem Post,* January 31, 2023, https://www.jpost.com/opinion/article-730098.

Traiman, Alex, "I Intend to Achieve Peace with Saudi Arabia," *Israel Hayom,* October 24, 2022, https://www.israelhayom.com/2022/10/24/i-intend-to-achieve-peace -with-saudi-arabia/.

Truzman, Joe, "Houthis Warn Israel, Touts Military Training," *FDD's Long War Journal,* March 7, 2022, https://www.longwarjournal.org/archives/2022/03/houthis -warn-israel-touts-military-training.php.

"USCIRF Releases New Report on Religious Freedom in Saudi Arabia," USCIRF, December 28, 2022, https://www.uscirf.gov/release-statements/uscirf-releases -new-report-religious-freedom-saudi-arabia.

Vassiliev, Alexei, *The History of Saudi Arabia* (New York: New York University Press, 2000).

Zaken, Danny, "Al-Monitor: The Israelis Have Started Making Deals in Saudi Arabia," *Al Mayadeen,* June 3, 2022, https://www.almayadeen.net/press/%D8%A7 %D9%84%D9%85%D9%88%D9%86%D9%8A%D8%AA%D9%88%D8%B1:- %D8%A7%D9%84%D8%A5%D8%B3%D8%B1%D8%A7%D8%A6%D9%8A %D9%84%D9%8A%D9%88%D9%86-%D8%A8%D8%AF%D8%A3%D9%88 %D8%A7-%D8%B9%D9%82%D8%AF-%D8%B5%D9%81%D9%82%D8%A7 %D8%AA-%D9%81%D9%8A-%D8%A7%D9%84%D8%B3%D8%B9%D9%88 %D8%AF%D9%8A%D8%A9.

Chapter 8

Oman-Israel Relations

Established, Not Yet "Historic"

Robert Mason

Oman is historically linked across the Strait of Hormuz to parts of Iran and Pakistan, and to Eastern Africa through a maritime-based Omani Empire. The country has long sat as a bridge between regions. Moreover, Sultan Qaboos (July 23, 1970–January 10, 2020) offered a long-standing and consistent set of policies, including avoiding internal and external political entanglements, embracing tolerance as an extension of its religious creed, Ibadhiyyah, and implementing modernizations which have now passed to Sultan Haitham bin Tariq.[1]

The Sultan of Oman also derives some of his political confidence from a centuries-long tradition of centralized authority.[2] Sultan Qaboos pursued an independent foreign policy during his reign (1970–2020), and Oman has acted as a "facilitator" of regional dialogue and attempts at de-escalation for much of that time under the stewardship of Yusuf bin Alawi bin Abdullah, Oman's minister responsible for foreign affairs.[3] The Arabian country is notable for its steadfast rather than glossy approach, and its balancing or "intermediate" position between larger powers such as Saudi Arabia and Iran to create space for its own actions.[4] As a lynchpin of informal trade to Iran and a bastion of pragmatism, Oman manages to punch above its weight in Gulf politics.

Omni-balancing again becomes a key feature when considering Oman's strategy of balancing internal and external threats, including unusually, relations with Saudi Arabia, Iran, and Israel simultaneously.[5] This regional-wide approach only works because Oman is able to simultaneously reconcile competing demands through a high concentration of power in the Sultan, something which Saudi Arabia and the UAE appear to be replicating. Such an active balancing approach only works due to Oman's established position as a regional facilitator, its moderate Islamic identity, diplomatic assiduousness, consistency of approach, and relations with international powers such as the United States and the United Kingdom. Oman, unlike Saudi Arabia and Iran, does not derive its political legitimacy from Islamic leadership credentials.

Oman continues to play a bridging role between the majority of the Arab world that still boycotts Israel and those Arab states that have signed up to the Abraham Accords. It does this having built positive relations with Israel over decades while still insisting on the established parameters of the Middle East peace process (i.e., the two-state solution) and refusing to normalize ties. As a small state and regional facilitator, Oman has managed to chart this independent course with relative ease. Its approach has paid dividends on many occasions, including by assisting in Israeli-Syrian diplomacy[6] and by building bridges between the United States and Iran in the lead-up to the Joint Comprehensive Plan of Action (JCPOA) in 2015.[7] Oman has also been involved in mediating between the protagonists involved in the war in Yemen[8] (as it did in 1994 by hosting the parties to the Yemen civil war and supporting Yemeni unity), and at the outset of the Qatar Crisis.[9] Whether Oman's policy position will prove similarly valuable in the Israel-Palestine conflict remains to be seen. But its good offices have been invaluable over many years, especially during periods of escalation in the Gulf.[10]

One of five small states in the Gulf Cooperation Council (GCC), Oman has been pushing for self-sufficiency in the GCC since the 1990s, primarily through a stronger Peninsula Shield Force (the military arm of the GCC).[11] A GCC Counter-Terrorism Agreement was signed in May 2005 which provided for intelligence sharing and cross-border cooperation. A proposal for a centralized command and decentralized forces has never been taken forward probably due to a lack of trust and state-based interests within the GCC, but a joint naval force was created in 2009 to combat piracy. Thus, while there have been notable developments in GCC defense cooperation, including a GCC unified Military Command in 2013, a military alliance with Egypt, Jordan, and Morocco in 2014, and a series of large-scale GCC-wide military exercises from 2016, centrifugal forces still exist in the GCC which cause its members to seek insurances with other international allies.

What follows is a brief history of Oman's diplomatic engagement with Israel and Palestine with special reference to the Israel-Palestine conflict. Further sections examine the Omani response to the Abraham Accords at the political and social levels, including during the transition from Sultan Qaboos to Sultan Haitham. The penultimate sections outline intelligence, security, and military cooperation; the potential for enhanced socioeconomic linkages should Oman normalize relations in future; and potential points of US, Israeli, and GCC economic influence given the fiscal constraints that Oman has experienced in recent years. The conclusion teases out the main elements which affect Oman's positioning on normalization with Israel, clearly delineating the relationship which is established, but not yet historic.

SITUATING OMAN IN THE ISRAEL-PALESTINE CONFLICT

Oman's relations with Israel are deep-rooted, security-centric, and increasingly visible. Oman-Israel links were established during the Dhofar Rebellion when Israel provided military advice and possibly some weapons.[12] Israel was motivated in its intervention in the same way that it supported Yemeni royalists fighting Egyptian-backed rebels in the 1960s, that is, building ties toward normalization, highlighting its usefulness as an ally alongside the United States, and managing regional competition. Israel also played an indirect role in Oman, because Cairo's support for the Dhofar rebels decreased after the defeat of Egypt in the immediate aftermath of the 1967 Arab-Israel War. Egypt was instead forced to focus on liberating the Sinai over aiding liberation movements.[13] Following President Anwar Sadat's visit to Israel in 1977 and the conclusion of the Egypt-Israel Peace Treaty in 1979, Oman was one of just three Arab states, along with Sudan and Somalia, to maintain ties with Egypt rather than follow the Arab consensus of cutting ties.

After the 1993 Oslo Accords, Oman welcomed Yasser Arafat to Muscat at a time when he was being shunned by most of the Arab world. Unofficial contact between Omani and Israeli representatives took place at the United Nations in New York in 1993. In February 1994, the Israeli deputy foreign minister at the time, Yossi Beilin, met with a special Oman envoy to discuss contacts between the two countries.[14] Oman then hosted the April 1994 meeting of the Middle East multilateral working group on water resources. The Omani government encouraged Israel to send a representative to the event since Israel was a member of the group, which was the first-ever visit of an Israeli delegate to an Arab state.[15] Ties became even more high profile when Israeli prime minister Yizhak Rabin visited Muscat briefly (for less than twenty-four hours) in 1994, the first visit by an Israeli leader to a Gulf capital. Oman could afford to be receptive to Israel because it had also been so welcoming to the Yasser Arafat and the Palestinian Liberation Organization before.

Oman's foreign minister attended Rabin's funeral in Israel in 1996. The same year, trade offices were opened. Shimon Peres, Rabin's successor, was also welcomed in Muscat. Oman then closed its office in Tel Aviv after the onset of the Second Intifada in 2000 while Israel's office in Oman remained open but operated discreetly. Visible contact was effectively frozen until 2018, although Israeli experts continued to regularly visit the Middle East

Desalination Research Center based in Muscat. The Israeli representative on its council is usually the head of the Foreign Ministry's Middle East and Peace Process division.[16] This highlighted how seriously Israel took an opportunity represented through even relatively benign channels of cooperation. In 2008, Yusuf bin Alawi bin Abdullah met with Israeli foreign minister Tzipi Livni during their respective visits to Qatar, but it would take another decade for a high-level visit to occur.

In the lead-up to Prime Minister Netanyahu's surprise visit to Oman with his wife Sara in October 2018, Palestinian Authority president Mahmoud Abbas paid a three-day visit to Oman in what appears to be an Omani attempt at diplomacy rather than an Israel-first policy spun by the Israeli government (there was no explicit Israeli reference to Palestine after the meeting). Prime Minister Netanyahu's visit to Oman occurred just weeks after the Khashoggi murder (which the Israeli government has remained silent about), and with apparent Saudi tacit approval for the visit since the Israeli delegation flew through Saudi airspace. Saudi Arabia permanently opened up its airspace to Israeli commercial aviation in July 2022. Air space may have been on Netanyahu's agenda in Oman, because without Oman opening up its airspace to Israeli commercial aviation, Israeli commercial flights to Asia and Australia would have to continue to take a detour via the Red Sea to the Indian Ocean, extending flight times and adding extra cost.

Palestinian officials cited Netanyahu's visit, along with other developments such as a visit by Chad's president to Israel, and reports that Israel was attempting to strengthen relations with Sudan and Bahrain, as a reason to seek an emergency Arab League session and the Organization of Islamic Cooperation to address Israel's growing ties in the Arab world.[17]

The day after Netanyahu's visit, Yusuf bin Alawi bin Abdullah, then minister of foreign affairs of Oman, used the opportunity to push for an end to the Israel-Palestine conflict ahead of the anticipated "Deal of the Century" pursued by the Trump administration.[18] Jason Greenblatt, US Middle East envoy at the time, tweeted that it was a "helpful step for our peace efforts & essential to create an atmosphere of stability, security & prosperity between Israelis, Palestinians & their neighbors."[19] Domestic critics on social media said the Omani move to welcome Netanyahu in Muscat in 2018 was "shameful" and not in accordance with the parameters of the Arab Peace Initiative.[20] Notably, no Arab government criticized the meeting and Bahrain publicly supported it. Less than a week later, the Omani foreign minister traveled to Ramallah to deliver a letter from Sultan Qaboos regarding Prime Minister Netanyahu's visit.[21] With such conscientious and high-level attention on the Israel-Palestine issue, it is possible that Oman will be better placed than some other states to manage the competing optics of their dual engagement.

However, since Omani engagement occurred without any Israeli attempt to implement the Saudi-led Arab Peace Initiative in 2002, which Oman supports, it has been vulnerable to criticism. While it is clear that Mossad, the Israeli intelligence agency has played an important, if not pivotal, role in the development of tacit Omani-Israeli relations, there appears to be little quid pro quo since Oman is intent on advancing diplomacy in the two-state solution. Yossi Cohen, head of Mossad, said in 2019 that a representative office in Muscat was "only the visible tip of a much broader secret effort" that includes "a community of interests, broad cooperation and open channels of communication."[22] This "talking up" of the bilateral contacts has simply played into the hands of Prime Minister Netanyahu (2009–2021), followed by his successor Naftali Bennett (from June 13, 2021, to June 30, 2022, and as a third alternative prime minister from July 1, 2022, to November 8, 2022), and then again of Prime Minister Netanyahu (from December 2022), of enjoying broader relations with Arab states without any commitment whatsoever to a two-state solution.

The last attempt at restoring the Middle East peace process was led by John Kerry in US-brokered talks in 2014. After his visit to Oman, Prime Minister Netanyahu went so far as to mention that opening relations with the Arab world could open doors for an eventual reconciliation and peace with the Palestinians, effectively turning the Arab Peace Initiative on its head.[23] Still, some Israelis believe that without concessions to the Palestinians, the prospects for further normalization in the Arab world will be limited. Around 40 percent of Israeli Jews surveyed in 2020 still supported the two-state solution.[24] There also appears to be an awareness in Israel that the United States may demand concessions to the Palestinians and on other issues, but Israel will only deal with that eventuality when it occurs.[25]

After the 2018 visit, President Abbas visited Oman again in 2019 when Omani officials began to follow up on procedures to set up a diplomatic mission in the West Bank. The Abraham Accords may therefore represent a rising tide for states such as Oman to utilize, engaging both parties on equal or near equal terms. As for the former Israeli foreign minister Gabi Ashkenazi, from his telephone conversation with Yusuf bin Alawi bin Abdullah in August 2020, it appears that his hope was to strengthen bilateral relations and that Oman would be next to join the Abraham Accords.

OMANI POLITICAL, SOCIAL, AND MEDIA RESPONSES TO THE ABRAHAM ACCORDS

Sultan Qaboos passed away at the age of seventy-nine in January 2020, just months before the Abraham Accords were signed. Sultan Haitham who succeeded him is Oxford-educated, a former minister of heritage and culture, and was secretary-general at the Omani foreign minister from 1994 to 2002. He is maintaining continuity with Sultan Qaboos's policies,[26] including by not recognizing Israel. Yusuf bin Alawi stepped down from his position in 2020 after thirty years as minister responsible for foreign affairs, but his successor, Sayyid Badr bin Hamad bin Hamood Al Busaidi, who was appointed on August 18, 2020, was Alawi's deputy. Al Busaidi already stated in July 2021 that Oman will not be the third Gulf nation to normalize ties with Israel.[27]

Given the history of engagement between Oman and Israel and Oman's refusal to take action over President Sadat's peace agreement with Israel,[28] it is unsurprising that Oman welcomed the Abraham Accords in principle, with the hope that it would contribute momentum behind the Israel-Palestine peace process. A government statement said that "[Oman] hopes this new strategic path taken by some Arab countries will contribute to bringing about a peace on an end to the Israeli occupation of Palestinian lands and on establishing an independent Palestinian state with East Jerusalem as capital."[29] In December 2020, Oman again welcomed Morocco-Israel normalization.

However, moving forward Oman is unlikely to normalize relations with Israel for a number of reasons. These relate to the ongoing lack of resolution of the Israel-Palestine conflict, Oman's balancing position and cordial relations as a small state in the regional system, especially its relations with Saudi Arabia and Iran, and its role conception as a facilitator of solutions to local problems. Oman's balanced approach to regional affairs adds another constraint. Omani recognition of Israel will always be a thorny issue. First, it would upend Omani diplomacy with the Palestinian Authority. Oman has spent decades and significant political capital attempting to resolve the Israel-Palestine conflict, including by maintaining good relations with Hamas. Although relations did temporarily become strained in 2019 after then Omani foreign minister Yusuf bin Alawi stated that Arab countries should reassure Israel that it is not under threat in the Middle East.[30]

In 2022, the Omani ambassador to the UN noted "the Sultanate of Oman's denunciation and condemnation of the provocative and illegal practices of Israel and its occupying forces in the Palestinian territories, as well as its incursions into the blessed Al-Aqsa Mosque and the Al-Haram Al-Sharif."[31] Oman maintains that reports of international bodies confirm the situation in the occupied Palestinian territories is escalating and that this is in breach of international law and decisions of the UN Security Council such as resolutions 242 and 338.[32] These resolutions were passed after the 1967 and 1973 Arab-Israeli wars, respectively, and were designed to provide a framework based on a "land-for-peace" formula which has become a foundation for all subsequence peace negotiations. However, Oman, like Qatar,[33] within a rubric supported by the Arab League appears to take a more flexible view of the land for peace formula by returning to pre-1967 borders provided the Palestinians agree to it. The Oman Foreign Ministry stated that "the Sultanate of Oman is committed to its support to the Arab Peace Initiative within the framework of the Arab support for this initiative, at the same time Oman will support the Palestinian position when it comes to their land."[34] On December 26, 2022, the Omani Shura Council, the lower house of the Council of Oman (the main parliament) was reported to have been discussing amending the 1972 Israel boycott law which bans contact with any Israeli entity or person.[35] Discussions are said to have centered on expanding the scope of the boycott to include technical, cultural, economic, and sports relations, whether physical, virtual, or other.[36] This could have been political cover to communicate to Israel a decision about a boycott that other branches of government may have found it difficult to do. Nevertheless, by February 2023, Oman announced that

> As part of the Sultanate of Oman's continuous efforts to fulfil its obligations under the Chicago Convention of 1944, the Civil Aviation Authority affirms that the Sultanate's airspace is open for all carriers that meet the requirements of the Authority for overflying.[37]

Although representative of another form of tacit relations, it is still not tantamount to normalization and reflects US intervention on the issue.[38] Normalizing relations with Israel could significantly damage Oman's relations with other members of the Islamic World, most notably Iran, with which it has also built up close political relations over many years. Oman is highly cognizant that any move toward Israel, no matter how small, could be highly destabilizing for the country. Iranian diplomatic pressure coupled with incidents such as the attack on an Israeli oil tanker off the coast of Oman in November 2022 appears to have swayed the Omani government to sustain its boycott against Israel. If Iran already feels encircled by the US in the Gulf, the normalization of Omani-Israeli relations would extend Israeli influence the full length of the Persian Gulf and to the Gulf of Oman, creating the impression of a new axis against Iranian national security interests. In the wake of the Middle East Strategic Alliance which was announced during the Trump administration in May 2017, and was also viewed as anti-Iranian, and the escalation in the Gulf from 2019 to 2021, the move would be unacceptable to Iran. Iran has already voiced criticism over Prime Minister Netanyahu's visit to Oman in 2018. Special Aide on International Affairs of the Islamic Parliament, Hosein Amir Abdollahian, said, "The meeting of Netanyahu the Criminal with the Sultan Qaboos in the Sultanate of Oman is far from the usual wisdom of His Majesty the Sultan."[39]

Domestically, Omani demographics are roughly 45 percent Ibadi, 45 percent Sunni, 5 percent Shia, and 5 percent other faiths. The Ibadi sect of Islam is renowned for being tolerant and helps to inform Oman's foreign policy. Furthermore, unlike other GCC states such as Bahrain or Saudi Arabia, the Shia community is not securitized, and therefore the government has more domestic autonomy to pursue its chosen foreign policy agenda. The Omani government allows freedom of worship at temples and churches on land donated by the government. Offending any Abrahamic religion is an offense, giving Muslims, Jews, and Christians equal protection with a view to maintaining relative harmony and avoiding irritants which could compromise open channels of communication between states.

Omani public pressure for normalization with Israel is rather weak, reflecting a number of variables. First, there is no indigenous Jewish population to lobby for change within Oman. Second, limited private ownership of television and radio stations and Internet blockage on content that the government decides is objectionable may be a factor in moderating pro-normalization views, although private media are reported to have occasionally published anti-Semitic cartoons.[40] Third, as has already been noted, social media was rife with criticism for the 2018 visit of Prime Minister Netanyahu to Oman. It would probably take a similarly high-profile visit to demonstrate progress in Omani-Israeli relations for similar criticism to be voiced again. Fourth, the most trenchant public views appear to be reserved for issues related to Omani political representation and jobs. Though Israeli innovations, such as Bar-Ilan University offering an online class in biblical archaeology, meant that the Israeli government working in partnership with education institutions was able to attract student participation from Pakistan, the UAE, and Oman in 2018, despite none of these states recognizing Israel at the time.[41]

The pace of Omani political reform has not always matched public expectations, and protestors have consistently called for more job opportunities and a fully elected legislature.[42] Measures aimed at containing internal political dissent were used in Muscat, Sur, Sohar, and Salalah in 2011, including the use of rubber bullets and tear gas, arrests and prison sentences, and temporary shutdowns of government organizations. In the case of Sohar, it came under military control for a week. In tandem, the government has expanded the powers of the Oman Council, created more public sector jobs, reduced pension contributions in the public sector, increased the minimum wage in the private sector, raised allowances for students living away from home, established unemployment benefits, and pledged to raise expenditures to provide more welfare benefits.[43] Journalists and others arrested for "defaming the Sultan," for "illegal gatherings," or for violating the country's cyber laws were subsequently released and those dismissed from public or private sector jobs were reinstated.[44] Small protests also took place in 2018 and 2019 again calling for jobs and political reform.[45] The Omani government is likely to face pressure again in future to deliver more widespread economic gains, but unlike neighboring states which face more of an Islamist threat of aerial attack, Oman appears to be relatively insulated from wider sources of instability.

As Oman moves from a welfare state to a readjustment of the social contract, including increasing dependence on taxes, shrunken social services, and job opportunities, the state-society relationship is being altered. Mays Al Farsi, an Omani political rights defender notes that this will translate into more pressure for popular participation, the empowerment of municipal councils to manage local affairs, and a greater emphasis on citizens in political decision-making.[46] For the Oman-Israel relationship, the impact is rather muted since the focus is primarily on other pressing regional concerns such as Saudi-Iranian interactions as well as Oman's own internal affairs.

INTELLIGENCE, SECURITY, AND MILITARY COOPERATION BETWEEN OMAN AND ISRAEL

Due to historic ties to the UK, Oman has been reliant on the British military to first command the Omani military, and later provide advice on military issues. Having bought mainly British arms, Oman has shifted to purchase the majority of its arms from the United States, including F-16s and associated munitions (alongside Eurofighter "Typhoon" aircraft), AVENGER and Stinger air defense systems, tanks, patrol boats and hardware for maritime security such as de-mining equipment, and antitank weapons such as "Javelin" antitank guided missiles.[47] Thus, Oman is less reliant on states such as Israel for its evolving security needs, especially when considering its ability to balance a series of conflictual and dichotomous relations across the region. In 2016, the UK and Oman signed a memorandum of understanding to build a base near Al Duqm port for British naval and other forces, costing around $110 million, and a further 23.8 million in a UK logistics hub at Duqm port in 2020.[48] In 2018, India also signed an agreement to give its navy access to the port. As Oman internationalizes its military cooperation, it signifies to Iran, a key stakeholder, the benign nature of such relations and its emphasis on defense rather than offensive capabilities. In 2021, all GCC states but Oman signed defense industry cooperation agreements with Turkey, showing its reticence to develop close security ties with regional partners.[49] On the other hand, Oman appears to prefer to build on close defensive relations with international actors, which perhaps represent a less contentious and stable option in being less susceptible to currents of regional instability, for example, in reinstating joint military training with the UK in 2022.

US CONDITIONING ROLE IN OMAN-ISRAEL RELATIONS

Following the 1979 Iranian revolution, Sultan Qaboos continued to assert that the United States was the security guarantor of the region. In 1980 Oman signed a "facilities access agreement" that allows US forces to access Omani military facilities. Oman's Masirah Island air base was used within days by US forces attempting to rescue hostages from the US embassy in Tehran.[50] The agreement was renewed in 2010, giving the US access to airfields in Muscat, Thumrait, Masirah Island, and Musnanah.[51] In 2019, the United States and Oman extended access to US forces by signing the "Strategic Framework Agreement" which gives US forces access to Omani facilities and ports in Al Duqm (large enough to handle US aircraft carriers) and Salalah.[52] The agreement was deemed important by the Trump administration in countering Iran.

International actors engaging in Oman can be viewed through the prism of Oman needing to secure its remote borders with Saudi Arabia and Yemen and its long coastline and the building capacity through investments in infrastructure and hardware. Omani's near-term interests therefore concern homeland security rather than the regional balance of power, of which it has relatively little influence. Since the visit of then-US defense secretary, James Mattis, in 2018 to discuss ways to secure the Oman-Yemen border, Omani officials have said that the "file" of Iran smuggling weaponry to the Houthis via Oman was "closed," suggesting it had comprehensively been addressed.[53] The remote and sparsely populated enclave of Musandam, one of the governorates of Oman, sits close to consumer centers in the UAE and has played host to smuggling operations to Iran, especially during a period of intense sanctions imposed by the United States on Iran.[54] The timeline of the JCPOA, sanctions relief, and the war in Yemen therefore correlates closely with Omani national security and political economy. Oman did not contribute forces to the US-led coalition against Islamic State; it did not help armed groups fighting against Bashar Al Assad in Syria and has maintained neutrality during the war in Yemen where it sees no military solution. The ongoing conflict in Yemen continues to impinge on Omani national security and economic interests at a critical time of economic transition, a conflict that Israel has very limited influence.

In 2022, Israel, Saudi Arabia, and Oman took part together in a US-led naval exercise. The International Maritime Exercise 2022 involved sixty countries and is important for Saudi Arabia and the UAE in particular, which have sustained a series of Houthi (and probably Iranian) missile and drone attacks. The inclusion of Israel for the first time, alongside Saudi Arabia and Oman which do not recognize Israel, is another form of US-led tacit cooperation which is aimed at sustaining meaningful interactions. The exercises began at the US Fifth Fleet headquarters in Bahrain and extended across the Arabian Gulf, Arabian Sea, Gulf of Oman, Red Sea, and North Indian Ocean.[55] Should Israel and the United States be able to maintain and normalize such interactions, at least there will be a semblance of de-facto normalization, even if it is a multilateral framework, ever more reducing Israel's isolation and engagement with target states for normalization and with which it values contact.

ADVANTAGES AND DISADVANTAGES OF OMANI-ISRAELI SOCIOECONOMIC LINKAGES

There is much to build upon between Israel, an innovation hub, and Oman, a logistics hub. With oil production less than 1 million b/d, Oman is a late rentier state[56] with less oil and gas reserves than its neighbors. Oil accounted for 47.2 percent of Omani GDP in 2014[57] but just 19.37 percent in 2021.[58] Oman turned to debt markets for the first time in 2016 by selling $2.5 billion in bonds.[59] Oman has also implemented subsidy cuts, reduced benefits for public sector workers, increased fees, taxed Liquefied Natural Gas exports, and increased royalties paid for mineral exploitation.[60] Therefore, Oman, more than any other GCC state, has the most to gain from increasing revenues through non-oil sources, including establishing and expanding trade, tourism, and investment links with countries such as Israel. In light of the higher oil and gas prices caused by the Russian war in Ukraine, Oman has benefited from a period of higher revenues and budget surplus ($930 million at the end of the first quarter in 2022[61]). This should alleviate socioeconomic pressure if public spending cuts are not too deep, and reduce deficit concerns in the near term (expected to decline to 60 percent of GDP by 2024[62]). Depending on the speed of recovery in international energy markets and other impacts, such as the renewed nuclear agreement with Iran which should spur on higher Iranian oil exports and lower oil prices, Oman will still need to finance its budget increasingly through non-oil sectors.

Vision 2020 and Vision 2040 lay out Oman's developmental ambitions in areas such as education, health, citizenship, well-being, economic leadership, economic diversification, labor market, the private sector, development of governorates, environment, legislative and judicial oversight, and governance.[63] There are many areas of the Omani economy to which Israel could potentially contribute, such as training and building entrepreneurship, technology for agriculture and defense. Like its northern Arab Gulf neighbors, Oman is interested in building opportunities in renewable energy (such as Hydrogen Development Oman), in cyber and artificial intelligence, tech start-ups, and security. It is also interested in fostering more infrastructure projects and is aiming to increase educational and vocational training opportunities. While valuable, Israel is not the exclusive source of such possible programs.

Foreign direct investment represents about 10 percent of Omani GDP, and most of that comes from the United Kingdom and the United States.[64] Building on a long friendship, Oman and the UK signed the UK-Oman Comprehensive Agreement in 2019 with a focus on joint cooperation across a number of sectors including science, health, technology, and innovation.[65] The UK and Oman also signed a Sovereign Investment Partnership in 2021 to boost investment in each other's economy, especially in areas such as clean energy and technology, already part of the £1 billion per year trading relationship.[66] The United States and Oman entered into a Free Trade Agreement in January 2009, and their economic relations included $3.2 billion in bilateral trade in 2021, mainly in vehicles, aircraft and engines, industrial engines, and machines. US imports were mainly in industrial supplies, bauxite and aluminum, fertilizers, jewelry, plastics, and fuel oil.[67]

The GCC states are also important contributors. The UAE is the largest GCC state investor, while Kuwait and Qatar are also significant investors. Manufacturing and real estate are particularly important. Highlighting the importance of socioeconomic connections between Oman and India, vehicle and infrastructure opportunities, major foreign investors in the Omani economy include SV Pittie Textiles (India), Moon Iron & Steel Company (India), Sebacic Oman (India), BP (UK), Sembcorp (Singapore), Daewoo (Korea), Veolia (France), Huawei (China), SinoHydro (China), and Vale (Brazil).[68] With growing economic links between Oman and India, and India also being a member of the Indo-Pacific Quad with Israel, the UAE, and the United States, it is theoretically easy to see how Oman could take a half step toward normalization with Israel through membership of this Quad. That might have been the case if Oman wasn't simultaneously developing multimodal connectivity with Iran, as illustrated during President Raisi's visit to Oman in May 2022.[69] The Persian Gulf and Gulf of Oman forms part of the International North-South Transport Corridor (INSTC), which includes India's connection to Europe, the Baltic, Nordic and Arctic region, and its investment in Chabahar port in Iran. The INSTC is also part of China's Belt and Road Initiative.

Israel has been cognizant of infrastructure opportunities in particular as a political, economic, and strategic opening into the Arabian Peninsula. Following Prime Minister Netanyahu's visit to Oman, Israeli's then intelligence and transportation minister, Israel Katz, pushed for a rail link in November 2018. It was called "tracks of regional peace" and was expected to connect Haifa's seaport with Jordanian and Saudi rail networks, potentially linking up to the Omani network, ending at Oman's Sohar port.[70] At the 42nd

GCC Summit held in December 2021, the leaders of the GCC approved the creation of the GCC Railways Authority, tasked with bringing the GCC rail network into fruition. Expected to link Kuwait City to Muscat by 2025, the project remains susceptible to differences in implementation across each GCC state, with the UAE and Saudi Arabia leading the way. Although the project will no doubt boost regional connectivity, tourism, and lower the cost of trade, the project, estimated to cost $200 billion, also remains susceptible to budgetary constraints and political influence.[71]

The drop in the international oil price and COVID19, while providing an opportunity to replace some expatriate labor with more Omanis, drew attention to the erosion of Oman's fiscal balance in 2020.[72] Economic support from other GCC members designed to prevent contagion to their own economies could also come with foreign policy strings attached which could compromise Omani foreign policy independence and undermine the role it traditionally plays in helping to manage regional tensions.[73] At the onset of the Arab Spring, the GCC states launched a $20 billion fund for Oman and Bahrain in 2011.[74] But given internal demand for financing, it is unlikely such a large sum could be raised again. In 2019, Kuwait's Supreme Petroleum Council approved $2 billion to finance the $8.5 billion Duqm refinery.[75] Saudi Arabia and the UAE also play important roles in ports such as Duqm and Salalah in Oman, but it is their investment in Omani jobs which is most significant and was more than other major economic partners such as China in 2020.[76] The Saudi Fund for Development began funding three projects in Oman with a total value of $244 million from February 2022.[77]

Oman also maintains close economic relations with Iran. For example, Omani banks, including Bank Muscat, which held around $5.7 billion in Iranian funds in 2015, were used to support the implementation of the JCPOA.[78] Oman-Iran trade stood at $1.3 billion from 2021 to 2022, and Iran, like Oman, is seeking to boost non-oil exports.[79] Oman's position as a re-exporter of Iranian goods and interest in boosting Gulf connectivity also has to be factored into the equation of normalization of relations with Israel. Iran's agreement in May 2022 to revive a long-stalled undersea gas pipeline to Oman underscores this issue and the codependence that Oman and Iran exhibit.[80]

CONCLUSION

Oman-Israel connections are decades old and the process of normalizing Omani-Israeli began thirty years ago at the UN. In cultivating relations between East and West, and across the Persian Gulf and the Levant, Oman has been ahead in its thinking that balanced relations and regional stability are inherently valuable to a small state, especially those attempting to transition to a post-rentier economy. The combinations of role conception, political transition, the impacts of COVID-19, and an ongoing economic crisis in Oman, all favor growing relations with traditional security guarantors such as the United Kingdom and the United States, expanding ties with long-time allies across the Indian Ocean, and a status quo approach in relations with Israel. Since the United States has led the normalization process with Israel through the Abraham Accords, its close economic, political, and military ties to Oman could feasibly be used as part of an incentivization campaign for Oman to build closer relations with Israel. Much hinges on factors such as the regional and international threat perception of Iran with or without a new nuclear agreement in place, domestic Omani and US politics, and the state of the Omani economy.

Oman should be valued as an important interlocutor whose credentials would be seriously compromised should it sign onto the Abraham Accords without adequate thought to the regional ramifications of doing so. In this sense, Oman may look to the reintegration of Syria back into the Arab fold and learn lessons about conditionality and sequencing for normalized relations to be successful. This chapter identifies that Oman's inclusion into the Indo-Pacific Quad could have been a halfway house to building economic relations with Israel, India, the United States, and the UAE without foregoing its principled and pragmatic foreign policy, but growing relations with Iran will probably stymie such links. The Russian intervention in Ukraine and higher oil prices are relieving some fiscal pressure, at least in the short term. However, further economic shocks or protests may change the economic or national security calculation, especially Oman's future need for cutting-edge cyber security. Oman sits at an important crossroads in West Asia and given the unpredictable regional and inter-regional security environment, its good offices and traditional role of facilitator need not be gambled on expanding normalization with Israel without clear-eyed strategic thinking about how balance can be sustained and benefits extended to vital regional parties.

NOTES

1. Joseph A. Kéchichian, *A Sultanate that Endures: Oman in the World from Qaboos bin Sa'id to Haitham bin Tariq* (Liverpool: Liverpool University Press, 2023).

2. Gawdat Bahgat, "Security in the Gulf: The View from Oman," *Security Dialogue,* 30(4) (1999): 445–458.

3. "Oman Minister Describes Role as 'Facilitator' of Diplomacy in Turbulent Region," *Al-Monitor*, September 26, 2019, https://www.al-monitor.com/originals/2019/09/interview-oman-foreign-minister-bin-alawi-iran-syria-israel.html.

4. Badr Bin Hamad Al Bu Said, "'Small States' Diplomacy in the Age of Globalization: An Omani Perspective," *Review of International Affairs*, 3(2) (2007): 352–357.

5. Marc J. O'Reilly, "Omnibalancing: Oman Confronts an Uncertain Future," *Middle East Journal*, 52(1) (Winter 1998): 70–84.

6. Yossi Melman, "The 'Oman File': Inside the Mossad's Alliance with Muscat, Israel's Window into Iran,'" *Haaretz*, January 23, 2020, https://www.haaretz.com/israel-news/.premium-the-oman-file-inside-the-mossad-s-alliance-with-muscat-israel-s-window-into-iran-1.8414861.

7. Shohini Gupta, "Oman: The Unsung Hero of the Iranian Nuclear Deal," *Foreign Policy Journal*, July 23, 2015, https://www.foreignpolicyjournal.com/2015/07/23/oman-the-unsung-hero-of-the-iranian-nuclear-deal/.

8. Stacey Philbrick Yadav, "Oman is a Mediator in Yemen. Can it Play the Same Role in Qatar?" *The Washington Post*, July 22, 2017, https://www.washingtonpost.com/news/monkey-cage/wp/2017/07/22/oman-is-a-mediator-in-yemen-can-it-play-the-same-role-in-qatar/.

9. Ibrahim Fraihat, "Superpower and Small-State Mediation in the Qatar Gulf Crisis," T*he International Spectator*, 55(2) (2020): 79–91.

10. "Trump Asks Oman to Help Counter Iran's 'Destablizing' Activities," *Arab News*, July 19, 2017, https://www.arabnews.com/node/1131996/middle-east; "Secretary Pompeo's Call With Omani Sultan Qaboos bin Sa'id Al Sa'id," *US Department of State*, May 16, 2019, https://2017-2021.state.gov/secretary-pompeos-call-with-omani-sultan-qaboos-bin-said-al-said/index.html.

11. Robert Mason, "The Omani Pursuit of the Peninsula Shield Force: A Case Study of a Small State's Search for Security," *British Journal of Middle Eastern Studies*, 41(4) (2014): 355–367.

12. Elie Podeh, "Israel's Renewed Affair with Oman," *The Jerusalem Post,* November 8, 2018, https://www.jpost.com/opinion/israels-renewed-affair-with-oman-571410

13. Khalid Sulaiman Salim Al Kharusi, "The Dhofar War 1965-1975," PhD Thesis, May 2018, p. 97, http://clok.uclan.ac.uk/24029/1/24029%20Al-Kharushi%20Khalid%20Final%20e-Thesis%20%28Master%20Copy%29.pdf.

14. Robert H. Pelletreau, Jr, "US Foreign Policy and Oman" at Contemporary Oman and US-Oman Relations Symposium, Middle East Policy Council, Washington DC, October 12, 1995, http://www.oman.org/conf22.htm.

15. Ibid.

16. Ambassador Haim Regev served from August 2016 to August 2021, and Ambassador Oded Joseph from 2021, supported by Mr. Oded Fixler from the Israeli Water Authority, Mission of Israel to the EU and NATO, https://embassies.gov.il/eu/AboutTheEmbassy/Pages/The-ambassador.aspx; MEDRC, https://www.medrc.org/about-us/.

17. Jack Khoury, "Palestinians Seek Emergency Arab League Session Over Israel's Warming Ties with Arab States," *Haaretz,* November 26, 2018, https://www.haaretz.com/middle-east-news/palestinians/.premium-palestinians-seek-arab-league-session-on-israel-s-growing-ties-with-arab-world-1.6695112.

18. Katie Paul, "Oman Says Time to Accept Israel in the Region, Offers Help for Peace," *Reuters*, October 27, 2018, https://www.reuters.com/article/us-bahrain-summit-oman/oman-says-time-to-accept-israel-in-region-offers-help-for-peace-idUSKCN1N10BH.

19. "US Mission to the Kingdom of Saudi Arabia," *Twitter (X)*, October 28, 2018, https://twitter.com/USAinKSA/status/1056497507289759745?ref_src=twsrc %5Etfw.

20. Ian Black, "Netanyahu's Oman Talks Shed New Light on Israel's Ties with the Gulf," *LSE Middle East Center*, October 29, 2018, https://blogs.lse.ac.uk/mec/2018 /10/29/netanyahus-oman-talks-shed-new-light-on-israels-ties-with-the-gulf/.

21. Adam Rasgon, "Omani FM Visits Ramallah After Netanyahu's Visit to Muscat," *The Times of Israel,* October 31, 2018, https://www.timesofisrael.com/omani-fm -visits-ramallah-after-netanyahus-visit-to-muscat/.

22. "Mossad Chief Declares Israel Renewing Oman Ties; Foreign Ministry Won't Comment," *The Times of Israel,* July 2, 2019, https://www.timesofisrael.com/israel -renewing-oman-ties-says-mossad-chief/.

23. Tovah Lazaroff, "Netanyahu Makes Historic Visit to Oman," *The Jerusalem Post*, October 26, 2018, https://www.jpost.com/israel-news/netanyahu-makes-his- toric-visit-to-oman-570388.

24. "The Palestinian/Israeli Pulse, A Joint Poll Summary Report," Palestinian Center for Policy and Survey Research, https://www.pcpsr.org/en/node/823.

25. "A Changing Middle East: The View from Israel, a Conversation with Chuck Freilich," Crown Center for Middle East Studies, Brandeis University, February 9, 2022, https://www.brandeis.edu/crown/publications/crown-conversations/cc-12 .html.

26. "Meet Oman's New Sultan. How Will He Navigate the Region's Turmoil?" *The Washington Post,* January 15, 2020, https://www.washingtonpost.com/politics /2020/01/15/meet-omans-new-sultan-how-will-he-navigate-regions-turmoil/.

27. "Oman's Foreign Minister: We Won't be 3rd Gulf Country to Normalize Israel Ties," *The Times of Israel,* July 10, 2021, https://www.timesofisrael.com/omans-for- eign-minister-we-wont-be-3rd-gulf-country-to-normalize-israel-ties/.

28. Oman was just one of three states, including Sudan and Somalia, not to take action against Egypt over its peace with Israel. Christopher S. Wren, "Sudan Reap- praising Close Ties to Egypt," *The New York Times,* December 7, 1979, https://www .nytimes.com/1979/12/07/archives/sudan-reappraising-close-ties-to-egypt-implies-a -curtailment-if.html.

29. "Oman Welcomes Bahrain-Israel Normalization Decision," *Reuters*, Sep- tember 13, 2020, https://www.reuters.com/article/uk-israel-gulf-usa-oman-bahrain -idUKKBN26407G.

30. Kifah Zboun, "Hamas Leader Arrives in Oman Amid Abbas Visit," *Asharq Al- Awsat,* January 13, 2020, https://english.aawsat.com//home/article/2080101/hamas -leader-arrives-oman-amid-abbas-visit.

31. "Oman Calls for Effective International Role to End Israeli Occupation of Palestine," April 27, 2022, https://fm.gov.om/oman-calls-for-effective-international -role-to-end-israeli-occupation-of-palestine/.

32. Ibid.

33. "Arab League Backs Israel-Palestinian Land Swaps," *VOA News,* April 29, 2013, https://www.voanews.com/a/arab-league-backs-israeli-palestinian-land-swaps /1651398.html.

34. Interview with the Omani Foreign Ministry, July 16, 2022.

35. Hamed Al-Ghaithi, "Expanding the Scope of Oman's Israel Boycott?," Carnegie Endowment for International Peace, February 28, 2023, https://carnegieendowment.org/sada/89160.

36. Ibid.

37. Molly Russel, "Oman Opens its Airspace to Israeli Airlines," *Simple Flying,* February 23, 2023, https://simpleflying.com/oman-airspace-open-israeli-carriers/.

38. Rina Bassist, "Oman Opens Airspace to Israeli Flights, Following Saudi Arabia," *Al-Monitor,* February 23, 2023, https://www.al-monitor.com/originals/2023/02/oman-opens-airspace-israeli-flights-following-saudi-arabia.

39. Habib Toumi, "Bahrain Hails, Iran Condemns Oman's Wisdom in Receiving Netanyahu," *Gulf News,* October 27, 2018, https://gulfnews.com/world/gulf/bahrain/bahrain-hails-iran-condemns-omans-wisdom-in-receiving-netanyahu-1.2294535.

40. Kenneth Katzman, "Oman: Politics, Security, and US Policy," Congressional Research Service, May 19, 2021, p. 8, https://sgp.fas.org/crs/mideast/RS21534.pdf.

41. Amanda Borschel-Dan, "Students from Pakistan, UAE, Oman Join Israeli Online Biblical Archaeology Class," *The Times of Israel,* December 11, 2018, https://www.timesofisrael.com/students-from-pakistan-uae-oman-join-israeli-online-biblical-archaeology-class/.

42. Saleh al-Shaibany, "Protestors Across Oman Demand Reform, Jobs," *Reuters*, March 4, 2011, https://www.reuters.com/article/us-oman-protests-idUSTRE7234LK20110304.

43. Yasmina Abouzzohour, "Oman, Ten Years After the Arab Spring: The Evolution of State-Society Relations," Arab Reform Initiative, February 9, 2021, https://www.arab-reform.net/publication/oman-ten-years-after-the-arab-spring-the-evolution-of-state-society-relations/.

44. James Worall, "Oman: The 'Forgotten' Corner of the Arab Spring," *Middle East Policy*, 39 (September 2012): 98–115.

45. Abouzzohour, "Oman, Ten Years after the Arab Spring."

46. Rafiah Al Talei, "The Arab Youth: Aspirations for the New Year," *Sada*, Carnegie Endowment for International Peace, January 11, 2022, https://carnegieendowment.org/sada/86063.

47. Kenneth Katzman, "Oman: Politics, Security, and US Policy," Congressional Research Service, May 19, 2021, pp. 15–16.

48. Ibid., 15; "Defense Secretary Announces Investment in Strategic Omani Port," UK Government, September 12, 2020, https://www.gov.uk/government/news/defence-secretary-announces-investment-in-strategic-omani-port.

49. Ali Bakir, "Turkey's Defense Industry is on the Rise. The GCC is One of its Top Buyers," *Atlantic Council*, 4 August 2023, https://www.atlanticcouncil.org/blogs/menasource/turkey-defense-baykar-gcc-gulf/

50. Katzman, "Oman: Politics, Security, and US Policy," *Congressional Research Service*, May 19, 2021, p. 14.

51. Ibid.

52. Ibid, 14–15.

53. Ibid, 12.

54. Alexander Balas, "The Smugglers of Musandam," *The Interpreter,* Lowry Institute, November 14, 2017, https://www.lowyinstitute.org/the-interpreter/smugglers-musandam.

55. "Israel Takes Part in Naval Exercise with Saudi Arabia, Oman," February 2, 2022, https://www.al-monitor.com/originals/2022/02/israel-takes-part-naval-exercise -saudi-arabia-oman.

56. Matthew Grey, "A Theory of "Late-Rentierism" in the Arab States of the Gulf," Center for International and Regional Studies, Georgetown University Qatar, Occasional Paper 7, 2011, https://repository.library.georgetown.edu/bitstream/handle /10822/558291/CIRSOccasionalPaper7MatthewGray2011.pdf .

57. "Oman Diversifies Economy as Oil Revenues Shrink," Oxford Business Group, https://oxfordbusinessgroup.com/overview/renewed-efforts-oil-revenues -shrink-government-seeking-further-diversify-economy-boost-employment.

58. "Oman: Oil Rents (% of GDP)," https://tradingeconomics.com/oman/oil-rents -percent-of-gdp-wb-data.html#:~:text=Oil%20rents%20(%25%20of%20GDP)%20i n%20Oman%20was%20reported%20at,Bank%20on%20May%20of%202022.

59. "How is Oman Reacting to Low Oil Prices?," The World Bank, July 2016, https:// www.worldbank.org/en/country/gcc/publication/economic-brief-oman-july-2016.

60. Ibid.

61. Charles Kennedy, "Oman Sees $930M Budget Surplus As Oil Revenues Soar," *Oil Price,* May 9, 2022, https://oilprice.com/Latest-Energy-News/World -News/Oman-Sees-930M-Budget-Surplus-As-Oil-Revenues-Soar.html

62. "Oman Budget 2022," *KPMG*, January 2022, 10, https://assets.kpmg/content/ dam/kpmg/om/pdf-2022/01/analysis-of-oman-budget-2022.pdf.

63. "Vision 2040: Vision Document," Omani Government, p. 17, https://isfu.gov .om/2040/Vision_Documents_En.pdf.

64. "Oman's Top Foreign Investors Committed to Economic Growth," *Times of Oman*, August 11, 2021, https://timesofoman.com/article/105261-omans-top-foreign -investors-committed-to-economic-growth.

65. "Oman: UK and Oman Sign Comprehensive Agreement," *UK Government*, May 23, 2019, https://www.gov.uk/government/news/oman-uk-and-oman-sign-comprehensive-agreement.

66. "UK and Oman Kickstart Sovereign Investment Partnership to Boost Investment Links," January 11, 2022, https://www.gov.uk/government/news/uk-and-oman -kickstart-sovereign-investment-partnership-to-boost-investment-links.

67. "US Relations with Oman," *US Department of State*, May 12, 2022, https:// www.state.gov/u-s-relations-with-oman/#:~:text=Bilateral%20Economic%20Rela tions&text=Total%20bilateral%20U.S.%2DOman%20trade,%2C%20plastics%2C %20and%20fuel%20oil.

68. "2021 Investment Climate Statements: Oman," US Department of State, https://www.state.gov/reports/2021-investment-climate-statements/oman/.

69. "Oman to Join Chabahar Agreement During Iran President's Visit," *Mehr News Agency,* May 22, 2022, https://en.mehrnews.com/news/187064/Oman-to-join -Chabahar-Agreement-during-Iran-president-s-visit.

70. "Israel Transport Minister Visits Oman to Promote 'Tracks for Regional Peace,'" *I24 News,* November 6, 2018, https://www.i24news.tv/en/news/international/187966-181105-israel-transport-minister-visits-oman-to-promote-tracks-for-regional-peace.

71. Jon Whiteaker, "The GCC Railway Really Should be Built (But Might Not Be)," *Railway Technology*, May 15, 2022, https://www.railway-technology.com/analysis/gcc-railway-built-infrastructure/.

72. Sebastian Castelier, "Oman Weighs Costs of Bailout from Gulf Neighbors," *Al-Monitor,* June 25, 2020, https://www.al-monitor.com/originals/2020/06/oman-bailout-public-finances-cost-regional-role-gcc.html.

73. Ibid.

74. Ulf Laessing and Cynthia Johnston, "Gulf States Launch $20 Billion Fund for Oman and Bahrain," *Reuters*, March 10, 2011, https://www.reuters.com/article/us-gulf-fund/gulf-states-launch-20-billion-fund-for-oman-and-bahrain-idUSTRE7294B120110310.

75. "Kuwait Allocates $2bn to Oman's Duqm Refinery," January 27, 2019, https://english.mubasher.info/news/3405554/Kuwait-allocates-2bn-to-Oman-s-Duqm-refinery/%7B%7Bsection.url%7D%7D.

76. Karen Young, "China is not the Middle East's High Roller," *Bloomberg Opinion*, July 2, 2020, https://www.aei.org/op-eds/china-is-not-the-middle-easts-high-roller/.

77. "Saudi Fund for Development, Oman Sign Three Deals to Finance Projects Worth $244mln," *Zawya*, February 3, 2022, https://www.zawya.com/en/business/saudi-fund-for-development-oman-sign-three-deals-to-finance-projects-worth-244mln-i8v5ecp3.

78. Katzman, "Oman: Politics, Security, and US Policy," 10.

79. "Iran-Oman Annual Trade Hits Record High of $1.3b, Growing 53%," *Tehran Times*, April 18, 2022, https://www.tehrantimes.com/news/471819/Iran-Oman-annual-trade-hits-record-high-of-1-3b-growing-53.

80. "Iran to Revive Gas Pipeline Project to Oman, IRNA Reports," *Reuters*, May 21, 2022, https://www.reuters.com/world/middle-east/iran-agrees-revive-gas-pipeline-project-oman-irna-2022-05-21/.

REFERENCES

Abouzzohour, Yasmina, "Oman, Ten Years After the Arab Spring: The Evolution of State-Society Relations," *Arab Reform Initiative*, February 9, 2021, https://www.arab-reform.net/publication/oman-ten-years-after-the-arab-spring-the-evolution-of-state-society-relations/.

Al Bu Said, Badr Bin Hamad, "'Small States' Diplomacy in the Age of Globalization: An Omani Perspective," *Review of International Affairs,* 3(2) (2007): 352–357.

Al-Ghaithi, Hamed, "Expanding the Scope of Oman's Israel Boycott?" Carnegie Endowment for International Peace, February 28, 2023, https://carnegieendowment.org/sada/89160.

Al Kharusi, Khalid Sulaiman Salim, "The Dhofar War 1965-1975," PhD Thesis, May 2018, http://clok.uclan.ac.uk/24029/1/24029%20Al-Kharushi%20Khalid%20Final%20e-Thesis%20%28Master%20Copy%29.pdf.

Al-Shaibany, Saleh, "Protestors Across Oman Demand Reform, Jobs," *Reuters*, March 4, 2011, https://www.reuters.com/article/us-oman-protests-idUSTRE7234LK20110304.

Al Talei, Rafiah, "The Arab Youth: Aspirations for the New Year," *Sada*, Carnegie Endowment for International Peace, January 11, 2022, https://carnegieendowment.org/sada/86063.

"Arab League Backs Israel-Palestinian Land Swaps," *VOA News*, April 29, 2013, https://www.voanews.com/a/arab-league-backs-israeli-palestinian-land-swaps/1651398.html.

Bahgat, Gawdat, "Security in the Gulf: The View from Oman," *Security Dialogue*, 30(4) (1999): 445–458.

Bakir, Ali, "Turkey's Defense Industry is on the Rise. The GCC is One of its Top Buyers," *Atlantic Council*, August 4, 2023, https://www.atlanticcouncil.org/blogs/menasource/turkey-defense-baykar-gcc-gulf/.

Balas, Alexander, "The Smugglers of Musandam," *The Interpreter*, Lowry Institute, November 14, 2017, https://www.lowyinstitute.org/the-interpreter/smugglers-musandam.

Bassist, Rina, "Oman Opens Airspace to Israeli Flights, Following Saudi Arabia," *Al-Monitor*, February 23, 2023, https://www.al-monitor.com/originals/2023/02/oman-opens-airspace-israeli-flights-following-saudi-arabia.

Black, Ian, "Netanyahu's Oman Talks Shed New Light on Israel's Ties with the Gulf," *LSE Middle East Center*, October 29, 2018, https://blogs.lse.ac.uk/mec/2018/10/29/netanyahus-oman-talks-shed-new-light-on-israels-ties-with-the-gulf/.

Borschel-Dan, Amanda, "Students from Pakistan, UAE, Oman Join Israeli Online Biblical Archaeology Class," *The Times of Israel*, December 11, 2018, https://www.timesofisrael.com/students-from-pakistan-uae-oman-join-israeli-online-biblical-archaeology-class/.

Castelier, Sebastian, "Oman Weighs Costs of Bailout from Gulf Neighbors," *Al-Monitor*, June 25, 2020, https://www.al-monitor.com/originals/2020/06/oman-bailout-public-finances-cost-regional-role-gcc.html.

"A Changing Middle East: The View from Israel, a Conversation with Chuck Freilich," Crown Center for Middle East Studies, Brandeis University, February 9, 2022, https://www.brandeis.edu/crown/publications/crown-conversations/cc-12.html.

"Defense Secretary Announces Investment in Strategic Omani Port," UK Government, September 12, 2020, https://www.gov.uk/government/news/defence-secretary-announces-investment-in-strategic-omani-port.

Fraihat, Ibrahim, "Superpower and Small-State Mediation in the Qatar Gulf Crisis," *The* International Spectator, 55(2) (2020): 79–91.

Grey, Matthew, "A Theory of "Late-Rentierism" in the Arab States of the Gulf," Center for International and Regional Studies, Georgetown University Qatar,

Occasional Paper 7, 2011, https://repository.library.georgetown.edu/bitstream/handle/10822/558291/CIRSOccasionalPaper7MatthewGray2011.pdf.

Gupta, Shohini, "Oman: The Unsung Hero of the Iranian Nuclear Deal," *Foreign Policy Journal,* July 23, 2015, https://www.foreignpolicyjournal.com/2015/07/23/oman-the-unsung-hero-of-the-iranian-nuclear-deal/.

"How is Oman Reacting to Low Oil Prices?," The World Bank, July 2016, https://www.worldbank.org/en/country/gcc/publication/economic-brief-oman-july-2016.

"Iran-Oman Annual Trade Hits Record High of $1.3b, Growing 53%," *Tehran Times*, April 18, 2022, https://www.tehrantimes.com/news/471819/Iran-Oman-annual-trade-hits-record-high-of-1-3b-growing-53.

"Iran to Revive Gas Pipeline Project to Oman, IRNA Reports," *Reuters*, May 21, 2022, https://www.reuters.com/world/middle-east/iran-agrees-revive-gas-pipeline-project-oman-irna-2022-05-21/.

"Israel Takes Part in Naval Exercise with Saudi Arabia, Oman," February 2, 2022, https://www.al-monitor.com/originals/2022/02/israel-takes-part-naval-exercise-saudi-arabia-oman.

"Israel Transport Minister Visits Oman to Promote 'Tracks for Regional Peace,'" *I24 News,* November 6, 2018, https://www.i24news.tv/en/news/international/187966-181105-israel-transport-minister-visits-oman-to-promote-tracks-for-regional-peace.

Katzman, Kenneth, "Oman: Politics, Security, and US Policy," Congressional Research Service, May 19, 2021, https://sgp.fas.org/crs/mideast/RS21534.pdf.

Kéchichian, Joseph A., *A Sultanate that Endures: Oman in the World from Qaboos bin Sa'id to Haitham bin Tariq* (Liverpool: Liverpool University Press, 2023).

Kennedy, Charles, "Oman Sees $930M Budget Surplus As Oil Revenues Soar," *Oil Price,* May 9, 2022, https://oilprice.com/Latest-Energy-News/World-News/Oman-Sees-930M-Budget-Surplus-As-Oil-Revenues-Soar.html.

Khoury, Jack, "Palestinians Seek Emergency Arab League Session Over Israel's Warming Ties with Arab States," *Haaretz,* November 26, 2018, https://www.haaretz.com/middle-east-news/palestinians/.premium-palestinians-seek-arab-league-session-on-israel-s-growing-ties-with-arab-world-1.6695112.

"Kuwait Allocates $2bn to Oman's Duqm Refinery," *Mubasher*, January 27, 2019, https://english.mubasher.info/news/3405554/Kuwait-allocates-2bn-to-Oman-s-Duqm-refinery/%7B%7Bsection.url%7D%7D.

Laessing, Ulf, and Cynthia Johnston, "Gulf States Launch $20 Billion Fund for Oman and Bahrain," *Reuters*, March 10, 2011, https://www.reuters.com/article/us-gulf-fund/gulf-states-launch-20-billion-fund-for-oman-and-bahrain-idUSTRE7294B120110310.

Lazaroff, Tovah, "Netanyahu Makes Historic Visit to Oman," *The Jerusalem Post*, October 26, 2018, https://www.jpost.com/israel-news/netanyahu-makes-historic-visit-to-oman-570388.

Mason, Robert, "The Omani Pursuit of the Peninsula Shield Force: A Case Study of a Small State's Search for Security," *British Journal of Middle Eastern Studies,* 41(4) (2014): 355–367.

MEDRC, https://www.medrc.org/about-us/.

"Meet Oman's New Sultan. How Will He Navigate the Region's Turmoil?" *The Washington Post,* January 15, 2020, https://www.washingtonpost.com/politics /2020/01/15/meet-omans-new-sultan-how-will-he-navigate-regions-turmoil/.

Melman, Yossi, "The 'Oman File': Inside the Mossad's Alliance with Muscat, Israel's Window into Iran," *Haaretz,* January 23, 2020, https://www.haaretz.com/israel -news/.premium-the-oman-file-inside-the-mossad-s-alliance-with-muscat-israel-s -window-into-iran-1.8414861.

Mission of Israel to the EU and NATO, https://embassies.gov.il/eu/AboutTheEm-bassy/Pages/The-ambassador.aspx.

"Mossad Chief Declares Israel Renewing Oman Ties; Foreign Ministry Won't Com-ment," *The Times of Israel,* July 2, 2019, https://www.timesofisrael.com/israel -renewing-oman-ties-says-mossad-chief/.

"Oman Budget 2022," KPMG, January 2022, https://assets.kpmg/content/dam/kpmg /om/pdf-2022/01/analysis-of-oman-budget-2022.pdf.

"Oman Calls for Effective International Role to End Israeli Occupation of Palestine," Oman's Foreign Ministry, April 27, 2022, https://fm.gov.om/oman-calls-for-effec-tive-international-role-to-end-israeli-occupation-of-palestine/.

"Oman Diversifies Economy as Oil Revenues Shrink," Oxford Business Group, https://oxfordbusinessgroup.com/overview/renewed-efforts-oil-revenues-shrink -government-seeking-further-diversify-economy-boost-employment.

"Oman Minister Describes Role as 'Facilitator' of Diplomacy in Turbulent Region," *Al-Monitor,* September 26, 2019, https://www.al-monitor.com/originals/2019/09/ interview-oman-foreign-minister-bin-alawi-iran-syria-israel.html.

"Oman: Oil Rents (% of GDP)," https://tradingeconomics.com/oman/oil-rents-per-cent-of-gdp-wb-data.html#:~:text=Oil%20rents%20(%25%20of%20GDP)%20 in%20Oman%20was%20reported%20at,Bank%20on%20May%20of%202022.

"Oman to Join Chabahar Agreement During Iran President's Visit," *Mehr News Agency,* May 22, 2022, https://en.mehrnews.com/news/187064/Oman-to-join-Cha-bahar-Agreement-during-Iran-president-s-visit.

"Oman: UK and Oman Sign Comprehensive Agreement," UK Government, May 23, 2019, https://www.gov.uk/government/news/oman-uk-and-oman-sign-comprehen-sive-agreement.

"Oman Welcomes Bahrain-Israel Normalization Decision," *Reuters,* Septem-ber 13, 2020, https://www.reuters.com/article/uk-israel-gulf-usa-oman-bahrain -idUKKBN26407G.

"Oman's Foreign Minister: We Won't be 3rd Gulf Country to Normalize Israel Ties," *The Times of Israel,* July 10, 2021, https://www.timesofisrael.com/omans-foreign -minister-we-wont-be-3rd-gulf-country-to-normalize-israel-ties/.

"Oman's Top Foreign Investors Committed to Economic Growth," *Times of Oman,* August 11, 2021, https://timesofoman.com/article/105261-omans-top-foreign -investors-committed-to-economic-growth.

O'Reilly, Marc J., "Omnibalancing: Oman Confronts an Uncertain Future," *Middle East Journal,* 52(1) (Winter 1998): 70–84.

"The Palestinian/Israeli Pulse, A Joint Poll Summary Report," Palestinian Center for Policy and Survey Research, https://www.pcpsr.org/en/node/823.

Paul, Katie, "Oman Says Time to Accept Israel in the Region, Offers Help for Peace," *Reuters,* October 27, 2018, https://www.reuters.com/article/us-bahrain -summit-oman/oman-says-time-to-accept-israel-in-region-offers-help-for-peace -idUSKCN1N10BH.

Pelletreau, Robert H., Jr., "US Foreign Policy and Oman" at Contemporary Oman and US-Oman Relations Symposium, Middle East Policy Council, Washington DC, October 12, 1995, http://www.oman.org/conf22.htm.

Podeh, Elie, "Israel's Renewed Affair with Oman," *The Jerusalem Post,* November 8, 2018, https://www.jpost.com/opinion/israels-renewed-affair-with-oman-571410.

Rasgon, Adam, "Omani FM Visits Ramallah After Netanyahu's Visit to Muscat," *The Times of Israel,* October 31, 2018, https://www.timesofisrael.com/omani-fm-visits -ramallah-after-netanyahus-visit-to-muscat/.

Russel, Molly, "Oman Opens its Airspace to Israeli Airlines," *Simple Flying,* February 23, 2023, https://simpleflying.com/oman-airspace-open-israeli-carriers/.

"Saudi Fund for Development, Oman Sign Three Deals to Finance Projects Worth $244mln," *Zawya,* February 3, 2022, https://www.zawya.com/en/business/saudi -fund-for-development-oman-sign-three-deals-to-finance-projects-worth-244mln -i8v5ecp3.

"Secretary Pompeo's Call With Omani Sultan Qaboos bin Sa'id Al Sa'id," US Department of State, May 16, 2019, https://2017-2021.state.gov/secretary-pom peos-call-with-omani-sultan-qaboos-bin-said-al-said/index.html.

Toumi, Habib, "Bahrain Hails, Iran Condemns Oman's Wisdom in Receiving Netanyahu," *Gulf News,* October 27, 2018, https://gulfnews.com/world/gulf/bahrain/ bahrain-hails-iran-condemns-omans-wisdom-in-receiving-netanyahu-1.2294535.

"Trump Asks Oman to Help Counter Iran's 'Destablizing' Activities," *Arab News,* July 19, 2017, https://www.arabnews.com/node/1131996/middle-east.

"2021 Investment Climate Statements: Oman," US Department of State, https://www .state.gov/reports/2021-investment-climate-statements/oman/.

"UK and Oman Kickstart Sovereign Investment Partnership to Boost Investment Links," UK Government, January 11, 2022, https://www.gov.uk/government /news/uk-and-oman-kickstart-sovereign-investment-partnership-to-boost-invest ment-links.

"US Mission to the Kingdom of Saudi Arabia," *Twitter (X)*, October 28, 2018, https:// twitter.com/USAinKSA/status/1056497507289759745?ref_src=twsrc%5Etfw.

"US Relations with Oman," US Department of State, May 12, 2022, https://www .state.gov/u-s-relations-with-oman/#:~:text=Bilateral%20Economic%20Relations &text=Total%20bilateral%20U.S.%2DOman%20trade,%2C%20plastics%2C %20and%20fuel%20oil.

"Vision 2040: Vision Document," Omani Government, https://isfu.gov.om/2040/ Vision_Documents_En.pdf.

Whiteaker, Jon, "The GCC Railway Really Should be Built (But Might Not Be)," *Railway Technology*, May 15, 2022, https://www.railway-technology.com/analysis /gcc-railway-built-infrastructure/.

Worall, James, "Oman: The 'Forgotten' Corner of the Arab Spring," *Middle East Policy*, 39 (September 2012): 98–115.

Wren, Christopher S., "Sudan Reappraising Close Ties to Egypt," *The New York Times,* December 7, 1979, https://www.nytimes.com/1979/12/07/archives/sudan -reappraising-close-ties-to-egypt-implies-a-curtailment-if.html.

Yadav, Stacey Philbrick, "Oman is a Mediator in Yemen. Can it Play the Same Role in Qatar?" *The Washington Post,* July 22, 2017, https://www.washingtonpost.com /news/monkey-cage/wp/2017/07/22/oman-is-a-mediator-in-yemen-can-it-play-the -same-role-in-qatar/.

Young, Karen, "China is not the Middle East's High Roller," *Bloomberg Opinion*, July 2, 2020, https://www.aei.org/op-eds/china-is-not-the-middle-easts-high-roller/.

Zboun, Kifah, "Hamas Leader Arrives in Oman Amid Abbas Visit," *Asharq Al-Awsat,* January 13, 2020, https://english.aawsat.com//home/article/2080101/hamas -leader-arrives-oman-amid-abbas-visit.

Chapter 9

Kuwait's Boycott of Israel

Internal and Bilateral Dynamics

Robert Mason

Kuwait's boycott of Israel contrasts with the policy position of many of the other Gulf Cooperation Council (GCC) members. A combination of Arab nationalism, semi-democratic system of governance allowing Sunni and Shia Islamist and other voices to be heard, and historic ties to the Palestinian community and solidarity with them, all play important roles in shaping Kuwaiti policy. With reference to Israel, Islamist voices and Kuwaiti pan-Arab solidarity deliver a consistent political attitude and environment that favors Palestine. The approach of the late emir, elder statesman, and commander of the Kuwait Military Forces, Sabah Al-Ahmad Al-Jaber Al-Sabah, also brought consistency to Kuwait's outlook, as has Kuwait's position in the regional and international system on the issue of Israel.

According to the Kuwaiti newspaper *Al-Qabas*, government sources confirmed in 2020 that Kuwait "will be the last country to normalize with Israel."[1] Kuwait refuses entry to anyone with a passport issued by Israel or with documented evidence of travel to Israel. Kuwait also bans Israeli citizens from traveling on its national airline. Kuwait policy in this respect was publicized by Israeli passport holder "Adar M" who booked a flight with Kuwait Airways for travel from Frankfurt to Bangkok, had his flight canceled, and was offered to be booked on a different airline. However, he refused and sued for discrimination in 2016. A German court ruled in favor of the airline, although the German foreign ministry said in 2017 that it would push for a change of heart by the Kuwaitis.[2]

There have been two major impacts on Kuwaiti foreign policy: oil and the Iraqi invasion of Kuwait in 1990–1991, with both formal institutions (e.g., National Assembly) and informal ways in which these have operated, playing a role in Kuwaiti politics.[3] Political life has been termed "segmented pluralism" which attempts to reconcile religious and ideological diversity with civic cohesion whereby social movements, educational associations, and political parties organize along religious and ideological lines.[4] Kuwait's foreign policy, or what has been termed *Dinar Diplomacy*,[5] incorporates a generous foreign aid program, a strong mediation role familiar to small states in this part of the world, and support for the Palestinian cause. This latter point has been informed a great deal by Kuwait's Arabism, the large Palestinian community in Kuwait, the presence and penetration of Palestinian advisors and influences in Kuwaiti society, and relationships built between the Kuwaiti and Palestinian elites.

This chapter elucidates the historic and contemporary patterns of Kuwaiti engagement with Palestinians which makes Kuwaiti normalization with Israel an emotive subject. It progresses to discuss the role played by the Kuwaiti National Assembly in managing competing narratives but still giving voice to the dominant solidarity that exists for Palestinians. The chapter then turns to the established role played by Sheikh Sabah Al-Ahmad Al-Jaber Al-Sabah and, more recently, Emir Nawaf Al-Ahmad Al-Jaber Al-Sabah who is also commander of Kuwaiti Military Forces, in upholding key tenets of Kuwaiti policy such as mediation and a comprehensive solution to the Palestinian issue along the lines of a two-state solution. It then offers a glimpse into Kuwaiti society and the diversity of opinion that exists in the Kuwaiti media on normalization of relations with Israel. Next, it outlines the potential for Kuwaiti socioeconomic and defense ties with Israel with reference to its position in the regional system, between the larger states of Saudi Arabia, Iran, and Iraq. The chapter concludes with remarks about the sustainability of the status quo regarding Kuwait's boycott of Israel.

HISTORIC KUWAITI TIES TO PALESTINIANS

The ruling Al Sabah established good relations with the British East India Company as early as 1775, and in the Anglo-Ottoman Convention of 1913, Kuwait was defined as an autonomous *kaza* or administrative region. During the First World War, in exchange for support during the Mesopotamian Campaign, the British government recognized Kuwait as an "independent government under British protection."[6] Kuwait, like other small states in the region, prefers extra-regional alliances that would only have a limited impact on its domestic and foreign policy. It has understood the value that the UK's military presence in the southern Gulf provided and was dissatisfied with the UK's withdrawal "East of Suez" announced in 1968 and implemented by 1971. Its vulnerability has translated into "rhetorical and practical expressions of solidarity with key causes."[7] In addition, due to the limited direct role of the British in Kuwait's internal administration after oil was discovered in 1938, Kuwait has relied more on Arab technical assistance than its neighbors.[8]

In 1922, the Mufti of Jerusalem visited Kuwait to collect donations to rebuild Al-Aqsa Mosque. In the 1930s, the Kuwaiti Youth Association formed a committee to study the Palestine issue, and in 1936 the first Palestinian education mission, including four school teachers, came to Kuwait.[9] Palestinian immigration to Kuwait began in the 1940s and Palestinians assumed positions as teachers, judges, and doctors later on. Yasser Arafat also traveled to Kuwait and formed Fatah with his comrades when he was a refugee there in 1959. Kuwait has, since joining the United Nations in May 1963, lobbied on behalf of the Palestinians and expressed displeasure with US military support for Israel. On October 16, 1973, Kuwait hosted separate meetings of the Organization of Arab Petroleum Exporting Countries (OAPEC) and the Persian Gulf members of OAPEC, including Iran, and leveraged their collective oil supplies in the form of an embargo against states deemed friendly with Israel. Kuwait was also one of the eighteen countries, including Saudi Arabia, Jordan, Bahrain, Qatar, and the UAE, that imposed sanction on Egypt for its peace treaty with Israel in 1979. More than half a million Palestinians moved to Kuwait after the first Intifada (1987–1993).

Following Arafat's alleged alignment with Saddam Hussein during the Gulf War (1990–1991), Kuwaiti-Palestinian Liberation Organization (PLO) relations fractured and the resident Palestinian population of 200,000 was expelled. The impact of withdrawing Gulf support from the PLO had immediate and profound consequences, almost making the group irrelevant had the 1993 Israel-PLO accord not been signed.[10] From the Gulf War onwards, Kuwaiti-US relations have been generally close and cordial, making Kuwait less overtly critical of US policy vis-à-vis the Israel-Palestine conflict. Kuwait's brief occupation by Saddam Hussein's Iraqi forces has left a legacy of territorial sensitivity in its foreign policy dealings, including its stance on the Israeli occupation of Palestine. Kuwait has maintained a consistent policy that only a comprehensive peace treaty with Israel would bring peace to the region. Mohammad Sabah Al-Salem Al-Sabah, former Kuwaiti prime minister and foreign minister, confirmed in October 1993 when he was Kuwaiti ambassador to the United States, that Kuwait rejected a separate treaty between any Arab state and Israel.[11] Kuwait supported the Saudi-led 2002 Arab Peace Initiative while emphasizing the need to adhere to pre-1967 borders.

Although Kuwaiti support for Arab nationalism as a nationalist ideology has declined, Kuwait and the Palestinian Authority have tried to maintain unity and mend fences. In 2013, the Palestinian National Authority opened an embassy in Kuwait City and Palestinian Ambassador Rami Tahboub has expressed appreciation for Kuwait being "proactive in supporting the Palestinian cause."[12] Some 80,000 Palestinian residents remain in Kuwait and represent a vital source of Kuwaiti solidarity with the State of Palestine.

Included in this is the legacy of prominent Arab intellectuals and media figures who have sustained the Palestinian cause in the public sphere. In 2016,
Kuwait passed a law in an attempt to encourage Palestinians to once again
participate as teachers in Kuwait's state education system in 2017. However,
supply from the West Bank and Gaza outstrips demand, with some 1,173
applications for just 180 positions.[13]

In January 2018, Kuwait announced plans to open an embassy in Palestine and did so in October 2019 with the appointment of Aziz Al-Daihani,
non-resident ambassador of Kuwait to Palestine. Kuwait continues to play a
mediation role between Hamas and some Middle Eastern states, including
asking Saudi Arabia in 2019 to release dozens of Hamas members who had
spent months in Saudi prisons without charge.[14]

Kuwait's position that only a comprehensive peace treaty with Israel would
bring peace has been proven to be a prudent one in the context of continued
flare-ups in Israeli-Palestinian violence in 2021 and the Gaza War in 2023.
Kuwait and Bahrain took the Palestinian cause to the UN General Assembly
during the Israeli-Palestinian crisis in 2021. Kuwaiti foreign minister, Ahmad
Nasser Al-Mohammad Al-Sabah, condemned the policies carried out by
Israeli forces in May 2021 "with the strongest terms" and said he "denounces
all of Israel's illegal settlement schemes, its bid to seize Palestinians' houses
and properties, particularly citizen's assets in Jerusalem, namely in Sheikh
Jarrah neighborhood."[15] In the meantime, the Bennett government was working hard to expand the Abraham Accords. Indeed, if another Arab state or two
were to normalize relations with Israel it would have enhanced his personal
political standing. But the normalization enterprise has continued to be simultaneously undermined by Israel's annexation policies, intercommunal violence, and the Gaza War. As annexation and conflict continues, it only leaves
room to develop relations with states which no longer rely on solidarity with
the Palestinians as part of their political legitimacy or foreign policy strategy.

NATIONAL ASSEMBLY'S ROLE IN KUWAITI
POLICY ON ISRAEL

Kuwait has an old communal order and oil revenues tend to perpetuate old
alliances.[16] The Al Sabah family has ruled Kuwait since 1716 and as such its
modern politics are informed by a tribal authority system through which the
Al Sabah co-opted groups at the periphery through intermediaries to counter Kuwait's Najdi merchants with whom they shared power.[17] The system
was inherently coherent except for episodes such as 1938 during a period of
Najdi opposition when they and others demanded that Kuwait set up legislative councils that would give citizens a voice in how the Sheikhdoms were

governed. Herb picks up this point and notes that merchants in other locales such as Dubai and Bahrain demanded the same, as these were states with substantial trade and merchant classes.[18] The *majlis* movement in Bahrain failed due to British opposition and did so generally when its power started to usurp the ruler's control of oil revenues.[19] In Kuwait, there was said to be no broad-based coalition but a takeover of the state by the ruling family.[20]

Patron-client relations, therefore, best describe the Kuwaiti system in which parliament provided the ideal forum and the main intermediary amid a growing circle of old and new elites. While some transnational connections lead to Saudi Arabia or an imagined past where pan-Arab identity and values still reign supreme, they do not directly gain purchase with stakeholders involved in the Abraham Accords, except for relations with the United States. Iraqi irredentism toward Kuwait discussed in terms of its "19th province" made clear in Iraq's announcement that a new government would be formed in the country during the Gulf War,[21] and has also been a constant since Kuwait's independence in 1961. Thus, the national parliament and the 1962 constitution helped to bolster the state's nationhood, claim to sovereignty, and political legitimacy against foreign threats. It is not a perfect system and the parliament has been dissolved twice, between 1976 and 1981 and between 1986 and 1992. Following the Arab Spring, a new electoral law was introduced in 2012 that limited the opposition's ability to succeed by moving electoral competition into precincts, limiting crosscutting pan-sectarian appeal and the ability of parliamentary blocs from campaigns, sparked protest, and a four-year election boycott by the opposition. Nevertheless, the system still remains relatively consultative and participatory in comparison to the other GCC states.

The prospect of rapid normalization with Israel based on the configuration of the Kuwaiti parliament as it stands, and under the new law, looks slim. Shiite Islamic blocs represented the largest contingent in parliament between 2012 and 2016 and isolating them would have been counterproductive.[22] But the National Assembly still represents more diversity of opinion and influence than other small GCC states yet to conclude normalization agreements of their own. In 2013, for example, Hammad al-Dosari, an independent MP, commented that "the sharia permits us to have dealings with the Israelites. We follow the example of the prophet Muhammad, who died while his shield was mortgaged with a Jew."[23] Nabil al-Fadhl, another MP at the time and former Kuwait Airways pilot and columnist, said he "loves" Israel for selling military equipment to Kuwait.[24]

Speaker Marzouq al-Ghanim called Israeli Knesset members "occupiers and murderers of children" after discussing the Israeli imprisonment of Palestinian politicians in 2017.[25] He demanded that Israeli parliament representatives then leave the Inter-Parliamentary Union in Saint Petersburg.[26]

Another parliamentarian, Osama al-Shaheen, said in April 2020 that "Kuwait is against any cultural, political, or social normalization with the 'Zionist entity.'" As of August 18, 2020, thirty-nine out of fifty of Kuwait's parliamentarians signed a statement against normalization with Israel.[27] At the same time, Kuwait's former information minister, Sami Abdullatif Al-Nesf, said that nobody has harmed the Palestinian cause over the years more than Arab extremists and that the Sinai was not regained through war but through peace.[28] These statements highlight the confluence of traditional solidarity with Palestine, a view expressed in line with Sunnah, along with a certain amount of exasperation at the degree to which extremist elements and a lack of diplomatic progress have helped to undermine Kuwait's position in the advancement of a two-state solution.

LEADERSHIP TRANSITION IN KUWAIT AND CONTINUITY IN PALESTINE

Alsayed finds that Kuwait's foreign policy under Sheikh Sabah Al-Ahmad Al-Jaber Al-Sabah in the first decades after independence was "progressive, pan-Arab, and anti-colonial."[29] Kuwait has a deep historical memory based on the former emir and crown prince, Sheikh Sabah Al-Ahmad Al-Jaber Al-Sabah, having lived through the era of the Arab-Israeli conflict. He was Kuwait's foreign minister for four decades (1963–2003) and emir for fourteen years (2006–2020). He was widely regarded as a bridge-builder, including under his direction, mediating Saudi-Egyptian tensions in North Yemen in 1968. He was also a leader in the provision of foreign aid in times of crisis. The late emir was what UAE crown prince Mohammad bin Zayed called "a great pioneer of Gulf cooperation."[30] He remained neutral during the 2017–2021 Qatar Crisis and led reconciliation efforts. He also helped a former enemy state. In 2018, he hosted a large donor conference where $30 billion was pledged to help Iraq.[31] This shows the degree to which multilateralism, mediation, and reconciliation are favored by Kuwait, even if the results fall somewhat short, and the general support for incremental positive changes through diplomacy rather than the potential backlash from more risky and assertive foreign policy maneuvers.

The Israeli foreign ministry referred to Sheikh Sabah as bringing modernity and stability to Kuwait.[32] Such statements from the Israeli government do leave the door open to more positive political relations in future and support existing relations in the Arab world by conforming to general Arab governmental pronouncements about this leader. Still, Kuwait has shown no intention of normalizing relations. To do so without the implementation of the two-state solution in place would undermine the diplomacy that Kuwait and neighbors such as Saudi Arabia have engaged in over decades, including at the UN. It would also undermine and potentially upend state-society relations and invite instability in relations with Iran and Iraq. Iran remains tied to the Palestinian cause to avoid isolation in the Sunni-dominated region and as part of its "resistance" modus operandi, including in a (shadow) war with Israel across the region. The Iraqi parliament adopted the "Criminalizing Normalization and Establishment of Relations with the Zionist Entity Law" in June 2022, facilitated by a conference held in Erbil aimed at exploring Iraqi diplomatic and other relations with Israel.[33] The move potentially undermines relations with the GCC states that have signed the Abraham Accords thereby sustaining Iranian influence over the country, apparent since the US invasion in 2003. Unlike the transitions to more youthful leaders in other parts of the GCC, changing foreign policy assertiveness, and social engineering taking place in Saudi Arabia and UAE, Kuwait remains tied to a traditional and more pluralistic form of governance, role conception and pan-Arab principles. This suggests two tiers are opening up in the GCC, in which certain states choose to engage with Israel whilst others refrain.

In September 2020, President Trump floated the suggestion that Kuwait may be the next country in the Middle East to sign onto the Abraham Accords.[34] There was no factual basis for this assessment, with Kuwaiti officials stating publicly that its policy toward Israel had not changed. The suggestion therefore appears to be based on the fact that Kuwait remains dependent on the United States for its security. Still, there is no evidence that the United States has pressed Kuwait to normalize relations with Israel. The United States has had a series of military bases in Kuwait since the 1990–1991 Gulf War, and there is cooperation on terrorism. Kuwait has been, and remains, supportive of the Middle East peace process, having participated in multilateral talks and without direct confrontation with Israel. Kuwait appreciates the restraint that Israel exhibited during the Gulf War, but there is little appetite for unilateral movement on normalization with Israel until Syria-Israel and Lebanon-Israel negotiations have been completed and after whatever final deal the Palestinian Authority accepts.[35]

Kuwait discovered a massive Hezbollah weapons cache and a terrorist sleeper cell in the country in 2015, which is said to have existed for sixteen years prior.[36] Despite this and Hezbollah being proscribed as a terrorist organization by both the GCC and Arab League in March 2016, Kuwait still accused Israel of exaggerating the danger posed by Hezbollah's tunnels crossing from Lebanon to northern Israel in December 2018. Focusing instead on what it claimed were new levels of Israeli violations, the Kuwaiti delegation at the United Nations called for an end to Israeli violation of UN Security Council Resolution 1701, including the ongoing occupation of Lebanese territory.[37] The suggestion made by President Trump may therefore have been in the context of the ill health of Emir Sheikh Sabah Al-Ahmad Al-Jaber Al-Sabah at the time and an attempt to influence his successor. It may also have been an effort to support the perception in the region that momentum in the normalization of relations between Israel and the Arab world was gathering pace. If it required vigorous mediation by the United States for states predisposed to normalizing relations with Israel such as Bahrain and the UAE, it would have required unprecedented and counterproductive pressure on Kuwait with a radically different domestic political situation.

The passing of Sheikh Sabah Al-Sabah on September 29, 2020, was met with a high-level delegation sent by President Trump and led by Defense Secretary Mark Esper to offer condolences in Kuwait. Sheikh Nawaf's succession to the throne occurred without undue obstruction. He has made little change to Kuwaiti foreign policy and maintained space for Islamist movements in Kuwait's governmental institutions. Public opinion is relatively unchanged about Israel and Kuwait's foreign policy vision remains relatively constant.

Amid the Israeli-Palestinian violence in 2021, Sheikh Nawaf affirmed that

the State of Kuwait stands with the Palestinian people and supports all efforts aimed at reaching a just and comprehensive solution to the Palestinian issue in a way that enables the Palestinian people to establish their independent Palestinian state with East Jerusalem as its capital in accordance with United Nations resolutions and the Arab Peace Initiative.[38]

This position was further reaffirmed by Sheikh Salem Abdullah Al-Jaber, the Kuwait foreign minister, when he said in February 2023 that "the situation for the Palestinians is still as dire as it was ever before . . . I don't see how the Abraham Accords are bringing us closer to a two-state solution."[39]

In contrast to President Biden's increasingly tense relations with Saudi Arabia and the UAE, he has expressed gratitude to Kuwait for generous support for the evacuation of US citizens and US partner nations from Afghanistan in 2021. President Biden has thanked the emir for contributing to de-escalation in the Middle East and welcomed cooperation between neighboring states.[40] Kuwait has played an important coordination role in fora such as the GCC Iran Working Group and did not support President Trump's triumphant withdrawal from the Joint Comprehensive Plan of Action in 2018, unlike Saudi Arabia, the UAE, Bahrain, and Israel.

While Saudi Arabia remains non-committal in terms of its normalization with Israel, at least until Mohammad bin Salman accedes to the throne, Kuwait completely avoids difficult choices that threaten GCC unity. Changes in Saudi policy could have a significant but not necessarily definitive bearing on Kuwait's position. Kuwait, which remains highly cognizant of political developments among its larger neighbors, could find itself at odds if there is a Saudi policy shift and suddenly an outlier in the GCC. It is not clear where Saudi policy stands, but a deal is not beyond the realms of possibility within the wider strategic context of rebuilding relations with the US and post-Gaza War planning.[41] Should Saudi Arabia sign onto the Abraham Accords, Kuwait still looks to be in a strong position of autonomy given its established position as a mediator, including six decades of involvement in conflict resolution. The limited number of GCC trade and investment ties as sources of potential leverage over its national interests gives Kuwait further insulation.

Areas of possible future effect on Kuwait's position vis-à-vis Israel include the emergence of shifting popular alliances and competing factions in the ruling elite which reorientate Kuwaiti politics in pursuit of new opportunities in the regional environment. Parliamentary alliances tend to be fluid: in 2021 Kuwait announced three new governments, with the health, interior, commerce, and housing ministers replaced with selections made by the prime minister which no parliamentary bloc supported.[42]

By not following primogeniture, Kuwait opens itself up to ruling family competition, which has been intense at times. Al-Saif noted that the Kuwaiti government in 2022 had one of the lowest Al Sabah ruling family representations of any government (defense, interior, and foreign affairs).[43] There is a slow promotion of younger family members to ministerial positions, but there is also said to be a distinct lack of planning in terms of government operating as a team.[44] Sheikh Mishaal al-Ahmad al-Jaber al-Sabah became crown prince a few days after the accession of Sheikh Nawaf al-Ahmad al-Jaber to the throne in 2020. Sheikh Mishal was eighty-one then and has spent his career as head of State Security (1967–1980), in the Ministry of Interior and then as deputy chief of the National Guard with the rank of acting minister until 2004. When Sheikh Nawaf passed away in December 2023, he left his eighty-three-year-old half-brother, Sheikh Mishaal al-Ahmad al-Jaber al-Sabah to take over with immediate effect, and then formalized by the Kuwait parliament. Sheikh Mishal has been directing Kuwaiti policy since Sheikh Nawaf's health began to fail in 2021.[45] As such there will be a continuation of policy. While corruption, freedom of expression, and other economic and political reforms remain as key concerns, the focus will remain on internal issues.

It's not clear how slow paced reforms, an over-reliance on hydrocarbons, and a range of socioeconomic issues including health, education, and housing issues will impact on Kuwait's external relations but stresses to the social contract could create political pressure which will bog down Kuwaiti politics for many years to come. If a crisis does appear, it may lead to more robust government responses, including a greater emphasis on surveillance, which may favor closer ties with Israel as a leading source of this technology. Since the Arab Spring, peaceful dissent has been criminalized in Kuwait, and Amnesty International states that scores have been arrested, prosecuted, or imprisoned in recent years.[46] Undermining or questioning the emir is punishable with a five-year prison sentence, a punishment that can extend to MPs.

DISSENTING KUWAITI MEDIA AND SOCIETY VIEWS ON NORMALIZATION WITH ISRAEL

The majority of Kuwaitis still feel a degree of Arab solidarity, including solidarity with Palestinians, and public support is in response to Palestinian suffering under Israeli occupation. *Diwaniyya* gatherings have spurred on Kuwait's distinct political culture by sitting at the nexus of political campaigning and social commentary and could have been a forum where normalization with Israel might first be discussed. But there is little evidence that civil society as a whole deviates significantly from the ruling elite and is therefore not eager to discuss or debate the issue of normalizing relations with Israel. The Bar Association, Teachers' Association, and the Kuwaiti Economic Association have all been critical of the UAE's normalization with Israel.[47] In a 2020 poll, 88 percent of Kuwaitis rejected normalization with Israel.[48] Although state law prohibits the collection of funds for charity without a government permit, public support for Hamas is more difficult to calculate and control, meaning that funds collected in a legal way for Palestine may still end up in Hamas's coffers. Private funds are said to being given often without there necessarily being a clear understanding of the differences between Fatah, Hamas, and the PLO.[49] This appears to be an area of continuity in Kuwaiti social differences on Palestinian solidarity which have existed in one shape or form for more than a century.

After the bombardment of Gaza in 2021, hundreds of Kuwaitis protested in support of Palestinians and burned the Israeli flag. One protestor said, "We send a message to our friends in GCC countries that any normalization with the Zionists will not help. It helps the killer against the Palestinian people."[50] Some Kuwaitis also appealed to others across the Gulf to post their support for Palestinians through social media and symbolic sit-ins in their homes.[51] The effect a sit-in would have is not clear. The war in Gaza has underscored to Kuwaitis that its preference for a two-state solution was the correct course of action.[52] At the official level, Kuwait like many other Arab Gulf States has publicly declared that its top priority is ending the war and ensuring the well-being of Palestinians.[53]

A brief survey suggests that there have been examples of dissenting opinion on the Abraham Accords evident in Kuwaiti media, reflecting perhaps wide access to local and international media outlets. However, reasons given for normalizing relations in the media are shown to be disparate and ephemeral. In 2000, Kuwaiti national identity was found to be reflected in and impacted by new media, making any assumption about the causality of positive or negative media coverage of Israel impacting public perceptions problematic.[54] In 2021, tribalism and tribal identity, and the degree to which it hinders or advances popular participation in government and to what extent they exert domestic political power in rentier environments are found to be vital in conceptualizing Kuwait's political system, including through electoral tribalism.[55]

In 2016, Kuwaiti media personality, Yousuf Abd Al-Karim Al-Zinkawi, in a privately run *Al-Seyassah* magazine, called on all Muslim nations to recognize Israel, writing that Arab and Muslim nations already recognize Israel because they work "under the same roof as the Israeli delegation" at the UN General Assembly.[56] In 2017, a Kuwaiti writer, appearing on Middle East Media Research Institute (MEMRI) TV, a pro-Israeli advocacy group, said that the countries that don't recognize Israel are "the countries of tyranny and oppression," citing North Korea as an example.[57] These personalities appear to be not only fringe from the mainstream media and provocative but also active participants in the Israeli campaign for normalization by cooperating with organizations such as MEMRI, whether knowingly or not.

There are also questions about the independence of Kuwaiti media from foreign interference. For example, in 2019, then-Israeli prime minister Benjamin Netanyahu was accused of planting a story in the Kuwait-based online news site *Al-Jarida* in an effort to boost his security credentials during an election by using it as an excuse to respond with strong rhetoric.[58] At the time of the Abraham Accords in 2020, Kuwaiti TV host Fajer Alsaeed, called the Palestinian rejection of the UAE peace agreement with Israel a "historic mistake" and said she hoped "they [Palestinians] will deal with it reasonably and do away with the revolutionary spirit that is not suitable for this day and age."[59] In January 2022, in an editorial in the *Arab Times* titled "Normalize, Let Insulters Fend for Themselves," editor-in-chief Ahmed al-Jarallah wrote:

> They [Palestinians] stood with the Iranian Houthi aggressor against Saudi Arabia and the Gulf. They slandered and cursed the leaders and governments of the Gulf Cooperation Council countries because they did not mourn the assassination of the head of the terrorist snake Qasem Soleimani. . . . All the Gulf states should normalize relations with Israel due to the fact that peace with this most advanced country is the right thing to do. Let the foolish defend themselves.[60]

POTENTIAL SOCIOECONOMIC CONNECTIONS AND DEFENSE TIES BETWEEN KUWAIT AND ISRAEL

With a small population of around 4.3 million, oil and gas accounting for more than half of GDP and 92 percent of export revenues, Kuwait is a rentier economy.[61] Its GDP was approximately \$136 billion in 2019.[62] While the country remains heavily dependent on oil production and is dominated by public ownership, diversification of the Kuwait economy is considered in National Vision 2035 which aims to attract foreign investment into non-oil sectors. The main areas have been identified as Information and Communications Technology (ICT), renewable energy, and healthcare, among others, into which Kuwait has attracted \$3.4 billion of foreign investment from 2015 to 2020.[63] With high GDP per capita and Internet penetration for remote working, good access to public health facilities, and the lowest public debt levels in the GCC combined with one of the world's largest Sovereign Wealth Funds, Kuwait was relatively well prepared for the COVID-19 crisis. Although COVID-19 has created economic disruption and an incentive to reform, the war in Ukraine has pushed up oil prices which staves off immediate concerns. While economic tie-ups similar to those between the UAE and Israel could potentially impact favorably on Kuwaiti economic activities, they would not be enough to exclusively sustain Kuwaiti diversification plans alone. Many states will have a role to play if these are to be successfully implemented.

Kuwait has not so far implemented the wide-ranging reforms required to absorb large-scale and sustained investment. For example, the government sector still accounts for about two-thirds of all economic activity, with a nascent private sector still taking shape.[64] Kuwait also lacks the tourism potential of Abraham Accords states such as the UAE. On paper, closer relations with a new regional partner which can help facilitate reform and help ease the transition from a wasta-based economy where personal connections are relied upon to find a job, to one with more opportunities in a reformed economy, looks desirable.[65]

The Kuwaiti Ministry of Trade and Industry boycotts Israeli products and closed eight stores in 2020, one of which sold Israeli products.[66] Kuwait has, in the past, boycotted conferences in other parts of the region which were attended by Israeli representatives, such as the 2014 World Future Energy Summit held in Abu Dhabi.[67] Kuwait-Israeli trade and investment ties have been vanquished further following the decision by the Kuwaiti minister of public works Rana al-Fares in 2021, who revived an Emiri decree dating back to 1957 that imposes sanctions on parties which "financially deal with Israel."[68] The move could simultaneously undermine intra-GCC economic cooperation with key import/export states such as the UAE and therefore does not appear to be in Kuwait's best long-term interests as it attempts to diversify.

As a small state intent on sustaining its regional approach of mediation, caution, and solidarity, Kuwait lacks the regional geostrategic imperative to work with Israel against Iran through the importation of, for example, high-tech weapons. There are, of course, some exceptions and the situation could change if there is a repeat of growing escalation in the region as witnessed in 2019–2021. Kuwait's interior ministry has been monitoring the country's Yemen community since 2015, and the National Guard is preparing for any emergency. To that end, the Kuwaiti National Guard is said to have been outfitted with Israeli-made Multi-Threat Detection System which alerts armored vehicles if they are being targeted by anti-tank weapons or laser-guided munitions.[69] But these imports, probably as part of a deal with the United States and without close attention to the origin of the technology, fall within a more traditional framework of military modernization rather than the outreach of other GCC states toward Israel aimed at addressing a range of clear and present dangers. Kuwait, through virtue of tolerating dissenting parliamentary and public opinion through the media, lacks the need for repression seen in other parts of the GCC. It also helps to reduce the focus on state-of-the-art surveillance technology which Israel could provide.

CONCLUSION

The independent and ideational power of Kuwait is notable in the case of Israel, Palestine, and the Abraham Accords. Kuwait is one of the few Arab States where the question of Palestine and the two-state solution still resonates loudly. There are a limited number of dissenting views in Kuwait on normalization with Israel, and within that a diversity of opinion as to why normalization with Israel should occur, based variously on history, Israel's role in the UN, recognition from other states, and the role Israel has played in selling military equipment to Kuwait. At the parliamentary level where calls for normalization have been limited, a combination of lower regional threat perception and Israel-Palestine clashes has reinforced the notion that no normalization will take place. Kuwait, traversing a slow transition to a post-rentier economy, subsumed by government instability, and lacking GCC connectivity, looks to have less to lose from an official boycott affecting economic connectivity with Israel. While the country has maintained consistency on the need to find a durable two-state solution, the analysis in this chapter shows that as soon as that solution presents itself Kuwait will be well served to reach out and connect with a range of regional and international partners to boost its economic diversification, reform, and growth prospects.

NOTES

1. Hamad Al Salama and Mahmoud Ezzahi, "Government Sources Confirmed to 'Al-Qabas' the Firmness of its Positions: Kuwait is the Last to Normalize with Israel," *Al-Qabas,* August 15, 2020, https://alqabas.com/article/5793787-%D9%85%D8%B5%D8%A7%D8%AF%D8%B1-%D8%AD%D9%83%D9%88%D9%85%D9%8A%D8%A9-%D8%A3%D9%83%D8%AF%D8%AA-%D9%84-%D8%A7%D9%84%D9%82%D8%A8%D8%B3-%D8%AB%D8%A8%D8%A7%D8%AA-%D9%85%D9%88%D9%82%D9%81%D9%87%D8%A7-%D8%A7%D9%84%D9%83%D9%88%D9%8A%D8%AA-%D8%A2%D8%AE%D8%B1-%D9%85%D9%86-%D9%8A%D8%B7%D8%A8%D8%B9-%D9%85%D8%B9-%D8%A5%D8%B3%D8%B1%D8%A7%D8%A6%D9%8A%D9%84.

2. Sarah Wildman, "A German Court Just Ruled that Kuwait's National Airline Can Refuse Service to Israelis," *Vox,* November 17, 2017, https://www.vox.com/world/2017/11/17/16670038/kuwait-airways-israeli-germany-discrimination.

3. Jill Crystal, *Kuwait: The Transformation of an Oil State* (London: Routledge, 1992).

4. Daniel L. Tavana, "The Evolution of the Kuwaiti 'Opposition': Electoral Policies After the Arab Spring," Issue Brief 08.07.18, Rice University's Baker Institute for Public Policy, Houston, TX, https://www.bakerinstitute.org/files/13359/.

5. Abdul-Reda Assiri, *Kuwait's Foreign Policy: City-State in World Politics* (Abingdon: Routledge, 1990).

6. B. J. Slot, "Mubarak's Last Years, 1913-1915," in *Mubarak Al-Sabah: Founder of Modern Kuwait, 1896-1915* (London: Arabian Publishing Ltd, 2005), 406–409.

7. Neil Partrick, ""Introduction," Kuwait's Foreign Policy (1961-1977): Non-Alignment, Ideology and the Pursuit of Security," PhD Thesis (London: London School of Economics, 2006), 8.

8. See, for example, Andrew B. Loewenstein, "'The Veiled Protectorate of Kuwait': Liberalized Imperialism and British Efforts to Influence Kuwaiti Domestic Policy During the Reign of Sheikh Ahmad al-Jaber, 1938-50," *Middle Eastern Studies*, 36(2) (2000): 103–123.

9. Abdul-Reda Assiri, "Pragmatism and Balance (1963-1979)," in *Kuwait's Foreign Policy: City-State in World Politics* (Abingdon: Routledge, 1990).

10. Philip Mattar, "The PLO and the Gulf Crisis," *Middle East Journal,* 48(1) (Winter 1994): 31–46.

11. Chookiat Panaspornprasit, "US-Kuwaiti Relations under the Carter Administration," in *US-Kuwaiti Relations, 1961-1992: An Uneasy Relationship* (London: Routledge, 2005), 70.

12. "Tahboub: Kuwait is a Pioneer in Supporting the Palestinian Cause," *Al-Qabas,* June 11, 2020, https://alqabas.com/article/5779445-%D8%B7%D9%87%D8%A8%D9%88%D8%A8-%D8%A7%D9%84%D9%83%D9%88%D9%8A%D8%AA-%D8%B3%D8%A8%D8%A7%D9%82%D8%A9-%D9%81%D9%8A-%D8%AF%D8%B9%D9%85-%D9%82%D8%B6%D9%8A%D8%A9-%D9%81%D9%84%D8%B3%D8%B7%D9%8A%D9%86.

13. Huda Baroud, "Palestinian Teachers Seize Golden Opportunity in Kuwait," *Al-Monitor,* April 4, 2017, https://www.al-monitor.com/originals/2017/04/palestine-teachers-employment-kuwait.html.

14. Rasha Abou Jalal, "Kuwait Asks Saudi Arabia to Release Palestinian Detainees," *Al-Monitor,* September 26, 2019, https://www.al-monitor.com/originals/2019/09/hamas-detainees-saudi-arabia-kuwait-mediation.html.

15. "Bahrain, Kuwait Take Palestinian Cause to UN General Assembly, Jordan Ruler Seeks De-escalation in Gaza," *Arab News,* May 21, 2021, https://www.arabnews.com/node/1862166/middle-east.

16. Rivka Azoulay, *Kuwait and Al-Sabah: Tribal Politics and Power in an Oil State* (London: I. B. Tauris, 2020).

17. Ibid.

18. Michael Herb, "The Origins of Kuwait's National Assembly," LSE Middle East Center, Kuwait Paper Series 39, March 13, 2016, https://eprints.lse.ac.uk/65693/1/39_MichaelHerb.pdf.

19. Ibid.

20. Ibid, 14.

21. Mohammed A. Al-Yahya, "The World Response," in *Kuwait: Fall and Rebirth* (London: Routledge, 1993), 99.

22. Courtney Freer, "How Politics at Home Shapes Kuwait's Foreign Policy," *Brookings*, November 19, 2020, https://www.brookings.edu/blog/order-from-chaos/2020/11/19/how-politics-at-home-shapes-kuwaits-foreign-policy/.

23. "Kuwaiti Legislator Says He 'Loves' Israel for Helping Keep His Country Safe," *Times of Israel*, July 2, 2013, https://www.timesofisrael.com/kuwaiti-legislators-defend-financial-ties-with-israel/.

24. Ibid.

25. Naser Al Wasmi, "Kuwait Speaker Calls Knesset Members 'Occupiers and Murderers of Children,'" *The National,* October 19, 2017, https://www.thenationalnews.com/world/gcc/kuwait-speaker-calls-knesset-members-occupiers-and-murderers-of-children-1.668679.

26. Ibid.

27. Osama al-Shaheen, https://twitter.com/OALSHAHEEN/status/1295661040424845312.

28. "Kuwait Ex-Minster: Nobody Has Harmed Palestinian Cause More Than Extremist Groups," *The Algemeiner*, August 2, 2018, https://www.algemeiner.com/2018/08/02/kuwaiti-ex-minister-nobody-has-harmed-palestinian-cause-more-than-extremist-groups/.

29. Wafa Alsayed, "Kuwait Foreign Policy Under Sabah al-Ahmed," The Arab Gulf States Institute in Washington, October 5, 2020, https://agsiw.org/kuwaiti-foreign-policy-under-sabah-al-ahmed/.

30. "Leaders of Arab World and Beyond Mourn Sheikh Sabah," *Arab News,* September 29, 2020, https://www.arabnews.com/node/1741966/middle-east.

31. Freer, "How Politics at Home Shapes Kuwait's Foreign Policy."

32. "Death of Kuwait Ruler Draws Outpouring of Tributes, From Israel to Iran," *The Times of Israel,* September 30, 2020, https://www.timesofisrael.com/death-of -kuwait-ruler-draws-outpouring-of-tributes-from-israel-to-iran/.

33. Yerevan Saeed and Hussein Ibish, "Iraq's Anti-Normalization Law Could Prove a Risky Political Stunt," The Arab Gulf States Institute in Washington, June 6, 2022, https://agsiw.org/iraqs-anti-normalization-law-could-prove-a-risky-political -stunt/.

34. "Trump Says Kuwait May be Next in Middle East to Sign Peace Deal with Israel," *I24 News,* September 14, 2020, https://www.i24news.tv/en/news/middle-east /1600497870-trump-says-kuwait-may-be-next-in-middle-east-to-sign-peace-deal -with-israel.

35. Greg Saiontz, "Kuwait and the Gulf: Five Years After Desert Storm," Policy Watch 185, The Washington Institute for Near East Policy, February 21, 1996, https:// www.washingtoninstitute.org/policy-analysis/kuwait-and-gulf-five-years-after-desert -storm.

36. Khalaf Ahmad Al Habtoor, "Hezbollah Sleeper Cells in Kuwait Are a Wake-Up Call," Middle East Policy Council, https://mepc.org/commentary/hezbollah -sleeper-cells-kuwait-are-wake-call.

37. "Kuwait at UNSC: Israel is Exaggerating the Danger from Hezbollah Tunnels," *The Jerusalem Post,* December 19, 2018, https://www.jpost.com/Breaking -News/Kuwait-at-UNSC-Israel-is-exaggerating-the-danger-from-Hezbollah-tunnels -574807.

38. "The Emir of Kuwait Condemns Israeli Escalation Against Worshippers in Al-Aqsa Mosque," *WAFA News Agency,* May 11, 2021, https://english.wafa.ps/Pages /Details/124408.

39. John Irish, "Kuwait Foreign Minister Sees Progress on Maritime Border with Iraq," *Reuters*, February 18, 2023, https://www.reuters.com/world/middle-east/ kuwait-foreign-minister-sees-progress-maritime-border-with-iraq-2023-02-18/.

40. "Readout of President Joseph R. Biden, Jr's Call with Emir Nawaf Al-Ahmad Al-Jaber Al-Sabah of Kuwait," *The White House*, September 1, 2021, https://www.whitehouse.gov/briefing-room/statements-releases/2021/09/01/readout -of-president-joseph-r-biden-jr-s-call-with-emir-nawaf-al-ahmad-al-jaber-al-sabah -of-kuwait/.

41. "Biden Aide, Saudi Crown Prince Discussed Israel Normalization: Report," *Al-Monitor,* October 20, 2021, https://www.al-monitor.com/originals/2021/10/biden -aide-saudi-crown-prince-discussed-israel-normalization-report.

42. Bader Al-Saif, "Old Playbook for New Kuwaiti Government Signals Further Stasis," The Arab Gulf States Institute in Washington, January 10, 2022, https://agsiw .org/old-playbook-for-new-kuwaiti-government-signals-further-stasis/.

43. Ibid.

44. Ibid.

45. Gerald M. Feierstein, "Following Emir's Death, Sheikh Mishal Al Sabah Named Kuwait's New Ruler, Signalling Continuity," Middle East Institute, December 18, 2023, https://www.mei.edu/blog/following-emirs-death-sheikh-mishal-al -sabah-named-kuwaits-new-ruler-signaling-continuity.

46. "Kuwait at Risk of Sliding into a Deeper Repression Amid Growing Clampdown on Critics," *Amnesty International*, December 14, 2015, https://www.amnesty.org/en/latest/news/2015/12/kuwait-at-risk-of-sliding-into-deeper-repression-amid-growing-clampdown-on-critics/.

47. "Israel and the Gulf: Future Prospects for Normalization," Moshe Dayan Center for Middle Eastern and African Studies, September 15, 2020, https://dayan.org/content/israel-and-gulf-future-prospects-normalization.

48. Dana El Kurd, "What do Ordinary Arabs Think About Normalizing Relations with Israel," *The Washington Post,* October 26, 2020, https://www.washingtonpost.com/politics/2020/10/26/what-do-ordinary-arabs-think-about-normalizing-relations-with-israel/.

49. Interview with an analyst who asked not to be named, May 16, 2022.

50. Ahmed Hagagy, "Kuwaiti Protestors Burn Israeli Flag, Reject Normalisation Deals," *US News,* May 19, 2021, https://www.usnews.com/news/world/articles/2021-05-19/kuwaiti-protesters-burn-israeli-flag-reject-normalisation-deals.

51. @Gulf_can, May 11, 2021, https://twitter.com/gulf_can/status/1391878894110842887.

52. Vivian Nereim, "Across the Mideast, a Surge of Support for Palestinians as War Erupts in Gaza," *The New York Times,* October 9, 2023, https://www.nytimes.com/2023/10/09/world/middleeast/mideast-palestine-support-gaza.html.

53. "Kuwait's Top Priority: Ending Gaza War and Well-Being of Palestinians," *Times Kuwait,* March 23, 2024, https://timeskuwait.com/kuwaits-top-priority-ending-gaza-war-and-well-being-of-palestinians/

54. Deborah Wheeler, "New Media, Globalization and Kuwaiti National Identity," *Middle East Journal,* 54(3) (Summer 2000): 432–444.

55. Courtney Freer and Alanoud al-Sharekh, *Tribalism and Political Power in the Gulf: State-Building and National Identity in Kuwait, Qatar and the UAE* (London: Bloomsbury, 2021).

56. "Arab Media Personality Calls on Muslims to Accept Nation of Israel," *CBN News*, April 14, 2016, https://www1.cbn.com/cbnnews/israel/2016/april/arab-media-personality-calls-on-muslims-to-accept-nation-of-israel.

57. Eric Sumner, "Watch: Kuwaiti Writer Says Israel is a Legitimate State, Not an Occupier," *The Jerusalem Post,* November 23, 2017, https://www.jpost.com/arab-israeli-conflict/watch-kuwaiti-writer-says-israel-is-a-legitimate-state-not-an-occupier-514993.

58. Ian Black, "Just Below the Surface: Israeli, The Arab Gulf States and the Limits of Cooperation," LSE Middle East Center Report, March 2019, 35, https://eprints.lse.ac.uk/100313/.

59. "Kuwaiti TV Host Fajar Alsaeed: Palestinian Rejection of UAE Peace Agreement with Israel A Historic Mistake," *MEMRI TV*, August 17, 2020, https://www.memri.org/tv/kuwaiti-host-fajer-alsaeed-palestinian-rejection-of-uae-isreal-peace-historic-mistake.

60. Ahmed Al-Jarallah, "Normalize, Let Insulters Fend for Themselves," *Arab Times,* January 28, 2022, https://www.arabtimesonline.com/news/normalize-let-insulters-fend-for-themselves/.

61. "2022 Index of Economic Freedom: Kuwait," Heritage, https://www.heritage .org/index/country/kuwait.
62. "Kuwait," https://datacommons.org/place/country/KWT?utm_medium =explore&mprop=amount&popt=EconomicActivity&cpv=activitySource%2CGross DomesticProduction&hl=en.
63. Wendy Atkins, "Kuwait Pins Hopes on Diversification with Vision 2035," *FDI Intelligence*, April 16, 2020, https://www.fdiintelligence.com/article/77070.
64. Amirah El-Haddad, "Kuwait Small Businesses After the Pandemic: Time for a New Social Contract," *Economic Research Forum*, June 1, 2021, https://theforum.erf .org.eg/2021/05/31/kuwaiti-small-businesses-pandemic-time-new-social-contract/.
65. Bader al-Saif, "Another Invasion of Kuwait," *Carnegie Endowment for International Peace*, August 11, 2020, https://carnegieendowment.org/publications/?fa =82453.
66. "Kuwait in Hard Fight Over Normalisation with Israel," *The Arab Weekly*, November 3, 2020, https://thearabweekly.com/kuwait-hard-fight-over-normalisation -israel.
67. Sharon Udasin, "Israel Shrugs Off Kuwaiti Boycott, Joins Arab States, Iran at Abu Dhabi Conference," *The Jerusalem Post,* January 19, 2014, https://www.jpost .com/National-News/Kuwait-boycotts-Abu-Dhabi-energy-conference-attended-by -Zionist-regime-338624.
68. "Kuwait Issues Decision Hindering Neighbors' 'Economic Peace' with Israel," *The Arab Weekly*, December 12, 2021, https://thearabweekly.com/kuwait -issues-decision-hindering-neighbours-economic-peace-israel.
69. Grant Turnbull, "Israeli Military Technology Discovered in Kuwait, Despite Ban," *Shephard,* January 9, 2018, https://www.shephardmedia.com/news/landwarfa-reintl/israeli-military-technology-discovered-kuwait-desp/.

REFERENCES

@Gulf_can, May 11, 2021, https://twitter.com/gulf_can/status/1391878894110842887.
Al Habtoor, Khalaf Ahmad, "Hezbollah Sleeper Cells in Kuwait Are a Wake-Up Call," Middle East Policy Council, https://mepc.org/commentary/hezbollah -sleeper-cells-kuwait-are-wake-call.
Al-Jarallah, Ahmed, "Normalize, Let Insulters Fend for Themselves," *Arab Times,* January 28, 2022, https://www.arabtimesonline.com/news/normalize-let-insulters -fend-for-themselves/.
Al-Monitor, "Biden Aide, Saudi Crown Prince Discussed Israel Normalization: Report," *Al-Monitor,* October 20, 2021, https://www.al-monitor.com/originals /2021/10/biden-aide-saudi-crown-prince-discussed-israel-normalization-report.
Al-Qabas, "Tahboub: Kuwait is a Pioneer in Supporting the Palestinian Cause," *Al-Qabas,* June 11, 2020, https://alqabas.com/article/5779445-%D8%B7%D9%87 %D8%A8%D9%88%D8%A8-%D8%A7%D9%84%D9%83%D9%88%D9%8A %D8%AA-%D8%B3%D8%A8%D8%A7%D9%82%D8%A9-%D9%81%D9

%8A-%D8%AF%D8%B9%D9%85-%D9%82%D8%B6%D9%8A%D8%A9-
%D9%81%D9%84%D8%B3%D8%B7%D9%8A%D9%86.

Al-Saif, Bader, "Another Invasion of Kuwait," Carnegie Endowment for International Peace, August 11, 2020, https://carnegieendowment.org/publications/?fa=82453.

Al-Saif, Bader, "Old Playbook for New Kuwaiti Government Signals Further Stasis," The Arab Gulf States Institute in Washington, January 10, 2022, https://agsiw.org/old-playbook-for-new-kuwaiti-government-signals-further-stasis/.

Al Salama, Hamad, and Mahmoud Ezzahi, "Government Sources Confirmed to "Al-Qabas" the Firmness of its Positions: Kuwait is the Last to Normalize with Israel," *Al-Qabas*, August 15, 2020, https://alqabas.com/article/5793787-%D9%85 %D8%B5%D8%A7%D8%AF%D8%B1-%D8%AD%D9%83%D9%88%D9%85 %D9%8A%D8%A9-%D8%A3%D9%83%D8%AF%D8%AA-%D9%84-%D8 %A7%D9%84%D9%82%D8%A8%D8%B3-%D8%AB%D8%A8%D8%A7%D8 %AA-%D9%85%D9%88%D9%82%D9%81%D9%87%D8%A7-%D8%A7%D9 %84%D9%83%D9%88%D9%8A%D8%AA-%D8%A2%D8%AE%D8%B1- %D9%85%D9%86-%D9%8A%D8%B7%D8%A8%D8%B9-%D9%85%D8%B9- %D8%A5%D8%B3%D8%B1%D8%A7%D8%A6%D9%8A%D9%84.

Alsayed, Wafa, "Kuwait Foreign Policy Under Sabah al-Ahmed," *The Arab Gulf States Institute in Washington*, October 5, 2020, https://agsiw.org/kuwaiti-foreign -policy-under-sabah-al-ahmed/.

Al-Shaheen,   Osama,   https://twitter.com/OALSHAHEEN/status /1295661040424845312.

Al Wasmi, Naser, "Kuwait Speaker Calls Knesset Members 'Occupiers and Murderers of Children,'" *The National,* October 19, 2017, https://www.thenationalnews .com/world/gcc/kuwait-speaker-calls-knesset-members-occupiers-and-murderers -of-children-1.668679.

Al-Yahya, Mohammed A., *Kuwait: Fall and Rebirth.* (London: Routledge, 1993).

Amnesty International, "Kuwait at Risk of Sliding into a Deeper Repression Amid Growing Clampdown on Critics," *Amnesty International*, December 14, 2015, https://www.amnesty.org/en/latest/news/2015/12/kuwait-at-risk-of-sliding-into -deeper-repression-amid-growing-clampdown-on-critics/.

Arab News, "Bahrain, Kuwait Take Palestinian Cause to UN General Assembly, Jordan Ruler Seeks De-escalation in Gaza," *Arab News,* May 21, 2021, https://www .arabnews.com/node/1862166/middle-east.

Arab News, "Leaders of Arab World and Beyond Mourn Sheikh Sabah," *Arab News,* September 29, 2020, https://www.arabnews.com/node/1741966/middle-east.

Assiri, Abdul-Reda, *Kuwait's Foreign Policy: City-State in World Politics* (Abingdon: Routledge, 1990).

Atkins, Wendy, "Kuwait Pins Hopes on Diversification with Vision 2035," *FDI Intelligence*, April 16, 2020, https://www.fdiintelligence.com/article/77070.

Azoulay, Rivka, *Kuwait and Al-Sabah: Tribal Politics and Power in an Oil State* (London: I. B. Tauris, 2020).

Baroud, Huda, "Palestinian Teachers Seize Golden Opportunity in Kuwait," *Al-Monitor,* April 4, 2017, https://www.al-monitor.com/originals/2017/04/palestine -teachers-employment-kuwait.html.

Black, Ian, "Just Below the Surface: Israeli, The Arab Gulf States and the Limits of Cooperation," LSE Middle East Center Report, March 2019, https://eprints.lse.ac.uk/100313/.

CBN News, "Arab Media Personality Calls on Muslims to Accept Nation of Israel," *CBN News*, April 14, 2016, https://www1.cbn.com/cbnnews/israel/2016/april/arab-media-personality-calls-on-muslims-to-accept-nation-of-israel.

Crystal, Jill, *Kuwait: The Transformation of an Oil State* (London: Routledge, 1992).

"Death of Kuwait Ruler Draws Outpouring of Tributes, From Israel to Iran," *The Times of Israel,* September 30, 2020, https://www.timesofisrael.com/death-of-kuwait-ruler-draws-outpouring-of-tributes-from-israel-to-iran/.

El-Haddad, Amirah, "Kuwait Small Businesses After the Pandemic: Time for a New Social Contract," *Economic Research Forum*, June 1, 2021, https://theforum.erf.org.eg/2021/05/31/kuwaiti-small-businesses-pandemic-time-new-social-contract/.

El Kurd, Dana, "What do Ordinary Arabs Think About Normalizing Relations with Israel," *The Washington Post,* October 26, 2020, https://www.washingtonpost.com/politics/2020/10/26/what-do-ordinary-arabs-think-about-normalizing-relations-with-israel/.

"The Emir of Kuwait Condemns Israeli Escalation Against Worshippers in Al-Aqsa Mosque," *WAFA News Agency,* May 11, 2021, https://english.wafa.ps/Pages/Details/124408.

Freer, Courtney, "How Politics at Home Shapes Kuwait's Foreign Policy," *Brookings*, November 19, 2020, https://www.brookings.edu/blog/order-from-chaos/2020/11/19/how-politics-at-home-shapes-kuwaits-foreign-policy/.

Freer, Courtney, and Alanoud al-Sharekh, *Tribalism and Political Power in the Gulf: State-Building and National Identity in Kuwait, Qatar and the UAE* (London: Bloomsbury, 2021).

Feierstein, Gerald M. "Following Emir's Death, Sheikh Mishal Al Sabah Named Kuwait's New Ruler, Signalling Continuity," *Middle East Institute,* December 18, 2023, https://www.mei.edu/blog/following-emirs-death-sheikh-mishal-al-sabah-named-kuwaits-new-ruler-signaling-continuity.

Hagagy, Ahmed, "Kuwaiti Protestors Burn Israeli Flag, Reject Normalisation Deals," *US News,* May 19, 2021, https://www.usnews.com/news/world/articles/2021-05-19/kuwaiti-protesters-burn-israeli-flag-reject-normalisation-deals.

Herb, Michael, "The Origins of Kuwait's National Assembly," LSE Middle East Center, Kuwait Paper Series 39, March 13, 2016, https://eprints.lse.ac.uk/65693/1/39_MichaelHerb.pdf.

Heritage, "2022 Index of Economic Freedom: Kuwait," Heritage, https://www.heritage.org/index/country/kuwait.

I24 News, "Trump Says Kuwait May be Next in Middle East to Sign Peace Deal with Israel," *I24 News,* September 14, 2020, https://www.i24news.tv/en/news/middle-east/1600497870-trump-says-kuwait-may-be-next-in-middle-east-to-sign-peace-deal-with-israel.

Irish, John, "Kuwait Foreign Minister Sees Progress on Maritime Border with Iraq," Reuters, February 18, 2023, https://www.reuters.com/world/middle-east/kuwait-foreign-minister-sees-progress-maritime-border-with-iraq-2023-02-18/.

Jalal, Rasha Abou, "Kuwait Asks Saudi Arabia to Release Palestinian Detainees," *Al-Monitor,* September 26, 2019, https://www.al-monitor.com/originals/2019/09/hamas-detainees-saudi-arabia-kuwait-mediation.html.

"Kuwait," https://datacommons.org/place/country/KWT?utm_medium=explore&mprop=amount&popt=EconomicActivity&cpv=activitySource%2CGrossDomesticProduction&hl=en.

"Kuwait at UNSC: Israel is Exaggerating the Danger from Hezbollah Tunnels," *The Jerusalem Post,* December 19, 2018, https://www.jpost.com/Breaking-News/Kuwait-at-UNSC-Israel-is-exaggerating-the-danger-from-Hezbollah-tunnels-574807.

"Kuwait Ex-Minster: Nobody Has Harmed Palestinian Cause More Than Extremist Groups," *The Algemeiner*, August 2, 2018, https://www.algemeiner.com/2018/08/02/kuwaiti-ex-minister-nobody-has-harmed-palestinian-cause-more-than-extremist-groups/.

"Kuwait in Hard Fight Over Normalisation with Israel," *The Arab Weekly*, November 3, 2020, https://thearabweekly.com/kuwait-hard-fight-over-normalisation-israel.

"Kuwait Issues Decision Hindering Neighbors' 'Economic Peace' with Israel," *The Arab Weekly*, December 12, 2021, https://thearabweekly.com/kuwait-issues-decision-hindering-neighbours-economic-peace-israel.

"Kuwaiti Legislator Says He 'Loves' Israel for Helping Keep His Country Safe," *The Times of Israel*, July 2, 2013, https://www.timesofisrael.com/kuwaiti-legislators-defend-financial-ties-with-israel/.

"Kuwait's Top Priority: Ending Gaza War and Well-Being of Palestinians," *Times Kuwait,* March 23, 2024, https://timeskuwait.com/kuwaits-top-priority-ending-gaza-war-and-well-being-of-palestinians/.

Loewenstein, Andrew B. "'The Veiled Protectorate of Kuwait': Liberalized Imperialism and British Efforts to Influence Kuwaiti Domestic Policy During the Reign of Sheikh Ahmad al-Jaber, 1938-50," *Middle Eastern Studies*, 36(2) (2000): 103–123.

Mattar, Philip, "The PLO and the Gulf Crisis," *Middle East Journal,* 48(1) (Winter 1994): 31–46.

MEMRI TV, "Kuwaiti TV Host Fajar Alsaeed: Palestinian Rejection of UAE Peace Agreement with Israel A Historic Mistake," *MEMRI TV*, August 17, 2020, https://www.memri.org/tv/kuwaiti-host-fajer-alsaeed-palestinian-rejection-of-uae-isreal-peace-historic-mistake.

Moshe Dayan Center for Middle Eastern and African Studies, "Israel and the Gulf: Future Prospects for Normalization," Moshe Dayan Center for Middle Eastern and African Studies, September 15, 2020, https://dayan.org/content/israel-and-gulf-future-prospects-normalization.

Nereim, Vivian. "Across the Mideast, a Surge of Support for Palestinians as War Erupts in Gaza," *The New York Times,* October 9, 2023, https://www.nytimes.com/2023/10/09/world/middleeast/mideast-palestine-support-gaza.html

Panaspornprasit, Chookiat, "US-Kuwaiti Relations under the Carter Administration," in *US-Kuwaiti Relations, 1961-1992: An Uneasy Relationship* (London: Routledge, 2005), 65–85.

Partrick, Neil, "Kuwait's Foreign Policy (1961-1977): Non-Alignment, Ideology and the Pursuit *of* Security," PhD Thesis (London: London School of Economics, 2006).

"Readout of President Joseph R. Biden, Jr's Call with Emir Nawaf Al-Ahmad Al-Jaber Al-Sabah of Kuwait," The White House, September 1, 2021, https://www.whitehouse.gov/briefing-room/statements-releases/2021/09/01/readout-of-president-joseph-r-biden-jr-s-call-with-emir-nawaf-al-ahmad-al-jaber-al-sabah-of-kuwait/.

Saeed, Yerevan, and Hussein Ibish, "Iraq's Anti-Normalization Law Could Prove a Risky Political Stunt," *The Arab Gulf States Institute in Washington*, June 6, 2022, https://agsiw.org/iraqs-anti-normalization-law-could-prove-a-risky-political-stunt/.

Saiontz, Greg, "Kuwait and the Gulf: Five Years After Desert Storm," Policy Watch 185, The Washington Institute for Near East Policy, February 21, 1996, https://www.washingtoninstitute.org/policy-analysis/kuwait-and-gulf-five-years-after-desert-storm.

Slot, B. J., "Mubarak's Last Years, 1913-1915," in *Mubarak Al-Sabah: Founder of Modern Kuwait, 1896-1915* (London: Arabian Publishing Ltd, 2005), 406–409.

Sumner, Eric, "Watch: Kuwaiti Writer Says Israel is a Legitimate State, Not an Occupier," *The Jerusalem Post,* November 23, 2017, https://www.jpost.com/arab-israeli-conflict/watch-kuwaiti-writer-says-israel-is-a-legitimate-state-not-an-occupier-514993.

Tavana, Daniel L., "The Evolution of the Kuwaiti 'Opposition': Electoral Policies After the Arab Spring," Issue Brief 08.07.18, Rice University's Baker Institute for Public Policy, Houston, TX, https://www.bakerinstitute.org/files/13359/.

Turnbull, Grant, "Israeli Military Technology Discovered in Kuwait, Despite Ban," *Shephard,* January 9, 2018, https://www.shephardmedia.com/news/landwarfareintl/israeli-military-technology-discovered-kuwait-desp/.

Udasin, Sharon, "Israel Shrugs Off Kuwaiti Boycott, Joins Arab States, Iran at Abu Dhabi Conference," *The Jerusalem Post,* January 19, 2014, https://www.jpost.com/National-News/Kuwait-boycotts-Abu-Dhabi-energy-conference-attended-by-Zionist-regime-338624

Wheeler, Deborah, "New Media, Globalization and Kuwaiti National Identity," *Middle East Journal,* 54(3) (Summer 2000): 432–444.

Wildman, Sarah, "A German Court Just Ruled that Kuwait's National Airline Can Refuse Service to Israelis," *Vox,* November 17, 2017, https://www.vox.com/world/2017/11/17/16670038/kuwait-airways-israeli-germany-discrimination.

Conclusion

Robert Mason

In this book, the authors have sought to analyze and assess the leading drivers of normalization, non-normalization, or anti-normalization within the Abraham Accords, and for those participating in the accords, whether they are sustainable. We have approached these questions in two ways: First through individual studies of each country in the Gulf Cooperation Council (GCC), as well as Iran, Israel, and the Palestinians. Second, by adopting a common conceptual framework to review multiple factors affecting elite decision-making, popular sentiment, and the accords.

Our examination of GCC states and normalization with Israel reveals that the subject is not a new one. Normalization with Israel has been a topic of ongoing discussion for political elites and societies across the GCC for decades. The Abraham Accords is simply the most recent and notable manifestation.

In this conclusion, some general observations and developments are presented. At the conceptual level, the realist approach initially laid out for this book, which prioritizes threat perception and security matters, is found to be somewhat limited in its application to the signatories of the Abraham Accords. Iran is indeed a primary driver of GCC state normalization with Israel, and states such as the UAE value Israeli intelligence, arms, and other emerging forms of security cooperation, such as in the maritime domain. But, the case of Bahrain highlights both the pertinence and the limitations of the broader realist perspective. For Bahrain, and several of the other GCC states, constructivist accounts—especially those that focus on identity, religion, and the self-interest of leaderships—have also appeared to play a major role in their respective positions toward Israel.

The situation is nuanced, and even GCC states involved in the Abraham Accords are acutely aware of the need to balance their relations with Israel, on the one hand, and with Iran, where possible, on the other. Iran is geographically closer and the risk of further escalation could affect the smaller GCC states far more than any benefits secured from closer relations with Israel. Nevertheless, the Abraham Accords are, intrinsically, a response to regional factors, in particular, as part of a deterrence against an Iranian threat. This has become increasingly necessary due to Tehran's accumulation of material power in conjunction with its apocalyptic worldview. Tehran's ballistic missile program, nuclear program, and regional behavior, which have blurred defensive and offensive components, significantly complicate the process of regional de-escalation. Unlike the 2001 Saudi-Iranian security deal when the two states saw security issues in the same light, a point partially acknowledged in the 2023 normalization and subsequent contact between Saudi and Iranian officials, Iran and Israel threat perception has never meshed post-1979 and has consistently been a zero-sum game. Although Iran constitutes a threat to some GCC states, both the nature and degree of the threat vary between states and over time. Such variation therefore affects how GCC states choose to respond to Iran and in their choice of whether or not to normalize with Israel. Related considerations include Iranian irredentist claims and religious influence over resident Shia, which enhances the sense of ontological threat felt in both Abu Dhabi and Manama.

States such as Qatar and Oman favor cordial relations with Iran but still find ways to engage with Israel without normalization, mainly to enlarge the space in which they can conduct their mediation activities. With an onus on political leadership and its religious identity, Muscat has been able to offset its actions toward Israel by pairing them with equally close political and economic relations with the Palestinian Authority and Iran.

Small states such as Qatar, Kuwait, and Oman have religious, ideological, and demographic reasons not to engage with Israel, as well as some political, security, and economic rationales and incentives for prioritizing Iran across the Strait of Hormuz. Unlike Saudi Arabia and the UAE, these states have not traveled as far in their journey toward late rentierism and social engineering, or in the case of Qatar, Doha remains tied to the status quo through its deep ties to the United States, Iran, and Turkey, as well as its working relationship with various Islamist groups.

If overall threat perception remains high, closer GCC state relations (for collective bargaining) and GCC state relations with external security guarantors such as the United States might translate into greater pressure to normalize relations with Israel. But for some states in the GCC and beyond, while these issues are a concern, they do not necessarily directly affect them. For others, such as Saudi Arabia, the issues of aerial defense, nuclearization, and nuclear deterrence are a primary concern.

There is a certain amount of tension between the realist and constructivist positions, exacerbated following the installation of the Israeli far-right government in December 2022 and the Israel-Hamas War in October 2023. A new fragility is evident in Israeli politics, such as ongoing social unrest, IDF focus on the destruction on Gaza, and political turmoil, which could significantly complicate and undermine a host of foreign policies, including the Abraham Accords and further normalization. Omni-balancing is elucidated as being a key conceptual framework in that the balance between the domestic, regional, and international have influenced the Abraham Accords decisively for or against the GCC states. While bandwagoning, balancing, and hedging are all on show in the case of GCC normalization (or not) with Israel, there is a risk that a focus on the international system overlooks other drivers of behavior. Indeed, as the chapters illustrate, often the threat perception of GCC states is driven by domestic concerns, especially state-society relations and regime survival.

The degree of political consolidation, pluralism, stage of rentierism, and positions on state repression could be determining factors regarding normalization with Israel and possibly represent a fork developing in the road. This aspect could be enhanced if the regime and state survival by means of authoritarian upgrading (e.g., technology transfer) become more paramount in the GCC states, which might occur if various "Visions" strategies are found to have failed or significantly lag behind domestic expectations. The GCC states' ability to manage or control socioeconomic pressure going forward, reflecting stage and success of diversification and perceived requirement for repression, could be determining factors regarding normalization or sustaining normalization with Israel. Social forces may demand a greater voice in public policy, especially if the current social contract ends. Should that happen, then there may be a greater push for (foreign) policies attuned toward a more populist agenda.

Were Saudi Arabia to normalize relations with Israel, and there is no indication it will in the short term, it would immediately lose leverage vis-à-vis Israel and the United States. Furthermore, normalization would send shockwaves through the regional balance of power and undermine its newly forged relations with Iran. Although Riyadh has pivoted away from Wahabbism, it is still the predominant Islamic power and its current leadership is in the middle of a process of political consolidation, so it must tread carefully. Islamic challenger states could use Saudi normalization with Israel, especially at an inopportune time, as a weapon against the kingdom to undermine its Islamic credentials and influence. The instability caused by further normalization without implementation of the API could undermine much of the hard-won diplomacy that many of the GCC states have been involved in. Lessons concerning the further rollout of the Abraham Accords might be learned from the normalization of relations with Syria where there has been no apparent prerequisite action required from the Assad regime.

Other important considerations regarding whether to normalize relations with Israel or not may depend on the trajectory of Palestinian prospects for self-determination and rights. Against that concern, however, is the issue of self-interest. Whether GCC states choose to normalize with Israel or not—and whether they opt to bandwagon, balance, or hedge—will be largely based on the regimes' assessment of what will ensure not only their survival but also their ability to thrive in an unstable regional context. In this regard, the Palestinians constitute a more marginal factor than they previously did, especially in the years following several of these states' independence when they have been vulnerable to exogenous and endogenous pressures.

The boycott and criminalization of contact with Israel suggests Arab-Palestinian solidarity in some quarters, but may also harm contacts and regionalism emanating from within the Gulf. As regionalism and inter-regional relations become more important to diversifying GCC state trade and investment relations, Israel, Palestine, and Syria will continue to represent both obstacles and opportunities in forging direct overland connections with states such as Turkey and Greece, and the wider European Union.

Time will tell whether a division of labor—Qatari and Omani mediation, Saudi, UAE, and Kuwaiti economic statecraft, along with Bahraini and UAE diplomacy with Israel—can advance peace in Gaza. UAE's and Qatar's economic engagement in Gaza has provided a tantalizing glimpse of how support for reconstruction, security sector reform, and the right of return or definitive resettlement might work. Whether this is in line with a two-state solution depends largely on the United States as the primary security guarantor.

Throughout the globalization process in the 1980s and 1990s, the United States accumulated significant soft and hard power capabilities, especially in projecting influence into the Gulf and the wider Middle East. These capabilities were utilized more effectively during the George. H. W. Bush administration to address the issue of Palestine after the Iran-Iraq War and Gulf War had occupied some US foreign policy bandwidth since. Due to the transition to a unipolar world after the dissolution of the Soviet Union in 1991, the United States had an unrivaled scope and capacity for leverage and change. Overall, regional and small states in the Gulf had limited options in terms of balancing against US policy. Instead, they generally bandwagoned with Washington, looking to attract and maintain support. At the same time, however, the US position within the Middle East, the GCC states included, has not been perceived as always consistent. In recent years five major changes have taken place affecting US policy which challenge its status as an (honest) peace broker in the Israel-Palestine conflict have affected GCC state threat perception or enhanced the US role in Gulf affairs, which have created the conditions for the Abraham Accords to occur.

The first is the role of the Jewish lobby in the formulation of policy on the Israel-Palestine conflict. Whereas the Middle East is generally considered to be a penetrated region, so too is US politics, by special interests that have generally favored Israeli government policy. Some GCC state attempts at interfaith dialogue, tolerance, and mediation, while cornerstones of Islam, also serve to deflect or dispel criticism post 9/11 about anti-Semitism and intolerance, and contribute to more positive interreligious and public relations in the West that are aimed particularly at the American public beyond Washington, D.C.

The second factor is the negative experience of past presidents such as President Bill Clinton in his attempts at peacemaking which has arguably discouraged other presidents from following in his footsteps. Indeed, after President Obama's limited effort in 2010, he delegated the task of Mideast peace to his secretary of state, John Kerry, who attempted to force a resolution through an eventually failed attempt at shuttle diplomacy in 2013–2014.

Third is the role that CENTCOM (the US Central Command) has played in bringing the United States into the Gulf as a local power after the 1990–1991 Gulf War, especially in locating the Fifth Fleet in Bahrain. In so doing, the United States has been well placed to leverage its interests. By bringing Israel within the purview of CENTCOM from 2021, the United States has effectively facilitated Israeli and GCC state contact through multilateral military exercises. In 2023, the limits to the perceived value of GCC states working directly with CENTCOM on some activities in the maritime sphere have become evident. By working solely with the United States in areas perceived to be mainly about countering Iran or with risk of direct clashes, they have intruded on the delicate balancing act described above, a risk to de-escalation, as well as a possible constraint to the autonomy that the GCC states seek.

Fourth, the change in the international environment toward multipolarity, where new entrants to Middle East policy such as China, are of growing economic and diplomatic relevance, especially through part brokering (along with Iraq and Oman) a deal for Saudi Arabia and Iran to reestablish diplomatic relations in early 2023. Such a presence may impinge on US policy by being seen to be more balanced toward Iran due to its lack of political baggage and underscores US deficiencies in this respect. Against this trend, however, is another perspective: the fact that while both global and regional politics are becoming more multipolar, power is not distributed evenly. It remains the case that notwithstanding its relative decline, the United States is still the principal power in the Middle East. The power of other external actors like China, especially in the security sphere, remains more symbolic and potential rather than actual. Because of this, then, the United States has yet to be fully replaced as the Arab Gulf states' security guarantor.

Fifth is the transactional nature of US policy, especially during the Trump administration. The Abraham Accords were at once politicized and were a wealth of balancing opportunities where participation could be traded as a commodity to maximize state concessions and national interests. As already noted, in September 2019, Prime Minister Netanyahu said that if he were reelected he would annex West Bank settlements and a large segment of the Jordan Valley. The Trump administration stated support for the policy. President Donald J. Trump's so-called Deal of the Century included offers to end the Palestinian conflict, building on a demilitarized Palestinian state subject to Israel's security interests, control of the Jordan Valley, and the annexation by Israel of settlements in the West Bank. In January 2020, Netanyahu and President Trump unveiled this Mideast plan, recognizing Israeli sovereignty over its West Bank settlements despite Palestinian rejection of it, and proceeded later in the year to announce the deal between Israel and the UAE to normalize ties, with Bahrain following a month after to normalize its relations with Israel in September 2020. While the Abraham Accords was an innovative direct form of diplomacy that would lead to a renewed Arab-Israeli peace normalization process, it has been slow to affect the Gulf regional balance of power through an over-the-horizon security guarantee by the United States. Israel's refusal to engage with Iran directly in a regional act of strategic balancing, and Iranian regional behavior, meant that the accords, like the Middle East Strategic Alliance, were only building more insecurity along the regional corridors of conflict that Tehran could influence or benefit from. Without a full US commitment to the region, this meant that Israel and the GCC were unable to fully control emerging (in)security trends, despite the accords. Consequently, the Abraham Accords seemed to exacerbate the region's security challenges.

This brings us to a further consideration: whether GCC states' decision to normalize or not and what position that entails in relation to external parties, like Israel, the United States, and Iran can be judged a success. The authors have sought to set out the past and present state of affairs between GCC states and Israel, in an effort to provide an objective account. Consequently, such questions have not been central to the chapters in this book, meaning that assessments of the relative success or failure of normalization or its rejection have not been addressed. To do so would require setting out criteria, which may be "thin" (i.e., that the policy option, once adopted, has lasted) or "thick" (by perhaps applying some of the elements summarized in each chapter). If we opt for the first, the "success" of full normalization with Israel must be uncertain, given the short period of time that has passed since the signing of the Abraham Accords. By contrast, rejection of normalization or a more ambiguous informal type of normalization has been a long-established position for several GCC states; consequently, they may be judged to have succeeded as well.

Were the thicker, more substantive approach be applied, again, this remains open to debate. For example, the UAE's normalization with Israel has advanced further in terms of material economic and security outcomes than that of Bahrain. This may also be due to the relative size and scale of opportunities available to the UAE compared to Bahrain. Similarly, Bahrain's exposure to Iran as a threat is a more existential one, thereby limiting the scope for normalization. Meanwhile, Saudi ambivalence over normalization may be "successful" insofar as it generates both tangible and perceived benefits for the regime, in the form of greater military assistance or consideration by their US ally, for example.

The issue of "success" may also be applied to the realist options adopted by the GCC states over whether to normalize. Whether states choose to bandwagon, balance, or hedge entails individual agency considerations as well as structural ones. So long as they are judged to be realizing regimes' aims, they will be perceived as successful. In so doing, such assessments stress the importance of subjective perceptions, thereby reiterating the limits of objective analysis and resorting to realist accounts. In sum then, as the Abraham Accords become a principal (perhaps permanent?) feature of GCC politics and international relations, we would do well to acknowledge these different ways in which Israeli normalization can be viewed and judged.

Looking ahead and beyond the scope of this book, there is much more to be explored in relation to Israeli normalization and the GCC states. Given the limited amount of time that has passed since the Abraham Accords were signed, much of what has been written about their current state remains provisional and subject to further developments and institutionalization. For instance, in the short term, the policies of Israel's far-right government have put pressure on the Abraham Accords and acted as a break that has slowed the rollout of further deals. Further deals may be possible if President Donald J. Trump is reelected, pending the containment of the regional conflagration that looked apparent in 2024. For the mainly realist and late-rentier pressures highlighted earlier, and the small populations involved, the accords as they stand probably are sustainable. However, the constructivist interpretations highlight the subtle and nuanced influences that should not be underestimated in sustaining the status quo positions of non-signatories. Indeed, as the work on the individual countries has shown, the question of whether to normalize with Israel or not is entrenched. Moreover, whether GCC states have chosen to do so—formally, informally, or not at all—has been shaped by a range of factors, from the structure of the international system in which they are located to other regional and domestic concerns. Many of these elements are deep and durable and may well influence the future course of GCC states' relations with Israel.

Index

About the Authors

Dr. Guy Burton has researched and taught at universities in Brussels, Dubai, Malaysia, Iraq, and Palestine and has been a visiting fellow at the LSE Middle East Centre and Lancaster University. His research interests cover the international politics of the Middle East, including the role and impact of emerging, external powers in the region. He has written numerous journal articles and book chapters on these subjects, including the books *China and Middle East Conflicts* and *Rising Powers and the Arab-Israeli Conflict since 1947*.

Dr. Banafsheh Keynoush is a scholar of international relations and Middle East studies, a nonresident scholar at the DC-based Middle East Institute, a fellow at Rasanah (The International Institute for Iranian Studies in Saudi Arabia), and a team member of the Carnegie-funded Sectarianism, Proxies and De-sectarianization Project. She conducted fieldwork in the Middle East for two decades, was recently a visiting scholar at Princeton University, and was previously a visiting fellow at the King Faisal Center for Research and Islamic Studies in Riyadh. She is the author of *Saudi Arabia and Iran: Friends or Foes?* (2016, also available in Arabic and Persian), the editor and an author of *Iran's Interregional Dynamics in the Near East* (2021), and the author of *The World Powers and Iran: Before, During and After the Nuclear Deal* (2022). Her latest report, the *Archival History of Iran's Diplomatic Relations with Saudi Arabia* (September 2023) reviews the shared history of the two regional countries from 1913 to 1979, explores the history and legacy of nationalism and colonialism, border dynamics, and the interplay between religious memory and ideology, statehood, society, and politics

Dr. Robert Mason, FHEA, FRSA, is a nonresident fellow with the Arab Gulf States Institute in Washington and a nonresident senior fellow with the Gulf Research Center in Jeddah. Previously, he served as Associate Professor and Director of the Middle East Studies Center at the American University in Cairo. Dr. Mason has held visiting positions at the University of Oxford, Princeton University, the London School of Economics, Sciences Po Paris, New York University, and the King Faisal Center for Research and Islamic Studies. Additionally, he has received research funding from the European Union, LSE Middle East Centre, and the British Institute of Persian Studies. Robert has published numerous books, chapters, and articles concerning the international relations of the Middle East. His most recent book is *Saudi Arabia and United Arab Emirates Foreign Policy: Strategic Alliances in an Uncertain World.*